IEEE
COMPUTER
SOCIETY

IEEE Computer Society Publications

The world-renowned IEEE Computer Society publishes, promotes, and distributes a wide variety of authoritative computer science and engineering texts. These books are available from most retail outlets. Visit the Online Catalog, *http://computer.org*, for a list of products.

IEEE Computer Society Proceedings

The IEEE Computer Society also produces and actively promotes the proceedings of more than 141 acclaimed international conferences each year in multimedia formats that include hard and softcover books, CD-ROMs, videos, and on-line publications.

For information on the IEEE Computer Society proceedings, send e-mail to *cs.books@computer.org* or write to Proceedings, IEEE Computer Society, P.O. Box 3014, 10662 Los Vaqueros Circle, Los Alamitos, CA 90720-1314. Telephone +1 714-821-8380. FAX +1 714-761-1784.

Additional information regarding the Computer Society, conferences and proceedings, CD-ROMs, videos, and books can also be accessed from our web site at *http://computer.org/cspress*

Revised 9 November 1999

Iterative Computer Algorithms with Applications in Engineering

Iterative Computer Algorithms with Applications in Engineering

Solving Combinatorial Optimization Problems

Sadiq M. Sait
Habib Youssef

IEEE
COMPUTER
SOCIETY

Los Alamitos, California

Washington • Brussels • Tokyo

Library of Congress Cataloging-in-Publication Data

Sait, Sadiq M., 1957-
   Iterative computer algorithms with applications in engineering : solving combinatorial optimization problems / Sadiq M. Sait, Habib Youssef.
      p.   cm.
   Includes bibliographical references and index.
   ISBN 0-7695-0100-1
   1. Combinatorial optimization – Data processing.   I. Title: Solving combinatorial optimization problems.   II. Youssef, Habib.   III. Title.

QA402.5 .S23 1999
519.3 — dc21

99-049500
CIP

IEEE Computer Society Press Order Number BP00100
Library of Congress Number 99-049500
ISBN 0-7695-0100-1

Additional copies may be ordered from:

IEEE Computer Society Press	IEEE Service Center	IEEE Computer Society
Customer Service Center	445 Hoes Lane	Watanabe Building
10662 Los Vaqueros Circle	P.O. Box 1331	1-4-2 Minami-Aoyama
P.O. Box 3014	Piscataway, NJ 08855-1331	Minato-ku, Tokyo 107-0062
Los Alamitos, CA 90720-1314	Tel: +1-732-981-0060	JAPAN
Tel: +1-714-821-8380	Fax: +1-732-981-9667	Tel: +81-3-3408-3118
Fax: +1-714-821-4641	mis.custserv@computer.org	Fax: +81-3-3408-3553
Email: cs.books@computer.org		tokyo.ofc@computer.org

Executive Director and Chief Executive Officer: T. Michael Elliott
Publisher: Angela Burgess
Manager of Production, CS Press: Deborah Plummer
Advertising/Promotions: Tom Fink
Production Editor: Denise Hurst

IEEE
COMPUTER
SOCIETY

IEEE

Dedication

To

our wives Sumaiya and Leila
whose care, patience, and understanding made it possible.

Sadiq M. Sait and Habib Youssef

This book represents a joint effort of both authors who closely cooperated on all chapters. The names of authors have been listed in alphabetical order. This does not imply any senior-junior relationship.

Contents

List of Figures

List of Tables

Preface

Motivation

Combinatorial optimization problems are encountered everywhere, in science, engineering, as well as in industrial management, economics, and so on. Most engineering and business schools offer several courses in algorithms and optimization. The advent of the digital computer is credited for this explosion in the number of algorithmic solutions to combinatorial optimization problems. Such solution techniques were unthinkable before this magnificent invention. This book in concerned with one class of combinatorial optimization algorithms: *general iterative nondeterministic algorithms.* The growing interest in this class of algorithms is attributed to their generality, ease of implementation, and mainly, the many success stories reporting very positive results. We shall limit ourselves to five dominant iterative nondeterministic algorithms, which, in order of popularity are: (1) Simulated Annealing (SA), (2) Genetic Algorithm (GA), (3) Tabu Search (TS), (4) Simulated Evolution (SimE), and (5) Stochastic Evolution (StocE). All five search heuristics have several important properties in common.

1. They are blind, in that they do not know when they have reached the optimal solution. Therefore they must be told when to stop.

2. They are approximation algorithms, that is, they do not guarantee finding an optimal solution.

3. They have "hill climbing" property, that is, they occasionally accept uphill (bad) moves.

4. They are easy to implement. All that is required is to have a suitable solution representation, a cost function, and a mechanism to traverse the search space.

5. They are all *"general."* Practically, they can be applied to solve any combinatorial optimization problem.

6. They all strive to exploit domain-specific heuristic knowledge to bias the search toward "good" solution subspace. The quality of subspace searched depends to a large extent on the amount of heuristic knowledge used.

7. Although they asymptotically converge to an optimal solution, the rate of convergence is heavily dependent on the adequate choice of several parameters.

The last two properties are the hidden bone in the five combinatorial optimization strategies. Our main goal in this book is to address this aspect by compiling in a single source the extensive research work related to the problem of intelligently setting the required parameters of these five heuristics.

Most books on computer algorithms mainly address deterministic heuristics. Recently, due to the increase in size and complexity of a large number of combinatorial optimization problems, there has been a growing interest in general iterative nondeterministic algorithms. There are several books dedicated to one particular iterative algorithm. For example, there are at least three books that introduce the theory and concepts of simulated annealing. They are rigorous in mathematics and go far beyond the level of concepts required by engineers (and scientists). There is at least one excellent textbook that introduces the theory and concepts of genetic algorithms. The field of genetic algorithms is relatively new and the technique has only recently attempted to solve several NP-hard problems. Other nondeterministic techniques such as tabu search, simulated evolution, and stochastic evolution are now gaining ground and applications of such techniques have begun to appear in scientific literature. Tabu search has recently been the subject of an excellent book by F. Glover and M. Laguna (Kluwer Publishers, 1997). Currently, to our knowledge there are no books that address the last two techniques. And, no book is available that contains an integrated and up-to-date description of all the above techniques, with case studies and examples.

All five heuristics described in this book constitute very general and effective optimization techniques. Recently, SA, GA, and TS have been designated by the Committee of the Next Decade of Operations Research as "extremely promising" for the future treatment of practical applications.[1] It is our belief that simulated evolution and stochastic evolution are equally promising techniques for a wide array of combinatorial optimization problems.

Organization of the Book

The book is organized into seven chapters. The introductory chapter motivates the student toward a study of iterative algorithms. The definitions of NP-hard

---

[1] F. Glover, E. Taillard, and D. de Werra. "A user's guide to tabu search." *Annals of Operations Research*, 41:3–28, 1993.

and NP-complete are introduced, and some "hard" problems are illustrated with examples.

To make the book self contained, a brief review of Markov processes and chains is also provided in Chapter 1. Chapters 2 through 6 examine the five iterative algorithms, namely, simulated annealing, genetic algorithm, tabu search, simulated evolution, and stochastic evolution. In order to achieve a uniformity in treatment, each of these topics is examined in the following light. The introductory section intuitively presents the reader with the essence of the heuristic. Then the required mathematical notation is introduced, followed by a section presenting the heuristic with details on how to implement it on a digital computer. Next, the mathematical model needed to study the *convergence* properties of the heuristic and how to set its parameters is presented. Case studies follow which illustrate the application of the technique to well-known combinatorial optimization problems. All steps, from formulation of cost function to final results are illustrated with examples.

All five iterative algorithms are very greedy with respect to execution time no matter how well tuned the parameters are. The proliferation of a large number of parallel computers has forced extensive research on the parallelization of these algorithms. For each technique, a section is dedicated to this issue of parallelization. A bibliography is provided at the end of each chapter, followed by *exercises*. In Chapter 7 we provide a comparative analysis of the five algorithms including similarities, differences, solution qualities, and look into hybridization aspects. We also provide a brief introduction to fuzzy logic and neural networks, and show how fuzzy logic can help ease the formulation of multicriteria optimization problems.

This book is intended as a text for senior undergraduates and first-year graduate students in computer engineering, computer science, systems/industrial engineering, and electrical engineering. It is also a good reference book for researchers and practitioners in combinatorial optimization.

How to Use this book?

The book can serve as a text for a one-semester first year graduate course on nondeterministic approximation algorithms. It should be possible to cover all material in detail in the 15 weeks of the semester. One week is required to motivate the students to the need for such algorithms (Chapter 1). Approximately two weeks are spent on each chapter thereafter (Chapters 2 through 7). As an undergraduate text, the depth and pace of coverage will be different. Advanced material such as convergence and parallelization aspects would be omitted.

Acknowledgments

The book took over three years to complete, and was supported by many people. Acknowledgments and thanks are due to our friends and colleagues at KFUPM,

Drs. Mohammad H. Al-Suwaiyel, Hassan R. Barada, Korvin Gabor, and Subbarao Ghanta, for reading all or parts of the initial manuscript, and providing suggestions, editing comments, and corrections for the book. In particular, we wish to thank Dr. Korvin Gabor for thoroughly reading the entire manuscript and promptly providing us with his feedback. We are also thankful to the five IEEE CS Press anonymous reviewers for their thorough review of the earlier draft of this book.

Special thanks are due to Drs. Fred Glover and Youssef Saab for promptly responding to our request for literature on tabu search and stochastic evolution heuristics, respectively.

We used parts of this book as supporting material for senior and graduate courses. Our thanks and appreciation to the following graduate students of the Computer Engineering department of KFUPM: Ahmad Al-Yamani, Naved Baig, Hussain Ali, Salman Khan, and Ahsan Siddiqui, who contributed with corrections to the text. In particular we acknowledge Hussain Ali for his meticulous work and patience in making and editing most of the illustrations of this book.

The editors and staff of IEEE CS Press were extremely helpful in providing timely feedback on reviewers' comments. We particularly thank Ms. Cheryl Baltes, Project Editor; Ms. Deborah Plummer, Manager of Productions; and Ms. Denise Hurst, Production Editor, for their help and cooperation during the writing of this book.

To our parents, we gratefully acknowledge the principles they instilled in us. To our wives, Sumaiya Sadiq and Leila Youssef Braham, and children Afrah, Aakif, and Arwa Sadiq, Elias, Osama, and Amin Youssef, we owe a great depth of thanks for showing even greater patience and indulgence than during the writing of our previous book.

The book was initially typeset in LaTeX at KFUPM using the computing facilities of the Computer Engineering Department. We thank the Department of Computer Engineering and the College of Computer Sciences & Engineering for providing us with the resources and environment to undertake the writing of such a book. Finally, we acknowledge the support provided by King Fahd University of Petroleum and Minerals under Project Code # COE/ITERATIVE/187.

Sadiq M. Sait
Dhahran, May 1999
sadiq@kfupm.edu.sa

Habib Youssef
Dhahran, May 1999
youssef@kfupm.edu.sa

CHAPTER 1

Introduction

1.1 Combinatorial Optimization

Combinatorial optimization constitutes one specific class of problems. The word *combinatorial* is derived from the word *combinatorics*, which is a branch of mathematics concerned with the study of arrangement and selection of discrete objects. In *combinatorics* one is usually concerned with finding answers to questions such as *"does a particular arrangement exist?"* or *"how many arrangements of some set of discrete objects exist?"* Finding the number of orderings of some set of discrete objects usually consists of deriving a mathematical formula or relation which, when evaluated for the parameters of the problem leads to the answer. On the other hand, *combinatorial optimization* is not concerned with whether a particular arrangement or ordering exists but rather, concerned with the determination of an *optimal* arrangement or order [Law76].

In most general terms, a problem is a question whose answer is a function of several parameters. Usually the problem is stated by articulating the properties that must be satisfied by its solution. A particular instance of the problem is obtained by fixing the values of all its parameters. Let's take a simple example.

Example 1.1 *The shortest path problem.*
Problem: Given a connected graph[1] $G = (V, E)$, where V is a set of n vertices and E is a set of edges. Let $D = [d_{i,j}]$ be a distance matrix, where $d_{i,j}$ is the distance between vertices v_i and v_j (weight or length of the edge $(v_i, v_j) \in E$). For convenience, we assume $d_{i,j} = d_{j,i} > 0$, $d_{i,i} = 0$, $\forall v_i, v_j \in V$, and $d_{i,j} = \infty$ if there is no edge between v_i and v_j.

---

[1]For definition of terms from graph theory the reader is referred to the text *Algorithmic Graph Theory* by Alan Gibbons, Cambridge University Press, 1985.

Objective: Find the shortest path from some source node v_i to some target node v_j. A path $\pi(v_i, v_j)$ from v_i to v_j is a sequence of the form $[v_i, v_{i_1}, v_{i_2}, \ldots, v_{i_l}, v_j]$, such that $(v_i, v_{i_1}) \in E$, $(v_{i_k}, v_{i_{k+1}}) \in E$, $1 \leq k \leq l - 1$, and $(v_{i_l}, v_j) \in E$. The length of the path is the sum of the length of its constituent edges. That is,

$$length(\pi(v_i, v_j)) \; = \; d_{i,i_1} + \sum_{k=1}^{l-1} d_{i_k,i_{k+1}} \; + \; d_{i_l,j}$$

                                                                           ■

A particular instance of the above problem is defined when one fixes the graph, the distance measure, and decides the source and target vertices. For example, Figure 1.1 is one instance of the shortest path problem.

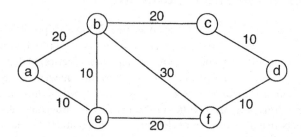

Figure 1.1: An instance of the shortest path problem: The shortest a-to-d path is $\pi(a, d) = [a, e, f, d]$ and $length(\pi(a, d)) = d_{a,e} + d_{e,f} + d_{f,d} = 10 + 20 + 10 = 40$.

A solution (optimal or not) to a *combinatorial optimization problem* usually requires that one comes up with a suitable algorithm, which when applied to an instance of the problem produces the desired solution.

An *algorithm* is a finite step-by-step procedure for solving a problem or to achieve a required result. The word *algorithm* is named after the ninth-century scholar *Abu-Jaafar Muhammad Ibn Musa Al-Khowarizmi* who authored among other things a book on mathematics.

Combinatorial optimization problems are encountered everywhere, in science, engineering, operation research, economics, and so forth. The general area of *combinatorial optimization* came to the fore with the advent of the digital computer. Algorithmic solutions to typical combinatorial optimization problems involve an extremely large number of computational steps and are impossible to execute by hand. The last 30 years have witnessed the development of numerous algorithms for almost any imaginable combinatorial optimization problem. Such algorithmic solutions were unthinkable before the advent of the era of modern computing.

Let us consider three examples of combinatorial problems.

Example 1.2 *Sorting.*
Problem: Given an array of n real numbers A[1:n].
Objective: Sort the elements of A in ascending order of their values.

There are $n!$ possible arrangements of the elements of A. In case all elements are distinct only one such arrangement is the answer to the problem. Several algorithms have been designed to sort n elements. One such algorithm is the *Bubble-Sort* algorithm.

Algorithm BubbleSort (A[1:n]);
Begin /* Sort array A[1:n] in ascending order */
  var integer i, j;
    For $i = 1$ **To** $n - 1$ **Do**
      For $j = i + 1$ **To** n **Do**
        If A[i] > A[j] **Then**
            swap (A[i],A[j]);
      EndFor;
    EndFor;
End Algorithm;

                                                 ■

Example 1.3 *Maximum set bipartitioning.*
Problem: Given a set of n positive integers $x_1, x_2, \ldots, x_n$ (n even).
Objective: Partition the set X into two subsets Y and Z such that
    1. $|Y| = |Z| = \frac{n}{2}$,
    2. $Y \cup Z = X$, and
    3. the difference between the sums of the two subsets is maximized.

There are $\binom{n}{\frac{n}{2}}$ possible bipartitions of the set X. To find the required bipartition, we can follow the steps of the following algorithm.

Algorithm MaxBipartition (X[1:n]);
Begin
  BubbleSort(X[1:n]) /* Sort array X[1:n] in ascending order */
  Put the $\frac{n}{2}$ smaller integers in Y;
  Put the $\frac{n}{2}$ larger integers in Z;
  Return (Y, Z)
End Algorithm;

                                                 ■

Example 1.4 *Minimum set bipartitioning.*

Problem: Given a set of n positive integers $x_1, x_2, \ldots, x_n$ (n even).

Objective: Partition the set X into two subsets Y and Z such that

1. $|Y| = |Z| = \frac{n}{2}$,
2. $Y \cup Z = X$, and
3. the difference between the sums of the two subsets is minimized.

∎

The two problems of set bipartitioning appear to be similar; only one word has changed (maximized became minimized). However the minimum set bipartition problem is much more difficult to solve. Actually, the two problems belong to two different classes of problems: maximum set bipartitioning belongs to the class of *easy problems* for which there are several efficient algorithms, whereas minimum set bipartitioning belongs to the class of *hard problems* with no known efficient algorithm (typically only full enumeration will guarantee finding an optimal solution).

Before we clarify the distinction between *easy* and *hard problems*, we first need to define the notions of *time* and *space complexity* of algorithms and how we measure them.

1.1.1 Complexity of Algorithms

Two important ways to characterize the *effectiveness* of an algorithm are its *space complexity* and *time complexity*. *Time complexity* of an algorithm concerns determining an expression of the number of steps needed as a function of the problem size. Since the step count measure is somewhat coarse, one does not aim at obtaining an exact step count. Instead, one attempts only to get asymptotic bounds on the step count [SB80]. Asymptotic analysis makes use of the Big-Oh notation.

Big-Oh Notation

We say that $f(n) = O(g(n))$ if there exist positive constants n_0 and c such that for all $n > n_0$, we have $f(n) \leq c \cdot g(n)$. Alternately, we say that $f(n)$ is *upper bounded* by $g(n)$. The Big-Oh notation is used to describe the space and time complexity of *algorithms*.

Example 1.5 Consider the "BubbleSort" algorithm to sort n real numbers (page 3). The procedure "BubbleSort" requires $O(n)$ storage (for the array A) and $O(n^2)$ running time (two nested **for** loops). The above statement should be taken to mean that the BubbleSort procedure requires no more than linear amount of storage and no more than a quadratic number of steps to solve the sorting problem. In this sense, the following statement is also equally true: the procedure BubbleSort takes $O(n^2)$ storage and $O(n^3)$ running time! This is because the Big-Oh notation only captures the concept of "upper bound." However, in order to be informative, it is customary to choose $g(n)$ to be as small a function of n as one can come up with, such that $f(n) = O(g(n))$. Hence, if $f(n) = a \cdot n + b$, we will state that $f(n) = O(n)$ and not $O(n^k)$, $k > 1$.

■

Big-Ω and Big-Θ Notation

The Big-Oh notation is one of several convenient notations used by computer scientists in the analysis of algorithms. Two other notational constructs are frequently used: Big-Ω (Big-Omega) and Big-Θ (Big-Theta) notation.

The Big-Oh notation is easier to derive. Typically, we prove that an algorithm is $O(f(n))$ and try to see whether it is also $\Omega(f(n))$.

Definition 1   Big-Omega Notation.
We say that $f(n) = \Omega(g(n))$ if there exist positive constants n_0 and c such that for all $n > n_0$, we have $f(n) \geq c \cdot g(n)$. Alternately, we say that $f(n)$ is *lower bounded* by $g(n)$.

Definition 2   Big-Theta Notation.
We say that $f(n) = \Theta(g(n))$ if there exist positive constants c_1, c_2, and n_0 such that for all $n > n_0$, we have $c_1 \cdot g(n) \leq f(n) \leq c_2 \cdot g(n)$.

The Θ notation is used to state an exact bound on the time complexity of a given algorithm. For example, the time complexity of BubbleSort is $O(n^2)$, $\Omega(n^2)$, as well as $\Theta(n^2)$.

How useful are these complexity functions? For example, can we use them to find out how much time the algorithm would run? Asymptotic analysis does not tell us the execution time of an algorithm on a particular problem instance, it barely characterizes the growth rate of the algorithm runtime as a function of the problem size. For example, if the sorting of 1,000 real numbers with the BubbleSort algorithm takes 1 millisecond on a particular computer, then we expect the sorting of 5,000 numbers by the same algorithm will require 25 milliseconds on the same computer. The complexity functions are also used to compare algorithms. For example, if algorithm A_1 has time complexity $\Theta(n \log n)$ and algorithm A_2 has time complexity $\Theta(n^2)$, then A_1 is a better algorithm (more efficient or superior to A_2).

In many situations, the runtime of the algorithm is data dependent. In that case, one talks of the best case, the worst case, and average time complexity.

1.1.2 Hard Problems versus Easy Problems

An algorithm is said to be a *polynomial-time* algorithm if its time complexity is $O(p(n))$, where n is the problem size and $p(n)$ is a polynomial function of n. The BubbleSort algorithm of Example 1.2 is a polynomial-time algorithm. The function $p(n)$ is a polynomial of degree k if $p(n)$ can be expressed as follows:

$$p(n) = a_k n^k + \cdots + a_i n^i + \cdots + a_1 n + a_0$$

where $a_k > 0$ and $a_i \geq 0$, $1 \leq i \leq k - 1$. In that case, the time complexity function of the corresponding algorithm is said to be $O(n^k)$.

In contrast, algorithms whose time complexity cannot be bounded by polynomial functions are called exponential time algorithms. To be more accurate, an *exponential-time* algorithm is one whose time complexity is $O(c^n)$, where c is a real constant larger than 1. A problem is said to be *tractable* (or *easy*) if there exists a polynomial-time algorithm to solve the problem. From Example 1.2 above, we may conclude that the sorting of real numbers is tractable, since the Bubble-Sort algorithm given on page 3 solves it in $O(n^2)$ time. Similarly, maximum set bipartitioning is tractable since the algorithm given on page 3 solves it in $O(n^2)$ time.

Unfortunately, there are problems of great practical importance that are not computationally easy. In other words, polynomial-time algorithms have not been discovered to solve these problems. The bad news is that it is unlikely that a polynomial-time algorithm will ever be discovered to solve any of these problems. Such problems are also known as "hard problems" or "intractable problems." For example, the minimum set bipartitioning introduced on page 4 is intractable since finding an optimum partition requires the exploration of $\binom{n}{\frac{n}{2}}$ bipartitions, which is a function that grows as an exponential function of n.[2]

Below, we recall several representative hard problems which find numerous applications in various areas of science and engineering. We shall be using these and other problems throughout the book. Readers interested in a thorough discussion of the subject of NP-completeness are referred to the classic work of Garey and Johnson [GJ79].

Example 1.6 *The traveling salesman problem* (TSP).
Problem: Given a complete graph $G(V, E)$ with n vertices. Let $d_{u,v}$ be the length of the edge $(u, v) \in E$ and $d_{u,v} = d_{v,u}$. A path starting at some vertex $v \in V$, visiting every other vertex exactly once, and returning to vertex v is called a *tour*.

---

[2]By Stirling's formula we can show that $\binom{n}{\frac{n}{2}} \approx 2^n$. The proof is left as an exercise (see Exercise 1.1).

Objective: Find a *tour* of minimum length, where the length of a *tour* is equal to the sum of lengths of its defining edges.

■

Example 1.7 *Hamiltonian cycle problem* (HCP).
Problem: Given a graph $G(V, E)$ with n vertices.
A *Hamiltonian cycle* is a simple cycle which includes all the n vertices in V. A graph containing at least one *Hamiltonian cycle* is called a *Hamiltonian graph*. A complete graph on n vertices contains $n!$ Hamiltonian cycles.

Objective: Find a Hamiltonian cycle on the n vertices of the graph.

■

Example 1.8 *The vehicle routing problem* (VRP).
Problem: Given an unspecified number of identical vehicles, having a fixed carrying capacity Q, we have to deliver from a single depot quantities q_i ($i = 1, \ldots, n$) of goods to n cities. A distance matrix $D = [d_{ij}]$ is given, where d_{ij} is the distance between cities i and j ($i, j = 1, \ldots, n$, and city 0 is the depot).

Objective: Find tours for the vehicles (a vehicle tour starts and terminates at the depot) such that

1. the total distance traveled by the vehicles is minimized,
2. every city is serviced by a unique vehicle, and
3. the quantity carried by any vehicle during any single delivery does not exceed Q.

There are several other variations of the VRP problem. For example, the distances may be Euclidean or non-Euclidean, there may be several depots, the vehicles may be different, and the goods may be delivered as well as picked up. Furthermore, there may be timing constraints for each delivery, that is, each customer at a particular (city) has a time window for service. A delivery outside its time window may be acceptable but incurs a penalty, or it may be unacceptable altogether [BGAB83, DLSS88, GPR94, Tai93].

■

Example 1.9 *The graph bisection problem* (GBP).
Problem: Given a graph $G(V, E)$ where, V is the set of vertices, E the set of edges, and $|V| = 2n$. Partition the graph into two subgraphs $G_1(V_1, E_1)$ and $G_2(V_2, E_2)$ such that, (1) $|V_1| = |V_2| = n$, (2) $V_1 \cap V_2 = \emptyset$, and (3) $V_1 \cup V_2 = V$.

Objective: Minimize the number of edges with vertices in both V_1 and V_2.

■

Example 1.10 *Quadratic assignment problem* (QAP).
Problem: Given a set M of $\mid M \mid$ modules and a set L of $\mid L \mid$ locations, $\mid L \mid \geq \mid M \mid$. Let $c_{i,j}$ be the number of connections between elements i and j, and $d_{k,l}$ be the distance between locations k and l.

Objective: Assign each module to a distinct location so as to minimize the wire-length needed to interconnect the modules.

■

Example 1.11 *Minimum set partitioning problem.*
Problem: Given a set of n positive integers $X = \{x_1, x_2, \ldots, x_n\}$.

Objective: Partition the set into two subsets Y of size k and Z of size $n - k$ ($1 \leq k \leq \frac{n}{2}$) such that the difference between the sums of the two subsets is minimized.

■

Example 1.12 *Vertex cover problem.*
Problem: Given a graph $G(V, E)$.
A *vertex cover* of a graph $G(V, E)$ is a subset $V_c \subseteq V$ such that, for each edge $(i, j) \in E$, at least one of i or $j \in V_c$.

Objective: Find a vertex cover of minimum cardinality.

■

All of the above problems are NP-hard [GJ79]. The only way to deal with NP-hard problems is to be satisfied with an approximate solution to the problem. Such an approximate solution must satisfy the constraints, but *may not* necessarily possess the best cost.

1.2 Optimization Methods

There are two general categories of combinatorial optimization algorithms: (1) *exact algorithms*[3] and (2) *approximation algorithms*. Most well known among the first category are linear programming, dynamic programming, branch-and-bound, backtracking, and so forth [HS84].

---

[3] Several exact algorithms tend to be enumerative.

The linear programming approach formulates the problem as the minimization of a linear function subject to a set of linear constraints. The linear constraints define a convex polytope. The vertices of the polytope correspond to feasible solutions of the original problem. The number of vertices in the polytope is extremely large. For example, an $n \times n$ assignment problem would require $2n$ linear inequalities, together with non-negativity constraints on n^2 variables, which describe a convex polytope with $n!$ vertices, corresponding to the extreme points of the feasible region of the assignment problem [Law76].

Dynamic programming is a stage-wise search method suitable for optimization problems whose solutions may be viewed as the result of a sequence of decisions. During the search for a solution, dynamic programming avoids full enumeration by pruning early partial decision sequences that cannot possibly lead to optimal sequences. In many practical situations, dynamic programming hits the optimal sequence in a polynomial sequence of decision steps. However, in the worst case, such a strategy may end up performing full enumeration.

Branch-and-bound search methods explore the state space search tree in either a depth-first or breadth-first manner. Bounding functions are used to prune subtrees that do not contain the required optimal state.

Many of the significant optimization problems encountered in practice are NP-hard. For relatively large instances of such problems, it is not possible to resort to optimal enumerative techniques; instead, we must resort to *approximation algorithms*. Approximation algorithms are also known as *heuristic* methods. Insight into the problem through some observations, when properly exploited, usually enables the development of a reasonable heuristic that will quickly find an "acceptable" solution. A heuristic algorithm will only search inside a subspace of the total search space for a "good" rather than the best solution which satisfies design constraints. Therefore, the time requirement of a heuristic is small compared to that of full enumerative algorithms. A number of heuristics have been developed for various problems. Examples of approximation algorithms are the *constructive greedy method, local search*, and the modern general iterative algorithms such as *simulated annealing, genetic algorithms, tabu search, simulated evolution*, and *stochastic evolution*.

The greedy method constructs a good feasible solution in stages. It starts from a seed input. Then other inputs are selected in succeeding steps and added to the partial solution until a complete solution is obtained. The selection procedure is based on some optimization measure strongly correlated with the objective function. At each stage, the inputs that optimize the selection measure are added to the partial solution, hence the term *greedy*.

A common feature of all of the aforementioned search algorithms (whether exact or approximate) is that they constitute general solution methods for combinatorial optimization.

This book is concerned with iterative approximation algorithms. Solution techniques such as linear programming, dynamic programming, and branch-and-bound have been the subject of several other books (see, for example, [Fou84, HS84, Hu82, PS82]).

One of the oldest iterative approximation algorithms is the *local search* heuristic. All other more modern iterative heuristics such as *simulated annealing*, *tabu search*, or *genetic algorithms* are generalizations of *local search*. Before we describe *local search*, we need to explain several important concepts that are customarily encountered in combinatorial optimization.

1.3 States, Moves, and Optimality

In most general terms, *combinatorial optimization* is concerned with finding the best solution to a given problem. The class of problems we are concerned with in this book are those with finite discrete state space and which can be stated in an unambiguous mathematical notation.

Combinatorial optimization algorithms seek to find the extremum of a given objective function $Cost$. Without any loss of generality we shall assume that we are dealing with a minimization problem.

> **Definition 3** An *instance of a combinatorial optimization problem* is a pair $(\Omega, Cost)$, where Ω is the finite set of feasible solutions to the problem and $Cost$ is a *cost function*, which is a mapping of the form,
>
> $$Cost : \Omega \longrightarrow \Re$$
>
> The *cost function* is also referred to as an *objective* or *utility function*. The function $Cost$ assigns to every solution $S \in \Omega$ a (real) number $Cost(S)$ indicating its worth.

> **Definition 4** A feasible solution S of an instance of a combinatorial optimization problem $(\Omega, Cost)$ is also called a state ($S \in \Omega$). The set of feasible solutions Ω is called the *state space*.

The function $Cost$ allows us to establish an ordering relation. Let S_1 and S_2 be two solutions to the problem. S_1 is judged better than or of equal value to S_2 if $Cost(S_1) \leq Cost(S_2)$.

Solution configurations in the neighborhood of a solution $S \in \Omega$ can always be generated by performing small perturbations to S. Such local perturbations are called moves. For example, for the quadratic assignment problem (Example 1.10 on page 8), a move may consist of the swapping of the locations of two modules.

Definition 5 A neighborhood $\aleph(S)$ of solution S is the set of solutions obtained by performing a simple move $m \in \mathcal{M}$, where $\mathcal{M}$ is the set of simple moves that are allowed on solution S.

A property of most combinatorial optimization problems is that they possess noisy objective functions, that is, the function $Cost$ has several minima over the the state space Ω.

Definition 6 $\hat{S} \in \Omega$ is a *local minimum* with respect to $\aleph(S)$ if $\hat{S}$ has a lower cost than any of its neighboring solutions, that is,

$$Cost(\hat{S}) \leq Cost(S_m), \ \forall S_m \in \aleph(S), \ \forall m \in \mathcal{M}$$

Definition 7 $S^* \in \Omega$ is a *global minimum* iff

$$Cost(S^*) \leq Cost(S), \ \forall S \in \Omega$$

The objective of combinatorial search algorithms is to identify such a global optimum state S^*.

1.4 Local Search

The *local search* heuristic is one of the oldest and easiest optimization methods. Although the algorithm is simple, it has been successful with a variety of hard combinatorial optimization problems. The algorithm starts at some initial feasible solution $S_0 \in \Omega$ and uses a subroutine *Improve* to search for a better solution in the neighborhood of S_0. If a better solution $S \in \aleph(S_0)$ is found, then the search continues in the neighborhood $\aleph(S)$ of the new solution. The algorithm stops when it hits a local optimum. The subroutine *Improve* behaves as follows:

$$Improve(S) = \begin{cases} any \ T \in \aleph(S) & s.t. \ Cost(T) < Cost(S) \\ nil & otherwise \end{cases}$$

An outline of the general local search algorithm is given below.

Algorithm LocalSearch(S_0);
Begin
  $S_2 = S_0$;
  Repeat
    $S_1 = S_2$;
    $S_2 = Improve(S_1)$
  Until $S_2 = nil$;
  Return (S_1)
End /* of LocalSearch */

To use the *local search* heuristic one has to address several issues, namely, (1) how to construct the initial solution, (2) how to choose a good neighborhood for the problem at hand, and (3) the manner in which the neighborhood is searched, that is, the *Improve* subroutine.

(a) Initial solution.

Should one start from a good solution obtained by a constructive algorithm or from a randomly generated solution? Another possibility is to make several runs of *local search* starting from different initial solutions and to select the best among the obtained final solutions. These alternatives have varying computational requirements and would usually result in final solutions of varying quality.

(b) Choice of neighborhood.

Here one has to select the appropriate perturbation function to explore a good neighborhood around current solution. Elaborate perturbations (moves) are more complex to implement, require more time to execute, and usually result in large neighborhoods. In contrast, simple perturbation functions are easier to implement, require less time to execute, and would result in smaller neighborhoods. Hence, one can see a clear trade-off here: a larger neighborhood would require more time to search but holds the promise of reaching a good local minimum while a smaller neighborhood can be quickly explored but would lead to a premature convergence to a poor local minima. This issue can best be resolved through experimentation.

We should note here that if one decides to work with a small neighborhood then one has to start from a good initial solution; otherwise the search will end in a poor-quality local minima. In contrast, if one opts for a large neighborhood, then the initial solution would not have as much effect on the quality of final solution. In that case, starting from a quickly generated random solution or from a good initial solution would result in final solutions of similar quality.

(c) The subroutine "Improve."

The *Improve* subroutine can follow one of the following two strategies: (1) *first-improvement* strategy, where the first favorable cost change is accepted, or (2) the *steepest descent* strategy, where the entire neighborhood is searched, and then a solution with lowest cost is selected. The first strategy may converge sooner to a poorer local minima. However, the decision as to which strategy to use may best be made empirically.

1.4.1 Deterministic and Stochastic Algorithms

Combinatorial optimization algorithms can be broadly classified into *deterministic* and *stochastic* algorithms. A deterministic algorithm progresses toward the solution by making deterministic decisions. For example, *local search* is a deterministic algorithm. On the other hand, stochastic algorithms make random decisions in their search for a solution. Therefore deterministic algorithms produce the same solution for a given problem instance while this is not the case for stochastic algorithms.

Heuristic algorithms can also be classified as *constructive* and *iterative* algorithms. A constructive heuristic starts from a seed component (or several seeds). Then, other components are selected and added to the partial solution until a complete solution is obtained. Once a component is selected, it is never moved during future steps of the procedure. Constructive algorithms are also known as *successive augmentation algorithms*.

An *iterative* heuristic such as *local search* receives two things as inputs, one, the description of the problem instance, and two, an initial solution to the problem. The iterative heuristic attempts to modify the given solution so as to improve the cost function; if improvement cannot be attained by the algorithm, it returns a "NO," otherwise it returns an improved solution. It is customary to apply the iterative procedure repeatedly until no cost improvement is possible. Frequently, one applies an iterative improvement algorithm to refine a solution generated by a reasonable constructive heuristic. To come up with the best constructive algorithm requires far more insight into the problem and much more effort than to set up an iterative improvement scheme of the aforementioned type. Nevertheless, one may argue that it is always certain that if any iterative technique fares well on a problem, then a good constructive/deterministic heuristic has been overlooked. However, the elaboration of such good heuristics is not always possible for many practical problems.

Alternately, one could generate an initial solution randomly and pass it as input to the iterative heuristic. Random solutions are of course generated quickly; but the iterative algorithm may take a large number of iterations to converge to either a local or global optimum solution. On the other hand, a constructive heuristic takes up time; nevertheless the iterative improvement phase converges rapidly if started off with a constructive solution.

Figure 1.2 gives the flowchart of a constructive heuristic followed by an iterative heuristic. The "stopping criteria met" varies depending on the type of heuristic applied. In case of deterministic heuristics, the stopping criterion could be the first failure in improving the present solution. While in the case of nondeterministic heuristics the stopping criterion could be the runtime available, or, k consecutive failures in improving the present solution.

Typically, constructive algorithms are deterministic while iterative algorithms may be deterministic or stochastic.

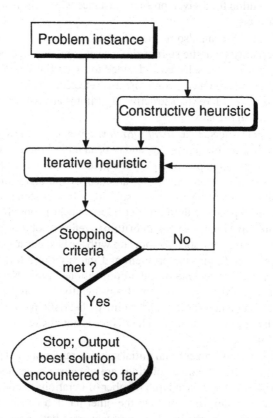

Figure 1.2: General structure combining constructive and iterative heuristics.

Justification of Iterative Improvement Approach

Constructive procedures have the advantage of being faster than iterative procedures such as those described in this book. However, at each decision step, due to its greedy nature, a constructive procedure has only a local view. Therefore, the procedure might reach the point where design constraints are not met. This will require several iterations to attempt various modifications to the solution to bring it to a feasible state. For practical problems, it is unthinkable to manually perform these modifications.

Automatic iterative improvement procedures which combine quality of constructive algorithms and iterative improvement procedures constitute effective approaches to produce feasible solutions with the desired performance. However, in order to speed up the search, care must be taken so that the iterative procedure is tuned to quickly converge to a solution satisfying all design constraints.

1.5   Optimal versus Final Solution

When is a problem solved? A key requirement of a combinatorial optimization algorithm is that it should produce a solution in a reasonably small number of computational steps. The approximation algorithms described in this book are recommended for hard combinatorial optimization problems. It will be unwise to use any of these iterative heuristics to solve problems with known efficient algorithms. For example, one should not use *local search* or *simulated annealing* (Chapter 2) to find the shortest path in a graph; we must instead use one of the known polynomial time algorithms such as *Dijkstra's* algorithm [Dij59].

Exact algorithms for hard problems require in the worst case an exponential (and sometimes a factorial) number of steps to find the optimal solution. For example, suppose that for a given hard problem, a computer is programmed to perform a brute force search for an optimal solution and that the computer is capable of examining one billion solutions per second. Assume that the search space consists of 2^n solutions. Then for $n = 20$ the optimal solution will be found in about 1 *millisecond*. For $n = 100$, the computer will need over 40,000 centuries! The situation would be much worse if we had a problem whose search space consisted of $n!$ solutions. Obviously, a combinatorial optimization problem will not be considered solved if one does not live to see the answer! Hence, a fundamental requirement of any reasonable optimization algorithm is that it should produce an answer to the problem (not necessarily the best) in a reasonably small amount of time. The words *reasonable* and *small* are fuzzy and usually are interpreted differently by different people (depending on the problem, what the answer is needed for, and how soon).

The approximation algorithms described in this book are all iterative, nondeterministic, and keep on searching the solution space until some stopping criteria are met. Examples of stopping criteria are: (1) the last k iterations did not identify a better solution, (2) a runtime limit has been exceeded, (3) some parameter of the iterative algorithm has reached a threshold limit; and so forth. Once the algorithm stops, it outputs the best solution found. For most practical applications, the runtime of such algorithms may be a few hours. Furthermore, none of these iterative algorithms guarantee finding the optimal solution (if such a solution exists) in a finite amount of time.

1.6   Single versus Multicriteria Constrained Optimization

Constrained optimization consists of finding a solution which satisfies a specified set of constraints and optimizes an analytically defined objective function. A solution which satisfies the problem constraints is a *feasible solution*. If it also optimizes the stated objective function then it is an *optimal solution*. The objective function is to be computed for each combination of the input variables. Values of the input variables change as the search moves from one solution to another. The solution with an optimal value of the objective function is an optimal solution.

A *single objective constrained optimization problem* consists of the minimization/maximization of a utility function $Cost$ over the set of feasible solutions Ω. For example, for a minimization problem we have something of the following form:

$$\min_{S \in \Omega} Cost(S) \tag{1.1}$$

If $Cost$ is linear and Ω is defined by linear constraints, the problem is *a single objective linear programming problem*. If in addition the problem variables are restricted to be integers, then the problem becomes an *integer programming problem*. In case either the utility function or any of the constraints are nonlinear the problem becomes *a single objective nonlinear optimization problem*.

In most practical cases, optimization problems are multiple objective problems. In such situations, one is typically confronted with several conflicting utility functions $Cost_1, \ldots, Cost_i, \ldots, Cost_n$, that is,

$$\min_{S \in \Omega} Cost_i(S) \quad 1 \le i \le n \tag{1.2}$$

Unlike single-objective optimization problems, no concept of optimal solution is universally accepted for multiobjective optimization. In practical cases, the rating of individual objectives reflects the preference of the decision-maker. At best, a compromise between competing objectives can be expected.

A commonly used approach to transform a multiobjective optimization problem into a single objective optimization problem is to define another utility function as a weighted sum of the individual criteria, that is,

$$Cost(S) = \sum_{i=1}^{n} w_i Cost_i$$

The w_i's are positive weights that reflect the relative importance of criteria or goals in the eyes of the decision maker. More important criteria are assigned higher weights. Usually, the weight coefficients sum to one. Furthermore, prior to computing the weighted utility function, the individual criteria are normalized to fall in the same range.

Another approach to tackle multicriteria optimization problems is to rely on the *ranking* of the individual objectives. In this approach one does not attempt to seek a solution that is minimum with respect to all objectives, since anyhow, in most cases such a solution does not exist; rather the objective function is seen as a vector function. Without loss of generality let us assume that $Cost_i$ is more important than $Cost_{i+1}$, $1 \leq i \leq n - 1$. Then a *preference relation* $\prec$ is defined over the solution space Ω as follows:

$\forall S \in \Omega,\ \forall S' \in \Omega :\ S \preceq S'$ if and only if
$\exists\, i,\ 1 \leq i \leq n$, such that $Cost_i(S) \leq Cost_i(S')$, and
$\forall\, j < i,\ Cost_j(S) = Cost_j(S')$

The above preference relation defines a partial order on the elements of the state space of feasible solutions Ω.

In many cases, it is not clear how one can balance different objectives by a weight function especially when the various objectives are defined over different domains. Also, it is not always possible to have a crisp ranking of the individual objectives. Another difficulty is that the outcome of such ranking is not always predictable especially when some of the criteria are correlated. Fuzzy logic provides a convenient framework for solving this problem [Zad65, Zad73, Zad75, Zim91]. It allows one to map values of different criteria into linguistic values, which characterize the level of satisfaction of the designer with the numerical values of objectives. Each linguistic value is then defined by a membership function which maps numerical values of the corresponding objective criterion into the interval [0,1]. The desires of the decision maker are conveniently expressed in terms of fuzzy logic rules and fuzzy preference rules. The execution/firing of such rules produces numerical values that are used to decide a solution goodness. In practice, this approach has been proven powerful for finding compromise solutions in different areas of science and engineering [KLS94, LS92, Ped89, RG90, TS85, Wan94, Zim87, Zim91]. We shall address in more detail the subject of using fuzzy logic for multicriteria optimization in Chapter 7.

The algorithms described in this book are general optimization techniques suitable for single as well as multiple objective problems. However, for the sake of simplicity, we shall confine ourselves to single-objective optimization problems.

Interested readers in the general subject of multi-criteria optimization may consult
the book by Steuer [Ste86].

1.7   Convergence Analysis of Iterative Algorithms

Unlike constructive algorithms, which produce a solution only at the end of the
design process, iterative algorithms operate with design solutions defined at each
iteration. A value of the objective function is used to compare results of consecutive iterations and to select a solution based on the maximal (minimal) value of
the objective function.

1.7.1   Configuration Graph

The state space being searched can be represented as a directed graph called the
configuration graph. Let Ω be the set of feasible configurations (states) for some
instance of a discrete minimization problem. Ω can be considered as the set of
vertices of a directed configuration graph C_G [Len90].

Definition 8   A directed graph $C_G=(\Omega, E)$ is called a configuration graph
where $S \in \Omega$, and $\aleph(S) = \{T \in \Omega | (S, T) \in E\}$; Ω is the set of legal
configurations and $E=\{(S, T) | S \in \Omega, T \in \Omega \text{ and } T \in \aleph(S)\}$. An edge
between two states indicates that they are neighbors. A state S is called a
"local minimum" if $Cost(S) \le Cost(T)$ for all $T \in \aleph(S)$. In addition, if S
is an optimal solution then it is called a "global minimum."

Example 1.13   An example of a configuration graph with eight states is
given in Figure 1.3. For the moment we will concentrate only on the structure
and the values in the circles and ignore the labels on the edges. The numbers
in the circles indicate the cost of the configurations. For example, the circle
with label 3 represents a state with cost equal to 3. State 3 is a local minimum
because it has no neighbors with a lower cost. State 1 is a global minimum
because it is a local minimum with the lowest cost, and is the optimal solution. It is not possible to go from state 3 to state 1 without going through
states with cost greater than 3, that is, through states with costs 4 and 7, or
through 5 (climbing the hill). On the other hand, starting in state 8 we can
apply a greedy heuristic that will take us to state 1 (that is, through states 5
and 2, or through state 6).

■

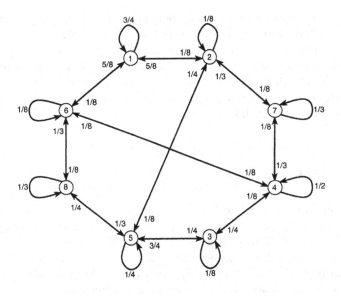

Figure 1.3: An example of a configuration graph.

A "search" from configuration $S \in \Omega$ is a directed path in C_G that starts at S and ends in the solution the search has found. The search is said to be "greedy" if the costs of successive vertices along the search path are decreasing.

The goal of the search is to find a solution that is as close as possible to the optimum. As illustrated in Figure 1.3, greedy heuristics such as *local search* usually lead to local optima and not global optima. The reason is that they provide no mechanism for the search to escape from a local optimum. Two possibilities exist that can help one avoid getting trapped in a local optimum.

1. Accommodate nongreedy search moves, that is, moves in which the cost increases

2. Increase the number of edges in the configuration graph

As for the first possibility, care must be taken to see that such moves are not too frequent. There are probabilistic and deterministic ways of doing so.

In the second possibility, for a configuration graph with many edges and a large neighborhood there are less chances to hit a local optimum. In addition, for a given initial configuration, shorter search paths to the "global optimum" may exist. An extreme case is when C_G is a fully connected directed graph. In that case, every local optimum is also a global optimum and a single step is enough to go from any state to the global optimum. However, the denser the configuration graph is, the more inefficient the search step will be. This is because in each search step we optimize over the neighborhood of the current configuration, and the larger the neighborhood is, the more time we need to find a good configuration to move to, from where the search can proceed. Therefore, it is important to keep the neighborhood small and not add too many edges to C_G. Researchers have been looking at such issues with mathematical rigor. The mathematical framework used to study the convergence properties of iterative approximation algorithms is the theory of Markov chains.

1.8   Markov Chains

A randomized local search technique operates on a state space. As mentioned above, the search proceeds step by step, by moving from a certain configuration (state) S_i to its neighbor S_j, with a certain probability $\text{Prob}(S_i, S_j)$ denoted by p_{ij}. At the end of each step the new state reached represents a new configuration. The states in $\aleph(S_i) = \{S_j \in \Omega | (S_i, S_j) \in E\}$ are said to be connected to S_i by a single move. We can assume that choices of all neighbors out of S_i are independent. The corresponding mathematical structure is a labeled configuration graph with edge labels corresponding to *transition* probabilities. Such a configuration graph is a Markov chain (see Figure 1.3).

1.8.1   Time-Homogeneous Markov Chains

Let $C_G = (\Omega, E)$ be a directed graph with $\Omega = \{S_1, S_2, \ldots, S_i, \ldots, S_n\}$ the set of all possible states, and $Cost : \Omega \to \Re$, be a function which assigns a real number $Cost_i$ to each state $S_i \in \Omega$, and $p : E \to [0, 1]$ be an edge-weighting function such that

$$\sum_{S_j \in \aleph(S_i)} p_{ij} = 1 \quad \forall S_i \in \Omega \tag{1.3}$$

(C_G, p) is a finite *time-homogeneous* Markov chain. In our case $Cost_i$ denotes the cost of configuration S_i, and p_{ij} represents the transition probability from state S_i to S_j. The restriction on p, the edge-weighting function, is that the sum of transition probabilities of edges leaving a vertex add up to unity (p is a probability distribution). Also, in a time-homogeneous Markov chain the transition probabilities are *constant* and independent of past transitions. The configuration graph C_G given in Figure 1.3 represents a time-homogeneous Markov chain.

Two numbers are associated with each pair of states. One is called the *selection probability* or the *perturbation probability*, denoted by p_{ij}, and the other is the acceptance probability A_{ij}.

1.8.2 Perturbation Probability

The number associated with each pair of states (edge label denoted by p_{ij}) is called the *perturbation probability*. This number actually gives the probability of generating a configuration S_j from S_i.

Let $\aleph(S_i)$ be the configuration subspace for state S_i which is defined as the space of all configurations that can be reached from S_i by a single perturbation. For pairs of states connected by at least a single move the perturbation probability p_{ij} is never zero. The probability p_{ij} depends on the structure of the configuration graph, and in the simplest case it is defined as follows:

$$p_{ij} = \begin{cases} \frac{1}{|\aleph(S_i)|} & \text{if } S_j \in \aleph(S_i) \\ 0 & \text{if } S_j \notin \aleph(S_i) \end{cases} \tag{1.4}$$

This is a uniform probability distribution for all configurations in the subspace. The probabilities p_{ij} can also be represented using a matrix P known as the *generation matrix* or *perturbation matrix*. Matrix P is a stochastic matrix.[4]

1.8.3 Ergodic Markov Chains

A Markov chain is called ergodic if and only if it is

1. irreducible, that is, all states are reachable from all other states;

2. aperiodic, that is, for each state, the probability of returning to that state is positive for all steps;

3. recurrent, that is, for each state of the chain, the probability of returning to that state at some time in the future is equal to one; and

4. non-null, that is, the expected number of steps to return to a state is finite.

Let $\pi(t) = (\pi_1(t), \pi_2(t), \ldots, \pi_i(t), \ldots, \pi_n(t))$ be the probability state vector, where $\pi_i(t)$ is the probability of being in state S_i at time t (iteration t).

The probability transition matrix P is used to describe how the process evolves from state to state. If at step t, the probability state vector is $\pi(t)$, then the probability state vector one step later is given by

$$\pi(t+1) = \pi(t) \cdot P \tag{1.5}$$

Hence, the probability $\pi_i(t+1)$ of being in state S_i at step $t+1$, is given by

$$\pi_i(t+1) = \sum_{j=1}^{n} \pi_j(t) \cdot p_{ji} \tag{1.6}$$

---

[4]A square matrix whose entries are non-negative, and whose row sums are equal to unity, is called a *stochastic* matrix. Sometimes an additional condition is that the column sums are also not zero.

For an ergodic Markov chain, the state probability vector changes at each step and is guaranteed to converge to a limit probability vector $\pi = (\pi_1, \ldots, \pi_i, \ldots)$, that is, $\lim_{t \to \infty} \pi(t) = \pi$. The probability state vector π, which no longer depends on the time step, is the steady-state distribution of the search process.

A fundamental theorem on Markov chains states that an ergodic Markov chain has a unique stationary distribution π which is a solution to the following equation [Kle75].

$$\pi = \pi \cdot P \tag{1.7}$$

The stationary distribution can also be obtained by finding the stationary matrix P_S given by

$$P_S = \lim_{k \to \infty} P^k \tag{1.8}$$

where P^k is the k-fold matrix product of P with itself. If the Markov chain is ergodic, then P_S will have the characteristic that all its rows are identical. We say that the Markov chain has converged to its stationary distribution.

If we start the Markov chain in any state S_i, it will converge to the distribution given by $\lim_{k \to \infty} I_i \cdot P^k$, where I_i is the ith unit vector (1 in the ith position and 0 elsewhere). Since $I_i \cdot P_S$ is equal to $I_j \cdot P_S$ for all i, j, at steady state, the probability of being in any state is independent of the initial state. We will now illustrate the above concepts with examples.

Example 1.14 Figure 1.3 is an example of an ergodic Markov chain. The labels on the edges connecting two states S_i and S_j indicate the transition probability from state S_i to state S_j. The corresponding transition matrix is given below.

$$P = \begin{Bmatrix} \frac{3}{4} & \frac{1}{8} & 0 & 0 & 0 & \frac{1}{8} & 0 & 0 \\ \frac{5}{8} & \frac{1}{8} & 0 & 0 & \frac{1}{8} & 0 & \frac{1}{8} & 0 \\ 0 & 0 & \frac{1}{8} & \frac{1}{8} & \frac{3}{4} & 0 & 0 & 0 \\ 0 & 0 & \frac{1}{4} & \frac{1}{2} & 0 & \frac{1}{8} & \frac{1}{8} & 0 \\ 0 & \frac{1}{4} & \frac{1}{4} & 0 & \frac{1}{4} & 0 & 0 & \frac{1}{4} \\ \frac{5}{8} & 0 & 0 & \frac{1}{8} & 0 & \frac{1}{8} & 0 & \frac{1}{8} \\ 0 & \frac{1}{3} & 0 & \frac{1}{3} & 0 & 0 & \frac{1}{3} & 0 \\ 0 & 0 & 0 & 0 & \frac{1}{3} & \frac{1}{3} & 0 & \frac{1}{3} \end{Bmatrix}$$

Let us raise the matrix P to a large power, say 100. Using Mathematica [Wol91], this can be achieved by the command

```
Q=MatrixPower[P,100];
Print[MatrixForm[N[Q]]]
```

which produces the following output.

$$
\mathbf{P}^{100} = \left\{
\begin{array}{cccccccc}
0.5334 & 0.1106 & 0.0385 & 0.0562 & 0.0786 & 0.1028 & 0.0313 & 0.0488 \\
0.5334 & 0.1106 & 0.0385 & 0.0562 & 0.0786 & 0.1028 & 0.0313 & 0.0488 \\
0.5334 & 0.1106 & 0.0385 & 0.0562 & 0.0786 & 0.1028 & 0.0313 & 0.0488 \\
0.5334 & 0.1106 & 0.0385 & 0.0562 & 0.0786 & 0.1028 & 0.0313 & 0.0488 \\
0.5334 & 0.1106 & 0.0385 & 0.0562 & 0.0786 & 0.1028 & 0.0313 & 0.0488 \\
0.5334 & 0.1106 & 0.0385 & 0.0562 & 0.0786 & 0.1028 & 0.0313 & 0.0488 \\
0.5334 & 0.1106 & 0.0385 & 0.0562 & 0.0786 & 0.1028 & 0.0313 & 0.0488 \\
0.5334 & 0.1106 & 0.0385 & 0.0562 & 0.0786 & 0.1028 & 0.0313 & 0.0488
\end{array}
\right\}
$$

■

From the above example we note that starting from any initial state, say state 3, denoted by the unit vector $I_3 = [0, 0, 1, 0, 0, 0, 0, 0]$, the probability of being in any state after 100 state transitions (or moves) is given by $I_3 \cdot \mathbf{P}^{100}$, that is, the third row of the matrix $\mathbf{P}^{100}$. The probability of being in state 1 after 100 moves is 0.5334, of being in state 2 is 0.1106, and so on. Note that in this case the value 100 can be defined as *large*. Sometimes the matrix will have to be raised to a larger power to get the stationary distribution.

Observe that since all rows are identical, irrespective of which row we start our search, we will always get the same probability of being in any state. We can also verify Equation 1.6. For example, when $i = 4$,

$$
\pi_4 = \sum_{j=1}^{8} \pi_j \cdot p_{j4} = \pi_3 \cdot p_{34} + \pi_4 \cdot p_{44} + \pi_6 \cdot p_{64} + \pi_7 \cdot p_{74}
$$

$$
\pi_4 = \frac{0.0385}{8} + \frac{0.0562}{2} + \frac{0.1028}{8} + \frac{0.0313}{3} = 0.0562
$$

which is the same as column 4 of our matrix $\mathbf{P}^{100}$ which gives the value of π_4, the steady-state probability of being in state S_4.

Example 1.15 For the same ergodic Markov chain of the previous example, the stationary distribution can be accurately obtained by solving the set of linear equations $\pi = \pi \cdot \mathbf{P}$, and the equation $\sum_{i=1}^{n} \pi_i = 1$. Again, using Mathematica, this can be obtained as follows.

Solution: Solve

```
[{
P[[1,1]]p1+P[[2,1]]p2+P[[3,1]]p3+P[[4,1]]p4+P[[5,1]]p5
                +P[[6,1]]p6+P[[7,1]]p7+P[[8,1]]p8==p1,
P[[1,2]]p1+P[[2,2]]p2+P[[3,2]]p3+P[[4,2]]p4+P[[5,2]]p5
                +P[[6,2]]p6+P[[7,2]]p7+P[[8,2]]p8==p2,
P[[1,3]]p1+P[[2,3]]p2+P[[3,3]]p3+P[[4,3]]p4+P[[5,3]]p5
                +P[[6,3]]p6+P[[7,3]]p7+P[[8,3]]p8==p3,
P[[1,4]]p1+P[[2,4]]p2+P[[3,4]]p3+P[[4,4]]p4+P[[5,4]]p5
```

```
                      +P[[6,4]]p6+P[[7,4]]p7+P[[8,4]]p8==p4,
P[[1,5]]p1+P[[2,5]]p2+P[[3,5]]p3+P[[4,5]]p4+P[[5,5]]p5
                      +P[[6,5]]p6+P[[7,5]]p7+P[[8,5]]p8==p5,
P[[1,6]]p1+P[[2,6]]p2+P[[3,6]]p3+P[[4,6]]p4+P[[5,6]]p5
                      +P[[6,6]]p6+P[[7,6]]p7+P[[8,6]]p8==p6,
P[[1,7]]p1+P[[2,7]]p2+P[[3,7]]p3+P[[4,7]]p4+P[[5,7]]p5
                      +P[[6,7]]p6+P[[7,7]]p7+P[[8,7]]p8==p7,
P[[1,8]]p1+P[[2,8]]p2+P[[3,8]]p3+P[[4,8]]p4+P[[5,8]]p5
                      +P[[6,8]]p6+P[[7,8]]p7+P[[8,8]]p8==p8,
p1+p2+p3+p4+p5+p6+p7+p8==1},{p1,p2,p3,p4,p5,p6,p7,p8}];
Simplify[%]
```

Here $P[[i,j]]$ represents p_{ij} the elements of matrix P, and pi represents π_i (i=1,2,...,8). The distribution thus obtained is

$$\pi = \left(\begin{array}{cccccccc} \frac{3020}{5662} & \frac{626}{5662} & \frac{218}{5662} & \frac{318}{5662} & \frac{445}{5662} & \frac{582}{5662} & \frac{177}{5662} & \frac{276}{5662} \end{array} \right)$$

That is,

$$\pi = \left(\begin{array}{cccccccc} 0.5334 & 0.1106 & 0.0385 & 0.0562 & 0.0786 & 0.1028 & 0.0313 & 0.0488 \end{array} \right)$$

Note that this is identical to one of the rows of our matrix P^{100}.

■

1.8.4 Acceptance Probability

In many cases, the transition probabilities of a random process depend on a control parameter T which is a function of time. The probabilities now take the form $f(Cost_i, Cost_j, T)$, where T is a parameter that depends on the step number of the Markov chain, and $Cost_i$ and $Cost_j$ are the costs of the current and next states, respectively. The corresponding Markov chains are called *time-inhomogeneous* Markov chains. Let $\Delta Cost_{ij} = Cost_j - Cost_i$. Then the acceptance probability A_{ij} may be defined as

$$A_{ij}(T) = \begin{cases} f(Cost_i, Cost_j, T) & \text{if } \Delta Cost_{ij} > 0 \\ 1 & \text{if } \Delta Cost_{ij} \leq 0 \end{cases} \tag{1.9}$$

Thus the probability that the generated new state will be the next state depends on its cost, the cost of the previous state, and the value of the control parameter T. We always accept cost-improving moves. A move that deteriorates the cost will be accepted with a probability $f(Cost_i, Cost_j, T)$. The sequence of states thus generated corresponds to a *time-inhomogeneous Markov chain*. We have a Markov chain because of the important property that the next state depends only on where we are now and does not depend on the states that have preceded the current state. Therefore, for this time-inhomogeneous Markov chain, given S_i as the current state, the probability $\Theta_{ij}(T)$ to transit to state S_j is defined as follows:

$$\Theta_{ij}(T) = \begin{cases} A_{ij}(T)p_{ij} & \text{if } i \neq j \\ 1 - \sum_{k,k\neq i} A_{ik}(T)p_{ik} & \text{if } i = j \end{cases} \quad (1.10)$$

where p_{ij} is the perturbation probability, that is, the probability of generating a configuration S_j from configuration S_i (usually independent of T); $A_{ij}(T)$ is the acceptance probability, (see Equation 1.9), i.e., the probability of accepting configuration S_j if the system is in configuration S_i; and T is the control parameter.

The transition probabilities for a certain value of T can be conveniently represented by a matrix $\Theta(T)$, called the *transition matrix*. The probabilities $A_{ij}(T)$ can also be represented using a matrix $A(T)$ (*acceptance matrix*). Like the perturbation matrix P, the transition matrix Θ is also stochastic. The acceptance matrix $A(T)$ however, is not stochastic.

1.8.5 Transition Probability

Let $\Theta_{ij}(T)$ be the transition probability from state S_i to state S_j for a particular value of the control parameter T, that is, $\Theta_{ij}(T) = p_{ij} \cdot A_{ij}(T)$. At a particular value of the parameter T, the transition matrix $\Theta(T)$ is constant and thus corresponds to a *homogeneous* Markov chain.

Under the assumption that all states of current neighborhood $\aleph(S_i)$ are equally likely, p_{ij} is equal to the following:

$$p_{ij} = \frac{1}{|\aleph(S_i)|}$$

Therefore, in summary, we have the following expressions for the probabilities $\Theta_{ij}(T)$:

$$\Theta_{ij}(T) = \begin{cases} \frac{1}{|\aleph(S_i)|} & \text{if } \Delta Cost_{ij} \leq 0 \quad S_j \in \aleph(S_i) \\ \frac{1}{|\aleph(S_i)|} f(Cost_i, Cost_j, T) & \text{if } \Delta Cost_{ij} > 0 \quad S_j \in \aleph(S_i) \\ 1 - \sum_{k,k\neq i} p_{ik} A_{ik}(T) & \text{if } i = j \qquad\quad S_j \in \aleph(S_i) \\ 0 & \qquad\qquad\qquad\quad S_j \notin \aleph(S_i) \end{cases} \quad (1.11)$$

As we shall see, in the following chapter in the case of the simulated annealing algorithm, a steady-state distribution $\pi(T)$ exists for each value of the parameter T, provided T is maintained constant for a large enough number of iterations. The steady-state probability vector $\pi(T)$ satisfies the following equation:

$$\pi(T) = \pi(T) \cdot \Theta(T)$$

Furthermore, following an adequate updating schedule of the parameter T, the process will converge to the steady state whose stationary distribution π (also called *optimizing distribution*) satisfies the following equality:

$$\pi = \pi \cdot \Theta$$

1.9 Parallel Processing

In this section, we introduce the necessary terminology that will be used in the discussion of the parallel implementations of the various iterative algorithms that are described in this book.

Need for Parallel Processing

Exact as well as approximate iterative algorithms for hard problems have large runtime requirements. There is ever increasing interest in the use of parallel processing to obtain greater execution speed. Parallel computation offers a great opportunity for sizable improvement in the solution of large and hard problems that would otherwise have been impractical to tackle on a sequential computer. A general problem with parallel computers is that they are harder to program. Every computer scientist knows how to design and implement algorithms that run on sequential computers. In contrast, only relatively few have the skill of designing and implementing parallel algorithmic solutions.

A *parallel computer* is one that consists of a collection of processors, which can be programmed to cooperate together to solve a particular problem. In order to achieve any improvement in performance, the processors must be programmed so that they work concurrently on the problem. The goal, of course, is usually to reach, in much less time, a solution of similar quality to that obtained from running a sequential algorithm. Actually, the ratio of the sequential runtime to parallel runtime is an important performance measure called the *speed-up*. Sometimes, parallel search is used to find a better solution in the same time required by the sequential algorithm rather than to reach a similar quality solution in shorter time.

Parallel Algorithm Evaluation Measures

Let A_1 and A_p, respectively, be a sequential algorithm and a parallel algorithm for p processors to solve the same problem. The goodness of the parallel algorithm is usually characterized by several measures, such as

1. The time t_p taken to run A_p.

2. The space s_p required to run A_p.

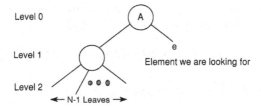

Figure 1.4: Imbalanced tree. Sequential depth first for element e would require $N + 1$ operations. If the search is split among two processors, each looking in a subtree, then element e will be returned in two steps.

3. *Speed-up*: how much did we gain in speed by using p processors. If t_1 is the runtime of the sequential algorithm, then the *speed-up* $\mathcal{S}_p$ is defined as follows:

$$\mathcal{S}_p = \frac{t_1}{t_p} \tag{1.12}$$

Normally, $0 < \mathcal{S}_p \leq p$. However, this is not always the case. For instance, assume that we would like to look for a particular node in a tree using the *depth-first* search algorithm. Assume that the tree has N nodes. Then the maximum time that will be taken by the sequential *depth-first* algorithm will be $t_1 = N + 1$. This happens in case the tree is imbalanced with all the $N - 1$ nodes in the left subtree and being at the second level (root at level 0), and the node we are looking for is the only node in the right subtree (Figure 1.4). Suppose we have two processors and that each processor takes a subtree and expands it. In that case $t_2 = 2$. Therefore the *speed-up* is $\mathcal{S}_p = \frac{N+1}{2}$, which is greater than 2, the number of processors. One might wonder why this is happening? The answer is simply because in the first place one should not have used *depth-first* search to locate a particular node in a tree, that is, one must use the best possible sequential algorithm for the problem at hand. The parallel algorithm should not mimic the sequential algorithm nor should the sequential algorithm be a simple serialization of the parallel algorithm.

The above definition of *speed-up* applies to deterministic algorithms only. For a nondeterministic iterative algorithm such as simulated annealing, *speed-up* is defined in a different manner. It is equal to the number of parallel tasks into which each move is divided [RK86]. Sometimes, the number of processors that are concurrently working is taken as a measure of the speed-up achieved.

Another suggested definition [DRKN87] bears closer resemblance to the definition of *speed-up* for deterministic algorithms. *Speed-up* is defined as the ratio of the execution time of the serial algorithm to that of the parallel implementation of the algorithm, averaged over several runs and various final values of the cost function.

4. *Efficiency* E_p: this performance measure indicates how well we are using the p processors,

$$E_p = \frac{S_p}{p} \tag{1.13}$$

Under normal conditions, $0 < E_p \leq 1$.

5. *Isoefficiency* ie_p: this measure is an estimate of the efficiency of the algorithm as we change the number of processors, while maintaining the problem instance fixed. It is desirable to have parallel algorithms with ie_p close to p (linear in p). Hence, we guarantee no processor starvation as we increase the number of processors.

Amdahl's Law

Amdahl's law was introduced to convince the computing community that parallelism is not good after all.

Let f be the fraction parallelized in the algorithm. Then, with p processors, the best possible parallel algorithm would require the following runtime given by

$$t_p = (1 - f)t_1 + \frac{f}{p}t_1 \tag{1.14}$$

Therefore, the maximum speed-up in this case would be

$$S_p = \frac{1}{(1 - f) + \frac{f}{p}} \tag{1.15}$$

For example, for $f = 0.5$, according to Amdahl's law, the speed-up cannot exceed 2 even if an infinite number of processors are made available! This is indeed a disturbing conclusion both to the manufacturers of parallel machines, as well as to researchers in parallel algorithms. Fortunately, a closer examination of Amdahl's law uncovers a major flaw. The main problem with Amdahl's law is that it does not capture how much time the algorithm spends in the parallelized fraction of the code. If, for example, 90 percent of the time is spent in the parallelized piece of code, then the speed-up can be as high as $0.9p$. Hence, parallelism can indeed be extremely good!

Parallel Computer Models and Properties

There are several ways one can classify computers. A possible classification is that of *multiprocessor* versus *multicomputer*. A *multiprocessor* machine is a computer with several processors that are tightly coupled, that is, they either have a shared memory or a shared memory address space. When programming a multiprocessor machine one does not have to explicitly indicate from which processor he or she wants the data. An example of such a machine is the Butterfly [Lei92].

A *multicomputer* also consists of several processors; however, the processors have no shared memory or shared address space. When programming a multi-computer, one has to explicitly request/send data from/to a given processor. An example of a multicomputer machine is the NCUBE [Lei92]. In practice, we may find combinations that fit in both categories. Both classes of parallel computer models are illustrated in Figure 1.5.

A classification of parallel machine models based on the work of Flynn [Fly66] distinguishes between the parallel machine models on the basis of the number of instructions and data streams concurrently accepted by the machine. Flynn identified four classes of parallel machine models.

1. SISD—Single Instruction, Single Data Stream
   Here one instruction at a time is executed on one data set at a time. The classic sequential Von Neumann machines fall into this class.

2. SIMD—Single Instruction, Multiple Data Stream
   For this class, one instruction at a time is executed concurrently on several data sets. Examples of machines that fall into this class are *vector computers* and *array processors*.

3. MISD—Multiple Instructions, Single Data Stream
   These machines are capable of executing concurrently several instructions at a time on one data set.

4. MIMD—Multiple Instructions, Multiple Data Stream
   Multiple instructions at a time are concurrently executed on multiple data sets. MIMD machines can be either synchronous or asynchronous. The processors of a synchronous MIMD machine are synchronized on a global clock, thus forcing the execution of each successive group of instructions simultaneously. For asynchronous MIMD machines the processors execute the instructions independently of each other. Typical examples of MIMD machines are hypercube computers (such as the NCUBE) [Lei92].

The four machine models are illustrated in Figure 1.6. The reader should note, however, that machines that perform some lower level of parallelism, such as *pipelining,* do not fit into Flynn's classification.

1.10   Summary and Organization of the Book

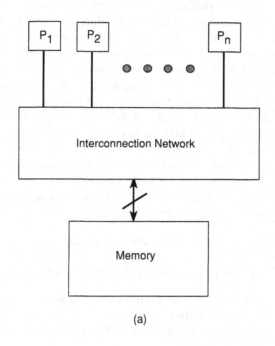

(a)

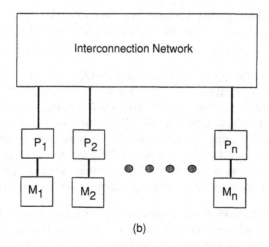

(b)

Figure 1.5: Models of parallel computers: (a) tightly coupled multiprocessor; (b) loosely coupled multicomputer.

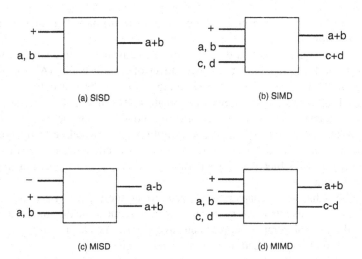

Figure 1.6: Classification of parallel machine models: (a) SISD—Single Instruction, Single Data Stream; (b) SIMD—Single Instruction, Multiple Data Stream; (c) MISD—Multiple Instructions, Single Data Stream; (d) MIMD—Multiple Instructions, Multiple Data Stream.

This chapter has introduced basic concepts of combinatorial optimization and algorithm complexity. There are two general categories of algorithms for combinatorial optimization: (1) exact or full-enumeration algorithms, and (2) approximation algorithms, also known as heuristics. In this book, we are concerned with hard problems. For such class of problems, exact algorithms are impractical as they have prohibitive runtime requirements. Approximation algorithms constitute the only practical alternative solution method.

Approximation algorithms can further be classified into problem-specific heuristics and general heuristics. As their names indicate, problem-specific algorithms are tailored to one particular problem. A heuristic designed for one particular problem would not work for a different problem. General heuristics on the other hand can be easily tailored to solve (reasonably well) any combinatorial optimization problem. There has been increasing interest in such heuristic search algorithms.

In the following chapters the reader will find detailed descriptions of five well-thought-out general iterative approximation algorithms, namely, *simulated annealing, genetic algorithms, tabu search, simulated evolution,* and *stochastic evolution.* Simulated annealing mimics the thermodynamic process of annealing. Genetic algorithms, simulated evolution, and stochastic evolution simulate biological processes according to the Darwinian theory of evolution. Tabu search attempts to imitate intelligent search processes through the use of a memory component in order to learn from its (long- or short-term) past, thus making better search decisions.

This is the only book that describes these five heuristics in a single volume. Two of these heuristics have been the subject of several books [AK89, Aze92, Dav91, Gol89, OvG89]. The tabu search algorithm has been widely used in the literature [GL97, Ree95]. However, the remaining two heuristics, simulated evolution and stochastic evolution, have not witnessed yet similar success. We believe that simulated evolution and stochastic evolution are extremely effective general combinatorial optimization techniques that deserve much more attention than they have received. The objective of this book is to provide a uniform treatment of all these techniques.

The book has seven chapters organized around these five iterative heuristics. The purpose of this introductory chapter has been to motivate the student to study and use the general iterative approximate algorithms. The chapter also introduced the basic terminology needed in the remaining chapters.

The following five chapters are dedicated to the five selected heuristics. For each search heuristic, we start by providing a historical account of the search method. We then describe the basic algorithm and its parameters and operators. This will be followed by addressing the convergence aspects of the algorithm. Examples are included to illustrate the operation of the heuristic on a number of practical problems. Parallelization strategies of the algorithm will also be presented. In each chapter, the final section, "Conclusions and Recent Work," discusses several other relevant variations of the described techniques (recent or otherwise).

Finally, in Chapter 7, we shall touch upon some work that has been reported in the area of hybridization. This area concerns combining key features of various heuristics to design new effective search techniques. In this chapter we also discuss multiobjective optimization, and give a brief overview of how fuzzy logic is used to represent multiobjective cost functions. Optimization using neural networks, and other relevant issues such as solution quality, measure of performance, and so forth are also covered.

The body of available literature on some of the techniques, namely, *simulated annealing* and *genetic algorithms*, is enormous. Therefore, it is impossible to describe and discuss every single reported work. Rather, we concentrate on describing those works we are most familiar with and which we feel are the most significant.

References

[AK89]   E. Aarts and J. Korst. *Simulated Annealing and Boltzmann Machines: A Stochastic Approach to Combinatorial Optimization and Neural Computing.* John Wiley & Sons, 1989.

[Aze92]   R. Azencott, editor. *Simulated Annealing Parallelization Techniques.* John Wiley & Sons, 1992.

[BGAB83]   L. Bodin, L. Goldin, A. Assad, and M. Ball. Routing and scheduling of vehicles and crews: The state of art. *Computers & Operations Research*, 10:63–211, 1983.

[Dav91]   L. Davis, editor. *Handbook of Genetic Algorithms.* Van Nostrand Reinhold, New York, 1991.

[Dij59]   E. W. Dijkstra. A note on two problems in connection with graphs. *Numerische Mathematik*, 1:269–271, 1959.

[DLSS88]   M. Desrochers, J. K. Lenstra, M. W. P. Savelsbergh, and F. Soumis. Vehicle routing with time windows: Optimization and approximation. In B. L. Goldin and A. A. Assad, editors, *Vehicle Routing: Methods and Studies*, pages 65–84. North Holland, Amsterdam, 1988.

[DRKN87]   F. Darema-Rogers, S. Kirkpatrick, and V. A. Norton. Parallel algorithms for chip placement by simulated annealing. *IBM Journal of Research and Development*, 31:391–402, May 1987.

[Fly66]   ·M. J. Flynn. Very high-speed computing systems. *Proceedings of IEEE*, 54:1901–1909, 1966.

[Fou84]   L. R. Foulds. *Combinatorial Optimization for Undergraduates.* Springer-Verlag, 1984.

[GJ79]   M. Garey and D. Johnson. *Computer and Intractability: A Guide to the Theory of NP-completeness.* W. H. Freeman, San Francisco, 1979.

[GL97]   F. Glover and M. Laguna. *Tabu Search.* Kluwer, MA, 1997.

[Gol89]   D. E. Goldberg. *Genetic Algorithms in Search, Optimization and Machine Learning.* Addison-Wesley, 1989.

[GPR94]   B.-L. Garica, J.-Y. Potvin, and J.-M. Rousseau. A parallel implementation of the tabu search heuristic for vehicle routing problems with time window constraints. *Computers & Operations Research*, 21(9):1025–1033, November 1994.

[HS84]   E. Horowitz and S. Sahni. *Fundamentals of Computer Algorithms.* Computer Science Press, Rockville, MD, 1984.

[Hu82]   T. C. Hu. *Combinatorial Algorithms.* Addison-Wesley, 1982.

[Kle75]   L. Kleinrock. *Queueing Systems, Volume I: Theory.* Wiley-Interscience, New York, 1975.

[KLS94]   E. Kang, R. Lin, and E. Shragowitz. Fuzzy logic approach to VLSI placement. *IEEE Transactions on VLSI Systems*, 2:489–501, Dec. 1994.

[Law76]   E. L. Lawler. *Combinatorial Optimization: Networks and Matroids.* Holt, Rinehart and Winston, 1976.

[Lei92]   F. Thomson Leighton. *Introduction to Parallel Algorithms and Architectures: Arrays - Trees - Hypercubes.* Morgan Kaufmann, San Mateo, CA, 1992.

[Len90]   T. Lengauer. *Combinatorial Algorithms for Integrated Circuit Layout.* B. G. Teubner and John Wiley & Sons, 1990.

[LS92]   R. Lin and E. Shragowitz. Fuzzy logic approach to placement problem. *Proceedings of the ACM/IEEE 29th Design Automation Conference*, pages 153–158, 1992.

[NSS89]   S. Nahar, S. Sahni, and E. Shragowitz. Simulated annealing and combinatorial optimization. *Journal of Computer-Aided Design*, 1:1–23, 1989.

[OvG89]   R.H.J.M. Otten and L.P.P.P. van Ginneken. *The Annealing Algorithm.* Kluwer, MA, 1989.

[Ped89]   W. Pedrycz. *Fuzzy Control and Fuzzy Systems.* John Wiley & Sons, New York, 1989.

[PS82]   C. Papadimitriou and K. Steiglitz. *Combinatorial Optimization: Algorithms and Complexity.* Prentice-Hall, 1982.

[Ree95]   C. R. Reeves, editor. *Modern Heuristic Techniques for Combinatorial Optimization Problems.* McGraw-Hill, Europe, 1995.

[RG90]   M. Razaz and J. Gan. Fuzzy set based initial placement for IC layout. *Proceedings of the European Design Automation Conference*, pages 655–659, 1990.

[RK86]   R. A. Rutenbar and S. A. Kravitz. Layout by simulated annealing in a parallel environment. *Proceedings of International Conference on Computer Design: VLSI in Computers & Processors, ICCD-86*, pages 434–437, 1986.

[Sah81] S. Sahni. *Concepts in Discrete Mathematics*. The Camelot Publishing Company, MN, 1981.

[SB80]   S. Sahni and A. Bhatt. The complexity of design automation problems. *Proceedings of the Design Automation Conference*, pages 402–410, 1980.

[Ste86] R. E. Steuer. *Multiple Criteria Optimization: Theory, Computation, and Application*. John Wiley & Sons, 1986.

[Tai93] E. Taillard. Parallel iterative search methods for the vehicle routing problem. *Networks*, 23:661–673, 1993.

[TS85]   T. Takagi and M. Sugeno. Fuzzy identification of systems and its applications to modeling and control. *IEEE Transactions on Systems, Man, and Cybernetics*, SMC-15(1), Jan 1985.

[Wan94] L.-X. Wang. *Adaptive Fuzzy Systems and Control*. Prentice-Hall, 1994.

[Wol91] S. Wolfram. *Mathematica–A System for Doing Mathematics by Computer*. Addison-Wesley, 1991.

[Zad65] L. A. Zadeh. Fuzzy sets. *Information and Control*, 8:338–353, 1965.

[Zad73] L. A. Zadeh. Outline of a new approach to the analysis of complex systems and decisions processes. *IEEE Transactions on Systems, Man, and Cybernetics*, SMC-3(1):28–44, Jan 1973.

[Zad75] L. A. Zadeh. The concept of a linguistic variable and its application to approximate reasoning. *Information Sciences*, 8:199–249, 1975.

[Zim87] H. J. Zimmermann. *Fuzzy Sets, Decision Making, and Expert Systems*, 2nd Ed. Kluwer Academic Publishers, 1987.

[Zim91] H. J. Zimmermann. *Fuzzy Set Theory and Its Applications*, 2nd Ed. Kluwer, 1991.

Exercises

Exercise 1.1
Stirling approximation of the factorial function is as follows [Sah81]:

$$n! \approx \sqrt{2\pi n}(\frac{n}{e})^n(1 + \frac{1}{12n})$$

Using the above approximation, show that for large n,

$$\binom{n}{\frac{n}{2}} \approx 2^n$$

Exercise 1.2
Given a set of n distinct positive integers $X = \{x_1, x_2, \ldots, x_n\}$. The objective is to partition the set into two subsets Y of size k and Z of size $n - k$ ($1 \le k \le \frac{n}{2}$) such that the difference between the sums of the two subsets is minimized. This problem is known as the set partitioning problem.

1. For a fixed k, how many partitions exist?
2. How many partitions are there for all possible values of k.
3. Assume that $k = \frac{n}{2}$. One possible heuristic algorithm for this problem is the following.

   Algorithm SetPartition(X, Y, Z);
   Begin
      Sort Array X[1:n] in descending order;
      For $i = 1$ **To** n **Do**
      Begin
         Assign X[i] to the set which has currently the smaller sum;
      EndFor;
      Return (Y, Z)
   End Algorithm;

   (a) Find the time complexity of the above algorithm.
   (b) Implement the above heuristic and experiment with it on several randomly generated problem instances.
   (c) Generalize the above heuristic to partition the set X for any value of $k \le \frac{n}{2}$.

Exercise 1.3
1. Experiment with the *local search* heuristic (page 11) on a number of randomly generated instances of the set partitioning problem. Compare quality of solutions obtained with those of the greedy heuristic outlined in Exercise 1.2.

2. The *Improve* subroutine can follow one of two strategies: (a) *first-improvement* strategy where the first favorable cost change is accepted, or (b) the *steepest descent* strategy where the entire neighborhood is searched, and then a solution with lowest cost is selected. Discuss the merits and demerits of both strategies.

3. Experiment with both strategies and report the effect of each strategy on quality of solution, runtime, and so forth.

Exercise 1.4
Given a graph $G(V, E)$ with n nodes and m edges. Show that there are at most:

1. 2^m subsets of E that might be *edge coverings*.

2. 2^m possible *cuts*.

3. 2^m possible *paths*.

4. $(2m)!$ possible *tours*.

5. n^{n-2} possible *spanning trees*.

Exercise 1.5
For an $n \times n$ quadratic assignment problem (QAP), show that there are at most $n!$ feasible solutions.

Exercise 1.6
Write a program to generate a random connected graph. The inputs to the program are the number of nodes, (an even number) and, the range of degree of the nodes (for example, between 2 and 5). In a graph $G(V, E)$, the *degree* d_i of a node $i \in V$ is defined as the number of (other) nodes i is connected to.

Exercise 1.7

1. Given a graph of $2 \cdot n$ elements, show that the number of *balanced* two-way partitions is $P(2n) = \frac{(2n)!}{2 \cdot n! \cdot n!}$.

2. Use Stirling's approximation for $n!$ to simplify the expression for $P(2n)$. Express $P(2n)$ using the Big-Oh notation.

3. A *brute force* algorithm for the two-way partition problem enumerates all the $P(2n)$ solutions and selects the best. Write a computer program which implements such a brute force algorithm. What is the time complexity of your program?

4. Plot the running time of the *brute force* partition program for $n = 1, \ldots, 10$. If the maximum permitted execution time for the program is 24 hours, what is the maximum value of n for which your program can run to completion?

Exercise 1.8

Suppose we are given a graph with $2n$ nodes, and a matrix C that specifies the connectivity information between nodes; for example, c_{ij} gives the number of connections between elements i and j. Let A and B represent a balanced partition of the graph, that is, $|A| = |B| = n$. Use the *local search* algorithm to divide the graph into a balanced partition such that the cost of edges cut is minimum. Experiment with the following neighbor functions.

1. Pairwise exchange. Here two elements, one from each partition are swapped to disturb the current solution.

2. Swap a subset of elements selected from each partition.

3. Select for swap those elements whose contribution to the external cost is high, or those that are internally connected to the least number of vertices.

Exercise 1.9

1. Repeat Exercise 1.8 using instead the *random-walk* search heuristic given below.

    Algorithm RandomWalk(S_0);
    Begin
      $S = S_0; BestS = S$;
      $BestCost = Cost(S_0)$;
      Repeat
        $S = Perturb(S)$; /* Generate another random feasible solution */
        $CostS = Cost(S)$
        If $CostS < BestCost$ **Then**
          $BestCost = CostS$;
          $BestS = S$
        EndIf
      Until *time-to-stop*;
      Return ($BestS$)
    End Algorithm;

2. Compare the *local-search* and *random-walk* heuristics.

Exercise 1.10

A variation of the *random-walk* heuristic is to adapt a *steepest descent* strategy. That is, a new feasible solution is accepted only if it improves the cost. A random search of this type is known as *random-sampling*.

Algorithm RandomSampling(S_0);
Begin
  $S = S_0; BestS = S$;
  $CostS = Cost(S_0)$;
  $BestCost = Cost(S_0)$;
  Repeat
    $NewS = Perturb(S)$; /* Generate another random feasible solution */
    $NewCost = Cost(NewS)$;
    If $NewCost < CostS$ **Then**
      $BestCost = NewCost$;
      $CostS = NewCost$;
      $S = NewS$
    EndIf
  Until *time-to-stop*;
  Return ($BestS$)
End Algorithm;

Using the problem instances and perturbation functions suggested in Exercise 1.8, do the following:

1. Experiment with *random-sampling* and compare it with *random-walk.*

2. Compare *random-sampling* with *local-search.*

Exercise 1.11
Another iterative search heuristic is known as *sequence-heuristic* [NSS89]. In this heuristic a new solution with a higher cost (uphill move) is accepted if the last k perturbations on current solution S failed to generate a $NewS$ with $Cost(NewS) < Cost(S)$. The *sequence-heuristic* algorithm is given below.

Algorithm SequenceHeuristic(S_0, L_0);
/* S_0 is initial solution and L_0 is initial sequence length. */
Begin
  $S = S_0; BestS = S$;
  $CostS = Cost(S_0)$;
  $BestCost = Cost(S_0)$;
  $L = L_0$;   /* initial sequence length */
  Repeat
    $length = 0$; /* current length of bad perturbations */
    Repeat

```
NewS = Perturb(S);
NewCost = Cost(NewS);
If NewCost < CostS Then
    CostS = NewCost;
    S = NewS;
    If NewCost < BestCost Then
        BestCost = NewCost;
        BestS = NewS
    EndIf
Else length = length + 1
EndIf
Until length > L;
L = UpdateLength(L)
Until time-to-stop;
Return (BestS)
End Algorithm;
```

The function $UpdateLength$ could perform an additive increase ($L = L + \beta$ for some $\beta > 0$) or geometric increase ($L = \beta \times L$ for some $\beta > 1$).

Experiment with *sequence-heuristic* and compare it with *random-walk*, *local-search*, and *random-sampling* heuristics. Use the problem instances and perturbation functions suggested in Exercise 1.8.

Exercise 1.12
Construct an example of a graph with 10 nodes, such that the nodes have a large degree, say 5–10.

1. Assume that all the nodes have unit sizes. Apply the *local-search* algorithm to obtain a two-way balanced partition of the graph.

2. Randomly assign weights to nodes say between 1 and 10 and generate an almost balanced partition with a minimum weighted cut-set using *local-search*. Since nodes have different sizes, a pairwise swap may not be the best move to generate the neighbor function. One possibility is to select a random partition (A or B), and to move the node to the other partition. Use the following cost function:

$$Cost(A, B) = W_c \times Cut - set\ Weight(A, B) + W_s \times Imbalance(A, B)$$

where,

$$Imbalance(A, B) = Size\ of\ A - Size\ of\ B$$
$$= \sum_{v \in A} s(v) - \sum_{v \in B} s(v)$$

$s(v)$ is the size of vertex (or node) v. W_s and W_c are constants in the range of $[0,1]$ which indicate the relative importance of balance and minimization of cut-set, respectively.

3. Experiment with different values of W_c and W_s. Does increasing the value of W_c (W_s) necessarily reduce the value of cut-set (imbalance)?

Exercise 1.13

1. Repeat Exercise 1.12 using the *random-walk* search heuristic.

2. Repeat Exercise 1.12 using the *random-sampling* search heuristic.

3. Compare the three heuristics with respect to runtime, quality of solution, and quality of solution subspace explored.

Exercise 1.14

1. Construct a connected graph with 10 nodes and 25 edges. Starting from a random partition, apply both the greedy pairwise exchange and the *local search* algorithm to this graph and generate balanced two-way partitions.

2. Starting from the solution obtained from the greedy pairwise technique, apply the *local search* algorithm. Comment on any noticeable improvement in quality of solution and runtime.

Exercise 1.15

Given n modules to be placed in a row, show that there are $\frac{n!}{2}$ unique linear placements of n modules. When n is large, show that the number of placements is exponential in n.

Exercise 1.16

Write a procedure *CALC-LEN* to evaluate the total connection length of a given assignment. The inputs to the procedure are,

1. The number of modules n,

2. the connectivity matrix C; C is an $n \times n$ matrix of non-negative integers, where c_{ij} indicates the number of connections between modules i and j,

3. The assignment surface is a uniform grid of dimensions $M \times N$. The array $P[1 \ldots M, 1 \ldots N]$ is used to represent the placement information. $P[i, j]$ contains the number of the module placed in row i and column j.

You may assume that $M \cdot N = n$. What is the complexity of your procedure?

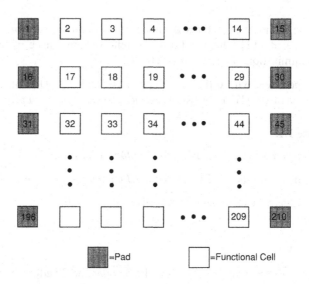

Figure 1.7: 210-cell mesh for Exercise 1.18.

Exercise 1.17

Suppose that n modules are placed in a row. The placement information is represented by array $p[1, \ldots, n]$, where $p[i]$ indicates the module placed in the ith location. If the modules are numbered $1, \ldots, n$, then p is simply a permutation of $1, \ldots, n$.

Write a procedure *DELTA-LEN* to compute the change in total wire-length when two modules in p are swapped. Assume that the connectivity information is represented by a connectivity matrix C as in Exercise 1.16.

Exercise 1.18

Implement a placement algorithm based on *local-search*. Assume that there are 210 modules to be placed on a 15×14 mesh. There are two types of modules, functional blocks and input/output (I/O) pads. The I/O pads must be placed only on the periphery of the mesh, whereas a functional block may be placed in any empty slot. Assume 28 I/O pads and 182 functional blocks.

Generate a random initial placement which satisfies the pad position constraint. Experiment with various perturbation functions. The *perturb* function must respect the pad position constraint. Use the *DELTA-LEN* procedure of Exercise 1.17 to evaluate the change in cost function Δc.

1. Test your program for the sample circuit shown in Figure 1.7. In other words, synthesize the connectivity matrix for the circuit and give it as input to your program.

2. Run your program for several *random* initial placements. Does the initial solution influence the final solution?

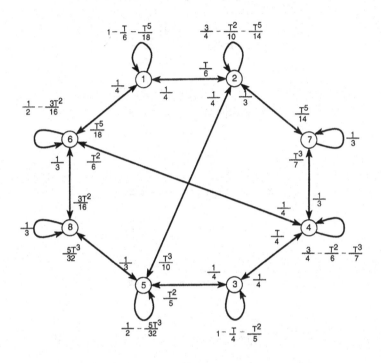

Figure 1.8: Configuration graph for Exercise 1.19.

Exercise 1.19

Consider the configuration graph of Figure 1.8 labeled with probabilities that are composed of uniform probabilities over each neighborhood and the acceptance function given by [Len90].

$$
f(Cost_i, Cost_j, T) = \begin{cases} \dfrac{Cost_i}{Cost_j} \cdot T^{Cost_j - Cost_i} & \text{if } \Delta Cost_{ij} > 0 \\ 1 & \text{if } \Delta Cost_{ij} \leq 0 \end{cases} \tag{1.16}
$$

The transition matrix $\Theta(T)$ is given on the following page.

$$\Theta(T)=\begin{pmatrix}
1-\dfrac{T}{6} & \dfrac{T}{6} & 1-\dfrac{T}{4} & \dfrac{T}{4} & 0 & \dfrac{T^5}{18} & 0 & 0\\[8pt]
\dfrac{1}{4} & \dfrac{3}{4}-\dfrac{T^3}{10} & \dfrac{1}{4} & \dfrac{3}{4}-\dfrac{T^2}{6} & \dfrac{T^3}{10} & 0 & \dfrac{T^5}{14} & 0\\[8pt]
0 & \dfrac{T^5}{14} & -\dfrac{T^2}{5} & \dfrac{T^3}{7} & \dfrac{T^2}{5} & 0 & 0 & 0\\[8pt]
0 & 0 & \dfrac{1}{4} & 0 & 0 & \dfrac{T^2}{6} & \dfrac{T^3}{7} & 0\\[8pt]
0 & 0 & \dfrac{1}{4} & \dfrac{1}{4} & \dfrac{1}{2}-\dfrac{5T^3}{32} & 0 & 0 & \dfrac{5T^3}{32}\\[8pt]
\dfrac{1}{4} & \dfrac{1}{4} & 0 & \dfrac{1}{3} & 0 & \dfrac{1}{2}-\dfrac{3T^2}{16} & 0 & \dfrac{3T^2}{16}\\[8pt]
0 & 0 & 0 & 0 & 0 & 0 & \dfrac{1}{3} & 0\\[8pt]
0 & \dfrac{1}{3} & 0 & 0 & \dfrac{1}{3} & \dfrac{1}{3} & 0 & \dfrac{1}{3}
\end{pmatrix}$$

1. Show that the stationary distribution at T is,

$$\pi(T) = \left(\frac{2520}{N}, \frac{1680\,T}{N}, \frac{840\,T^2}{N}, \frac{840\,T^3}{N}, \frac{672\,T^4}{N}, \frac{560\,T^5}{N}, \frac{360\,T^6}{N}, \frac{315\,T^7}{N} \right)$$

where

$$N = 2520 + 1680T + 840T^2 + 840T^3 + 672T^4 + 560T^5 + 360T^6 + 315T^7$$

2. Verify that the generating chain is time reversible. For a reversible Markov chain, the transition probabilities of the forward and reversed chains are identical ($\theta_{ij} = \theta_{ji}$). That is, a time reversible Markov chain is identical to itself when viewed in reverse time.

3. Show that the stationary distribution converges to an optimizing distribution given by

$$\lim_{T \to 0} \pi(T) = (1, 0, 0, 0, 0, 0, 0, 0)$$

Exercise 1.20
Consider the configuration graph of Figure 1.9 labeled with probabilities, and the acceptance function of Exercise 1.19. The corresponding transition matrix is given below. Answer the following questions.

$$\Theta(T) = \left\{ \begin{matrix} 1 - \frac{T}{6} - \frac{T^4}{15} & \frac{T}{6} & 0 & 0 & \frac{T^4}{15} & 0 \\ \frac{1}{3} & \frac{2}{3} - \frac{T^4}{9} & 0 & 0 & 0 & \frac{T^4}{9} \\ 0 & 0 & 1 - \frac{T}{4} - \frac{T^2}{5} & \frac{T}{4} & \frac{T^2}{5} & 0 \\ 0 & 0 & \frac{1}{3} & \frac{2}{3} - \frac{2\,T^2}{9} & 0 & \frac{2\,T^2}{9} \\ \frac{1}{4} & 0 & \frac{1}{4} & 0 & \frac{1}{2} - \frac{5\,T}{24} & \frac{5\,T}{24} \\ 0 & \frac{1}{4} & 0 & \frac{1}{4} & \frac{1}{4} & \frac{1}{4} \end{matrix} \right\}$$

(a) Verify the transition matrix representing the configuration graph in Figure 1.9.

(b) What is the stationary distribution ($\pi(T)$) and the optimizing distribution ($\pi = \lim_{T \to 0} \pi(T)$)?

(c) To the configuration graph of Figure 1.9 add an additional edge between states 2 and 3, rewrite the transition matrix, and find the stationary distribution. Should the distribution be different from the one obtained in part (b) of this question. Justify your answer.

(d) In the configuration graph obtained in part (c) above, delete edges between nodes 5 and 6 and between nodes 2 and 3, and add edges between nodes 2 and 5 and between nodes 3 and 6 and compute the stationary distribution. Is the stationary distribution obtained the same as in part (b) of this question? Why?

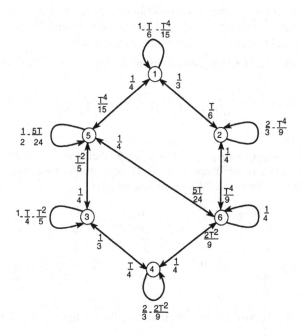

Figure 1.9: Configuration graph for Exercise 1.20.

Exercise 1.21

Consider the configuration graph given in Figure 1.10. The cost of the five states is as follows: $Cost_1 = 1$, $Cost_2 = 2$, $Cost_3 = 3$, $Cost_4 = 4$, $Cost_5 = 1$. $Cost_n$ represents the cost of state S_n. If the acceptance criterion used is as given in Equation 1.17 below,

$$f(Cost_i, Cost_j, T) = \begin{cases} e^{-\frac{\Delta Cost_{ij}}{T}} & \text{if } \Delta Cost_{ij} > 0 \\ 1 & \text{if } \Delta Cost_{ij} \leq 0 \end{cases} \tag{1.17}$$

determine the transition matrix and find the stationary distribution.

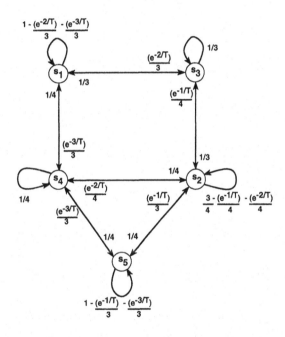

Figure 1.10: Configuration graph for Exercise 1.21.

Exercise 1.22

For the Markov chain given in Exercise 1.21, find the optimizing distribution.

CHAPTER 2

Simulated Annealing (SA)

2.1 Introduction

In this chapter we present *simulated annealing* (SA), one of the most well developed and widely used iterative techniques for solving optimization problems.

Simulated annealing is a general *adaptive* heuristic and belongs to the class of *nondeterministic* algorithms [NSS89]. It has been applied to several combinatorial optimization problems from various fields of science and engineering. These problems include the traveling salesman problem (TSP), graph partitioning, quadratic assignment, matching, linear arrangement, and scheduling. In the area of engineering, simulated annealing has been applied to very large–scale integration (VLSI) design (placement, routing, logic minimization, testing), image processing, code design, facilities layout [AK89], network topology design [EP93], and so forth.

One typical feature of simulated annealing is that, besides accepting solutions with improved cost, it also, to a limited extent, accepts solution with deteriorated cost. It is this feature that gives the heuristic the hill climbing capability. Initially the probability of accepting inferior solutions (those with larger costs) is large; but as the search progresses, only smaller deteriorations are accepted, and finally only good solutions are accepted. A strong feature of the SA heuristic is that it is both effective and robust. Regardless of the choice of the initial configuration it produces high-quality solutions. It is also relatively easy to implement.

We begin this chapter by first introducing annealing from an intuitive point of view. In Section 2.2 we present the operation of the simulated annealing algorithm. We then build the necessary mathematical background and the terminology required to discuss convergence related issues (Section 2.3). Aspects related to the parameters of the algorithm, also known as the "cooling schedule" are discussed in Section 2.4. Requirements for implementation of SA on a digital computer are

49

presented in Section 2.5. Case studies and examples that illustrate the implementation aspects of this powerful iterative technique are presented in Section 2.6.

Simulated annealing, like all other iterative techniques, is very greedy with respect to run time. The acceleration of simulated annealing has been an extensive area of research since the introduction of the algorithm. Among the widely researched acceleration techniques is parallelization. The various parallelization strategies of simulated annealing are also discussed in this chapter (Section 2.7).

2.1.1   Background

The term *annealing* refers to heating a solid to a very high temperature (whereby the atoms gain enough energy to break the chemical bonds and become free to move), and then slowly cooling the molten material in a controlled manner until it crystallizes. By cooling the metal at a proper rate, atoms will have an increased chance to regain proper crystal structure with perfect lattices. During this annealing procedure the free energy of the solid is *minimized.*

As early as 1953, Metropolis and his colleagues introduced a simple algorithm to simulate the evolution of a solid in a heat bath to its thermal equilibrium [M+53]. Their simulation algorithm is based on *Monte Carlo techniques* and generates a *sequence of states* of the solid as follows. Given a current state S_i of the solid with energy E_i, a subsequent state S_j with energy E_j is generated by applying a perturbation mechanism. This perturbation transforms the current state into a next state with slight distortion. For instance a new state can be constructed by randomly selecting a particle and displacing it by some random amount. If the energy associated with the new state is lower than the energy of the current state, that is, $\Delta E = E_j - E_i \leq 0$, then the displacement is accepted, and the current state becomes the new state. However, if the energy of the new state is higher (the energy difference greater than zero), then the state S_j is accepted with a certain probability, which is given by

$$\text{Prob(accept)} = e^{-\left(\frac{\Delta E}{K_B T}\right)} \tag{2.1}$$

where K_B is the Boltzmann constant and T denotes temperature. The acceptance rule described above is repeated a large number of times. The acceptance criterion is known as the *Metropolis step*, named after its inventor, and the procedure is known as the *Metropolis algorithm.*

In the early eighties, 30 years after the idea of the Metropolis loop was introduced, a correspondence between annealing and combinatorial optimization was established, first by Kirkpatrick et al. [KCGV83] in 1983, and independently by Černy [Čer85] in 1985. These scientists observed that there is a correspondence between, on one hand, *a solution to the optimization problem* and *a physical state of the material*, and between the *cost* of a solution of the combinatorial optimization problem and *free energy* in the molten metal. As a result of this analogy they introduced a solution method in the field of combinatorial optimization. This method is thus based on the simulation of the physical annealing process, and hence the name *simulated annealing* [Čer85, KCGV83].

As explained by Kirkpatrick et al. and Černy, a solution in combinatorial optimization is equivalent to a *state* in the physical system and the cost of the solution is analogous to the *energy* of that state. If we compare optimization to the annealing process, the attainment of global optimum is analogous to the attainment of a perfect crystal structure (a minimum-energy state for the material), and attainment of a structure with imperfections will correspond to getting trapped in a local optimum.

As discussed in Chapter 1, every combinatorial optimization problem may be discussed in terms of a *state space*. A *state* is simply a configuration of the combinatorial objects involved. For example, consider the problem of partitioning a graph of $2n$ nodes into two equal-sized subgraphs such that the number of edges with vertices in both subgraphs is minimized. In this problem, any division of $2n$ nodes into two equal-sized blocks is a configuration. There is a large number of such configurations (see Exercise 1.7 on page 37). Only some of these correspond to global optima, that is, states with optimum cost.

An iterative improvement scheme starts with some given state, and examines a *local neighborhood* of the state for better solutions. A local neighborhood of a state S, denoted by $\aleph(S)$, is the set of all states which can be reached from S by making a small change to S. For instance, if S represents a two-way partition of a graph, the set of all partitions which are generated by swapping two nodes across the partition represents a local neighborhood (see Exercise 1.8). The iterative improvement algorithm moves from the current state to a state in the local neighborhood if the latter has a better cost. If all the local neighbors have larger costs, the algorithm is said to have *converged* to a *local optimum*. This is illustrated in Figure 2.1. Here, the states are shown along the x-axis, and it is assumed that two consecutive states are local neighbors. It is further assumed that we are

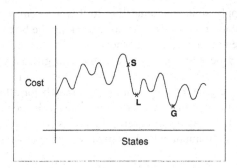

Figure 2.1: Local versus global optima.

discussing a *minimization* problem. The cost curve is *nonconvex*, that is, it has multiple minima. A greedy iterative improvement algorithm may start off with an initial solution such as **S** in Figure 2.1, then slide along the curve and find a local minimum such as **L**. There is no way such an algorithm can find the global minimum **G** of Figure 2.1, unless it "climbs the hill" at the local minimum **L**. In other words, an algorithm which occasionally accepts inferior solutions can escape from getting trapped in a local optimum. Simulated annealing is such a hill-climbing algorithm.

During annealing, a metal is maintained at a certain temperature T for a pre-computed amount of time, before reducing the temperature in a controlled manner. The atoms have a greater degree of freedom to move at higher temperatures than at lower temperatures. *The movement of atoms is analogous to the generation of new neighborhood states in an optimization process.* In order to simulate the annealing process, much flexibility is allowed in neighborhood generation at higher "temperatures," that is, many "uphill" moves are permitted at higher temperatures. The temperature parameter is lowered gradually as the algorithm proceeds. As the temperature is lowered, fewer and fewer uphill moves are permitted. In fact, at absolute zero, the simulated annealing algorithm turns greedy, allowing only downhill moves.

Example 2.1 We can visualize simulated annealing by considering the analogy of a ball placed in a hilly terrain, as shown in Figure 2.2. The hilly terrain is nothing but the variation of the cost function over the configuration space, as shown by Figure 2.1. If a ball is placed at point **S**, it will roll down into a pit such as **L**, which represents a local minimum. In order to move the ball from the local minimum to the global minimum **G** we do the following. We enclose the hilly terrain in a box and place the box in a water bath. When the water bath is heated, the box begins to shake, and the ball has a chance to climb out of the local minimum **L**.

If we are to apply simulated annealing to this problem, we would initially heat the water bath to a high temperature, making the box wobble violently. At such high temperatures, the ball moves rapidly into and out of local minima. As time proceeds, we cool the water bath gradually. The lower the temperature, the gentler the movement of the box, and lesser the likelihood of the ball jumping out of a minimum. The search for a local minimum is more or less random at high temperatures; the search becomes more greedy as temperature falls. At absolute zero, the box is perfectly still, and the ball rolls down into a minimum, which, hopefully, is the global minimum **G**.

■

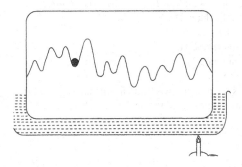

Figure 2.2: Design space analogous to a hilly terrain.

2.2   Simulated Annealing Algorithm

The simulated annealing algorithm is shown in Figure 2.3. The core of the algorithm is the *Metropolis* procedure, which simulates the annealing process at a given temperature T (Figure 2.4) [M+53]. The *Metropolis* procedure receives as input the current temperature T, and the current solution $CurS$ which it improves through local search. Finally, *Metropolis* must also be provided with the value M, which is the amount of time for which annealing must be applied at temperature T. The procedure *Simulated_annealing* simply invokes *Metropolis* at decreasing temperatures. Temperature is initialized to a value T_0 at the beginning of the procedure, and is reduced in a controlled manner (typically in a geometric progression); the parameter α is used to achieve this cooling. The amount of time spent in annealing at a temperature is gradually *increased* as temperature is lowered. This is done using the parameter $\beta > 1$. The variable *Time* keeps track of the time being expended in each call to the *Metropolis*. The annealing procedure halts when *Time* exceeds the allowed time.

The *Metropolis* procedure is shown in Figure 2.4. It uses the procedure *Neighbor* to generate a local neighbor $NewS$ of any given solution S. The function *Cost* returns the cost of a given solution S. If the cost of the new solution $NewS$ is better than the cost of the current solution $CurS$, then the new solution is accepted, and we do so by setting $CurS = NewS$. If the cost of the new solution is better than the best solution ($BestS$) seen thus far, then we also replace $BestS$ by $NewS$. If the new solution has a higher cost in comparison to the original solution $CurS$, *Metropolis* will accept the new solution on a *probabilistic* basis. A random number is generated in the range 0 to 1. If this random number is smaller than $e^{-\Delta Cost/T}$, where $\Delta Cost$ is the difference in costs, ($\Delta Cost = Cost(NewS) - Cost(CurS)$), and T is the current temperature, the uphill solution is accepted. This criterion for accepting the new solution is known as the *Metropolis criterion*. The *Metropolis* procedure generates and examines M solutions.

Algorithm Simulated_annealing($S_0, T_0, \alpha, \beta, M, Maxtime$);

      (*S_0 is the initial solution *)
      (*$BestS$ is the best solution *)
      (*T_0 is the initial temperature *)
      (*α is the cooling rate *)
      (*β a constant *)
      (*$Maxtime$ is the total allowed time for the annealing process *)
      (*M represents the time until the next parameter update *)

Begin

    $T = T_0$;
    $CurS=S_0$;
    $BestS = CurS$; /* $BestS$ is the best solution seen so far */
    $CurCost = Cost(CurS)$;
    $BestCost = Cost(BestS)$;
    $Time = 0$;

        Repeat

            Call Metropolis($CurS$, $CurCost$, $BestS$, $BestCost$, T, M);
            $Time = Time + M$;
            $T = \alpha T$;
            $M = \beta M$

        Until ($Time \geq MaxTime$);
        Return ($BestS$)

End. (*of Simulated_annealing*)

Figure 2.3: Procedure for simulated annealing algorithm.

Algorithm Metropolis($CurS$, $CurCost$, $BestS$, $BestCost$, T, M);
Begin

    Repeat

      $NewS = Neighbor(CurS)$; /* Return a neighbor from $aleph(CurS)$ */
      $NewCost = Cost(NewS)$;
      $\Delta Cost = (NewCost - CurCost)$;
      If ($\Delta Cost < 0$) **Then**
        $CurS = NewS$;
        If $NewCost < BestCost$ **Then**
          $BestS = NewS$
        EndIf
      Else
        If ($RANDOM < e^{-\Delta Cost/T}$) **Then**
          $CurS = NewS$;
        EndIf
      EndIf
      $M = M - 1$
    Until ($M = 0$)
End. (*of Metropolis*)

Figure 2.4: The Metropolis procedure.

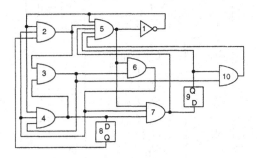

Figure 2.5: Circuit for Example 2.2.

The probability that an inferior solution is accepted by the *Metropolis* is given by $P(RANDOM < e^{-\Delta Cost/T})$. The random number generation is assumed to follow a *uniform distribution*. Remember that $\Delta Cost > 0$ since we have assumed that *NewS* is uphill from *CurS*. At very high temperatures, (when $T \to \infty$), $e^{-\Delta Cost/T} \simeq 1$, and hence the above probability approaches 1. On the contrary, when $T \to 0$, the probability $e^{-\Delta Cost/T}$ falls to 0.

In order to implement simulated annealing on a digital computer we need to formulate a suitable cost function for the problem being solved. In addition, as in the case of local search techniques we assume the existence of a neighborhood structure, and need *perturb* operation or *Neighbor* function to generate new states (neighborhood states) from current states. And finally, we need a control parameter to play the role of temperature and a random number generator. The actions of simulated annealing are best illustrated with the help of an example.

Example 2.2   Circuit Partitioning Using SA

A logic circuit can be represented using sets of nets. For example, $N_x = \{C_a, C_b, C_c, C_d\}$ denotes that cells C_a, C_b, C_c, and C_d, all have a common terminal point labeled N_x. All the cells in the set N_x have terminals with the same label N_x, and all the terminals with the same label are connected together by a wire. If *all* the cells of a particular net N_i are in the same partition (A or B), then no external wiring is required to connect across partitions. We then say that the net is not cut by the partition. Let w_n be the weight of net n, or the cost of the net if cut. And let $CutSet$ represent the set of nets that are cut, that is, those with terminals (or cells) in both A and B (see Exercise 2.7).

The circuit in Figure 2.5 contains 10 cells and 10 nets. Assume that all cells are of the same size. The nets of the circuit are indicated along with their weights in Table 2.1. Using the information below, it is required to use SA

Net	Weight
$N_1 = \{C_1, C_2, C_4, C_5\}$	$w_1 = 1$
$N_2 = \{C_2, C_3, C_5\}$	$w_2 = 1$
$N_3 = \{C_3, C_6, C_{10}, C_4\}$	$w_3 = 2$
$N_4 = \{C_4, C_8, C_3, C_7\}$	$w_4 = 1$
$N_5 = \{C_5, C_7, C_1, C_6\}$	$w_5 = 3$
$N_6 = \{C_6, C_4, C_7, C_2\}$	$w_6 = 3$
$N_7 = \{C_7, C_9, C_5\}$	$w_7 = 2$
$N_8 = \{C_8, C_2\}$	$w_8 = 3$
$N_9 = \{C_9, C_{10}, C_5\}$	$w_9 = 2$
$N_{10} = \{C_{10}, C_5\}$	$w_{10} = 4$

Table 2.1: Netlist for Example 2.2.

to divide the circuit of Figure 2.5 into two equal partitions A and B with the objective of minimizing the weighted sum of the nets cut.

Initial solution: Randomly assign cells $C_1, \ldots, C_5$ to block A;
Neighbor function: Pairwise exchange, that is, exchange a cell $a \in A$ with a cell $b \in B$;
Initial temperature: $T_0=10$ (this is high enough for this particular example);
Constants: $M=10$; $\alpha =0.9$; $\beta =1.0$;
Termination criterion: T reduces to 30 percent of its initial value.

Solution The objective function can be represented as

$$Cost(A, B) = \sum_{n \in CutSet} w_n$$

Table 2.2 shows results for some iterations, where (C_i, C_j) represents the two cells selected for swapping, one from each partition. Only the accepted moves are listed. For example, when $count = 9$, the temperature is equal to 10, the cells selected for pairwise interchange are (3,8), the cost of current solution S is $Cost(S) = 13$, and the cost of the new solution is $Cost(NewS) = 10$. Therefore the interchange is automatically accepted. For the next iteration at the same temperature, $count = 10$, the cells selected are (1,4), the cost of new solution $Cost(NewS) = 13$, which is larger than the cost of the current solution ($Cost(S) = 10$). In this case a random number is generated. Since the value of this number is 0.11618 which is less than $e^{-\Delta Cost/T} = e^{-3/10} = 0.74082$, the move is accepted.

Figure 2.6 is a plot of the *cost* versus iterations for both a greedy algorithm and for simulated annealing. When greedy pairwise exchange is applied only good moves are accepted, and uphill moves rejected. Note that for this example, using simulated annealing, the cost reduces to 10 in the 9th iteration. This is due to the acceptance of some previous bad moves. The plot of greedy pairwise exchange shows plateaus or a decrease and converges to 10 after 50 iterations. For this example, the final partition obtained by both deterministic pairwise exchange and simulated annealing procedures is the same, with $A=\{C_2, C_4, C_6, C_7, C_8\}$ and $B=\{C_1, C_3, C_5, C_9, C_{10}\}$. The cost of this partition is 10.

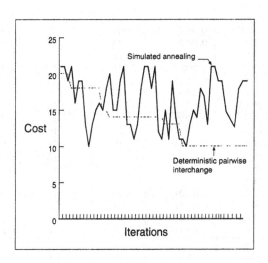

Figure 2.6: Variation of cost in Example 2.2.

2.3   SA Convergence Aspects

The convergence aspects of the simulated annealing algorithm have been the subject of extensive studies. Here we present a detailed summary of these studies. For a more thorough discussion of SA convergence we refer the reader to [AK89, AL85, OvG89].

The convergence analysis presented here follows the Markovian analysis developed in Section 1.8 of Chapter 1.

Recall from Chapter 1, that for pairs of states connected by at least a single move the perturbation probability p_{ij} is never zero. The probability p_{ij} depends

count	$\alpha * T$	(C_i, C_j)	$RANDOM$	$Cost(S)$	$Cost(NewS)$	$e^{-\Delta Cost/T}$
1		(1,6)	0.73222	20	21	0.90484
2		(1,2)		21	19	
3		(2,3)	0.13798	19	21	0.81873
4		(2,7)		21	16	
5	10.000	(1,3)	0.64633	16	19	0.74082
6		(2,3)	0.46965	19	19	1.00000
8		(3,5)		19	13	
9		(3,8)		13	10	
10		(1,4)	0.11618	10	13	0.74082
11		(2,4)	0.47759	13	15	0.80074
12		(3,4)	0.19017	15	16	0.89484
13		(4,6)		16	15	
14		(4,9)	0.26558	15	18	0.71653
15	9.000	(1,5)	0.19988	18	20	0.80074
16		(2,5)		20	15	
17		(3,5)	0.28000	15	15	1.00000
18		(4,5)	0.90985	15	15	1.00000
19		(5,7)	0.06332	15	19	0.64118
20		(5,10)		19	16	
21		(2,6)	0.15599	16	21	0.53941
22		(3,6)		21	19	
23		(4,6)	0.36448	19	21	0.78121
24		(5,6)		21	13	
25	8.100	(6,8)	0.53256	13	13	1.00000
26		(3,7)		13	11	
27		(4,7)	0.18104	11	13	0.78121
28		(5,7)	0.51371	13	18	0.53941
29		(7,8)	0.37249	18	21	0.69048
30		(7,9)	0.57933	21	21	1.00000
31		(1,8)		21	18	
32		(4,8)	0.10814	18	21	0.66264
33	7.290	(5,8)		21	12	
37		(1,9)		12	11	
39		(3,9)	0.14080	11	15	0.57770
41		(6,9)		15	11	
44		(2,10)	0.21728	11	19	0.29543
45	6.561	(3,10)		19	14	
49		(1,2)		14	11	
50		(1,3)	0.84921	11	11	1.00000
52	5.905	(1,7)		11	10	
53		(1,8)	0.54613	10	13	0.60167

Table 2.2: Table of execution run of Example 2.2.

on the structure of the configuration graph and may be defined as follows:

$$p_{ij} = \begin{cases} \frac{1}{|\aleph(S_i)|} & \text{if } S_j \in \aleph(S_i) \\ 0 & \text{if } S_j \notin \aleph(S_i) \end{cases} \quad (2.2)$$

Recall also that the acceptance probability A_{ij} of accepting a move from state S_i to state S_j has the following general expression:

$$A_{ij}(T) = \begin{cases} f(Cost_i, Cost_j, T) & \text{if } \Delta Cost_{ij} > 0 \\ 1 & \text{if } \Delta Cost_{ij} \leq 0 \end{cases} \quad (2.3)$$

where $\Delta Cost_{ij} = Cost_j - Cost_i$. In case of SA, downhill moves ($\Delta Cost_{ij} \leq 0$) are accepted with probability 1 while uphill moves ($\Delta Cost_{ij} > 0$) are accepted according to the Metropolis function. Hence,

$$A_{ij} = \begin{cases} e^{-\frac{\Delta Cost_{ij}}{T}} & \text{if } \Delta Cost_{ij} > 0 \\ 1 & \text{if } \Delta Cost_{ij} \leq 0 \end{cases} \quad (2.4)$$

That is, the probability that the generated new state will be the next state depends on its cost, the cost of the previous state, and the value of the temperature T. The sequence of states thus generated corresponds to a *time-inhomogeneous Markov chain*. This is because of the important property that the next state does not depend on the states that have preceded the current state. Therefore, for this time-inhomogeneous Markov chain, given S_i as the current state, the probability $\Theta_{ij}(T)$ of transit to state S_j is defined as follows:

$$\Theta_{ij}(T) = \begin{cases} A_{ij}(T)p_{ij} & \text{if } i \neq j \\ 1 - \sum_{k, k \neq i} A_{ik}(T)p_{ik} & \text{if } i = j \end{cases} \quad (2.5)$$

where p_{ij} is the perturbation probability, that is, the probability of generating a configuration S_j from configuration S_i (which is independent of T); $A_{ij}(T)$ is the acceptance probability (see Equation 2.4), that is, the probability of accepting configuration S_j if the system is in configuration S_i; and T is the control parameter.

Transition Probability

Let $\Theta_{ij}(T)$ be the transition probability from state S_i to state S_j at temperature T, that is, $\Theta_{ij}(T) = p_{ij} \cdot A_{ij}(T)$. These probabilities can be combined into a matrix $\Theta(T)$, called the transition matrix. The transition matrix of the Metropolis loop does not change from step to step (T does not change inside the loop). Markov chains with constant transition matrices are called *homogeneous*. The Metropolis loop can therefore be correctly modeled by a homogeneous Markov chain, characterized by the following transition probabilities.

$$\Theta_{ij}(T) = \begin{cases} \frac{1}{|\aleph(S_i)|} & \text{if } \Delta Cost_{ij} \leq 0 \quad S_j \in \aleph(S_i) \\[2mm] \frac{1}{|\aleph(S_i)|} e^{-\frac{\Delta Cost_{ij}}{T}} & \text{if } \Delta Cost_{ij} > 0 \quad S_j \in \aleph(S_i) \\[2mm] 1 - \sum_{k,k \neq i} p_{ik} A_{ik}(T) & \text{if } i = j \quad\quad\quad S_j \in \aleph(S_i) \\[2mm] 0 & \quad\quad\quad\quad\quad\quad S_j \notin \aleph(S_i) \end{cases} \quad (2.6)$$

Each time the body of the Metropolis loop is completed we say that the chain has completed a step. If the temperature T is lowered carefully, the solid can reach thermal equilibrium. Thermal equilibrium can be reached by generating a large number of transitions at a given temperature and applying the Metropolis acceptance criterion (Equation 2.1). The thermal equilibrium is then characterized by the *Boltzmann distribution* [AK89]. This distribution gives the probability of the solid being in state S_i with energy E_i, at temperature T, and is equal to

$$P(S_i) = \frac{1}{Z(T)} e^{-(\frac{E_i}{K_B T})} \quad (2.7)$$

where K_B is the Boltzmann constant, S_i is a variable denoting the current state of the solid, and $Z(T)$ is a normalizing function defined by

$$Z(T) = \sum_i e^{-(\frac{-E_i}{K_B T})} \quad (2.8)$$

where the summation is over all possible states.

SA for combinatorial optimization uses the following Metropolis acceptance probability:

$$A_{ij} = \begin{cases} e^{-(\frac{\Delta Cost_{ij}}{T})} & \text{if } \Delta Cost_{ij} > 0 \\[2mm] 1 & \text{if } \Delta Cost_{ij} \leq 0 \end{cases} \quad (2.9)$$

Using a suitable neighborhood structure and applying the above acceptance probability, the SA algorithm will have in the limit the following stationary-state probability distribution [AK89]:

$$P(S_i) = \frac{1}{N_o(T)} e^{-\frac{Cost_i}{T}} \quad (2.10)$$

where $N_o(T)$ is a normalizing function defined by

$$N_o(T) = \sum_{S_j \in S} e^{-\frac{Cost_j}{T}} \qquad (2.11)$$

The above conjecture states that, given enough time to run and an appropriate perturbation function, simulated annealing should hit a global optimum with a probability greater than zero [AK89]. Generation probabilities are chosen independent of T, and uniformly over the neighborhood $\aleph(S_i)$. It is assumed that all neighborhoods are of equal size, that is, $|\aleph(S_i)|$ is the same for all $S_i \in \Omega$ [AK89].

From the theory of Markov chains it follows that there exists a stationary distribution $\pi(T) \in [0, 1]^n$ that satisfies

$$\lim_{L \to \infty} e_i \Theta(T) = \pi(T) \qquad (2.12)$$

where e_i is the ith unit vector in $[0, 1]^n$, T is the temperature, and n is the number of states. If we start from any state S_i, and perform L perturbations, with $L \to \infty$, then the probability of ending up in state S_j is given by the component $\pi_j(T)$ of the stationary distribution π. Thus, the stationary distribution $\pi(T)$ gives the probability distribution for the occurrence of each state at equilibrium. The optimizing distribution can be obtained by finding the stationary distribution and then applying the limit $T \to 0$.

For the values of P and $A_{ij}(T)$ given in Equations 2.2 and 2.4, we have

$$\pi_j(T) = \pi_0(T) e^{-(\frac{\Delta Cost_{i_0 j}}{T})} \qquad (2.13)$$

where S_{i_0} is the optimal configuration, $Cost_{S_{i_0}} = Cost_{i_0}$ is the cost of the optimal configuration, and $\pi_0(T)$ is a normalization factor given by [AK89].

$$\pi_0(T) = \frac{1}{\sum_{k=1}^{n} e^{-(\frac{\Delta Cost_{i_0 k}}{T})}} \qquad (2.14)$$

Furthermore,

$$\lim_{\substack{T \to 0 \\ L \to \infty}} (e_i \Theta(T))_j = \lim_{T \to 0} \pi_j(T)$$

$$= \begin{cases} \frac{1}{|\Omega_0|} & \text{if } S_{i_0} \in \Omega_0 \\ 0 & \text{if } S_{i_0} \notin \Omega_0 \end{cases}$$

where Ω_0 is the set of optimal configurations; that is, $\Omega_0 = \{S_i \in \Omega | Cost_i = Cost_{i_0}\}$. Thus, if SA is given unlimited time the algorithm will achieve one of the optimal configurations with equal probabilities (uniform probability distribution) and the probability of achieving a suboptimal configuration is zero.

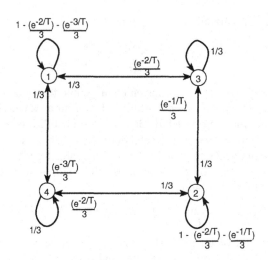

Figure 2.7: Configuration graph for Example 2.3.

Example 2.3 Consider the configuration graph corresponding to the Markov chain given in Figure 2.7. The cost of the four states is as follows: $Cost_1 = 1$, $Cost_2 = 2$, $Cost_3 = 3$, and $Cost_4 = 4$, where $Cost_n$ represents the cost of state S_n. The acceptance function is given by the Metropolis criterion $f(Cost_i, Cost_j, T) = e^{-\frac{\Delta Cost_{ij}}{T}}$. Verify that the transition matrix for the Markov chain is as given below and obtain the stationary distribution.

$$\Theta = \left\{ \begin{matrix} 1 - \frac{e^{-2/T}}{3} - \frac{e^{-3/T}}{3} & 0 & \frac{e^{-2/T}}{3} & \frac{e^{-3/T}}{3} \\ 0 & 1 - \frac{e^{-1/T}}{3} - \frac{e^{-2/T}}{3} & \frac{e^{-1/T}}{3} & \frac{e^{-2/T}}{3} \\ \frac{1}{3} & \frac{1}{3} & \frac{1}{3} & 0 \\ \frac{1}{3} & \frac{1}{3} & 0 & \frac{1}{3} \end{matrix} \right\}$$

Solution In the above matrix, the elements are $\Theta_{ij} = A_{ij} \cdot p_{ij}$. Let us verify the entry $\Theta_{2,3}$. Note that there exists an arc between states 2 and 3, and the transition is to a state with higher cost. We therefore apply Equation 2.6 with the condition $\Delta Cost_{ij} > 0$.

$\Theta_{2,3} = A_{2,3} \cdot p_{2,3}$; where $A_{2,3} = f(Cost_2, Cost_3, T) = e^{-\frac{(3-2)}{T}} = e^{-\frac{1}{T}}$, and $p_{2,3} = \frac{1}{\aleph(S_2)}$, where $\aleph(S_2)$ = number of neighbors of state 2, which is equal to 3 (Equation 2.2). Therefore, $\Theta_{2,3} = \frac{e^{-\frac{1}{T}}}{3}$.

As discussed earlier, $\pi = (\pi_1, \pi_2, \ldots, \pi_i, \ldots, \pi_n)$ denotes the stationary distribution, that is, π_i represents the probability of being in state i. The probability transition matrix Θ above describes how the process evolves from state to state. An ergodic Markov chain is guaranteed to reach a steady state, where the probability state vector no longer depends on the time step. Thus, at steady state we have

$$\pi = \pi \cdot \Theta \tag{2.15}$$

To obtain the stationary distribution, we solve the equation $\pi = \pi \cdot \Theta$ using Mathematica as illustrated below.

```
Solve
[{Theta[[1,1]]p1+Theta[[2,1]]p2+Theta[[3,1]]p3+
                          Theta[[4,1]]p4==p1,
  Theta[[1,2]]p1+Theta[[2,2]]p2+Theta[[3,2]]p3+
                          Theta[[4,2]]p4==p2,
  Theta[[1,3]]p1+Theta[[2,3]]p2+Theta[[3,3]]p3+
                          Theta[[4,3]]p4==p3,
  Theta[[1,4]]p1+Theta[[2,4]]p2+Theta[[3,4]]p3+
                          Theta[[4,4]]p4==p4,
  p1+p2+p3+p4==1},{p1,p2,p3,p4}];
Simplify[%]
```

Here Theta$[[i,j]]$ represents Θ_{ij} and pi represents π_i. Solving the equations to obtain the stationary distribution of the above Markov chain we get

$$\pi = \left(\frac{e^{-\frac{1}{T}}}{N_o(T)}, \frac{e^{-\frac{2}{T}}}{N_o(T)}, \frac{e^{-\frac{3}{T}}}{N_o(T)}, \frac{e^{-\frac{4}{T}}}{N_o(T)} \right)$$

where

$$N_o(T) = \sum_{i=1}^{4} e^{-\frac{Cost_i}{T}}$$

that is,

$$\pi_i = \frac{e^{-\frac{Cost_i}{T}}}{\sum_{i=1}^{4} e^{-\frac{Cost_i}{T}}}$$

Since in this example we have $Cost_i = i$,

$$\pi_i = \frac{e^{-\frac{i}{T}}}{\sum_{i=1}^{4} e^{-\frac{i}{T}}}$$

This is consistent with Equation 2.10.

■

Example 2.4 For the Markov chain given in Example 2.3, find the optimizing distribution.

Solution The optimizing distribution can be obtained by finding the stationary distribution and then applying the limit $T \to 0$. For this example, we have the stationary distribution given by

$$\pi = \left(\frac{e^{-\frac{1}{T}}}{N_o(T)}, \frac{e^{-\frac{2}{T}}}{N_o(T)}, \frac{e^{-\frac{3}{T}}}{N_o(T)}, \frac{e^{-\frac{4}{T}}}{N_o(T)} \right)$$

where

$$N_o(T) = \sum_{i=1}^{4} e^{-\frac{i}{T}} = e^{\frac{-1}{T}} \left(1 + e^{-\frac{1}{T}} + e^{-\frac{2}{T}} + e^{-\frac{3}{T}} \right)$$

If we apply the limit $T \to 0$, we get

$$\lim_{T \to 0} \pi(T) = (1, 0, 0, 0)$$

That is, the probability of achieving the optimal solution with lowest cost, $Cost_1 = 1$, is unity, and the probability of achieving a suboptimal solution is zero.

■

In order to clarify further, let us use an example of a configuration graph with two optimal states. In the example below we find the stationary and optimizing distributions to verify Equation 2.15.

Example 2.5 Consider the configuration graph given in Figure 2.8. The cost of the five states is as follows: $Cost_1 = 1$, $Cost_2 = 2$, $Cost_3 = 1$, $Cost_4 = 4$, $Cost_5 = 3$, $Cost_n$ represents the cost of state S_n. If the acceptance criterion used is Metropolis, determine the transition matrix and find the stationary distribution.

Solution Equation 2.6 is used to obtain the transition matrix. Let us define $t = e^{-\frac{1}{T}}$. Then the transition matrix Θ is given by

$$\Theta = \left\{ \begin{matrix} 1 - \frac{t}{3} - \frac{t^2}{3} & \frac{t}{3} & 0 & 0 & \frac{t^2}{3} \\ \frac{1}{3} & \frac{1}{3} & \frac{1}{3} & 0 & 0 \\ 0 & \frac{t}{3} & 1 - \frac{t}{3} - \frac{t^3}{3} & \frac{t^3}{3} & 0 \\ 0 & 0 & \frac{1}{3} & \frac{1}{3} & \frac{1}{3} \\ \frac{1}{3} & 0 & 0 & \frac{t}{3} & \frac{2}{3} - \frac{t}{3} \end{matrix} \right\}$$

As before, we can solve the equations for the stationary distribution ($\pi = \pi \cdot \Theta$) using Mathematica as follows.

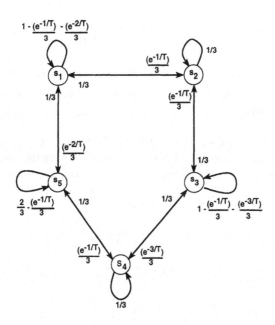

Figure 2.8: Configuration graph for Example 2.5.

```
Solve
[{Theta[[1,1]]p1+Theta[[2,1]]p2+Theta[[3,1]]p3+
                Theta[[4,1]]p4+Theta[[5,1]]p5==p1,
  Theta[[1,2]]p1+Theta[[2,2]]p2+Theta[[3,2]]p3+
                Theta[[4,2]]p4+Theta[[5,2]]p5==p2,
  Theta[[1,3]]p1+Theta[[2,3]]p2+Theta[[3,3]]p3+
                Theta[[4,3]]p4+Theta[[5,3]]p5==p3,
  Theta[[1,4]]p1+Theta[[2,4]]p2+Theta[[3,4]]p3+
                Theta[[4,4]]p4+Theta[[5,4]]p5==p4,
  Theta[[1,5]]p1+Theta[[2,5]]p2+Theta[[3,5]]p3+
                Theta[[4,5]]p4+Theta[[5,5]]p5==p5,
  p1+p2+p3+p4+p5==1}, {p1,p2,p3,p4,p5}];
Simplify[%]
```

Where, Theta[[i,j]] represents Θ_{ij} and pi represents π_i. Solving the equations to obtain the stationary distribution of the above Markov chain we get,

$$\pi = (\pi_1, \pi_2, \pi_3, \pi_4, \pi_5) = (\frac{1}{N_o}, \frac{t}{N_o}, \frac{1}{N_o}, \frac{t^3}{N_o}, \frac{t^2}{N_o})$$

where

$$N_o = 2 + t + t^2 + t^3$$

∎

Example 2.6 For the Markov chain given in Example 2.5, find the optimizing distribution.

Solution The optimizing distribution can be obtained by applying the limit to the stationary distribution. For this example, we have the stationary distribution given by: $\pi = (\pi_1, \pi_2, \pi_3, \pi_4, \pi_5)$, where (see Example 2.5),

$$\pi_1 = \frac{1}{2+t+t^2+t^3}$$

$$\pi_2 = \frac{t}{2+t+t^2+t^3}$$

$$\pi_3 = \frac{1}{2+t+t^2+t^3}$$

$$\pi_4 = \frac{t^3}{2+t+t^2+t^3}$$

$$\pi_5 = \frac{t^2}{2+t+t^2+t^3}$$

and $t = e^{-\frac{1}{T}}$. As $T \to 0$, we have $t \to 0$. And

$$\lim_{T \to 0} \pi(T) = (\frac{1}{2}, 0, \frac{1}{2}, 0, 0)$$

Note that since there are two optimal states, the probability of reaching either of them is half, and the probabilities of reaching an optimal state add up to unity, whereas the probability of reaching a suboptimal state is zero.

∎

2.4   Parameters of the SA Algorithm

In the previous paragraphs we demonstrated that, if simulated annealing is allowed to run for an infinitely long time, starting with a high value of T, and allowing $T \to 0$, then it will find a desired optimal configuration. In practice, however, simulated annealing is only run for a finite amount of time. A finite time implementation can be realized by generating homogeneous Markov chains of finite lengths for a sequence of decreasing values of temperature. To achieve this, a set of parameters that govern the convergence of the algorithm must be specified. This set of parameters is commonly referred to as the "cooling schedule" [AK89, KCGV83, OvG89].

The *Metropolis* procedure receives as input the current temperature T, the current solution $CurS$, and a value M, which is the amount of time for which annealing must be applied at temperature T. Temperature is initialized to a value T_0 at the beginning of the procedure, and is slowly reduced in a geometric progression; the parameter α is used to achieve this cooling. The amount of time spent in annealing at a given temperature is gradually *increased* as temperature is lowered. This is done using the parameter $\beta \geq 1$. The variable *Time* keeps track of the time being expended in each call to the *Metropolis*. The annealing procedure halts when *Time* exceeds the allowed time. The cooling schedule specifies the following:

1. A finite sequence of values of temperature which are given by the initial value T_0, a decrement factor (α), and the final value which is specified by the stopping criterion.

2. A finite number of transitions (denoted by βM) at each value of the temperature which corresponds to the finite length of each homogeneous Markov chain.

Therefore, a cooling schedule is completely specified by setting the values of parameters α, β, M, T_0, and $Time$. It is customary to determine the schedule by trial and error. However, some researchers have proposed cooling schedules that rely on some mathematical rigor.

2.4.1   A Simple Cooling Schedule

The cooling schedule discussed in this section was presented by Kirkpatrick et al. [KCGV83]. It is based on the idea that the initial temperature T_0 must be large to virtually accept all transitions and that the changes in the temperature at each invocation of the Metropolis loop are small. The scheme provides guidelines to the choice of T_0, the rate of decrements of T, the termination criterion and finally the length of the Markov chain at a particular temperature [KCGV83].

Initial temperature T_0: The initial temperature must be chosen so that almost all transitions are accepted initially. That is, the initial acceptance ratio $\chi(T_0)$ must be close to unity, where

$$\chi(T_0) = \frac{\text{Number of moves accepted at } T_0}{\text{Total number of moves attempted at } T_0} \qquad (2.16)$$

To determine T_0 we start off with a small value of initial temperature given by T_0'. Then, $\chi(T_0')$ is computed. If $\chi(T_0')$ is not close to unity, then T_0' is increased by multiplying it by a constant factor larger than one. The above procedure is repeated until the value of $\chi(T_0')$ approaches unity. The value of T_0' is then the required value of T_0. Increasing the value of T_0' by small amounts until $\chi(T_0')$ approximates to unity is analogous to heating the material until all atoms are randomly arranged in the molten phase.

Decrement of T: A decrement function is proposed to reduce the temperature in a geometric progression, and is given by

$$T_{k+1} = \alpha T_k, \quad k = 0, 1, \ldots, \tag{2.17}$$

where α is a positive constant less than one, since successive temperatures are decreasing. Further, since small changes are desired, the value of α is chosen very close to unity, typically $0.8 \leq \alpha \leq 0.99$.

Final T: The algorithm is terminated if the cost of the solution obtained in the last trial of a Markov chain remains unchanged for a number of consecutive chains.

Length of Markov chain M: This is equivalent to the number of times the Metropolis loop is executed at a given temperature.

If the optimization process begins with a high value of T_0, the distribution of relative frequencies of states will be close to the stationary distribution. In such a case, the process is said to be in quasi-equilibrium [AL85]. The number M is based on the requirement that at each value of T_k quasi-equilibrium is restored [AL85].

From an intuitive point of view it can be argued that quasi-equilibrium will be restored after acceptance of at least some fixed number of transitions. Since at decreasing temperatures uphill transitions are accepted with decreasing probabilities, one has to increase the number of iterations of the Metropolis loop with decreasing T (so that the Markov chain at that particular temperature will remain irreducible and with all states being non-null). A factor β may be used ($\beta > 1$) which, in a geometric progression, increases the value of M. That is, each time the Metropolis loop is called, T is reduced to αT, M is increased to βM.

2.4.2 A Statistical Polynomial Time Cooling Schedule

Based on statistical analysis a problem-independent cooling schedule can be devised. That is, one which can be applied to different problems without tuning. A book by Otten and Van Ginneken is devoted to developing such a schedule control [OvG89]. In this section we summarize the cooling schedules proposed by Aarts et al. [AK89, AL85], where a statistical analysis of the problem is used and the schedule is adjusted so as to make the execution time polynomial.

Initial temperature T_0: The requirement for T_0 is the same as before, that is, it must be chosen so that almost all proposed transitions are accepted at this temperature. This means that the temperature must be chosen to achieve a certain desired initial acceptance ratio χ_0. Let m^- be the number of moves with cost decrease and m^+ the number of moves with cost increase. A good estimate of the number of accepted uphill moves is

$$M_{up} = m^+ \times e^{-(\frac{\overline{\Delta Cost^+}}{T})} \tag{2.18}$$

where $\overline{\Delta Cost^+}$ is the average change in cost over all uphill moves, that is,

$$\overline{\Delta Cost^+} = \frac{1}{m^+} \times \sum_{S_i, S_j \in \Omega : Cost_j > Cost_i} (Cost_j - Cost_i) \tag{2.19}$$

Then the total number of configurations accepted is

$$M_a = m^- + m^+ \times e^{-(\frac{\overline{\Delta Cost^+}}{T})} \tag{2.20}$$

The acceptance probability χ is given by

$$\chi = \frac{M_a}{M} \tag{2.21}$$

where $M = m^- + m^+$. Solving the above for the temperature T we obtain

$$T = \frac{(\overline{\Delta Cost^+})}{\left\{ \ln(\frac{m^+}{\chi(m^- + m^+) - m^-}) \right\}} \tag{2.22}$$

Having derived the expression for T, we now proceed to calculate the required initial value T_0. To do this, initially T_0 is set to an extremely small value, then a sequence of M_0 trial moves are generated, where $M_0 = m^- + m^+$. After each trial, a new value of T is calculated using Equation 2.22, where χ is set to χ_0. That is, starting with $T_0 = 0$, after each perturbation a new value of T_0 is calculated from the above expression. The above process is repeated until χ as defined in Equation 2.21 approximates to unity.

The final value of T_0 obtained is taken as the initial temperature of the control parameter for the annealing algorithm. Experiments conducted indicate a fast convergence of the above procedure to a final value of T_0.

Decrement of T: Most schemes use predetermined temperature decrements, which are not optimal for all configurations.

For small steps in the reduction of temperature the subsequent distributions of the homogeneous Markov chains will be close to each other. As a consequence of this, after decreasing T_k to T_{k+1}, a small number of transitions may be sufficient for restoring quasi-equilibrium at T_{k+1}. To achieve quasi equilibrium, Aarts and van Laarhoven impose the condition [AL85]

$$\forall k \geq 0 : ||\pi(T_k) - \pi(T_{k+1})|| < \varepsilon \tag{2.23}$$

where

$$||\pi(T_k) - \pi(T_{k+1})|| = \sum_{S_i \in \Omega} |\pi_i(T_k) - \pi_i(T_{k+1})| \tag{2.24}$$

Equation 2.23 is equivalent to imposing the following condition [AL85]:

$$\forall S_i \in \Omega : \frac{1}{1+\delta} < \frac{\pi_i(T_k)}{\pi_i(T_{k+1})} < 1 + \delta \tag{2.25}$$

δ and ε are some small real positive numbers. δ is a measure of how close the equilibrium vectors of two successive iterations are to each other. Aart et al. [AL85] show that if $\pi(T_k)$ is the stationary distribution for the homogeneous Markov chain associated with the simulated annealing algorithm as described above, and T_k and T_{k+1} are two consecutive values of temperature with $T_{k+1} < T_k$, then the inequalities of Equation 2.25 are satisfied if the following condition holds:

$$\forall S_i \in \Omega : \frac{e^{-(\frac{\Delta Cost_{i_0,i}}{T_k})}}{e^{-(\frac{\Delta Cost_{i_0,i}}{T_{k+1}})}} < 1 + \delta, \quad k = 0, 1, \ldots, \tag{2.26}$$

$\Delta Cost_{i_0,i} = Cost_{S_i} - Cost_{S_{i_0}}$, where $Cost_{S_{i_0}} = Cost_{S_{opt}}$ is the cost of an optimal state. For proof of the above equation see [AL85]. The above equation can be rewritten to give the following condition on two subsequent values of temperature:

$$\forall S_i \in \Omega : T_{k+1} > \frac{T_k}{1 + \frac{T_k \ln(1+\delta)}{Cost_i - Cost_{opt}}} \quad k = 0, 1, \ldots, \tag{2.27}$$

If we assume that the values of the cost function are normally distributed for a given value of T, then the $\Delta Cost_{i_0,i}$ are normally distributed with mean $\overline{C}(T) - Cost_{i_0}$ and standard deviation σ_{T_k} (σ_{T_k} is the standard deviation of the cost function up to the temperature T_k). Hence

$$\text{Prob}\{\Delta Cost_{i_0,i} \leq \overline{C}(T) - Cost_{i_0} + 3\sigma_{T_k}\} = 0.99 \tag{2.28}$$

We therefore replace the condition in Equation 2.27 by the following condition:

$$T_{k+1} > \frac{T_k}{1 + \frac{T_k \ln(1+\delta)}{\overline{C}(T) - Cost_{i_0} + 3\sigma_{T_k}}} \tag{2.29}$$

and obtain the expression for T_{k+1} as

$$T_{k+1} = T_k \left\{ 1 + \frac{T_k \ln(1+\delta)}{\overline{C}(T) - Cost_{i_0} + 3\sigma_{T_k}} \right\}^{-1} \qquad (2.30)$$

For most optimization problems, however, $Cost_{i_0}$ and hence $\overline{C}(T) - Cost_{i_0}$ are not known, and therefore, we approximate $\overline{C}(T) - Cost_{i_0} + 3\sigma_{T_k}$ by $3\sigma_{T_k}$ to obtain the following final expression for the decrement:

$$T_{k+1} = T_k \left\{ 1 + \frac{T_k \ln(1+\delta)}{3\sigma_{T_k}} \right\}^{-1} \qquad (2.31)$$

Final T: The stopping criterion suggested is based on the relative reduction during the optimization process of the running average of the cost function [AL85]. Let $\overline{Cost}_s(T)$ be the smoothed average cost over all states visited at a fixed temperature T. The search is stopped when the following condition is satisfied:

$$\frac{d\overline{Cost}_s(T)}{dT} \frac{T}{\overline{C}(T_0)} < \varepsilon_s \qquad (2.32)$$

where ε_s is a small positive number called the stopping parameter, $\overline{C}(T_0)$ is the average value of the cost function at T_0. This condition is based on extrapolating the smoothed average cost $\overline{Cost}_s(T)$ obtained during the optimization process. This average is computed over a number of Markov chains in order to reduce the fluctuations of $\overline{Cost}(T_i)$.

Length of Markov chain M: If quasi-equilibrium is maintained during the optimization process, the chain length can be kept small. However, for larger problems, obtaining stationarity will take longer time than for small problems. Furthermore, the system should have the possibility of investigating all configurations belonging to the neighborhood of a given configuration. A good value of the chain length therefore is given by the maximum size of the configuration subspace $\aleph(S_i)$, that is,

$$M = \max_{S_i \in \Omega} |\aleph(S_i)| \qquad (2.33)$$

Running-time complexity: With the cooling schedule presented above the run time of the cooling algorithm is proportional to

$$\max_{S_i \in \Omega} |\aleph(S_i)| \cdot \ln |\Omega| \qquad (2.34)$$

where the term $\max_{S_i \in \Omega} |\aleph(S_i)|$ originates from the length of the Markov chain and the term $\ln |\Omega|$ is the upper bound on the number of temperature steps. The perturbation mechanism can always be carefully selected so that the size of the configuration subspace is polynomial in the number of variables of the problem. Further, $\ln |\Omega|$ can be shown to be a polynomial function. Consequently, the simulated annealing algorithm can always be designed to be of polynomial time complexity.

2.4.3   An Efficient General Cooling Schedule

Approaches that use the above type of statistical analysis to derive cooling schedules are termed adaptive simulated annealing algorithms. In adaptive annealing approaches, the schedule can be adapted for each problem being solved. Results similar to those presented above have also been reported by Huang et al. [HRSV86] who use (1) a dynamic temperature decrement control to avoid quenching, (2) a dynamic adjustment of the Markov chain length to assure the establishment of equilibrium, and (3) reliable detection of the frozen condition. Below we summarize some important results.

Initial temperature T_0: The condition proposed by White [Whi84] is used to determine the starting temperature. The system is considered hot enough when $T \gg \sigma$, where σ is the standard deviation of the cost function. Hence $T_0 = k\sigma$, where k is computed assuming a normal cost distribution and selecting a temperature high enough to accept, with a given probability P, a configuration whose cost is 3σ worse than the present one. This assumption leads to

$$k = -\frac{3}{\ln P} \tag{2.35}$$

A typical value of k is 20 for P=0.9. First the configuration space is explored to determine σ (the standard deviation) of the cost function, and then the starting temperature is calculated.

Decrement of T: The annealing curve, which is the curve of average cost versus the logarithm of the temperature is used to guide the temperature decrease. The idea is to control the temperature so that the average cost decreases in a uniform manner. The slope of the annealing curve is

$$\frac{d < C >}{d \ln(T)} = T \cdot \frac{d < C >}{dT} \tag{2.36}$$

Using the result in [Rei65] and equating the slope of the annealing curve to σ^2/T^2 leads to

$$T_{k+1} = T_k e^{\left(\frac{T_k \Delta Cost}{\sigma^2}\right)} \tag{2.37}$$

To maintain quasi-equilibrium, the decrease in cost must be less than the standard deviation of the cost. For instance, $\Delta Cost = -\lambda\sigma$, $\lambda \leq 1$,

$$T_{k+1} = T_k e^{-\left(\frac{T_k\lambda}{\sigma}\right)} \tag{2.38}$$

A typical value of λ is 0.7. In actual implementations the ratio $\frac{T_{k+1}}{T_k}$ is not allowed to go below a certain lower bound (typically 0.5) in order to prevent a drastic reduction in temperature caused by the flat annealing curve at high temperatures.

Stopping criterion: When equilibrium is established, the difference between the maximum and minimum costs among the accepted states at that temperature is compared with the maximum change in cost in any accepted move during that temperature. If they are the same, it means that all the states accessed are of comparable costs, and there is no need to use SA. When the above occurs, the temperature is set to zero and the algorithm becomes a standard greedy random selection algorithm.

The above adaptive heuristic has been tested on the TSP and two-dimensional (2-D) standard cell placement problems. For the TSP problem, a uniform speed-up of more than 5 times was reported. For the 2-D placement, the heuristic has also been tested on circuits of size 183–800 cells resulting in a 16 to 57 percent saving in CPU time compared to TimberWolf3.2 (see Section 2.6.1) for approximately the same quality of solution. For more details on the above heuristic and details on how the quasi-equilibrium is established, see Huang et al. [HRSV86].

2.5 SA Requirements

In order to use simulated annealing to solve a particular problem, a sequence of Markov chains is to be generated at descending values of temperature. As seen above, the inner loop of the annealing algorithm is a homogeneous Markov chain, and T does not change within the loop. Such Markov chains are generated by transforming a current solution to another one by applying a generation mechanism (perturbance or neighbor function) and using an acceptance function which is usually the Metropolis function. Application of the annealing algorithm therefore requires the following.

1. A concise representation of the state space, where each state represents a configuration, and a cost function that represents the cost-effectiveness of the solutions with respect to the optimization objectives. It is important that the solution representation be easy to manipulate. Furthermore, the cost function should be given by a *simple* expression that is *easy* to evaluate.

This requirement is important because the manipulation of current configurations to generate new neighborhood states and the evaluation of the cost of that solution are done a large number of times.

2. A mechanism for transforming the current solution into a subsequent one to which the search should move. This will involve two steps.

   (a) First, the neighbor function is applied to generate a new solution. As seen above, to guarantee asymptotic convergence to the set of optimal solutions the neighborhood structure must be properly chosen so that the corresponding generation mechanism induces an irreducible and aperiodic Markov chain.

   (b) Second, the cost of this new solution, and hence the difference in cost $\Delta Cost$ is computed. Then, a decision is made whether to accept or reject this new generated solution.

These two steps are the most time consuming and should be executed in a time efficient manner. Therefore, in practice, the neighbor functions are generally simple. For permutation problems such as the cell placement or quadratic assignment problem (QAP) (see page 8), one simple neighbor function is a pairwise interchange where two slots are chosen at random and their contents swapped.

The computation of the new cost must be done incrementally, taking into account only the differences due to local disturbances (see Exercise 1.17).

The decision to accept new solutions is based on the acceptance criterion. If we use the Metropolis criterion then we are *actually* simulating the annealing process. That is,

$$f(Cost_i, Cost_j, T) = \begin{cases} e^{-\frac{\Delta Cost_{ij}}{T}} & \text{if } \Delta Cost_{ij} > 0 \\ 1 & \text{if } \Delta Cost_{ij} \leq 0 \end{cases} \qquad (2.39)$$

where $\Delta Cost_{ij} = (Cost_j - Cost_i)$ and $Cost_i$ and $Cost_j$ are the old and new costs, respectively.

However, in order to obtain an optimizing distribution, the requirements on $f(Cost_i, Cost_j, T)$ are met not only by the Metropolis function, but also by other functions (see Exercise 1.19) such as the one given below [Len90].

$$f(Cost_i, Cost_j, T) = \begin{cases} \frac{Cost_i}{Cost_j} \cdot T^{Cost_j - Cost_i} & \text{if } \Delta Cost_{ij} > 0 \\ 1 & \text{if } \Delta Cost_{ij} \leq 0 \end{cases}$$
$$(2.40)$$

Nahar et al. [NSS85] experimented with 20 different probabilistic acceptance functions and temperature schedules. The list of functions, and the results of experimentation on a one-dimensional (1-D) cell placement problem are summarized in [SM91].

3. Finally, the success of a simulated annealing algorithm depends on the choice of a proper cooling schedule, that is, on the initial value of temperature, the decrement function, the length of the Markov chain and a suitable stopping criterion.

2.6 SA Applications

Annealing is generally easy to implement. All that is required is an adequate problem representation, a move set, and a cost function. Since its introduction, simulated annealing has been applied to several problems.

The first applications of simulated annealing was on placement [KCGV83]. Furthermore, the largest number of application of simulated annealing was on digital design automation problems. We begin this section by describing the application of simulated annealing to solve the VLSI placement problem [SY95]. This choice is biased by the background of the authors. Also, it is our own way of giving tribute to this very important VLSI physical design problem which was the first application of SA in engineering. This work triggered many more applications on several other hard optimization problems.

2.6.1 VLSI Placement and TimberWolf3.2

Placement is the process of arranging the circuit components on a layout surface. The placement problem is a generalization of the quadratic assignment problem, which is NP-complete [GJ79]. As an example, consider the circuit of Figure 2.9(a); suppose that we need to place the gates on a two-dimensional surface. Figure 2.9(b) shows one such placement [the same placement is shown in a symbolic form in Figure 2.9(c)]. The symbolic placement shows gates as black boxes and nets as lines. Note that the actual details of routing (or interconnection) are omitted from the symbolic placement. However, from a symbolic placement, it is possible to get an *estimate* of the routing requirements. In estimating the total wire-length, it is realistic to assume that routing uses Manhattan geometry, that is, one in which routing tracks are either horizontal or vertical (after the city of Manhattan, where the streets run either North-South or East-West). In Figure 2.9(d), we show another symbolic placement for which the total wire-length ω is 12. Finally, Figure 2.9(e) shows a one-dimensional placement of the circuit. The one-dimensional (1-D) placement also requires 10 units of wiring. The area of a layout consists of two parts—the functional area (the sum of the areas of the

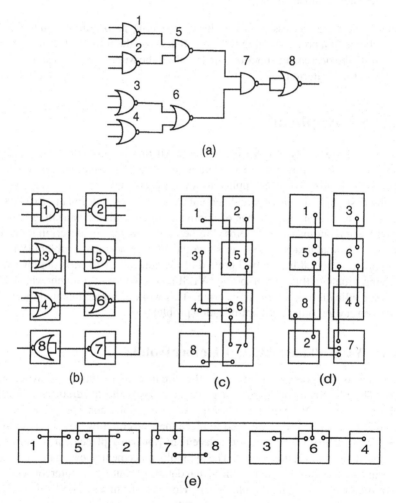

Figure 2.9: (a) A tree circuit. (b) A 2-D placement of gates. (c) A 2-D symbolic placement requiring 10 units of wiring. (d) A 2-D placement requiring 12 units of wiring. (e) A 1-D placement requiring 10 units of wiring.

functional cells) and the wiring area. The functional area remains unchanged for all placements. It is the wiring area which changes with the placement. This is because of *minimum separation* that must be maintained between two wires and between a wire and a functional cell.

A placement which requires a large amount of wiring space must necessarily involve long wires and hence a large value of total wire-length. Thus total wire-length ω is a good measure of the area of the layout. The advantage of using ω as a measure is that it is easy to compute. The overall wire-length of a given placement configuration P is defined as follows:

$$L(P) = \sum_{\text{Nets}} w_n \cdot d_n \qquad (2.41)$$

where

$$d_n = \text{estimated length of net } n, \text{ and}$$
$$w_n = \text{weight of net } n.$$

In this equation, since placement is performed before routing, the length of each net is just an estimate of the actual length. One popular approach to estimate the length is the semiperimeter method. In this approach, the length of the net is estimated as half the perimeter of the smallest box enclosing all the pins of the net. Having briefly introduced the VLSI cell placement problem, we now proceed to describe a package that uses simulated annealing for placement.

TimberWolf3.2

A popular package that uses simulated annealing for VLSI standard-cell placement and routing is the TimberWolf3.2 package [SSV86]. A standard-cell is a logic block that performs a standard function. Examples of standard-cells are two-input NAND gate, two-input XOR gate, D flip-flop, two-input multiplexer, and so on. A cell library is a collection of information pertaining to standard-cells. The relevant information about a cell consists of the name of the cell, its functionality, its pin structure, and a layout for the cell in a particular technology. Cells in the same library have standardized layouts, that is, all cells are constrained to have the same height (but different widths) so that they can be arranged in rows (see Figure 2.10). The space between two adjacent cell rows is used for routing (interconnecting the cells).

In the following paragraphs, we explain some of the features of the package and the algorithms employed by it.

The Algorithm

Based on the input data and parameters supplied by the user, TimberWolf3.2 constructs a standard-cell circuit topology. These parameters, in conjunction with the

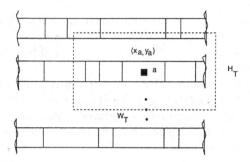

Figure 2.10: Limiter window centered around a cell.

total width of standard-cells to be placed, enable TimberWolf3.2 to compute the initial position and the target lengths of the rows. Following initial placement, the algorithm then performs placement and routing in three distinct stages. In the following discussion, we will be primarily concerned with the first stage which performs placement by simulated annealing.

The purpose of the first stage is to find a placement of the standard-cells such that the total estimated interconnect cost is minimized. A neighbor function called *generate* is used to produce new states by making a random selection from one of three possible perturb functions.

Perturb Functions

1. Move a single cell to a new location, for example, to a different row.

2. Swap two cells.

3. Mirror a cell about the x-axis.

TimberWolf3.2 uses cell mirroring less frequently than cell displacement or pairwise cell swapping. In particular, mirroring is attempted in 10 percent of the cases only (where cell movement is rejected).

Perturbations are limited to a region within a window of height H_T and width W_T. For example, if a cell must be displaced, the target location is found within a limiting window centered around the cell (Figure 2.10).

Therefore, two cells a and b, centered at (x_a, y_a) and (x_b, y_b) are selected for interchange only if $|x_a - x_b| \leq W_T$ and $|y_a - y_b| \leq H_T$. The dimensions of the window are decreasing functions of the temperature T. If current temperature is T_1 and next temperature is T_2, the window width and height are decreased as follows:

$$W(T_2) = W(T_1)\frac{\log(T_2)}{\log(T_1)} \tag{2.42}$$

$$H(T_2) = H(T_1)\frac{\log(T_2)}{\log(T_1)} \tag{2.43}$$

Cost Function

The cost function used by the TimberWolf3.2 algorithm is the sum of three components

$$\gamma = \gamma_1 + \gamma_2 + \gamma_3 \tag{2.44}$$

γ_1 is a measure of the total estimated wire-length. For any net i, if the horizontal and vertical spans are given by X_i and Y_i, then the estimated length of the net i is $(X_i + Y_i)$. This must be multiplied by the weight w_i of the net. Further sophistication may be achieved by associating two weights with a net—a horizontal component w_i^H and a vertical component w_i^V. Thus,

$$\gamma_1 = \sum_{i \in Nets} [w_i^H \cdot X_i + w_i^V \cdot Y_i] \tag{2.45}$$

where the summation is taken over all nets. The weight of a net is useful in indicating how *critical* the net is. If we want a particular net to be short we can increase its weight to achieve this goal. Independent horizontal and vertical weights give the user the flexibility to favor connections in one direction over the other.

When a cell is displaced or when two cells are swapped, it is possible that there is an overlap between two or more cells. Let O_{ij} indicate the area of overlap between two cells i and j. Clearly, overlaps are undesirable and must be minimized. The second component of the cost function, γ_2, is a penalty measure of overlaps.

$$\gamma_2 = w_2 \sum_{i \neq j} [O_{ij}]^2 \tag{2.46}$$

In the above equation w_2 is the weight for penalty. The reason for squaring the overlap is to provide much larger penalties for larger overlaps.

Because of cell displacements and pairwise exchanges of cells, the length of a row may become larger or smaller (Figure 2.11). The third component of the cost function represents a penalty for the length of a row R exceeding (or falling short of) the expected length $\overline{L_R}$.

$$\gamma_3 = w_3 \sum_{rows} |L_R - \overline{L_R}| \tag{2.47}$$

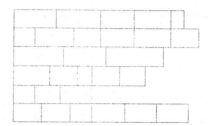

Figure 2.11: Uneven row lengths in standard-cell design.

where w_3 is the weight of unevenness. Uneven distribution of row lengths results in wastage of chip area. There is also experimental evidence indicating a dependence of both the total wire-length and the routability of the chip on the evenness of row lengths.

Annealing Schedule

Temperature is reduced as follows:

$$T_{i+1} = \alpha(T_i)T_i \qquad (2.48)$$

where $\alpha(T)$ is the cooling rate parameter which is determined experimentally. The annealing process is started at a high initial temperature, say 4×10^6. Initially, the temperature is reduced rapidly $[\alpha(T) \approx 0.8]$. In the medium range, the temperature is reduced slowly $[\alpha(T) \approx 0.95]$. Most processing is done in this range. In the low-temperature range, the temperature is reduced rapidly again $[\alpha(T) \approx 0.8]$. The algorithm is terminated when $T < 1$.

Inner Loop Criterion

At each temperature, a fixed number of moves are attempted. The optimal number of moves depends on the size of the circuit. From experiments, for a 200-cell circuit, 100 moves per cell are recommended, which calls for the evaluation of 2.34×10^6 configurations in about 125 temperature steps. For a 3,000-cell circuit, 700 moves per cell are recommended, which translates to a total of 247.5×10^6 attempts.

2.6.2 A Brief Overview of Other Applications

In addition to placement, there are several other problems to which SA has been applied successfully. These include classic problems such as the TSP [KCGV83], graph partitioning, matching problem, Steiner tree problems [Dow91], linear arrangement [NSS89], clustering problem [SAS91], quadratic assignment [Con90], various scheduling problems [OP89, OS90], graph coloring [CHdW87], and so forth. In the area of engineering SA has been applied extensively to solve various hard VLSI physical design automation problems [SY95]. In addition, it has been applied with success in other areas such as topology design of computer networks [EP93], image processing [GG84], test pattern generation, code design, and the like. A comprehensive list of bibliography of some of the above applications and some details of their implementation such as cost function formulation, move set design, parameters, and so on is available in [AK89, CEG88, Dow95, Egl90].

2.7   Parallelization of SA

In previous sections, several aspects of simulated annealing were discussed. By now, it should be obvious that overall, SA is a sound approximation algorithm. It is a general algorithm that is relatively easy to apply to almost any combinatorial optimization problem. However, simulated annealing requires some ingenuity on the part of the designer to cleverly anneal the problem in question, that is (1) the adoption of a good problem representation, so that the generation, execution, and evaluation of moves will be fast; (2) the choice of a good cost function so as to accurately characterize the goodness of solutions; and (3) the use of an adequate cooling schedule so as to have a high convergence rate. Nevertheless, simulated annealing is a greedy algorithm with respect to runtime, no matter how well tuned the algorithm is to the particular problem. The acceleration of the annealing algorithm has been an important area of research since the invention of the simulated annealing algorithm itself. Several accelerations techniques have been reported, which can be classified into three general categories [AK89, HRSV86]:

1. design of faster serial annealing, namely,

    (a) by using faster cooling schedule [CDV88, GS86, LA87, SH87]; and,

    (b) use of clever move sets [SSV86], approximate cost computation [Gro86], or changes in cost functions that reduce the chances of generating next states that may be rejected [GS86];

2. hardware acceleration which consists of implementing time-consuming parts in hardware [IKB83];

3. parallel acceleration, where execution of the algorithm is partitioned on several concurrently running processors [DKN87, DRKN87, KR87].

The most extensively studied approach is parallel acceleration. Parallel computation offers a great opportunity for sizable improvement in the solution of large and hard problems that would have otherwise been impractical to tackle on a sequential computer.

In this section we shall describe the basic techniques to parallelize simulated annealing. We will limit ourselves to the work we are most familiar with, and which we believe would be sufficient to indicate how to design a parallel version of the SA algorithm.

2.7.1 Parallel Annealing

The recent wide availability of parallel computing hardware attracted lots of research into the parallelization of simulated annealing in order to reduce its runtime requirements. Recall that a *move* or *trial* in simulated annealing consists of the following tasks:

1. perform a perturbation of the current solution to create a new solution;

2. compute the difference in the cost between the new and current solution;

3. decide whether to accept or reject the new solution;

4. if the new solution is accepted, then replace the current solution by the new solution; and

5. if the new solution is the best encountered so far, then replace the current best solution by the new solution.

A straightforward parallelization approach of SA could be as follows. Each processor is assigned a particular initial solution. Then each of the processors would be running sequential SA starting from its assigned initial solution. This simple approach would be good if the search subspaces of the various processors do not overlap (or have minimal overlap). In this case all processors would be concurrently searching distinct parts of the solution space. However, this would require that one has enough knowledge about the search space in order to partition it among the individual processors. In most cases this is an unrealistic assumption, and usually little is known about the search space. On the other hand, the subspace corresponding to the neighborhood of a particular solution is usually controlled by the algorithm designer (perturbation function), and can easily be searched in parallel by the available processors, with minimal overlap. It is for this reason that most of the suggested parallelization strategies force the various processors to always be working with the same current solution.

A close examination of the five tasks of a simulated annealing trial reveals that the first three tasks do not have any effect on the current solution and therefore, as long as the new solution is not accepted, the various processors can be concurrently evaluating distinct trials without affecting the correctness of the algorithm. However, the execution of the fourth and fifth tasks may change the global state of the problem. Thus, the parallel execution of tasks four and five would be a source of several problems. Assume that one processor rejects the new move, another accepts the new solution but does not update the current best, while a third processor accepts the new solution and updates both the current solution and the current best. The three processors would then have inaccurate information about the global state of the search. As we shall see later in this section, such problems can be avoided by providing some form of synchronization between the processors.

There are two general approaches that have been applied to parallelize simulated annealing: (1) *move acceleration*, also known as *single-trial parallelism*, and (2) *parallel moves*, also known as *multiple-trials parallelism* [AK89, Dur89].

In move acceleration, a trial is generated and evaluated faster by distributing the various tasks on several processors working in parallel. For parallel moves, several trials are generated and evaluated in parallel, where each trial is executed by a single processor. The difference between the two approaches is illustrated in Figure 2.12.

The speed-up that can be achieved by *single-trial parallelism* approach depends to a large extent on the problem instance.[1] For problems where a simulated annealing trial consists of central processing unit (CPU)-intensive tasks, such as floorplanning and placement in VLSI design or vehicle routing problem, sizable speed-up can be achieved when the various tasks of a trial are distributed among concurrently running processors [AK89, KR87]. However, we believe that this approach does not have good isoefficiency, that is, speed-up does not grow much with increasing number of processors. Furthermore, *single-trial parallelism* approaches must always be tailored to the particular problem instance.

Most work on the parallelization of simulated annealing have targeted the *multiple-trials parallelism* approach or a combination of the *single-* and *multiple-trials* approaches. In the remainder of this section, we shall confine ourselves to this class of approaches.

2.7.2   Multiple-Trials Parallelism

The multiple-trials parallelization approach of simulated annealing is general and can be tailored to any particular problem instance. In this strategy, several trials (moves) are generated and evaluated in parallel, where each trial is executed by a single processor. The processors are forced to concurrently search for an acceptable solution in the neighborhood of the same current solution (Figure 2.13). In order to ensure that all processors are always working with the same current solution configuration, one has to force them to communicate and synchronize their actions whenever at least one of the trials is successful (accepted move).

---

[1] See page 27 for definition of speed-up in the case of nondeterministic algorithm such as simulated annealing.

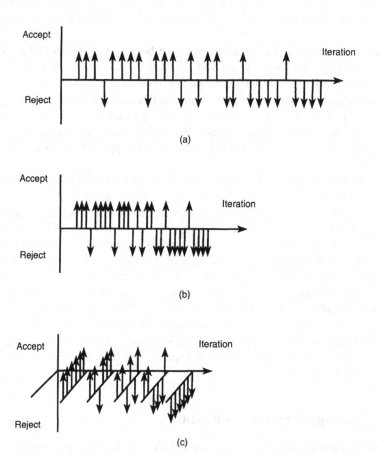

Figure 2.12: Parallelization of simulated annealing: (a) serial simulated annealing; (b) simulated annealing with move acceleration; (c) simulated annealing with parallel moves.

Figure 2.14 is a possible parallel simulated annealing algorithm following this multiple-trials parallelism approach.

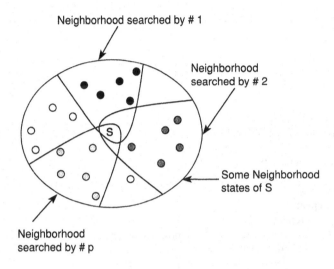

Figure 2.13: Multiple-trial parallel search of the neighborhood $\aleph(S)$ of current solution S.

In Figure 2.14, it is assumed that one master processor is ordering the concurrent execution of p trials, where p is the number of processors. The master evaluates the outcome from all trials. In case of no success, the master then orders the parallel evaluation of p new trials; otherwise, it selects the best new current solution among the accepted solutions, and updates the state of all processors. This process repeats until it is time to stop. Also at the end of each p new trials, the master processor checks to see whether equilibrium has been reached at current temperature. If the answer is yes, the algorithm parameters are updated.

A close examination of the algorithm in Figure 2.14 reveals that it is not a clever parallelization. The reason is that it is somehow a synchronous parallelization where the processors are forced to communicate and synchronize after each trial.

However, since the current solution will get updated only when a processor makes a successful trial, the various processors should be allowed to proceed asynchronously with their trials. Therefore, one can markedly improve the parallel algorithm of Figure 2.14 by making the following change. Synchronization is forced only when one of the processors performs a successful trial. In this new variation communication is minimal. Furthermore, it is a more efficient parallelization since no processor is forced to remain idle waiting for other processors with more elaborate trials to finish.

Algorithm Parallel_SA;
  (*S_0 is the initial solution *)
Begin
  Initialize parameters;
  $BestS = S_0$;
  $CurS = S_0$;
   Repeat
    Repeat
    Communicate $CurS$ to all processors;
    ParFor each processor i
     Perturb($CurS, NewS_i$);
     A_i = Accept($CurS, NewS_i$) (* A_i is true if $NewS_i$ is accepted *)
    EndParFor
    If Success **Then**
     (* Success = ($\bigvee_{i=1}^{p} A_i = True$) *)
     Select($NewS$);
     If $Cost(NewS) < Cost(BestS)$ **Then** $BestS = NewS$;
    EndIf
    Until Time to update parameters;
   Until Time to stop;
   Output Best solution found
End. (*$Parallel\_SA$*)

Figure 2.14: General parallel simulated annealing algorithm where synchronization is forced after each trial.

Both variations of this parallel algorithm can be implemented to run on a multicomputer or a multiprocessor machine. The parallel model assumed is a MISD or a MIMD machine. For both algorithms, it is assumed that each processor must be able to set a common variable to *True* whenever it accepts a move. Then the solution accepted by the processor is communicated to a master processor which will force all other processors to halt and to properly update the current solution. Here, there are two possibilities. If the processors do not halt immediately, but rather are allowed to complete the trials that were in progress when the request to stop was received, then more than one solution could be accepted, and therefore the master processor has to arbitrate between them, select the best, and pass a copy to each processor. The other possibility is when a processor is supposed to abort whatever activity in progress as soon as it receives a request to stop. In that case the first solution accepted by any of the processors would be the new solution of all the processors.

We believe that the first possibility would exhibit superior behavior. This is based on the following intuitive argument. Different trials usually have different time requirements. Trials that disturb the current solution more would usually require more time to complete. Although one cannot claim the existence of any correlation between the per-trial computing time and the probability of improving the current solution, the magnitude of improvement is positively correlated with the number of accepted trials.[2] Therefore, by letting all processors complete their current trials, it is expected to have a larger number of accepted moves, and by the same token a better chance of further improving the current solution.

As we have seen above, in the early regime (high temperature), the simulated annealing algorithm behaves close to a random search algorithm, where almost every move is accepted. This means that for the multiple-trials approach, the speed-up will be low (almost 1) at high temperatures since the processors will be forced to communicate after each trial. On the other hand, as the temperature is lowered, less and less moves are accepted, reducing by the same token the need for communication, thus allowing the p processors to concurrently be working most of the time. Therefore, in the cold regime, the speed-up will be approaching the number of processors (Figure 2.15).

This peculiar behavior of the simulated annealing algorithm has affected to a large extent most of the proposed parallel versions of annealing. A number of researchers have dealt with this problem by eliminating or minimizing communication between the processors [AK89, CRSV87, DRKN87].

In one approach, the processors are allowed to proceed concurrently with their search and to concurrently accept moves, with no interaction whatsoever. Algorithms following this strategy are known as *error algorithms*. The word "error" is used to highlight the fact that the processors have incorrect knowledge about the state of the parallel search. The major objection to this approach is the fact

---

[2]This observation deserves more rigorous analysis and some experimental evidence.

that the convergence properties of simulated annealing are affected. Experimental evidence revealed oscillation of the search when such strategy is adopted. Some authors gave intuitive explanations as to why error algorithms exhibit such behavior [AK89, KR87], but so far, no mathematical proof has been reported on the convergence or nonconvergence of error algorithms. Few studies have indicated, that by limiting the number of concurrent moves or by ensuring that the moves are always *noninteracting*, error is minimized and convergence is maintained [IKB83, KR87, UKH83]. Again, no mathematical proof of such claim has been provided. Furthermore, it is not always clear how one can go about restricting the moves to be of a particular type.

Another approach suggested by Kravitz and Rutenbar [KR87] is to restrict the set of concurrent moves to be *serializable*. A *serializable set* is a set of moves that would produce the same reject/accept decisions whether executed in parallel or in some serial order. For example, any set of rejected moves is a serializable set. Also, moves that are completely noninteracting are serializable too. In general, the identification of the largest possible serializable subset of moves (to maximize speed-up) is a difficult problem. Kravitz and Rutenbar suggested instead a subclass of serializable move-sets that are easy to identify. They refer to this move-set as the *simplest serializable set*. A simplest serializable set is formed by taking a number of rejected moves and appending to them an accepted move. Such move-set is always serializable. The expected size of the serializable move-set is a good estimation of the speed-up, since it is a measure of the average number of trials that are evaluated concurrently. The problem with this approach is that the size of the *simplest serializable* set is controlled by the temperature parameter. In the hot regime, the size of this set is extremely small (always close to 1) leading to unacceptably low speed-up (near 1). As a consequence of this behavior, different parallelization strategies are adopted at different regimes. In the following subsection, we shall describe this adaptive strategy.

Adaptive Multiple-Trials Parallel Simulated Annealing

Because the temperature control parameter has a marked effect on the behavior of simulated annealing, namely, on the acceptance ratio of attempted moves, a number of researchers suggested adaptive strategies, which apply different parallel approaches at different regimes [AK89, KR87].

One of the first adaptive strategies was suggested by Kravitz and Rutenbar [KR87]. The authors observed that the performance of the *move acceleration* is independent of temperature, while that of the *parallel moves* approach is sensitive to the temperature parameter. With the *move acceleration* approach, a 50 percent efficiency ($E_p \approx 0.5$) was attained on a four-processor shared memory computer. That is, with $P = 4$, the speed-up was near 2 ($S_P \approx 2$) at all temperatures. On the other hand, with the *parallel moves* approach the speed-up was near 1 at high temperature and near 4 (for $P = 4$) at extremely cold temperatures.

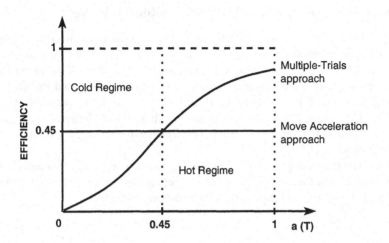

Figure 2.15: Achievable efficiency ($E_p = \frac{S_p}{p}$) in the hot and cold regimes for the multiple-trials approach; $p = 4$.

Furthermore, it was observed that at some temperature T^*, for which the move acceptance ratio $a(T^*) \approx 0.45$, the speed-up obtained with the *parallel moves* strategy became higher than that obtained with the *move acceleration* strategy. Kravitz and Rutenbar were also able to come up with an accurate estimation of the expected size of the *smallest serializable* move-set as a function of $a(T)$ and the number of parallel moves p, and the following adaptive strategy was adopted. At high temperature the *move acceleration* approach is used, that is, each move is decomposed into a number of fine-grained tasks executed concurrently by the available processors. Temperature is decreased whenever equilibrium is reached. As temperature is lowered, the fraction of accepted moves $a(T)$ at every temperature value T is constantly monitored. Then $a(T)$ is used to estimate the expected size of the smallest serializable move-set. When the expected size of this set reaches approximately half of the number of processors,[3] the algorithm dynamically switches to the *parallel moves* approach. The authors reported significant improvement over using either of the two static approaches [KR87].

Next, we shall briefly summarize the steps taken by Kravitz and Rutenbar to accurately estimate the size of the smallest serializable move-set.

---

[3] $\frac{P}{2}$ is the maximum observed speed-up with the *move acceleration* approach when $P = 4$. It remains to be proven whether this will hold for $P > 4$.

Expected Size of the Smallest Serializable Move-Set

The outcome of the p parallel trials can be represented by p independent and identically distributed random variables, m_i, $i = 1, 2, \ldots, p$. Each m_i is assumed to follow a Bernoulli distribution with parameter $a(T)$, where T is the current value of the temperature. Hence, $\text{Prob}[m_i = accept] = a(T)$ and $\text{Prob}[m_i = reject] = 1 - a(T)$. Similarly, let t_i, $i = 1, 2, \ldots, p$, be p independent and identically distributed random variables representing the completion times of the p trials. For simplicity, time is assumed to be normalized so that each t_i is uniformly distributed on $[0, 1]$.

Let R be the random variable representing the number of rejected moves. R takes on values in the interval $[0, p]$. $R = p$ represents the case when all p trials are rejected. Such event happens with the following probability:

$$\text{Prob}(R = p) = [1 - a(T)]^p \qquad (2.49)$$

In that case, the size of the serializable move-set is equal to p.

Before we find a general expression for $\text{Prob}[R = r], 0 \le r < p$, it is important to point out that, in the *multiple trial* implementation of Kravitz and Rutenbar, the first processor to accept a trial forces all remaining processors that have not yet completed their trials to stop. Therefore, none of the incomplete trials will be part of the serializable move-set.

Let τ be the time to get the first accepted trial. The event $R = r$, $r < p$, implies that at least one trial has been accepted and has finished first at time τ among all accepted moves. Furthermore, there are exactly r rejected trials which finish on or before τ, and $p - r - 1$ trials which do not finish by time τ and whose status do not concern us (since they will be forced to abort). Therefore, $\text{Prob}[R = r]$ can be expressed as follows:

$$\text{Prob}(R = r) = \binom{p}{1} \cdot a(T) \cdot \binom{p-1}{r} \cdot [1 - a(T)]^r \cdot \int_0^1 \tau^r (1 - \tau)^{p - r - 1} d\tau \quad (2.50)$$

One can easily show that the above equation can be simplified to the following:

$$\text{Prob}(R = r) = a(T)[1 - a(T)]^r, \ 0 \le r < p \qquad (2.51)$$

Let S be the random variable representing the size of the smallest serializable move-set. Then

$$S = \begin{cases} R + 1 & \text{if } 0 \le R < p \\ p & \text{if } R = p \end{cases} \qquad (2.52)$$

Therefore, the expected value of S can be expressed as follows:

$$E[S] = p[a(T)(1 - a(T))^{p-1} + (1 - a(T))^p] + \sum_{r=1}^{p-1} r \cdot a(T)[1 - a(T)]^{r-1}$$

$$(2.53)$$

The above expression for $E[S]$ can be simplified to the following closed form:

$$E[S] = \frac{1 - [1 - a(T)]^{p+1}}{a(T)} - [1 - a(T)]^p \qquad (2.54)$$

Kravitz and Rutenbar reported that the above equations overestimate by about 10 percent the value of $a(T)$ at which the *multiple trials* approach becomes superior to the *move acceleration* approach. As they indicated, the reason is that their statistical model does not account for any overhead due to the *multiple-trials* approach.

2.8 Conclusions and Recent Work

SA is a general-purpose optimization technique for combinatorial optimization problems. Theoretical studies have shown that the algorithm find global optimum provided a set of conditions on the annealing schedule are satisfied. For many hard problems, SA has produced excellent results but requires massive computing resources.

In addition to parallelization, various other approaches have been proposed to speed up SA. These approaches may be subdivided into two categories. One category is based on *move-set* design; they differ from the classic SA mainly in the perturbation mechanism that generates the next solution [Yao97]. Reported work in this category include fast SA [SH87], very fast SA [Ing89], a new SA [Yao95], and so forth. Most approaches based on move-set design are problem dependent; for example the move-set used in TimberWolf3.2 is based on range-limiting and is specific to the VLSI standard cell placement problem [SSV86]. Other techniques to speed up annealing based on changes to the cost function have also been reported [Gro86, GS86].

The second category is based on cooling schedule improvement [AL85, HRSV86]. Most annealing processes in the literature use predefined initial values of parameters such a initial temperature, predefined value of α, a fixed method to detect the equilibrium condition, and a predefined frozen condition. An annealing schedule is adaptive if the decrements of temperature and possibly the number of moves at each value of T are determined by the characteristic of the problem instance at hand. In this chapter we presented two *problem-independent* general annealing approaches whose parameters are determined automatically from measures of statistical quantities related to the problem being solved. The cooling schedule due to Aarts et al. [AL85] runs in polynomial time. Aarts et al. also proposed two parallel formulations (systolic, and a clustered algorithm) of the statistical cooling algorithm and showed that parallel algorithms can be executed in polynomial time. Both parallel algorithms are based on the requirement that quasi-equilibrium is preserved throughout the optimization process [AdBHL86].

For more on cooling schedules, adaptive annealing, parallel annealing, and results concerning optimal convergence see the work of Otten et al. [OvG89, OvG90], Azencott [Aze92], and Hajek [Haj88].

There is general agreement that the simulated annealing algorithm is difficult to parallelize because of its highly sequential nature. Each iteration depends on the outcome of the previous iteration. Some of the parallelization strategies described in this chapter allow the annealing process to proceed concurrently on all processors without forcing any synchronization among the processors. Such asynchronous parallel algorithms, which are referred to as the *error algorithms*, violate the serial decision sequence of simulated annealing. The main concern with this approach is that the convergence properties of simulated annealing are affected. Experimental evidence revealed oscillation of the search when such strategy is adopted [AK89, KR87]. Other parallelization approaches are synchronous and enforce that all processors be working with the same current solution. These synchronous approaches exploit parallelism within the phases of the simulated annealing algorithm. However, the amount of parallelism that can be exploited within the phases is both limited and problem-specific. In recent years, few researchers departed from these conventional parallelization strategies and followed the concurrency technique of speculative computation to parallelize the simulated annealing algorithm. This parallel realization of annealing is problem-independent. In this approach, concurrency is achieved by speculating the acceptance of each generated move before the move is actually made. Following this prediction, subsequent moves are made. To eliminate any decision errors, all moves subsequent to a wrong prediction are discarded. Statistics on previous moves are used to improve the prediction process. Speculative parallel annealing has been shown to result in significant speed-ups, much higher than speedups obtained with conventional strategies [SWJ93, SWJ94, WC96, WCF91]. The speculative parallel implementation reported in [WCF91] is referred to as *binary speculative computation*, where the processors are organized in a binary tree. Each node speculates on the computation of its parent node. If it is the left child it speculates that the result from the parent is an *accept*, otherwise it speculates that the result is a *reject*. The *reject node* assumes the parent processor will retain its current solution and thus expects the current solution from its parent. On the other hand, the *accept processor* expects the new solution after modification (after the move) from its parent. Communication among the processors is interleaved with the computation. The binary speculative computation approach suffers from the limitation that the maximum achievable speed-up is on the order of $\log_2 P$ on P processors. The work reported in [SWJ93, SWJ94] is a generalization of the binary speculative parallel annealing. The processors are no longer restricted to a binary tree organization. Instead, one of the processors is designated as the master (processor 0), the remaining P processors are slaves. At the beginning, all processors have the same initial solution. At the start, the master process transmits the current loop index to all slaves. The master then starts working on the evaluation and decision steps of the annealing algorithm. Each slave processor makes its own evaluation and decision and passes the result to the master processor. If more than one slave processor has reached an *accept decision*, the master processor accepts the decision of the processor with the lowest *ID* and rejects the *accept decisions* of the other slaves. The master updates the loop index, sends it with appropriate information to all slave processors, and modifies its own data structures. As soon as all slaves finish the updating step, the second round of parallel speculative annealing starts. Experimental results showed that *generalized speculative parallel annealing* can result in speed-ups of as much as P on P processors [SWJ93, SWJ94].

The work reported in [WC96] also employed speculative computation to parallelize the annealing algorithm. The authors introduced an effective prediction mechanism which relies on past moves to improve the accuracy of the speculative decision process. The authors also performed a thorough study of the various aspects of speculative computation which affect speedup. Interested readers should consult [WC96].

Although simulated annealing has been applied to several problems with success, there are some situations where it has not performed well. For example, application of annealing to the TSP has been considered by many researchers. This is one hard problem where heuristics have consistently outperformed simulated annealing [KCGV83, OvG89]. However, for many applications such as in VLSI physical design automation, image processing, and so forth, where no good heuristics exist, simulated annealing has produced excellent results [SSV86].

Finally, the performance of simulated annealing very much depends on the skill and effort put in the implementation of the algorithm. This includes the choice of an appropriate neighborhood structure, choice of cooling schedule and its parameters, the data structures use to represent and manipulate solutions, and so forth. All these have an effect on the runtime complexity and the quality of solutions produced [AK89].

References

[AdBHL86] E. H. L. Aarts, F. M. J. de Bont, E. H. A. Habers, and P. J. N. Van Laarhoven. Parallel implementations of the statistical cooling algorithm. *Integration, the VLSI Journal*, 4:209–238, 1986.

[AK89] E. Aarts and J. Korst. *Simulated Annealing and Boltzmann Machines: A Stochastic Approach to Combinatorial Optimization and Neural Computing.* John Wiley & Sons, 1989.

[AL85] E. H. L. Aarts and P. J. N. Van Laarhoven. Statistical cooling: A general approach to combinatorial optimization problem. *Philips Journal of Research*, 40(4):193–226, January 1985.

[Aze92]   Robert Azencott, editor. *Simulated Annealing Parallelization Techniques*. John Wiley & Sons, 1992.

[CDV88]   F. Catthoor, H. DeMan, and J. Vandewalle. Samurai: A general and efficient simulated-annealing schedule with fully adaptive annealing parameters. *Integration*, 6:147–178, 1988.

[CEG88]   N. E. Collins, R. W. Eglese, and B. L. Golden. Simulated annealing—an annotated bibliography. *AJMMS*, 8:209–307, 1988.

[Čer85]   V. Černy. Thermodynamical approach to the traveling salesman problem: An efficient simulation algorithm. *Journal of Optimization Theory and Application*, 45(1):41–51, January 1985.

[CHdW87]   M. Chams, A. Hertz, and D. de Werra. Some experiments with simulated annealing for coloring graphs. *European Journal of Operational Research*, 32:260–266, 1987.

[Con90]   D. T. Connolly. An improved annealing scheme for the QAP. *European Journal of Operational Research*, 46:93–100, 1990.

[CRSV87]   A. Casotto, F. Romeo, and A. L. Sangiovanni-Vincentelli. A parallel simulated annealing algorithm for the placement of macro-cells. *IEEE Transactions on Computer-Aided Design*, CAD-6:838–847, September 1987.

[D+92]   R. A. Dudek et al. The lessons of flowshop scheduling research. *Operations Research*, 40:7–13, 1992.

[DKN87]   F. Darema, S. Kirkpatrick, and V. A. Norton. Parallel techniques for chip placement by simulated annealing on shared memory systems. *Proceedings of International Conference on Computer Design: VLSI in Computers & Processors, ICCD-87*, pages 87–90, 1987.

[Dow91]   K. A. Dowsland. Hill climbing, simulated annealing, and the Steiner problem in graphs. *Eng. Opt.*, 17:91–107, 1991.

[Dow95]   K. A. Dowsland. Simulated annealing. In C. R. Reeves, editor, *Modern Heuristic Techniques for Combinatorial Optimization Problems*. McGraw-Hill Book Co., Europe, 1995.

[DRKN87]   F. Darema-Rogers, S. Kirkpatrick, and V. A. Norton. Parallel algorithms for chip placement by simulated annealing. *IBM Journal of Research and Development*, 31:391–402, May 1987.

[Dur89]   M. D. Durand. Accuracy vs. speed in placement. *IEEE Design & Test of Computers*, pages 8–34, June 1989.

[Egl90]   R. W. Eglese. Simulated annealing: A tool for operational research. *European Journal of Operational Research*, 46:271–281, 1990.

[EP93]   C. Ersoy and S. S. Panwar. Topological design of interconnected LAN/MAN networks. *IEEE Journal on Selected Areas in Communications*, 11(8):1172–1182, 1993.

[GG84]   S. Geman and D. Geman. Stochastic relaxation, Gibbs distribution, and the Bayesian restoration of images. *IEEE Transactions on Pattern Analysis and Machine Intelligence*, PAMI-6:721–741, 1984.

[GJ79]   M. R. Garey and D. S. Johnson. *Computers and Intractability: A Guide to the theory of NP-Completeness*. W. H. Freeman, San Francisco., 1979.

[Gro86]   L. K. Grover. A new simulated annealing algorithm for standard cell placement. *IEEE International Conference of Computer-Aided Design*, pages 378–380, 1986.

[GS86]   J. W. Greene and K. J. Supowit. Simulated annealing without rejected moves. *IEEE Transactions on Computer-Aided Design*, 5:221–228, 1986.

[Haj88]   B. Hajek. Cooling schedules for optimal annealing. *Mathematics of Operations Research*, 13:311–329, 1988.

[HRSV86]   M. D. Huang, F. Romeo, and A. L. Sangiovanni-Vincentelli. An efficient general cooling schedule for simulated annealing. *IEEE International Conference on Computer-Aided Design*, pages 381–384, 1986.

[HS78]   E. Horowitz and S. Sahni. *Fundamentals of Computer Algorithms*. Computer Science Press, 1978.

[IKB83]   A. Iosupovici, C. King, and M. Breuer. A module interchange placement machine. *Proceedings of 20th Design Automation Conference*, pages 171–174, 1983.

[Ing89]   L. Ingber. Very fast simulated re-annealing. *Mathl. Comput. Modeling*, 12(8):967–973, 1989.

[KCGV83]   S. Kirkpatrick, Jr. C. Gelatt, and M. Vecchi. Optimization by simulated annealing. *Science*, 220(4598):498–516, May 1983.

[Ker93]   A. Kershenbaum. *Telecommunications Network Design Algorithms.*
           McGraw-Hill, 1993.

[KR87]   S. A. Kravitz and R. A. Rutenbar. Placement by simulated annealing
           on a multiprocessor. *IEEE Transactions on Computer-Aided Design,*
           CAD-6(4):534–549, July 1987.

[LA87]   P. J. M. Laarhoven and E. H. L. Aarts. *Simulated Annealing: Theory
           and Applications.* Reidel, Dordrecht, 1987.

[Len90]   T. Lengauer. *Combinatorial algorithms for integrated circuit layout.*
           B. G. Teubner and John Wiley & Sons, 1990.

[M$^+$53] N. Metropolis et al. Equation of state calculations by fast computing
           machines. *Journal of Chem. Physics,* 21:1087–1092, 1953.

[MI94]   T. Murata and H. Ishibuchi. Performance evaluation of genetic al-
           gorithms for flowshop scheduling problems. *Proceedings of the
           first IEEE Conference on Evolutionary Computation, IEEE World
           Congress on Computational Intelligence,* pages 812–817, 1994.

[NSS85]   S. Nahar, S. Sahni, and E. Shragowitz. Experiments with simulated
           annealing. *Proceedings of 22nd Design Automation Conference,*
           pages 748–752, 1985.

[NSS89]   S. Nahar, S. Sahni, and E. Shragowitz. Simulated annealing and
           combinatorial optimization. *International Journal of Computer-
           Aided VLSI Design,* 1(1):1–23, 1989.

[OP89]   I. H. Osman and C. N. Potts. Simulated annealing for permutation
           flow-shop annealing. *OMEGA,* 17:551–557, 1989.

[OS90]   F. A. Ogbu and D. K. Smith. The application of the simulated an-
           nealing algortihm to the solution of the $n/m/c_{max}$ flowshop problem.
           Computers & Operations Research, 17:243–253, 1990.

[OvG89]   R. H. J. M. Otten and L. P. P. P. van Ginneken. *The Annealing Algo-
           rithm.* Kluwer, MA, 1989.

[OvG90]   R. H. J. M. Otten and L. P. P. P. van Ginneken. The complexity of
           adaptive annealing. *Proceedings of IEEE International Conference
           on Computer Design: VLSI in Computers and Processors,* pages
           404–407, 1990.

[Rei65]   F. Reif. *Statistical and Thermal Physics.* McGraw-Hill, New York,
           1965.

[SAS91]   S. Selim and K. S. Al-Sultan. A simulated annealing algorithm for the clustering problem. *Pattern Recognition*, 24(10):1003–1008, 1991.

[SH87]   H. Szu and R. Hartley. Fast simulated annealing. *Physics Letters, A*, 122:157–162, 1987.

[SM91]   K. Shahookar and P. Mazumder. VLSI cell placement techniques. *ACM Computing Surveys*, 23(2):143–220, June 1991.

[SSV86]   C. Sechen and A. L. Sangiovanni-Vincentelli. Timberwolf3.2: A new standard cell placement and global routing package. *Proceedings of 23rd Design Automation Conference*, pages 432–439, 1986.

[SWJ93]   A. Sohn, Z. Wi, and X. Jin. Parallel simulated annealing by generalized speculative computation. *Proceedings of 5th IEEE Symposium on Parallel and Distributed Processing*, pages 416–419, 1993.

[SWJ94]   A. Sohn, Z. Wi, and X. Jin. Parallel simulated annealing by generalized speculative computation. *Proceedings of the IEEE International Conference on Parallel Processing*, pages 8–11, 1994.

[SY95]   S. M. Sait and H. Youssef. *VLSI Design Automation: Theory and Practice*. McGraw-Hill Book Co., Europe (also copublished by IEEE Press), 1995.

[Tai90]   E. Taillard. Some efficient heuristic methods for the flow shop sequencing problem. *European Journal of Operational Research*, 417:65–74, 1990.

[UKH83]   K. Ueda, T. Komatsubara, and T. Hosaka. A parallel processing approach for logic module placement. *IEEE Transactions on Computer-Aided Design*, CAD-2(1):39–47, January 1983.

[WC96]   K. L. Wong and A. G. Constantinides. Speculative parallel simulated annealing with acceptance prediction. *IEE Proceedings: Computers and Digital Techniques*, 143(4):219–223, July 1996.

[WCF91]   E. E. Witte, R. D. Chamberlain, and M. A. Franklin. Parallel simulated annealing using speculative computation. *IEEE Transactions on Parallel and Distributed Systems*, 2(4):483–494, October 1991.

[Whi84]   S. R. White. Concept of scale in simulated annealing. *IEEE International Conference of Computer Design*, pages 646–651, 1984.

[Yao95]   X. Yao. A new simulated annealing algorithm. *International Journal of Computer Math*, 56:161–168, 1995.

[Yao97]   Xin Yao. Global optimization by evolutionary algorithms. *Proceedings of IEEE International Symposium on Parallel Algorithms Architecture Synthesis*, pages 282–291, 1997.

Exercises

Exercise 2.1

1. Why is simulated annealing called a nondeterministic algorithm?

2. Why is it called an adaptive algorithm?

3. Explain the term *cooling schedule* as applied to simulated annealing.

4. In implementing simulated annealing for your application, explain how you will choose the initial temperature and other parameters.

5. What is the significance of the comparison below in the simulated annealing

$$(random < e^{-\Delta h/T})$$

   where $\Delta h = (Cost(NewS) - Cost(S))$.

6. If you are to replace the exponential function $(e^{-\Delta h/T})$ by a (piecewise) linear function, what characteristic must this linear function have? (Illustrate with a figure.)

Exercise 2.2
Compare and contrast the simulated annealing algorithm with the local search iterative procedure discussed in Chapter 1.

Exercise 2.3
Does the quality of initial solution have any effect on the various parameters of the simulated annealing algorithm, such as initial temperature and the cooling rate? Explain.

Exercise 2.4
Propose a heuristic approach to estimate the number of iterations of the inner loop of the annealing algorithm (number of iterations in the Metropolis loop) as a function of the size of the neighborhood and the current temperature.

Exercise 2.5
Compare and contrast the various cooling schedules discussed in the text with respect to runtime complexity.

Exercise 2.6
Construct an example of a graph with 10 nodes, such that the nodes have a large degree, say 5–10 (see Exercise 1.6, page 37).

1. Assume that all the nodes have unit sizes. Apply the simulated annealing algorithm to obtain a two-way balanced partition of the graph. The objective is to minimize weight of the cut-set. Use pairwise swap as a move strategy.

2. Randomly assign weights to nodes say between 1 and 10 and generate an almost balanced partition with a minimum weighted cut-set using simulated annealing. Since nodes have different sizes, a pair-wise swap may not be the best move to generate the neighbor function. Use the neighbor and cost function suggested Exercise 1.12, page 40. Experiment with different values of W_c and W_s. Does increasing the value of W_c (W_s) necessarily reduce the value of cut set (imbalance)?

Exercise 2.7
A logic circuit can be represented by a set of nets as described in Example 2.2. Assume that all nets have a unit weight and all the nodes are of the same size. Write a program using SA to partition the circuit to reduce the number of nets cut. Every time you run the program you get a different result. Why?

Nets:

$N_1 = \{C_4, C_5, C_6\}$ $N_6 = \{C_4, C_7, C_9\}$ $N_{11} = \{C_2, C_6, C_7\}$
$N_2 = \{C_4, C_3, C_{12}\}$ $N_7 = \{C_2, C_8, C_{10}\}$ $N_{12} = \{C_{10}, C_{12}\}$
$N_3 = \{C_2, C_4\}$ $N_8 = \{C_1, C_7\}$ $N_{13} = \{C_4, C_7, C_9\}$
$N_4 = \{C_3, C_7, C_8\}$ $N_9 = \{C_3, C_5, C_9\}$ $N_{14} = \{C_3, C_9, C_{11}\}$
$N_5 = \{C_2, C_3, C_6\}$ $N_{10} = \{C_6, C_8, C_{11}\}$

Exercise 2.8

1. Construct a connected graph with 10 nodes and 25 edges. Starting from a random partition apply both the greedy pairwise exchange and the simulated annealing algorithm to this graph and generate balanced two-way partitions.

2. Starting from the solution obtained from the greedy pairwise technique, apply simulated annealing. Comment on any noticeable improvement in quality of solution and runtime.

Exercise 2.9
Given the following netlist with nine modules $m_1, \ldots, m_9$, and 13 nets N_1, $\ldots, N_{13}$. Assume that all cells are of the same size and that the layout surface is a checkerboard with three rows and three columns (nine slots).

Write a placement program using the SA algorithm in order to assign each cell to one of the nine slots, while minimizing the total Manhattan routing length. Use the *semiperimeter* method to estimate the wire-length [SY95].

Nets:

$$N_1 = \{m_4, m_5, m_6\} \qquad N_2 = \{m_4, m_3\} \qquad N_3 = \{m_2, m_4\}$$
$$N_4 = \{m_3, m_7, m_8\} \qquad N_5 = \{m_2, m_3, m_6\} \qquad N_6 = \{m_4, m_7, m_9\}$$
$$N_7 = \{m_2, m_8\} \qquad N_8 = \{m_1, m_7\} \qquad N_9 = \{m_3, m_5, m_9\}$$
$$N_{10} = \{m_6, m_8\} \qquad N_{11} = \{m_2, m_6, m_7\} \qquad N_{12} = \{m_4, m_7, m_9\}$$
$$N_{13} = \{m_3, m_9\}$$

(a) Apply sequential *pairwise exchange* as the *perturb* function. In sequential pairwise exchange, the cell in slot i is trial-exchanged in sequence with the cells in slots $i + 1, \ldots, n - 1, n$, for $1 \le i \le n - 1$. Use the following annealing schedule:

Initial temperature:	$T_0 = 10$;
Constants:	$M = 20$; $\alpha = 0.9$; $\beta = 1.0$.
Stopping criterion:	halt the program if no improvement at two consecutive temperatures.

(b) Suppress the condition that probabilistically accepts bad moves. This transforms the annealing to a deterministic greedy pairwise algorithm. Compare the results with those obtained in (a).

(c) Repeat parts (a) and (b) with random pairwise exchange. Tabulate the output as given in Table 2.2 and and compare the results.

Exercise 2.10
Modify the terminating condition of the simulated annealing algorithm so that the final annealing temperature is T_f. Estimate the time complexity of the SA procedure in terms of M, T_0, α, β, and T_f. (*Hint:* First estimate the number of temperatures during the annealing process.)

Exercise 2.11
Consider the configuration graph given in Figure 2.16. The cost of the five states is as follows: $Cost_1 = 1$, $Cost_2 = 2$, $Cost_3 = 3$, $Cost_4 = 4$, $Cost_5 = 1$, $Cost_n$ represents the cost of state S_n. If the acceptance criterion used is Metropolis, determine the transition matrix and find the stationary distribution.

Exercise 2.12
For the Markov chain given in Exercise 2.11, find the optimizing distribution.

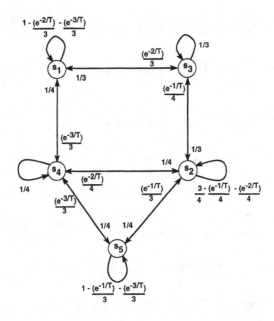

Figure 2.16: Configuration graph for Exercise 2.11.

Exercise 2.13

Implement a placement algorithm based on *simulated annealing*. Assume that there are 210 modules to be placed on a 15×14 mesh. There are two types of modules, functional blocks and input/output (I/O) pads. The I/O pads must be placed only on the periphery of the mesh, whereas a functional block may be placed in any empty slot. Assume 28 I/O pads and 182 functional blocks.

Generate a random initial placement which satisfies the pad position constraint. Use the following annealing schedule. $T_0 = 10.0$, $\alpha = 0.9$, $\beta = 1.0$, $T_f = 0.1$, $M = 200$. The *perturb* function must allow a circular shuffling of modules in λ slots, where λ is a user-specified constant. To test your program, you may set $\lambda = 2$ or $\lambda = 3$. The *perturb* function must respect the pad position constraint. Use the *DELTA-LEN* procedure of Exercise 1.17 to evaluate the change in cost function $\Delta Cost$.

1. Test your program for the sample circuit shown in Figure 2.17. In other words, synthesize the connectivity matrix for the circuit and give it as input to your program.

2. Run your program for several *random* initial placements. Does the initial solution influence the final solution?

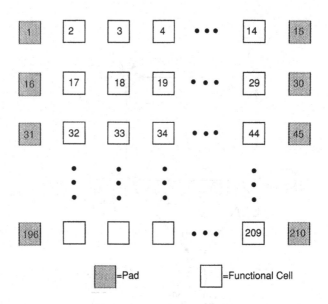

Figure 2.17: 210-cell mesh for Exercise 2.13.

3. Study the influence of the λ parameter on the quality of the final solution. Vary λ in the range 2 to 5. Does the runtime depend on λ?

4. In this book, we have been using the Metropolis function $(e^{-\Delta Cost/T})$ as the acceptance criterion. Can you suggest an alternate function for this purpose? Experiment with your alternative and compare the results.

Exercise 2.14

Consider the annealing schedule used in the TimberWolf3.2 placement algorithm. The initial temperature is T_1, the mid-range temperature starts at T_2, the low-range temperature starts at T_3, and T_4 is the final temperature. The cooling rate in the high-, middle-, and low-temperature ranges are α_1, α_2, and α_3 respectively. At each temperature, M moves are made per cell. Calculate the number of moves attempted by the algorithm if there are n cells in the circuit.

Compute the number of moves using your formula when $T_1 = 10^6$, $T_2 = 100$, $T_3 = 10$, $T_4 = 0.1$, $\alpha_1 = 0.8$, $\alpha_2 = 0.95$, $\alpha_3 = 0.8$, $M = 1000$, $n = 100$.

Exercise 2.15

Consider the vehicle routing problem (see Chapter 1, page 7) Propose a simulated annealing formulation for this problem.

Exercise 2.16
Flowshop Scheduling Problem:
Flowshop scheduling with the objective of minimizing the makespan is one of the well-known problem in the general area of scheduling (see also Chapter 4). Jobs are to be processed on multiple stages sequentially. There is one machine at each stage and machines are available continuously. There are n jobs and m machines. A job is processed on one machine at a time and a machine processes no more than one job at a time. Each job i requires $t_{i,j}$ time units of processing on machine j, $t_{i,j} \geq 0$, $1 \leq i \leq n$ and $1 \leq j \leq m$. The objective is to assign jobs to machines so as to minimize the makespan, that is, the finish time of the processing required by all the jobs. A general description of the problem is given by Taillard [Tai90]. For a more detailed description, see also [D$^+$92, MI94]. Propose a simulated annealing formulation for this problem.

Exercise 2.17
Terminal Assignment Problem:
Given n workstations and m hubs, the cost of assigning station i to hub j is c_{ij}. Each station consumes w_i units of hub capacity. The capacity of hub j is u_j. The objective is to find an assignment of minimum cost. Each station is to be assigned to exactly one hub. Let x_{ij} be a Boolean variable indicating whether station i is assigned to hub j ($x_{ij} = 1$) or not ($x_{ij} = 0$). This problem can be stated formally as follows.

$$
\begin{array}{ll}
\text{Minimize} & Z = \Sigma_{i,j} c_{ij} x_{ij} \\
\Sigma_{j=1}^{m} x_{ij} = 1 & i = 1, 2, \ldots, n \\
\Sigma_{i=1}^{n} w_i x_{ij} \leq u_j & j = 1, 2, \ldots, m \\
x_{ij} = 0, 1 & i = 1, 2, \ldots, n \text{ and } j = 1, 2, \ldots, m
\end{array}
$$

1. Provide English interpretation for each of the above constraints.
2. Develop a constructive greedy heuristic that will quickly find a feasible solution to this problem.
3. Develop a simulated annealing algorithm for this problem.
4. Implement the developed algorithms and test them on sample problem instances.

Exercise 2.18
Concentrator Location Problem:
Given a set of terminal locations i, $1 \leq i \leq n$, and a set of potential concentrator locations j, $1 \leq j \leq m$. The number of locations is assumed equal to the number of concentrators. The cost of connecting terminal i to location j is c_{ij}. Each terminal i requires w_i of concentrator capacity. For simplicity,

assume that all concentrators are of the same type and have a weight capacity of K. The cost of placing a concentrator at location j is d_j. Let x_{ij} be a Boolean variable indicating whether terminal i is connected to location j ($x_{ij} = 1$) or not ($x_{ij} = 0$), and y_j be such that $y_j = 1$ if a concentrator has been placed at location j and $y_j = 0$ otherwise. This problem can be stated formally as follows.

Minimize $\qquad Z = \Sigma_{i,j} c_{ij} x_{ij} + \Sigma_j d_j y_j$

$\Sigma_{j=1}^m x_{ij} = 1 \qquad i = 1, 2, \ldots, n$

$\Sigma_{i=1}^n w_i x_{ij} \leq K y_j \; j = 1, 2, \ldots, m$

$x_{ij}, y_j \in \{0, 1\} \quad i = 1, 2, \ldots, n \text{ and } j = 1, 2, \ldots, m$

1. Provide English interpretation for each of the above constraints.

2. Develop a constructive greedy heuristic that will quickly find a feasible solution to this problem.

3. Develop a simulated annealing algorithm for this problem.

4. Implement the developed algorithms and test them on sample problem instances.

Exercise 2.19

Constrained Minimum Spanning Tree Problem (CMST):

The objective is to connect a number of nodes (area hubs) to a central node (master hub) according to a spanning tree topology. Let c_{ij} be the cost of putting a link between nodes i and j. Assume that the master hub is node number 0, and the area hubs are numbered 1, 2, $\ldots$, n. The flow from area hub i to the master hub is w_i units. The flow on any link must not exceed a given bound c. Find a feasible minimum spanning tree interconnecting all the nodes, that is, a tree of minimum cost and where the flow on any of the links does not exceed the bound c.

1. Use the Esau-William algorithm to solve the above problem (see [Ker93] for a description of this algorithm).

2. Design a simulated annealing algorithm to solve the above CMST problem.

3. Compare your implementations on a number of randomly generated test problems.

Exercise 2.20

Mesh Topology Design Problem:

Given n routers numbered 1, 2, $\ldots$, n. Traffic flows between every pair of routers are given in the form of a traffic matrix $\Gamma = [\gamma_{i,j}]$, where $\gamma_{i,j}$ is the number of data units that are generated per unit of time from router i to router

j. Let c_{ij} be the cost of putting a link between routers i and j. Links can be of two types: (a) a higher grade link where the transmission time of a data unit takes only 0.5 unit of time, and (2) a lower grade link where the transmission time of a data unit takes 1 unit of time. The cost of a higher grade line is 1.5 times that of a lower grade line. Hence, the cost of putting a lower grade link between routers i and j is c_{ij}, and the cost is $1.5c_{ij}$ if the link is of a higher grade. Further, we assume that there is capacity constraint on the traffic volume transmitted over every link. A lower grade link can handle no more than L data units per unit of time while an upper grade link has twice that limit. Assume that the routers forward traffic along the path with the least transmission delays, and in case of a tie, the least cost path is preferred. The objective is to find a feasible topology of lowest possible cost and that which will incur minimum delays. A possible solution to this problem is to start from a feasible topology such as a minimum spanning tree or a complete mesh (where every router is connected to every other router), and then to keep modifying it by either adding or dropping links, while optimizing a figure of merit. The reader unfamiliar with this material should consult the book by Kershenbaum [Ker93].

1. Suggest criteria that can be used to select links for dropping or adding.

2. Design an SA algorithm to solve this problem.

3. Implement the developed algorithm and test it on sample problem instances.

Exercise 2.21
Weighted Matching/Semimatching Problem:

1. Let $W = (w_{ij})$ b an $m \times n$ non-negative matrix. The objective is to select a maximum-weight subset of elements subject to the constraint that no two elements are from the same row of the matrix. This problem is known as the *weighted semimatching problem*. Propose an optimal greedy algorithm for this problem.

2. Consider now the *weighted matching* problem, where we have the additional constraint that no two elements are to be chosen from the same column.

   (a) Show by example that the greedy algorithm proposed for the *Weighted Semimatching Problem* is not an optimal algorithm for the *Weighted Matching Problem*.

   (b) Design a simulated annealing algorithm for the *Weighted Matching Problem*.

   (c) Implement the developed algorithm and test it on sample problem instances.

Exercise 2.22
Plant Location Problem [HS78]:
Let $Site_i$, $1 \leq i \leq n$, be n possible sites at which plants may be located. At most one plant can be accommodated at each site. The cost of setting up a plant at $Site_i$ is F_i and its maximum capacity is C_i. There are m destinations, D_j, $1 \leq j \leq m$ to which products have to be shipped. The demand at D_j is d_j and the per unit cost of shipping a product from $Site_i$ to destination D_j is c_{ij}. A destination may be supplied from many plants. Define $y_i = 0$ if no plant is located at $Site_i$ and $y_i = 1$ otherwise. Let x_{ij} be the number of units of the product shipped from $Site_i$ to destination D_j. The objective is to assign plants to locations so as to minimize the cost of shipping required product quantities from sites to destinations. This can be expressed formally as follows:

Minimize $Z = \sum_i F_i y_i + \sum_i \sum_j c_{ij} x_{ij}$
$\sum_i x_{ij} = d_j$ $1 \leq j \leq m$
$\sum_j x_{ij} \leq C_i y_i$ $1 \leq i \leq n$
$x_{ij} \geq 0,\ y_j \in \{0, 1\}$ $1 \leq i \leq n, 1 \leq j \leq m$

1. Provide English interpretation for each of the above constraints.
2. Develop a constructive greedy heuristic that will quickly find a feasible solution to this problem.
3. Develop a simulated annealing algorithm for this problem.
4. Implement the developed algorithms and test them on sample problem instances.

Exercise 2.23
Discuss and compare the single- and multiple-trial parallelization approaches.

Exercise 2.24
In multiple-trial parallelization approach two possibilities were suggested in the text: (1) all processors are allowed to complete their trials and the best solution produced is adopted as the current solution, and (2) the first processor to accept new current solution forces all other processors to abort.

1. Discuss the merits and demerits of each possibility.
2. Does the value of temperature makes one possibility more suitable than the other?
3. Suggest with justifications other conditions to force processor synchronization.

Exercise 2.25

1. Prove the result of Equation 2.50.

2. Show that Equation 2.53 simplifies to the expression of Equation 2.54.

Exercise 2.26

Equation 2.54 applies when all incomplete trials are aborted once a processor accepts a move. Derive a similar expression for the case when all p processors are allowed to complete their trials and the serializable move-set is made of all rejected moves and the best accepted move.

CHAPTER 3

Genetic Algorithms (GAs)

3.1 Introduction

In this chapter we present the genetic algorithm (GA), a powerful, domain-independent, search technique that was inspired by Darwinian theory. It emulates the natural process of evolution to perform an efficient and systematic search of the solution space to progress toward the optimum. It is based on the theory of *natural selection* that assumes that individuals with certain characteristics are more able to survive, and hence pass their characteristics to their offspring.

The genetic algorithm is an *adaptive* learning heuristic. Similar to simulated annealing, it also belongs to the class of general *nondeterministic* algorithms. Several variations of the basic algorithm (modified to adapt to the problem at hand) exist. We will henceforth refer to this set as genetic algorithms (in plural).

Genetic algorithms (GAs) operate on a *population* (or set) of *individuals* (or solutions) encoded as strings. These strings represent points in the search space. In each iteration, referred to as a generation, a new set of strings that represent solutions (called offsprings) is created by crossing some of the strings of the current generation [Gol89c]. Occasionally new characteristics are injected to add diversity. GAs combine information exchange along with *survival of the fittest* among individuals to conduct the search.

Since their appearance, GAs have been applied to solve several combinatorial optimization problems from various fields of science, engineering, and business (see Section 3.7).

We begin this chapter by a brief introduction to background and terminology (Section 3.1.1), and subsequently present the basic genetic algorithm (Section 3.2). We then look at the fundamental theorem of GAs known as the Schema Theorem (Section 3.3) and discuss some convergence-related issues (Section 3.4). Following this, in Sections 3.5 and 3.6 we present some practical issues pertaining to implementation of GA on a digital computer. These include the various types of operators, schemes and suggestions for the choice of parameters, and so forth. In Section 3.7 we present a brief survey of some engineering applications, with case studies and examples, that further illustrate the implementation aspects of this powerful iterative technique. The various strategies proposed for parallel implementation are covered in Section 3.8. Other related issues and recent development in the area of GAs are covered in Section 3.9.

3.1.1 GA Basics

In living organisms, as members of the population mate, they produce offsprings that have a significant chance of retaining the desirable characteristics of their parents, and sometimes even combine or inherit the "best" characteristics of both parents. By establishing a correspondence between, on one hand, *a solution to the optimization problem* and the element of the population (represented by the *chromosome*), and between the *cost* of a solution and the *fitness* of an individual in the population, a solution method in the field of combinatorial optimization is introduced. The method thus simulates the process of natural evolution based on Darwinian principles, and hence the name *genetic algorithm* [Gol89c, Hol75].

Genetic algorithms (GAs) were invented by John Holland and his colleagues [Hol75] in the early 1970s. Holland incorporated features of natural evolution to propose a *robust*, computationally simple, and yet powerful technique for solving difficult optimization problems.

When employing GAs to solve a combinatorial optimization problem one has to find an efficient representation of the solution in the form of a chromosome (encoded string). Associated with each chromosome is its *fitness value*. If we simulate the process of natural reproduction, combined with the biological principle of survival of the fittest, then, as each generation progresses, better and better individuals (solutions) with higher fitness values are expected to be produced.

Robustness

The real world of search is filled with discontinuities and large multimodal noisy search spaces. Calculus-based methods and simple hill climbing are not robust, since they are local in scope and the optima they seek are the best in a neighborhood of the current point. Genetic algorithms, on the other hand, are both effective and *robust* [Dav91, Gol89c]. Independent of the choice of the initial configurations GAs always produce high quality solutions. They have proved to be effective because of their ability to exploit favorable characteristics of previous solution attempts to construct better solutions. Their power lies in the fact that as members of the population mate, they produce offsprings that have a significant chance of *inheriting* the best characteristics of both parents. Furthermore, GAs are computationally simple and easy to implement.

GAs are very different from other search algorithms. It is well known that techniques such as calculus-based methods, random search, and enumerative schemes (dynamic programming) are *inefficient* and perform poorly on some practical problems of moderate to large sizes. The main characteristics of GAs that make them different from other search heuristics are listed below.

They work with coding of parameters: GAs work with a coding of the parameter set, not the parameters themselves. Therefore, one requirement when employing GAs to solve a combinatorial optimization problem is to find an *efficient* representation of the solution in the form of a chromosome (encoded string).

They search from a set of points: In other optimization methods such as simulated annealing (Chapter 2) or tabu search (Chapter 4) we move from a single point in the search space, using some transition rule, to the next point. This type of point to point movement most often causes trapping in local optima. In contrast, GAs simultaneously work from a rich collection of points (a population of solutions). Therefore, the probability of getting trapped in false valleys (in case of minimization problem) is reduced.

They only require objective function values: GAs are not limited by assumptions about the search space (such as continuity, existence of derivatives, etc.,), and they do not need or use any auxiliary information. To perform an effective search for better and better structures, they **only** require *objective* (cost) *function* values.

They are nondeterministic: GAs use probabilistic transition rules, not deterministic rules. Mechanism for choice of parents to produce offsprings, or for combining of genes in various chromosomes are probabilistic.

They are blind: They are blind in the sense that they do not know when they hit the optimum, and therefore they must be told when to stop.

3.1.2   GA Terminology

In this subsection, we introduce the necessary terminology and illustrate some important concepts with examples.

Chromosome, Genes, and Alleles

The structure that encodes how the organism is to be constructed is called a *chromosome*. One or more chromosomes may be associated with each member of the population. The complete set of chromosomes is called a *genotype* and the resulting organism is called a *phenotype*. Similarly, the representation of a solution to the optimization problem in the form of an encoded string is termed as a *chromosome*. In most combinatorial optimization problems a single chromosome is generally sufficient to represent a solution, that is, the genotype and the chromosome are the same.

The symbols that make up a chromosome are known as *genes*. The different values a gene can take are called *alleles*.

Example 3.1 As an example, consider the problem of maximizing the function

$$f(x) = x^2 \qquad 0 \le x \le 63$$

We shall assume that this function measures the fitness of an individual phenotype x. The phenotype is a numerical value which we decode from the chromosome.

Let us encode the decision variables of the above problem as a string of finite length. For this example we can use chromosomes with binary alleles. A chromosome can be conveniently represented as a six-digit binary unsigned integer. For example, the string 1 0 0 1 0 0 is a possible chromosome. Also note that for the above problem we can guess the value of the chromosome that will maximize the given function. It is a string with all 1's. But in real problems, of course, there is no such advance knowledge [Fre94, Gol89c] (see Exercise 3.6).

∎

Example 3.2 As another example, consider an instance of the "scheduling problem." The problem consists of assigning and scheduling nodes (that correspond to tasks) of a task graph to a set of connected processors. Let the *Cost* of computation be the time to completion of the computation represented by the task graph. It is required to find an assignment and schedule that will reduce the total completion time (*Cost*).

For the graph shown in Figure 3.1(a), each node represents a task and the time required to execute it. Any of the five tasks may be assigned to one of the three connected processors [Figure 3.1(b)]. The values on the edges between nodes represent the time that must elapse after the completion of the first task, before the next task begins, if it is assigned to another processor. However, if the next task is assigned to the same processor as its predecessor task, then the time that must elapse is zero.

In our problem, each assignment can be encoded as a string containing n genes, where n is the number of tasks. The encoding divides each gene (g) into two fields T_j and p_k. If n is the number of tasks in the task graph, and m the number of processors, then field p_k ($1 \le k \le m$) specifies the processing element number and field T_j ($1 \le j \le n$) specifies the task that is assigned to

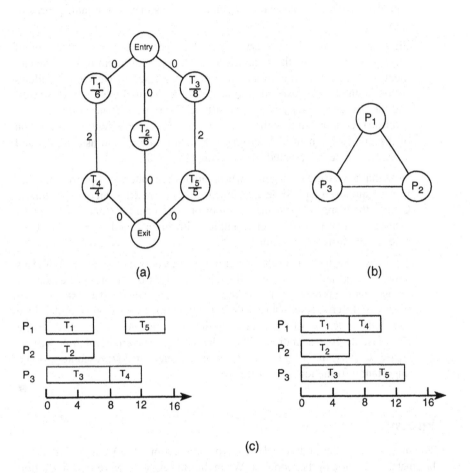

Figure 3.1: (a) Task graph. (b) Processing elements topology. (c) Two possible schedules.

it. For example, for our first assignment in Figure 3.1(c) we have the encoding $[(T_1, p_1), (T_2, p_2), (T_3, p_3), (T_4, p_3), (T_5, p_1)]$. Note that for this assignment, task T_5 begins 2 units after the completion of task T_3 since they are assigned to different processors (that is, T_5 to p_1 and T_3 to p_3). However, in the second assignment of Figure 3.1(c), task T_5 begins execution immediately after the completion of task T_3 since both T_3 and T_5 are assigned to the same processor (p_3).

Since we have associated every task with its processor, any permutation of these genes represents the same assignment. It is convenient to keep the elements of the string sorted in the order of task indexes. If we keep the alleles sorted on the task indexes, then it is no longer required to store the indexes, and the string $[p_1, p_2, p_3, p_3, p_1]$ is sufficient to represent our assignment (or solution). Or more simply the string [1 2 3 3 1] is a sufficient representation of the first assignment and schedule. Similarly the second assignment and schedule can be represented by the string [1 2 3 1 3].

Note that any string of n genes whose alleles are indexes of processors (between 1 and m) is a possible assignment, and a representation of our solution. Clearly there are m^n possible solutions or assignments of our task graph of n tasks to m processors. For example, with $m = 8$ and $n = 20$ we have 1.15×10^{18} different solutions.

The above chromosomal representation gives us only the assignment of tasks to processors, and does not give the schedule. That is, the order of execution of tasks on the processors is not known. We can always order tasks on each processor differently and have different completion times. For example, if we switch the order of tasks T_3 and T_4 in the first schedule of Figure 3.1(c), the chromosomal representation will not change, but the completion time will increase. Clearly, in trying to have a simple chromosomal representation some important information is lost (see Exercise 3.7).

∎

Fitness

The fitness value of an individual (genotype or a chromosome) is a *positive* number that is a measure of its goodness. When the chromosome represents a solution to the combinatorial optimization problem, the fitness value indicates the cost of the solution. In the case of a minimization problem, solutions with lower cost correspond to individuals that are more fit.

Example 3.3 For the chromosome representation of Example 3.1, since we would like to maximize the function $f(x) = x^2$, the square of the decimal value of the binary string is a measure of its fitness. For example, the fitness of the chromosome [1 0 0 1 0 0] is $36^2 = 1,296$. Since we are dealing with only unsigned integers, the integer value of x is also a possible measure of the fitness of the chromosome.

In the problem of Example 3.2, the objective is to find an assignment that will reduce the time to completion. Therefore, this is a minimization problem. Since genetic algorithms aim at maximizing the fitness, one trivial way to translate the completion time of a schedule (cost function in a minimization problem) to *fitness* is to consider fitness as the reciprocal of the completion time. Hence, the chromosome that represents the smallest elapsed execution time corresponds to the most fit individual in the population.

Fitness, denoted by σ, can therefore be expressed as the reciprocal of the maximum of the sum of the time required to execute all the tasks assigned to a given processor, plus its idle time. That is,

$$\sigma = \left[\max_{j=1,m} \left(\sum_{T_i \in p_j} \text{Time}(T_i) + \text{idle}(j) \right) \right]^{-1} \tag{3.1}$$

Applying the above definition, the fitness of schedule 1 in Figure 3.1(c) is $\frac{1}{15}$ and that of schedule 2 in the same figure is $\frac{1}{13}$. In the computation of fitness using Equation 3.1 above we have assumed that tasks ordering on processors (that is scheduling) is on their index values.

This is not the only way in which one can map costs to fitness values. There are other effective schemes which we discuss below in Section 3.5.2. ∎

Initial Population

Since GAs work on a population of solutions, an *initial population constructor* is required to generate a certain predefined number of solutions. The quality of the final solution produced by a GA depends on the size of the population and how the initial population is constructed. The initial population generally comprises random solutions. Later we elaborate on other schemes to construct the initial population (see Section 3.6.1).

Example 3.4 Construct a population of four individuals to solve the problems in Example 3.1 and 3.2 using the genetic algorithm.

Solution Let us assume that we have a random number generator that we use to generate binary patterns of 6 bits. Then a possible set of chromosomes for the problem in Example 3.1 is: $s_1 = [0\ 1\ 1\ 0\ 0\ 1]$; $s_2 = [1\ 0\ 1\ 1\ 0\ 0]$; $s_3 = [1\ 1\ 0\ 1\ 0\ 1]$; $s_4 = [1\ 1\ 1\ 0\ 0\ 0]$.

Similarly, for the assignment/scheduling problem in Example 3.2, a set of chromosomes that represent possible solutions to our optimization problem are: $s_1 = [2\ 3\ 3\ 1\ 2]$; $s_2 = [2\ 1\ 1\ 2\ 3]$; $s_3 = [3\ 2\ 1\ 1\ 2]$; $s_4 = [3\ 1\ 2\ 1\ 1]$. ∎

Parents, Genetic Operators, and Offsprings

GAs work on chromosomes or pairs of chromosomes to produce new solutions called offsprings. Common genetic operators are *crossover* (χ) and *mutation*. They are derived by analogy from the biological process of evolution. Crossover operator is applied to pairs of chromosomes. The two individuals selected for crossover are called *parents*. Mutation is another genetic operator that is applied to a single chromosome. The resulting individuals produced when genetic operators are applied on the parents are termed as *offsprings*.

Choice of Parents

The choice of parents for crossover from the set of individuals that comprise the population is probabilistic. In keeping with the ideas of natural selection, we assume that stronger individuals, that is those with higher fitness values, are more likely to mate than the weaker ones. One way to simulate this is to select parents with a probability that is directly proportional to their fitness values. That is, the larger the fitness of a certain chromosome, the greater is its chance of being selected as one of the parents for crossover.

To accomplish this type of selection we may use the *roulette wheel method*. In this method a wheel is constructed on which each member of the population is given a sector whose size is proportional to the relative fitness of that individual. To select a parent the wheel is spun, and whichever individual comes up becomes the selected parent. Therefore, in this method, individuals with lower fitness values also have a finite but lower probability of being selected for crossover [Gol89c]. Figure 3.2 illustrates the roulette wheel for the population of Example 3.4 whose fitness values and their percentages are given below:

$$s_1 = [0\ 1\ 1\ 0\ 0\ 1] = 25^2 = 625 = 7.35 \text{ percent}$$
$$s_2 = [1\ 0\ 1\ 1\ 0\ 0] = 44^2 = 1936 = 22.76 \text{ percent}$$
$$s_3 = [1\ 1\ 0\ 1\ 0\ 1] = 53^2 = 2809 = 33.02 \text{ percent}$$
$$s_4 = [1\ 1\ 1\ 0\ 0\ 0] = 56^2 = 3136 = 36.87 \text{ percent}$$

Crossover (χ)

Crossover is the main genetic operator. It provides a mechanism for the offspring to inherit the characteristics of both the parents. It operates on two parents (P_1 and P_2) to generate *offspring(s)*.

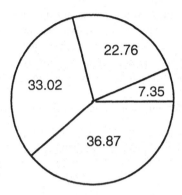

Figure 3.2: A roulette wheel for population of Example 3.4.

There are several crossover operators that have been proposed in the literature. Depending on the combinatorial optimization problem being solved some are more effective than others. One popular crossover that will also help illustrate the concept is the *simple crossover*. It performs the "cut-catenate" operation. It consists of choosing a *random* cut point and dividing each of the two chromosomes into two parts. The offspring is then generated by catenating the segment of one parent to the left of the cut point with the segment of the second parent to the right of the cut point.

Example 3.5 For the following two parent chromosomes from our previous example, $s_2 = [1\ 0\ 1\ 1\ 0\ 0]$ and $s_4 = [1\ 1\ 1\ 0\ 0\ 0]$, perform the simple crossover to generate an offspring.

Solution Let $P_1 = s_4$ and $P_2 = s_2$. If the crossover point is chosen after the 2nd gene from the left, then the offspring produced will contain the genes from the left of crossover point of parent P_1 and those from the right of crossover point of parent P_2. The offspring chromosome resulting from this operation is $[1\ 1\ |\ 1\ 1\ 0\ 0]$. ('|' indicates the randomly chosen cut point). The fitness of this chromosome is $60^2 = 3600$, which is larger than the fitness values of individual parent chromosomes! Such a chromosome has a good chance of being included in the population of next generation.

■

Mutation (μ)

Mutation produces incremental random changes in the offspring by randomly changing allele values of some genes. In case of binary chromosomes it corresponds to changing single bit positions. It is not applied to all members of the population, but is applied probabilistically only to some. Mutation has the effect of perturbing a certain chromosome in order to introduce *new* characteristics not present in any element of the parent population. For example, in case of binary chromosomes, toggling some selected bit produces the desired effect.

Example 3.6 Consider our population of chromosomes below.

$$
\begin{aligned}
s_1 &= [0\,1\,1\,0\,0\,1] = 25^2 = 625 = 7.35 \text{ percent} \\
s_2 &= [1\,0\,1\,1\,0\,0] = 44^2 = 1936 = 22.76 \text{ percent} \\
s_3 &= [1\,1\,0\,1\,0\,1] = 53^2 = 2809 = 33.02 \text{ percent} \\
s_4 &= [1\,1\,1\,0\,0\,0] = 56^2 = 3136 = 36.87 \text{ percent} \\
&\qquad\quad\ \uparrow
\end{aligned}
$$

The allele in the fifth position in the entire population is "0." Therefore, independent of the choice of cut point, and the choice of parents for crossover, this value will never become "1" in any offspring. In other words, if the parent chromosomes do not have a certain characteristic, then that characteristic *cannot* appear in the offsprings. The only way this gene can change its value is by mutation. That is, to have a mechanism where genes are chosen randomly, and their values changed probabilistically. By providing such a mechanism, there is a finite chance that those genes which are locked to a certain allele value will change, thus introducing new characteristics into the population. ∎

Is it guaranteed that the offsprings will inherit only the good characteristics? What would be the result in Example 3.5 if strings for P_1 and P_2 were swapped. Further, in our example to illustrate crossover (Example 3.5) we intentionally chose parents with high fitness values. Chromosomes with lower fitness values also have a finite nonzero probability of being selected as parents for crossover. And these may produce good or inferior offsprings. As will be evident shortly, if the new offsprings that are produced by crossover and mutated perform well (have large fitness), then they are retained and their characteristics spread throughout the entire population. If they do not perform well, then they have a smaller chance of survival.

Generation and Selection

A *generation* is an iteration of GA where individuals in the current population are selected for crossover and offsprings are created. Because of the addition of offsprings, the size of population increases. In order to keep the number of members in a population fixed, a constant number of individuals are selected from this set which consists of both the individuals of the initial population, and the generated offsprings. If M is the size of the initial population and N_o is the number of offsprings created in each generation, then, before the beginning of next generation, we select M new parents from $M + N_o$ individuals. A greedy selection mechanism is to choose the best M individuals from the total of $M + N_o$.

We will now summarize the main aspects of the basic genetic algorithm.

3.2   Genetic Algorithm

In order to implement the genetic algorithm on a digital computer, one of the most important steps is to encode the solution of the combinatorial optimization as a string of symbols, also known as a chromosome. This encoding must be amenable to genetic operations. In addition to this, unlike in other search techniques, GAs do not operate on one solution but a collection of solutions termed population. An *initial population constructor* is required to generate a certain predefined number of solutions. The quality of final solution depends upon the size of the population and how the initial population is constructed. The population comprises random solutions, or, a combination of random solutions and those produced using known constructive heuristics. We also need a mechanism to generate offsprings from parent solutions.

During each generation of the genetic algorithm a set of offsprings are produced by the application of the *crossover* operator. The crossover operator ensures that the offsprings generated have a mixture of parental properties. In order to introduce new alleles into the chromosome, with a certain probability, *mutation* is also applied. Following this, from the entire pool comprising both the parents and their offsprings, a fixed number of individuals are chosen that form the population of the new generation. If the M best individuals are chosen from this pool, then the fitness of the best individual, will be the same or better than the fitness of the best individual of the previous generation. Similarly, the average fitness of the population will be the same or higher than the average fitness of the previous generation. Thus the fitness of the entire population and the fitness of the best individual increase in each generation. The structure of the simple genetic algorithm is given in Figure 3.3.

3.3   Schema Theorem and Implicit Parallelism

In the previous sections we saw the operation of the basic genetic algorithm. We observed that crossover distinguishes GAs from all other optimization algorithms. In this section we throw more light on what is processed by GAs and show how this processing will lead to optimal results in our optimization problems. We will see how crossover, the critical accelerator of the search process, combines parts of good solutions from diverse chromosomes [Gol89c, Hol75].

Procedure $(Genetic\_Algorithm)$
    M= Population size.   (*# Of possible solutions at any instance.*)
    N_g= Number of generations.   (*# Of iterations.*)
    N_o= Number of offsprings.   (*To be generated by crossover.*)
    P_μ= Mutation probability.   (*Also called mutation rate M_r.*)
    $\mathcal{P} \leftarrow \Xi(\mathbf{M})$ (*Construct initial population $\mathcal{P}$.*)
                                   (*Ξ is population constructor.*)

    For j = 1 to **M**   (*Evaluate fitnesses of all individuals.*)
        Evaluate $f(\mathcal{P}[j])$ (*Evaluate fitness of $\mathcal{P}$.*)
    EndFor
    For i = 1 to N_g
        For j = 1 to N_o
           $(x, y) \leftarrow \phi(\mathcal{P})$ (*Select two parents x and y from current population.*)
           offspring[j] $\leftarrow \chi(x, y)$ (*Generate offsprings by crossover of parents x and y.*)
           Evaluate f(offspring[j]) (*Evaluate fitness of each offsprings.*)
        EndFor

        For j = 1 to N_o (*With probability P_μ apply mutation.*)
           mutated[j] $\leftarrow \mu(y)$
           Evaluate f(mutated[j])
        EndFor
    $\mathcal{P} \leftarrow Select(\mathcal{P},$ offsprings)   (*Select best **M** solutions from parents & offsprings.*)
    EndFor
    Return highest scoring configuration in $\mathcal{P}$.
End

Figure 3.3: Structure of a simple genetic algorithm.

To study the what and how of GAs performance, we resort to the notion of *schema*. A schema is a set of genes that make up a partial solution to our optimization problem. Schemata (plural) can be thought of as defining subsets of similar chromosomes, or as hyperplanes in an n-dimensional space, where n is the number of genes per individual. Schemata are only used to illustrate certain properties of GAs and are *not* explicitly processed. That is, when we implement the genetic algorithm, we do not have any strings in our population that represent partial solutions. All strings or chromosomes represent complete solutions.

If we are dealing with binary strings, a schema, also known as a *building block*, is a template made up of the ternary alphabet {0,1,*}, where the "*" is a metasymbol representing a don't care. We say that a chromosome has a building block if it matches the 1's and 0's on the schema exactly. Consider the population given below [Gol89c]:

$$s_1 = [0\ 1\ 1\ 0\ 0\ 1] = 25^2 = 625 = 7.35 \text{ percent}$$
$$s_2 = [1\ 0\ 1\ 1\ 0\ 0] = 44^2 = 1936 = 22.76 \text{ percent}$$
$$s_3 = [1\ 1\ 0\ 1\ 0\ 1] = 53^2 = 2809 = 33.02 \text{ percent}$$
$$s_4 = [1\ 1\ 1\ 0\ 0\ 0] = 56^2 = 3136 = 36.87 \text{ percent}$$

Let H_1, H_2, H_3, and H_4 be four schemata represented by the following strings: $H_1 = [1\ 1 * * * *]$, $H_2 = [1 * * * * 0]$, $H_3 = [1 * * * * *]$, and $H_4 = [0 * * * * 1]$. From the above we observe that schema H_1 matches two strings of our population, namely s_3 and s_4 since both these have a "1" in the first two positions. Similarly, schema H_2 with a "1" in first position and a "0" in the last position matches strings s_2 and s_4. Schema H_3 matches three strings s_2, s_3, and s_4. And finally, schema H_4 matches only string s_1. Associated with any schema are its *order* and its *defining length*. The order of a schema H, denoted by $o(H)$, is the number of non-* symbols it contains. Its defining length, denoted by $\delta(H)$, is the distance from the first non-* symbol position to the last non-* position. As an example, the order of the schema *1*011 is four and its defining length δ is four (6-2). Clearly, for binary strings (of length n), if the number of metasymbols in a schema is k ($k = n - o(H)$), then such a schema represents 2^k different chromosomes, and some of these may exist in our population. Also associated with each schema is its average fitness denoted by $f(H)$, which is equal to the average fitness of the schema representative in the population. For example, since H_1 matches two strings s_3 and s_4, $f(H_1)$ is given by $\frac{f(s_3)+f(s_4)}{2}$ $= \frac{2,809+3,136}{2} = 2,973$. Similarly, $f(H_3) = \frac{1,936+2,809+3,136}{3} = 2,627$.

During crossover, a schema may be cut. A schema is said to be *cut* if the crossover point is selected within its defining length. When a schema is cut we say that it is disrupted. The probability of disruption depends on its order $o(H)$ and its defining length $\delta(H)$. For example, consider the two schemata $H_1 = [1\ 1 * * * *]$ and $H_2 = [1 * * * * 0]$. H_2 is likely to be disrupted by crossover, but most probably H_1 will be left undisturbed. That is, the larger the value of δ, the greater is the chance of disruption. From the above we can say that schemata of short defining lengths are most probably left undisturbed by crossover. Also, since the selection for crossover is proportional to fitness, if the average fitness of a schema is high then there is a good chance that chromosomes represented by it will be selected for crossover. What is the effect of mutation on the schema? Since usually the mutation rate (M_r) is low, generally schemata are not disrupted by mutation. Using the above observations we can infer the following [Gol89c, Hol75]. Highly fit, short-defining-length schemata most likely remain undisturbed and are propagated from generation to generation.

Let us mathematically look into the details of the above observations, which will lead us to the fundamental theorem of GAs called the *schema theorem* [Hol75].

3.3.1   Schema Theorem

Schemata and their properties, in addition to helping in classifying string similarities, also provide a means for analyzing the effect of reproduction and genetic operations on building blocks. In this section we analyze the growth and decay of schemata contained in a population denoted by $\mathcal{P}(t)$, (population $\mathcal{P}$ at generation or time t), and consider the effect of reproduction and genetic operators on building blocks contained within the population [Gol89c].

Effect of Reproduction

Let the **M** individual strings of the population be denoted by $\mathcal{P}[j]$, with fitness values f_j, $j = 1, 2, \ldots, $ **M**. A generation of GA begins with reproduction, that is, the creation of the mating pool. Suppose during a given generation (or time step) t there are m chromosomes of a particular schema H contained within the population $\mathcal{P}(t)$. Let these samples be denoted by $m(H, t)$. During reproduction, a string from the current population is selected according to its fitness. That is, a string $\mathcal{P}[i]$ gets selected with a probability $p_i = \dfrac{f_i}{\sum_j f_j}$. If we do so then we *expect* to have $m(H, t+1)$ representatives of schema H in the population at time $(t + 1)$ given by

$$m(H, t+1) = m(H, t) \cdot \mathbf{M} \cdot \frac{f(H)}{\sum_j f_j} \tag{3.2}$$

where $f(H)$, as defined above, is the average fitness of strings represented by schema H at time t, and **M** is the population size. If the average fitness of the entire population is denoted by $\overline{f}$, then

$$\overline{f} = \frac{\sum_j f_j}{\mathbf{M}} \tag{3.3}$$

and

$$m(H, t+1) = m(H, t) \cdot \frac{f(H)}{\overline{f}} \qquad (3.4)$$

From the above equation we observe the following. "In each generation, a particular schema grows as the ratio of the average fitness $f(H)$ of the schema to the average fitness $\overline{f}$ of the population." In other words, if the average fitness of a schema is higher than the average of the population, the number of copies this schema will receive in the next generation is high [since $f(H) \geq \overline{f}$ implies $m(H, t+1) \geq m(H, t)$]. Similarly, schemata with fitness values below the population average will receive a lower number of samples.

Suppose that a particular schema H remains above average by a value $c \cdot \overline{f}$, where c is a positive constant, then, $f(H) = \overline{f} + c \cdot \overline{f}$. Equation 3.4 then simplifies to

$$m(H, t+1) = m(H, t) \cdot (1 + c) \qquad (3.5)$$

Starting from $t = 0$, and assuming a stationary value of c, we have

$$m(H, t) = m(H, 0) \cdot (1 + c)^t \qquad (3.6)$$

The effect of reproduction is now clear, it allocates an **exponentially** increasing (decreasing) number of trials to above (below) average schemata. This behavior of above average schema getting more copies and below average getting lesser copies is carried out with every schema H contained in a population $\mathcal{P}$ in parallel. All schemata grow or decay according to their schema averages under the operation of reproduction alone.

Effect of Crossover

Reproduction as discussed only allocates increasing (decreasing) number of schemata to future generations in parallel. It does nothing to explore new regions of the search space (since we only copy new structures into the mating pool without change). It is crossover that creates new structures with a minimum of disruption to the allocation strategy dictated by reproduction.

We discussed above that the survival or destruction of a schema is a function of its defining length. Consider the schema $H_1 = [11****]$ of length 6 with defining length $\delta(H_1) = 1$. If we assume a simple crossover then the cut point (crossover site) can occur at any one of the five positions. If it occurs between the first and second positions then it will disrupt the schema, else the schema remains intact. Since only one of these five positions will disrupt schema H_1, the probability of disruption of H_1 denoted by p_d is given by $\frac{1}{5}$. The probability of survival $p_s(H_1)$ of that schema is equal to $1 - p_d(H_1) = \frac{4}{5}$.

As another example, consider the following schema $H_2 = [1 * * * 0*]$ whose $\delta(H_2) = 4$. There are four positions (1 to 4) where a cross point can cut the schema and disrupt it, and one point (after position 5) that will keep the schema intact. Hence $p_s(H_2)$ is $\frac{1}{5}$ and the probability of disruption is $\frac{4}{5}$. We can therefore say, that for a schema of length n, the probability of survival $p_s(H)$ is given by

$$p_s(H) = 1 - \frac{\delta(H)}{n-1} \tag{3.7}$$

That is, a schema is disrupted whenever a crossover site is selected within its defining length from $n-1$ possible sites (n being the length of the chromosome).

If crossover is itself performed probabilistically, say with a probability p_c, then, assuming independence between crossover and reproduction, the survival probability of a schema may be given by the expression [Gol89c]

$$p_s(H) \geq 1 - p_c \cdot \frac{\delta(H)}{n-1} \tag{3.8}$$

Effect of Crossover and Reproduction

Assuming independence between reproduction and crossover, the estimate of the number of a particular type of schema H expected in the next generation due to the combined effect of reproduction and crossover is given by the product of Equations 3.4 and 3.8, and substituting for $m(H, t)$ from Equation 3.6, we get

$$m(H, t+1) \geq m(H, 0) \cdot (1+c)^t \cdot \frac{f(H)}{\bar{f}} \cdot \left[1 - p_c \cdot \frac{\delta(H)}{n-1} \right] \tag{3.9}$$

From the above expression we observe that those schemata with both above-average fitness and short defining lengths are going to be sampled at exponentially increasing rates [Gol89c, Ree95b].

Effect of Mutation

Mutation introduces random changes to single-bit positions. Recall that every schema has $o(H)$ fixed bit positions and those represented by '*' are don't cares. For a schema to survive, none of the $o(H)$ specified bit positions must be disturbed by mutation. If p_m is the probability of mutating a certain bit position, then the survival probability of that bit position is $1 - p_m$. Since mutation of an individual bit is statistically independent of other bits, a particular schema survives if each of the fixed $o(H)$ positions survives.

Thus, the probability of a schema H surviving mutation (or not losing its identity) denoted by $p_{sm}(H)$ is given by multiplying the survival probability $(1 - p_m)$ of one bit by itself $o(H)$ times, that is,

$$p_{sm}(H) = (1 - p_m)^{o(H)} \simeq 1 - o(H) \cdot p_m \qquad (p_m << 1) \tag{3.10}$$

Effect of Crossover, Mutation, and Reproduction

From the above discussion we conclude that a particular schema H, due to reproduction, crossover, and mutation receives an *expected* number of copies in the next generation given by

$$m(H, t+1) \geq m(H,0) \cdot (1 + c)^t \cdot \frac{f(H)}{\bar{f}} \cdot \left[1 - p_c \cdot \frac{\delta(H)}{n-1}\right] \cdot [1 - o(H) \cdot p_m]$$

Assuming that $\frac{o(H) \cdot p_m \cdot p_c \cdot \delta(H)}{n-1}$ is negligible, the above expression can be approximated to

$$m(H, t+1) \geq m(H,0) \cdot (1 + c)^t \cdot \frac{f(H)}{\bar{f}} \cdot \left[1 - p_c \cdot \frac{\delta(H)}{n-1} - o(H) \cdot p_m\right]$$

The conclusions drawn from the above expression leads to the fundamental theorem of genetic algorithms called the *schema theorem* which can be stated as follows:

Theorem 1 *Highly fit, short-defining-length schemata are most likely undisturbed and are propagated from generation to generation. These schemata receive exponentially increasing number of trials in subsequent generations* [Gol89c, Ree95b].

3.3.2 Implicit Parallelism

The genetic operators create a new generation of configurations by combining the schemata or subassignments of parents selected from the current generation. Due to the stochastic selection process, the fitter parents, which are expected to contain some good subassignments, are likely to produce more offspring, and the bad parents, which contain some bad subassignments, are likely to produce less offspring. Thus in the next generation, the number of good subsolutions (or high-fitness schemata) tend to increase, and the bad subsolutions (or low-fitness schemata) tend to decrease.

For binary representations of chromosomes, each string of length n is an instance of 2^n distinct schemata. Clearly, when we evaluate the fitness of a given chromosome, we are actually gathering information about the average fitness of each of the schemata of which it is an instance. Therefore, a population of **M** chromosomes can contain as many as $\mathbf{M} \cdot 2^n$ schemata. Surely not all of these schemata are equally represented, and some may not have any representatives at all. Now, by explicitly processing **M** chromosomes, we are implicitly processing a much larger number of schemata (as large as $\mathbf{M} \cdot 2^n$). That is, we are testing a large number of possibilities by means of few trials—this is the property of GAs which Holland called *implicit parallelism* (or intrinsic parallelism) [Hol75].

Despite disruptions of long high order schemata by crossover and mutation, GAs implicitly process a large number of schemata while processing a relatively small number of strings. It has been shown that in a population of size M, the algorithm effectively exploits some multiple of M^3 schema combinations. Therefore, for a population larger than a few individuals, this number, M^3, is far greater than the total number of alleles in the population. Due to the property of implicit parallelism there is a simultaneous allocation of search effort to many regions, resulting in speed-up in the rate of search [Ree95b].

3.4   GA Convergence Aspects

One of the desirable properties that a stochastic iterative algorithm should possess is the convergence property, that is, the guarantee of converging to one of the global optima if given enough time. In this section, we examine the convergence properties of the GA heuristic. Convergence aspects of GA using Markovian analysis has been addressed by several researchers [DP91, DP93, EAH90, GS87a, Mah93, NV93, Rud94]. Fogel [Fog95] provides a concise treatment of the main GA convergence results.

For convenience, GA convergence results reported in the literature assume that the solutions (chromosomes) are encoded as bit strings (the genes are 0's and 1's). In this section, we also assume binary encoding.

Let n be the number of solutions in the population, and l be the chromosome length. As GA proceeds from generation to generation, each population represents a state. Each such state depends on the previous state only. A state is a global optimum if at least one of its n chromosomes corresponds to a global optimum solution. Though there may be a large number of states, they are finite in number. Thus, the GA walk through the state space is a finite Markov chain. Furthermore, since the algorithm parameters are kept constant, the Markov chain is time homogeneous. Hence, Markovian analysis can be used to study the convergence aspects of GA algorithms.

Recall that a Markov chain is fully specified by a matrix of transition probabilities indicating how the chain moves from state to state in a single transition. For a homogeneous chain this matrix stays constant from generation to generation (state to state). The transition matrix raised to the power k yields a matrix whose entries represent probabilities of transiting in exactly k steps from a particular starting state to a particular ending state. For GA, the state space is usually extremely large. For a population of n strings of length l each, there are $\frac{(n+x)!}{n!x!}$, where $x = 2^l - 1$ (for proof see Exercise 3.11). For example, for ten strings, each 10 bits long, there are over 3×10^{23} states. Hence, it is unthinkable to compute the transition matrix of a Markov chain of such proportions.

A Markov chain is *regular* when all the entries of its transition matrix elevated to some power are positive. The chain is absorbing if, (1) it has at least one absorbing state and, (2) it is possible to transit (possibly in more than one transition) from each nonabsorbing state to an absorbing state. Recall that an absorbing state is one where, once there, it is impossible to move to another state. Absorbing Markov chains always drift to one of their absorbing states.

3.4.1 GA without Mutation or Inversion

The Markov chain corresponding to GA with only crossover and selection is an *absorbing Markov chain*. The density of absorbing states is equal to $\frac{1}{2^{l(n-1)}}$. For example, for a genetic population of two individuals encoded as 3-bit strings ($l = 3$ and $n = 2$), there will be $2^{3 \times 2} = 64$ states, which are:

(000, 000) (000, 001) (000, 010) (000, 011) (000, 100) (000, 101) (000, 110) (000, 111)
(001, 000) (001, 001) (001, 010) (001, 011) (001, 100) (001, 101) (001, 110) (001, 111)
$\vdots$
(111, 000) (111, 001) (111, 010) (111, 011) (111, 100) (111, 101) (111, 110) (111, 111)

Among the above states, there are exactly $2^3 = 8$ absorbing states, which are:

(000, 000) (001, 001) (010, 010) (011, 011) (100, 100) (101, 101) (110, 110) (111, 111)

In this example, the density of absorbing states is $\frac{2^3}{2^{3 \times 2}} = \frac{1}{2^3}$, that is, 12.5 percent. Notice that the density of absorbing states decreases exponentially with the length of the chromosome. Hence, if all state transitions are equally likely, the probability of hitting an absorbing state will be exponentially decreasing with increasing length of the chromosome. Furthermore, the likelihood that one of the absorbing states is a global optimum is also exponentially decreasing with chromosome length. Note also, that the absorbing states may not even be locally optimum.

The behavior of GA progress can be represented formally as follows. Each GA iteration forces a transition to either (1) an absorbing state, (2) a state from which it is possible to move in a single transition to an absorbing state, or (3) a state from which it is impossible to move in a single step to an absorbing state. Through careful indexing of the states, the matrix of transition probabilities can be written as follows [Fog95]:

$$P = \begin{bmatrix} I_a & \bigcirc \\ R & Q \end{bmatrix} \tag{3.11}$$

where I_a is an $a \times a$ identity matrix representing transitions among absorbing states of the Markov chain, Q is a $t \times t$ matrix describing transitions among transient states, R is a submatrix of transitions from transient states to absorbing states, and $\bigcirc$ is an $a \times t$ submatrix of zeros representing the impossibility of transiting out of any of the a absorbing states.

The n-step transition matrix P^n satisfies the following [Fog95]:

$$P^n = \begin{bmatrix} I_a & O \\ N_n R & Q \end{bmatrix} \tag{3.12}$$

where $N_n = I_t + Q + Q^2 + \ldots + Q^{n-1}$, and I_t is the $t \times t$ identity matrix. As n tends to infinity, the limit of P^n exists and satisfies the following [Goo88]:

$$\lim_{n \to \infty} P^n = \begin{bmatrix} I_a & O \\ (I_t - Q)^{-1} R & O \end{bmatrix} \tag{3.13}$$

and the matrix $(I_t - Q)^{-1}$ is guaranteed to exist [Goo88]. Therefore, given enough time, the chain is guaranteed to settle in an absorbing state. However, there is no guarantee that this state is a global optimum or even a local optimum. Hence, if the global optimum is one of the transient states, there is a large probability that the algorithm misses it.

3.4.2   GA with Crossover and Mutation

Mutation is introduced to help GA explore search subspaces that are unreachable with *crossover* alone. The use of the *mutation* operator eliminates all absorbing states. With *crossover* and *mutation*, the behavior of GA corresponds to a homogeneous ergodic Markov chain.

Definition 9   [EAH90] Let $\mathcal{P}_n$ be the set of individuals of GA population at the nth time step (generation), and $f(s)$ be the fitness of an individual $s \in \mathcal{P}_n$. The GA evolution is *monotone* if

$$\forall n \geq 0 : \quad \min_{s \in \mathcal{P}_{n+1}} f(s) \leq \min_{s \in \mathcal{P}_n} f(s)$$

Definition 10   [EAH90] Let Ω be the set of all possible populations. The set $succ(X)$ of *possible successors* of a population X is the set of all populations that are accessible from X in n generations, $n \geq 0$. That is,

$$succ(X) = \{Y \in \Omega | \exists n \geq 0 : Prob[\mathcal{P}_n = Y] > 0\}$$

Let S_{opt} be the set of optimal individuals, that is $S_{opt} = \{s \in S | f(s) = \min_{x \in S} f(x)\}$ Then the following theorems hold (for proofs, see [AEH89]):

Theorem 2   [EAH90] Let $X \in \Omega$ and let the following conditions be true:

(a) The GA evolution from X, denoted as $\{\mathcal{P}_n : n \geq 0\}_X$, is monotone,

(b) $\forall n_k \geq 0$ and $\varepsilon_k \in [0,1]$ are such that $n_k \to \infty$ $(k \to \infty)$ and $\prod_{k=0}^{\infty} \varepsilon_k = 0$, and

$$\forall k \geq 0, \forall\, Y \in succ(X) :\ Prob[\mathcal{P}_{n_{k+1}} \cap S_{opt} = \emptyset \,|\, X_{n_k} = Y] \leq \varepsilon_k$$

Then, $\{\mathcal{P}_n : n \geq 0\}_X$ almost surely reaches an optimum, that is,

$$Prob[\lim_{n \to \infty} \mathcal{P}_n \cap S_{opt} \neq \emptyset] = 1.$$

Theorem 3 [EAH90] Let $X \in S_{opt}$ be such that the following conditions hold:

(a) $\{\mathcal{P}_n : n \geq 0\}_X$, the GA evolution from X, is monotone and homogeneous.

(b) For every $Y \in succ(X)$, there exists at least one accessible optimum.

Then, $\{\mathcal{P}_n : n \geq 0\}_X$ almost surely reaches an optimum, that is,

$$Prob[\lim_{n \to \infty} \mathcal{P}_n \cap S_{opt} \neq \emptyset] = 1.$$

Next, we look at the conditions that will make the GA evolution reach an optimum.

Recall that GA has three basic steps: (1) a *choice* step where parents are picked for mating, (2) a *production* step where crossover operators are applied to produce offspring, and (3) a *selection* step where individuals of next generation are selected from the individuals of previous generation and their offspring.

Definition 11 [EAH90] The *selection* function is *conservative* if it always keeps one of the fittest individuals of any population.

Hence, the evolution of a *conservative* GA is *monotone*.

Definition 12 [EAH90] The neighborhood structure is *connective* if the neighbor to neighbor transitions allow the search to reach any given individual from any other individual of the solution space.

Definition 13 [EAH90] The *choice*, *production*, and *selection* steps of GA are called *generous* if they give a chance to every individual to become a parent, to be born, and to survive, respectively.

The reader should be able to observe that the *generousness* of the *choice* and *selection* functions implies that *mutation* is used.

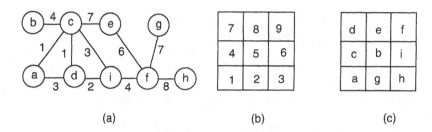

        (a)   (b)   (c)

Figure 3.4: (a) Graph whose nodes are to be assigned. (b) Position definition (labels of slots). (c) One possible assignment.

Theorem 4 [EAH90] A GA algorithm with homogeneous operators, a conservative *selection*, generous *choice*, *production* and *selection* functions, and *connective neighborhood* will find an optimum solution with probability one, regardless of the initial population. That is,

$$Prob[\lim_{n \to \infty} \mathcal{P}_n \cap S_{opt} \neq \emptyset] = 1.$$

What the above theorem states is that, running GA for a large enough number of generations, the algorithm will find one of the global optimum solutions. Since we are assuming a *conservative* GA, at least one of the global optimum solutions found during the search will be in the final population when GA stops. It will be the fittest individual.

3.5   GA in Practice

In the previous sections we presented a simple version of the genetic algorithm and saw how schema(ta) theory is used as a mathematical formalism to illustrate the implicit parallelism of GAs. Before we look into more examples and case studies of GAs in the field of science and engineering, we present some additional details pertaining to GA operators. Variations of the basic genetic algorithm, and other genetic operators, along with implementation specific details, are presented in this section. Other issues such as mapping cost function values to fitness, scaling of fitness values to prevent premature convergence, various schemes to select parents for new generation, and so forth, are also presented. We begin with the example of our classical module assignment problem.

Example 3.7 Consider the graph of Figure 3.4(a). The nine vertices represent modules and the numbers on the edges represent their weighted interconnection. Express the solution to the assignment of nodes to slots as a string of symbols.[1] Generate a population of four chromosomes and compute their

---

[1] see Example 1.10 in Chapter 1, page 8.

fitnesses using the reciprocal of weighted Manhattan distance[2] as a measure of fitness (see also page 365).

Solution The nine modules can be assigned to the nine slots as labeled in Figure 3.4(b). One possible solution is shown in Figure 3.4(c). Let us use a string to represent the solution as follows. Let the leftmost index (position 1) of the string correspond to slot "1" of Figure 3.4(b) and the rightmost to slot 9. Then the solution of Figure 3.4(c) can be represented by the string $\boxed{\text{aghcbidef}}$ ($\frac{1}{85}$). The number in parenthesis represents the fitness value and is obtained as follows. Consider the two modules g and f. They are connected by an edge of weight equal to 7. In the assignment they are 3 Manhattan units apart (2 vertically, and 1 horizontally). The cost to connect these two modules is therefore $7 \times 3 = 21$. Performing the above computation on the given assignment, for all edges in the graph, we get a total cost of 85. The reciprocal of the total weighted cost based on the Manhattan measure is the fitness of the solution.

If the lower left corner of the grid in Figure 3.4(b) is treated as the origin, then it is easy to compute the Cartesian locations of any module. For example the index of module i in the string is 6. Its Cartesian coordinates are given by $x = ((6 - 1) \mod 3) = 2$, and $y = \lfloor \frac{(6-1)}{3} \rfloor = 1$.

Any string (of length 9) containing characters $[a, b, c, d, e, f, g, h, i]$ represents a possible solution. There are 9! solutions equal to the number of *permutations* of length 9. Other possible solutions (chromosomes) are $\boxed{\text{bdefigcha}}$ ($\frac{1}{110}$), $\boxed{\text{ihagbfced}}$ ($\frac{1}{95}$), and $\boxed{\text{bidefaghc}}$ ($\frac{1}{86}$) (see Exercise 3.16).

∎

Example 3.8 From our previous example (Example 3.7) consider the two parents $\boxed{\text{bidefaghc}}$ ($\frac{1}{86}$), and $\boxed{\text{bdefigcha}}$ ($\frac{1}{110}$). If the cut point is randomly chosen after position 5, then the offspring produced is $\boxed{\text{bidef|gcha}}$. Verify that the weighted wire-length of the offspring is reduced to 63 and therefore the fitness of the offspring is (increased to) $\frac{1}{63}$.

∎

3.5.1 Genetic Operators

In the example above (Example 3.8), the elements to the left of the crossover point in one parent did not appear on the right of the second parent. If they had,

---

[2]Given two slots whose coordinates are (x_1, y_1) and (x_2, y_2), the Manhattan distance between them is given by $d_{12} = |x_1 - x_2| + |y_1 - y_2|$.

then some of the symbols in the solution string would be repeated. In cell assignment or in any other problem that uses a permutation representation for its solution, repetition of symbols (corresponding to conflicts due to two elements taking the same slot) do not represent a legal solution. There are crossovers that avoid the above problem, and are more suitable for permutation representations of solutions. Well-known among these are (a) *partially mapped crossover* (PMX) [GL85, Gol89c], (b) *order crossover* (OX), [Dav85a, Dav91], and (c) *cycle crossover* (CX), [OSH87], and their variations. Below, we discuss the details of these crossover operators and illustrate them with examples.

The Partially Mapped Crossover (PMX)

With the PMX, the offspring generated contains ordering information partially determined by its parents. The operation of this crossover is as follows. A random cut point is chosen in both the parents P_1 and P_2. The segment to the *right* of the cut point in both the strings acts as a partial mapping of the cells to be exchanged in P_1 to generate the offspring. To implement this crossover, following the selection of the cut point, a pair of cells in a certain location of both the segments are chosen. These pairs of cells are then exchanged in the first parent. This process is repeated for all the cells in the segment. Thus a cell in the segment of the first parent, and a cell in the same location in the second parent will define which cells in the first parent have to be exchanged to generate the offspring [GL85, SM91].

> **Example 3.9** Consider the two parents $\boxed{\text{dbcae}|\text{fghi}}$ and $\boxed{\text{efghi}|\text{dcba}}$. Let the random cut point chosen be after position 5. The pairs of alleles after the cut point situated in the same locations are (**f,d**), (**g,c**), (**h,b**), and (**i,a**). That is alleles **f** and **d** are situated in location 6 in both parents, alleles **g** and **c** in locations 7, and so on. These alleles are swapped in P_1, that is, allele **f** at location 6 in P_1 is swapped with **d** at location 1 in P_1. Similarly, the remaining three pairs of alleles are swapped in the first parent. The string resulting from these swaps in the first parent is $\boxed{\text{fhgiedcba}}$, which is the required offspring.
>
> ∎

The PMX crossover can also be alternately implemented as follows (see Exercise 3.20). Select two parents (P_1 and P_2) and choose a random cut point. As in the case of simple crossover, the entire right substring of P_2 is copied to the offspring (let us refer to this as a partial offspring). Next, the left substring of P_1 is scanned from the left, gene by gene, to the point of the cut. If a gene does not exist in the partial offspring then it is copied to it. However, if it already exists in the partial offspring, then its position in the partial offspring is determined and the gene from P_1 in the determined position is copied.

The Order Crossover (OX)

This crossover is similar to the PMX crossover, except that PMX respects absolute allele positions whereas the order crossover tends to respect *relative* allele positions. The *order* crossover is implemented as follows. Select two parents and choose a random cut point. Then the entire left substring of one parent (say P_1) is copied to the offspring. Next, the second parent P_2 is scanned from the left, gene by gene, from the beginning to the end. The remaining portion of the offspring is filled by taking those elements that were left out of P_1, but in *order* of their appearance in P_2 [Dav85a, Dav85b]. The example below illustrates these operations.

> **Example 3.10** Consider the two parents $\boxed{\text{bidcfgeha}}$ and $\boxed{\text{aghcbidef}}$. Let the parents crossover position be after 4. Then the partial offspring resulting from copying the left substring of P_1 is $\boxed{\text{bidc} | \text{*****}}$. The elements left out of this partial offspring are {fgeha}. The order in which these elements appear in the second parent is [aghef]. The complete offspring obtained as a result of *order* crossover, therefore, is the catenation of $\boxed{\text{bidc}}$ and $\boxed{\text{aghef}}$ resulting in $\boxed{\text{bidcaghef}}$.
>
> ■

The Cycle Crossover (CX)

This crossover also helps eliminate the conflicts that normally appear when permutation representations are used for chromosomes. Every allele in the offspring generated by this crossover is in the same location as in one of the parents. *A cycle contains a common subset of alleles in the two parents that occupy a common subset of positions.*

The operation of *cycle* crossover is as follows. We start with the cell in location 1 of P_1 and copy it to location 1 of the offspring. What will happen to the cell in location 1 of P_2? The offspring cannot inherit this cell from P_2, since location 1 in the offspring is already filled. So this cell must be located in P_1 and passed to the offspring from there. Suppose this cell is located in P_1 at location x, then it is passed to the offspring at location x. But then the cell in location x in P_2 cannot be passed to the offspring, so that cell is also passed from P_1. This process continues until we complete a cycle and reach a cell that has already been passed. Now we repeat the same process as above, but this time starting from a cell in P_2. We alternate between parents until the offspring is complete.

Thus in alternate cycles the offspring inherits cells from alternate parents, and the elements are placed in the same location as they were in the parents from which they where inherited. [OSH87, SM91]

Example 3.11 As an example of *cycle* crossover consider the two parents
c b a e d f , and a d f b e c . We will form the offspring by starting from P_1
and passing element **c** to the offspring in position 1. Since this position in P_2
is occupied by element **a**, it too has to be copied from P_1 and this is done in
position 3. Similarly P_2 in position 3 has element **f**, and therefore this too has
to be copied into the offspring from P_1 (from position 6). Finally, position 6
of P_2 has element **c** which is already in the offspring, therefore this completes
the cycle. The partial offspring formed is c * a * * f . The *cycle* formed is
c→a→f→c. In other words, elements {c,a,f} are in positions {1,3,6} in both
P_1 and P_2.

Now we move to P_2 and start another cycle from any unplaced gene. Let us
start from the element in second position (since this is the first element not
appearing in the offspring), which is **d**. Repeating the procedure as above, the
cycle created is d→b→e→d. The final offspring created is c d a b e f . Observe that in the offspring, elements of the first cycle are in the same position
as in P_1 and elements of the second cycle are in the same position as in P_2.
If the second cycle is completed without all elements copied to the offspring,
then we alternate back to P_1 and continue to search for another cycle.   ∎

Multipoint Crossovers and Other Variations

So far we have seen some important crossovers that are popularly used. There is
no hard and fast rule that they must be applied as discussed. The only requirement
is that they must ensure that the offsprings will inherit parental properties. There
are other variations of the same operators. For instance, we selected two parents
and generated an offspring. We could actually generate two offsprings by treating
the chromosome for P_2 as P_1 and vice versa. It was suggested that parents be
selected based on their fitness values. Generally one parent is selected based on
fitness and the other at random.

We also performed the simple crossover by generating a single cut point in
both parents. We could also generate two cut points in each parent, and swap the
cut segments. For example, for the two parent chromosomes $P_1 = [1 \mid 0\ 1\ 1 \mid 0\ 1]$
and $P_2 = [1 \mid 1\ 1\ 0 \mid 1\ 0]$, if the two cut points are chosen after the first and
fourth positions, then the two offsprings generated for the two parents are $O_1 = [1 \mid 1\ 1\ 0 \mid 0\ 1]$ and $O_2 = [1 \mid 0\ 1\ 1 \mid 1\ 0]$. Sometimes, the two-point crossover has
some advantages over the single-point crossover. Consider the two schemata $H_a = [*\ *\ 1\ 0\ 1\ *]$ and $H_b = [1\ *\ *\ *\ *\ 0]$. Let us assume that both are important in the
sense that they contain characteristics required in our optimal solution. Clearly
the single-point crossover will disrupt one or both the strings. With the two-point
crossover the chances of offsprings inheriting the goodness of the schemata are
higher.

Other examples of the multipoint crossover have also appeared in the literature. In general, the number of crossover points (CP) can be a parameter of the algorithm. With CP=1 the generalized crossover reduces to simple crossover. With values of CP $>$1 alternate segments are chosen from each of the parents to create offsprings [Gol89c, Jon75], that is, segments 1, 3, and so forth, from P_1 and segments 2, 4, and so on, from P_2. It has been shown that multipoint crossover with CP$>$2 has a poor performance because less structure and therefore fewer important schemata are preserved. In addition, runtime is also affected since more random numbers have to be generated and more time is involved in creating new strings.

Multipoint operations have also been applied to other advanced permutation crossovers. For example, the partially mapped crossover (also known as partially matched crossover) can also be a two-point operation. In this two-point crossover, first, two crossing sites are picked at random and these sites define the matching section (the middle section). This matching section is used to effect a cross-through position-by-position exchange operations as illustrated in the example below.

Example 3.12 As an example of the PMX two-point crossover, consider the two parents P_1= $\boxed{\text{bid} \mid \text{efg} \mid \text{cha}}$ and P_2= $\boxed{\text{agh} \mid \text{cbi} \mid \text{def}}$. First, two crossing sites are picked uniformly at random. Let these sites be after positions 3 and 6. These two positions define our matching section.

Pairs of alleles in the matching section in the corresponding location are picked. These alleles in our example are (e, c), (f, b), and (g, i) in positions 4, 5, and 6, respectively. We first map parent P_2 to parent P_1. This is done by exchanging places of our chosen pairs (e, c), (f, b) and (g, i) in P_1 resulting in the string OS_1= $\boxed{\text{fgd} \mid \text{cbi} \mid \text{eha}}$. Similarly, mapping parent P_1 to parent P_2, alleles (c, e), (b, f) and (i, g) exchange places in P_2, resulting in OS_2= $\boxed{\text{aih} \mid \text{efg} \mid \text{dcb}}$. Note that each offspring contains ordering information partially determined by each of its parents.

∎

There are cases where the simple one- or two-point crossover fails to inherit parental characteristics. Syswerda [Sys89] described an operator which he called the **uniform crossover**. In this crossover a binary string template is randomly generated. Then, for each bit position on the two selected parents, the value of the bit in the template will indicate which of the two parents will contribute its value in that position to the offspring. For example, if the template is the string [1 0 1 0 0 1] then the first bit, third bit, and the last bit of the offspring come from parent 1 and the remaining 3 bits from parent 2. A second offspring is similarly created by reversing P_2 and P_1. As you might have guessed, the main advantage of this crossover is that "building blocks" no longer have to be encoded as short schemata in order to survive. The survival of schemata in this case does not depend on its *defining length*, and all schemata of a given order have the same chance of being disrupted (or preserved).

The above uniform crossover of course does not work for strings with permutation representations. A generalization under the name of "**uniform order-based crossover**" which is a combination of the uniform crossover and order crossover was proposed by Davis [Dav91]. It is similar to the uniform crossover, where the 1's in the template define elements copied from the first parent, while the other elements are copied from the second parent *in the order* they appear in the chromosome. A second offspring is similarly generated.

Example 3.13 As an example of the uniform order-based crossover, consider the two parents $P_1=$ ⟨a b c d e f⟩ and $P_2=$ ⟨f d b e c a⟩. Let the defining template be [1 0 0 1 1 0]. Selecting elements of the first offspring O_1 from those positions in P_1 that have 1s in the template, and for O_2 from those positions in P_2 that have 0's in template, the partial offsprings generated are: $O_1=$ ⟨a - - d e -⟩ and $O_2=$ ⟨- d b - - a⟩. The missing elements in O_1 are {b c f}. The order they appear in P_2 is {f b c}. Filling these missing elements in the above order results in the offsprings $O_1=$ ⟨a f b d e c⟩. Similarly the second offspring O_2 is given by ⟨c d b e f a⟩. ■

Mutation

Mutation is a secondary genetic operator similar to the perturb function of simulated annealing (see Chapter 2). Unlike crossover, it does not produce any offsprings, but it produces random changes in the offsprings that are generated by the crossover. Mutation is important because crossover alone will not guarantee that a good solution will be obtained. Crossover is only an inheritance mechanism. The mutation operator generates "new" characteristics, thus assuring that crossover will have the complete range of all possible allele values to explore. Mutation also increases the variability in the population.

Following the selection of individuals for a new generation,[3] each gene position of each chromosome in the new population undergoes a random change with a small probability equal to the *mutation rate* denoted by M_r (also referred to as the mutation probability p_μ). Parameter M_r controls the rate at which new genes are introduced into the population. In order not to cause too much disruption to schemata, typical recommended values for M_r are generally very low (1 to 5 percent).

---

[3]In some implementations this is done after crossover and before the selection of individuals for the new generation.

In a population of size **M**, where each individual has n genes, approximately $\mathbf{M}_r \times \mathbf{M} \times n$ mutations occur per generation. A low level of mutation serves to prevent any given gene from remaining forever converged to a single allele value in the entire population. However, if mutation rate is low then infusion of new genes is also low, and many genes that would have been good would never be tried out. If mutation rate is high then there will be too much random disturbance, causing the offspring to lose resemblance to their parents, and the algorithm will lose its ability to learn from the history of the search [SM91, WSF89]. A high level of mutation essentially yields a random search. In some implementations mutation rate is varied as a function of population diversity (see Exercise 3.22).

In case of chromosomes represented by binary alleles a simple bit inversion mutates the chromosomes. This will not work for chromosomes that use permutation representations. In this case, generally two elements are chosen randomly and their positions are *exchanged* [Ree95b]. Or, two elements are chosen and one is moved to a position just before the other (similar to the insert move on page 232). A *scramble sublist* mutation was proposed by [Dav91] where two points are chosen on a string and the elements in the segment between them are randomly permuted. Obviously, in this case it is recommended that the length of the scrambled portion be limited since it has a larger tendency to disrupt the schema.

Inversion

Inversion is the third operator of GA and like mutation it also operates on a single chromosome. Its basic function is to laterally invert the order of alleles between two randomly chosen points on a chromosome. Its operation is as follows. Two points are randomly chosen along the length of the chromosome, and the string between the two points is inverted. For example, the string $\boxed{\text{bid} \mid \text{efgch} \mid \text{a}}$ (cut after positions 3 and 8) will become $\boxed{\text{bid} \mid \text{hcgfe} \mid \text{a}}$ after inversion.

3.5.2   Scoring/Fitness Function

Genetic algorithms work naturally on the maximization of fitness. In most optimization problems the objective is to minimize the cost. Therefore, it is required that the cost function is mapped to a fitness function. The fitness function assigns a *positive* value to each individual. In GAs, it is required that all fitness values must be positive.

In the subsequent paragraphs we will see several schemes that have been proposed to map *Cost* to fitness values. We will also see proposals to rank/scale fitness values to avoid premature convergence, which is a major problem in GAs.

Mapping Cost Function to Fitness

In earlier sections we proposed treating the fitness of an individual as the reciprocal of the cost. Another possibility is to multiply the costs by minus one. But this results in non-negative fitnesses. Generally, in GAs, the following transform is used:

$$f_i = \begin{cases} Cost_{\max} - Cost_i & \text{when} \qquad Cost_i < Cost_{\max} \\ 0 & \text{otherwise} \end{cases}$$

where $Cost_{\max}$ may be the maximum cost in the current population and $Cost_i$ is the cost of individual solutions. Other possible choices of $Cost_{\max}$ are the largest value of cost observed until the current iteration, or the largest observed in some last k generations.

When the objective function is not cost but profit or a utility function (u), u_i denoting the value of each individual solution, we still may have to transform it to avoid negative values. To accomplish this the following transform is proposed:

$$f_i = \begin{cases} u_i + Cost_{\min} & \text{when} \qquad u_i + Cost_{\min} > 0 \\ 0 & \text{otherwise} \end{cases}$$

where $Cost_{\min}$ is generally the absolute value of the the worst u_i in the current generation. Similar to the case of choosing $Cost_{\max}$, a possible choice of $Cost_{\min}$ is the absolute value of the worst u_i observed in some last k generations.

3.5.3 Scaling

The selection of parents is an important step in GA as it affects the population in the new generation. If selection is based on raw fitness values it may lead to premature convergence. This is because a few extraordinary individuals in the population would take over a large proportion of the finite population in a single generation. Further, in later runs there may be some diversity within the population, but most of the fitness values will be close to each other (that is, the average fitness may be close to the population best fitness). If this situation is left as is, then the average and best members will get the same number of copies. To avoid this situation, fitness values are *scaled* or *ranked*.

Several scaling methods have been proposed in the literature. One method is *linear scaling*. In this method, given a fitness f_i of individual i, the scaled fitness value f_i' is calculated as follows:

$$f_i' = a \times f_i + b \tag{3.14}$$

where a and b are chosen such that the averages of raw fitness and scaled fitness are equal.

Linear scaling runs into problems in later runs of GA when most of the fitness values are close to each other and some members have very low fitness values. This leads to negative fitness values which are unacceptable. To avoid this situation *sigma truncation* was proposed [For85]. In this method all the fitness values are preprocessed to calculate modified fitness values f_i'' as follows:

$$f_i'' = f_i - (f_{avg} - K_{mult} \times \sigma) \tag{3.15}$$

where σ is the standard deviation of the population and K_{mult} is a multiplying constant generally chosen to be between 1 and 3. The negative values ($f_i'' < 0$) are set to zero. After this truncation, linear scaling can proceed without the danger of negative results as follows.

$$f_i' = a \times f_i'' + b \tag{3.16}$$

Fitness scaling attempts to maintain the variation in the population which is necessary for further exploration of the search space. Once the population consists of the same type of individuals the GA loses its ability to explore the search space until the population gains some variation by the slow process of mutation. Yet another method of scaling has been suggested in the literature and is called *power law* scaling [Gil85]. In this method the scaled fitness is some specified power of the raw fitness given by

$$f_i' = f^k \tag{3.17}$$

The value of k is problem dependent and may be required to change during a GA run to stretch/shrink the range as needed.

3.5.4 Selection of Parents

Each generation of a GA begins with the creation of a mating pool from which offsprings are generated by probabilistically applying crossover on pairs of parents. This is followed by mutation.[4]

Stochastic Sampling:

We saw above that the *roulette wheel* method for selecting parents for crossover. This method is also known as *stochastic sampling with replacement*. For each application of crossover one or two offsprings are generated. Once a certain number of offsprings are generated, they are mutated and are used to replace some parents, thus becoming possible parents for the next generation.

---

[4]It is recommended that mutation follows selection otherwise the effect of mutation maybe severely decreased.

Another scheme is to choose parents based on an *expected* value (e_i) determined using string fitnesses. This method was designed [Jon75] to reduce the stochastic errors that are associated with the roulette wheel method of selection. It can use raw fitness or scaled fitness values (see Section 3.5.3). The value e_i determines the expected number of times an individual is to be selected as a parent, and is computed as follows:

$$e_i = \frac{f_i'}{\sum_i^M f_i'} \times M$$

where M is the population size. A sample space is defined based on the above e_i values. It is an array of records with two fields, a member identification number field, and a probability field. For example, if $e_j = 2.6$, then individual j will receive three slots $(j, 1.0)$, $(j, 1.0)$, and $(j, 0.6)$ in the sample space. Note that the first field in a slot is the individual's identification and the second field is the probability with which the slot should be accepted.

1	2	3	4	5	6	⋯	⋯	k
			e_j	e_j	e_j	⋯	⋯	
			1	1	0.6	⋯	⋯	

Assume that there are a total of k slots in the sample space. To select a parent, a random number is generated between 1 and k, and the individual corresponding to the slot is selected as a parent with the probability of that slot. Since fitter individuals will get more slots in the sample space, they will have a higher chance of being selected. Diversity is maintained because the selection is random over the sample space. The parents are thus selected randomly from the sample space and with consideration to the probability of the slot.

Another method of constructing the array is to assign a number of copies to it equal to the integer value of e_i. Then, the fractional parts of the expected number values are treated as probabilities. For each individual, Bernoulli trials are carried out using the fractional parts as success probabilities. This operation is repeated until the array is full. For example, if the expected number of copies of an individual i is 1.4, then this individual will receive a single copy surely in the array, and another with probability 0.4 [Jon75]. Following this preselect procedure, the parent selection procedure operates on the array. Each time a parent is needed for a crossover, it is randomly selected from the array. Then, the selected parent is removed from the list. This method of using expected values to build the array and select the parent is also known as *stochastic remainder without replacement*.

Ranking:

Selection methods such as roulette wheel, that use raw or scaled fitness values to select parents for new population and crossover can be problematic and work only on positive fitness values. As seen, the scaling methods proposed are ad hoc. Some researchers argue that a key to good GA performance is to maintain an adequate selective pressure on all the individuals by means of an appropriate *relative* fitness measure [Bak85, WSF89]. This can be accomplished by dissociating the fitness function from the underlying objective function using a method called *Ranking*. In ranking, the selection depends on the relative goodness of individuals and not the *actual* fitness values. Individuals are sorted in ascending order of their fitnesses. Then, depending on the rank, a function is used to assign a count to each chromosome [Bak85].

Ranking has been used to obtain improved results. For example, for the flow-shop sequencing problem [Ree95a], a selection procedure based on the probability distribution given below was used.

$$p([k]) = \frac{2k}{M(M+1)}$$

where $[k]$ is the kth chromosome in the *ascending* order. The best chromosome $(k = M)$ then has a chance of $\frac{2}{M+1}$ of being selected and the median a chance of $\frac{1}{M}$ [Ree95a, Yao97].

Tournament Selection:

Finally, we present a mechanism that combines both selection and ranking mechanisms. It can be thought of as a noisy form of ranking and is known as *tournament selection* [Gol90, Whi94]. It consists of the comparison (competition) of all individuals within a subgroup of the population.

This scheme treats the population as a permuted list of M chromosomes. The population is divided into sub-groups of $\mathcal{G}$ chromosomes each ($\mathcal{G} \geq 2$). The chromosomes with the highest fitness in each subgroup are then selected and chosen as parents. Then, the list is permuted and the entire procedure is repeated until M parents have been chosen. Each parent is then mated with another chosen randomly. As an example, consider the population of six individuals, with indexes 1 to 6. Let the index value also be its fitness. If the random permutation (of chromosomes) is [2 5 3 6 1 4], and the value of $\mathcal{G}$ chosen is 3, then, from the first three individuals, chromosome 5 wins, and from the next three chromosome 6. Now the list is permuted again. Let the permuted list be [1 2 4 6 3 5]. Then the parents selected are 4 and 6, respectively. The list is permuted one last time to select the final two parents. Let the permuted list be [6 5 4 3 2 1]. Then the parents selected are 6 and 3, respectively. Therefore the six chromosomes selected are 5, 6, 4, 6, 6, and, 3. Observe that in this method the best chromosome gets selected $\mathcal{G}$ times, the worst is never selected, and individuals with fitness below average still have a chance to "win" (to be selected as parents) [FW93, GD91, Gol90, Ree95b].

3.6   Parameters of GAs

Determining the parameters to be used in a GA can be difficult. Parameters to be set include: the n (M), the probabilities used for crossover (P_c) and mutation (P_μ or M_r), and so forth. The performance of a GA depends on the above parameters which are difficult to tune. The tuning of GA to a particular problem requires extensive experimentation. In the following paragraphs we elaborate on *some* of the ad hoc methods that have been proposed or adopted by GA practitioners.

3.6.1   Population

In this section we present some issues concerning initial population and its construction, and choice of population size.

Initial Population:

The choice of initial population affects both the quality of the solution and the number of generations needed to reach a good solution. This is because it is the characteristics of the elements of the initial population that are inherited by the offsprings produced in subsequent generations. And one of these offsprings is to be our desired solution. There are two issues that concern the initial population: (1) How should the individuals of the initial population be selected? and (2) What should be the size of the population? Generally the population size is maintained constant for the entire run of GA. In Section 3.9 we look at the effect of dynamically reducing the size of the population.

Construction:

The initial population is generally constructed randomly. Sometimes certain elements of the initial population may be solutions of some well known *constructive* heuristics. This method of including solutions of other known methods is called *seeding*. The initial population may also contain elements used as initial solution by other heuristics. Seeding has been reported [Dav91, Ree95b] to help obtain a better solution faster.

Population Size (M):

As discussed above, the number of schemata processed is a function of the population size M. In addition, the value M affects the runtime, the convergence rate, as well as the solution quality of the algorithm. That is, it has a direct effect on both the ultimate performance and the efficiency of GAs. GAs do poorly with smaller populations because a small population provides insufficient sample size for most hyperplanes. On the other hand, a large value of **M** is more likely to contain representatives from a large number of hyperplanes, and therefore GAs can perform a more informed search. As a result, large **M** discourages premature convergence to suboptimal solutions but requires more evaluations per generation, and may result in an unacceptably slow rate of convergence [GDC92].

Goldberg [Gol85] presented a heuristic to determine the optimal value of **M**. The expression obtained grows exponentially with the length of the chromosome (l) and is given by

$$\mathbf{M} = 1.65 \times 2^{0.21l} \tag{3.18}$$

The value of **M** obtained this way is impractical, as it exceeds the capabilities of today's machines. For example, with a value of $l = 200$, the population size is 7.3×10^{12} [HMS89].

Based on experimental work, a value between l and $2l$ has been suggested by Alander [Ala92] (where $l =$ length of the chromosome). In [HGL92], for the Traveling Salesman Problem (TSP) of N cities, a population size $\mathbf{M} = p \times N$ was proposed, $2 < p < 20$. Typical values of **M**, for most GA applications range between 10 and 50, although some applications have used values as large as 200.

3.6.2 Generation Gap

The percentage of the population to be replaced during each generation is controlled by a parameter called *generation gap* denoted by G ($0 < G \leq 1$). In each generation, M $\times$ G offsprings are generated and, using one of the several policies described below, some or all of them replace the parents to form the population of the next generation. Therefore, M $\times$ $(1 - G)$ individuals of the current population are chosen to survive intact in the population for the next generation.

A value of $G = 1.0$ means that the entire population is replaced during each generation. This indicates that there is no overlapping of population since no parents of the current generation survive into the next. Experimental evidence indicates that GAs perform better when nonoverlapping populations are used.

A value of $\frac{1}{M} < G < 1.0$ means that M $\times$ G offsprings are generated and are inserted into the population. There are several ways to do so. One trivial way is to randomly select **M** $\times$ G individuals from the population and replace them with the offsprings. Another possibility is to replace individuals with low fitness values. Or, a replacement based on a combination, where a certain percentage of those replaced are selected randomly, and the remaining based on their fitness values.

The third possibility is when $G = \frac{1}{M}$. In this case each offspring is inserted into the population as it gets generated. One of the elements in the existing population is randomly selected with probability $\frac{1}{M}$ and is replaced by the created offspring. This step is repeated as many times as required. This type of GA in which only one crossover operation is performed per generation is called *incremental* or *steady-state* GA. It corresponds to incremental replacement and has advantages in terms of implementation. (see also page 349). Several other proposals have been suggested to replace an element of the current population with a new offspring. One, of course, is to randomly choose a member of the population and replace it. Another method is known as *termination with prejudice.* In this method, the offspring replaces a randomly selected parent from those which currently have a certain below-average fitness [Ack87].

In some of the above strategies, there is a possibility of the best structure in the current population disappearing due to sampling error, crossover, or mutation. An *elitist strategy* was suggested [Jon75] in which the current best solution is forced to survive, and is included in the population for the next generation. GAs that keep the current best solution throughout the optimization process are referred to as *elitist* GAs. Recall from Section 3.4 (page 126) that elitist GA has monotonicity property which is a necessary property for convergence.

3.6.3   Operator Probabilities

Implementation of most GAs assumes a fixed rate of using the genetic operators (crossover or mutation). Generally mutation is applied with a very low probability (less than 1 percent) and crossover is always applied, that is, the probability of crossover is 1. Probabilities lower than 1 have also been used for crossovers.

As has been mentioned above, the population diversity decreases in every generation. In order to alleviate the problem of premature convergence that results due to the decrease in population diversity, the mutation rate can be made to vary inversely with the population diversity [Ree95b] (see Exercise 3.22). Another suggestion [Dav91] reported is to apply in each generation either crossover or mutation but not both. Thus, at each step, the algorithm chooses between operators on the basis of a probability which is known as *operator fitness.* For example, if the crossover has a fitness of 90 percent and mutation 10 percent, crossover is applied nine times more often than mutation. A modification to this idea is to change the operator fitness values as the algorithm proceeds [Dav91]. More weight is given to crossover when population diversity increases, and more weight to mutation as the solutions start converging [Ree95b].

Sometimes more than one crossover operator is available. In such a case, during each generation, one of the available crossovers is chosen based on a probability distribution. In [Y+95] a multiobjective function is optimized using GA. In order to satisfy different objectives, different characteristics need to be inherited, and for each characteristic a different crossover is proposed. Similarly, in [S+95] several mutation operators are proposed, and one of them is chosen in a generation on the basis of its probability.

Is there a theoretical optimal value for the mutation rate? In [Jon75] a mutation rate equal to n^{-1} (where n is the string length) has been recommended. And in [S+89], based on experimentation, the optimal rate was estimated to be proportional to $1/M^{0.9318}n^{0.4535}$. But most GA practitioners ignore string length in their choice of mutation probabilities [Ree95b].

3.6.4 Other Issues

The runtime efficiency of a GA can be greatly improved by giving careful consideration to some issues. One important issue is the design of the chromosome. For example, the chromosome may be efficiently designed so as to ensure inheritance of good characteristics. However, the same representation may not be good for computing the solution (chromosome) fitness. Consider the example of assigning tasks to processors in Example 3.2. The chromosome representation is elegant, a simple string. But each time a new offspring is generated, the fitness cannot be known until the entire schedule is constructed. The expression given in Equation 3.1 seems simple, but it is not easy to incrementally determine the change in the finish time (new fitness value) as a result of crossover. Other researchers have solved the same scheduling problem with a different chromosome representation, and more efficient implementation [HAH94]. *As a rule of thumb, the computational requirements for both, the genetic operations and the fitness calculation must be kept low.*

The data structure used to store the chromosome must also be efficient. It must be easily accessible, and easy to manipulate. An inefficient data structure results in waste of time and memory usage. Sometimes, one has to trade off between storage efficiency and manipulation time.

The type of chromosome encoding adopted is also important. Binary encoding may not always be the best solution. Even if nonbinary encoding is employed, whenever possible, any available knowledge of the problem or the search space must be incorporated to help obtain optimal solutions quickly. One-dimensional strings are not the only chromosomal representation that can be used. For some applications, researchers have found 2-D chromosomes [HGL92] to be more amenable to genetic operations, and useful in inheriting parental characteristics. In the next section, we use two examples to further illustrate both these points.

Another issue is the design and usage of genetic operators. Consider the crossover operator. Since crossover is applied several hundred times, it must not consume too much time. Generation of random numbers is extremely time consuming. Time is also wasted if crossover is not guaranteed to generate legal offsprings. On the other hand, restricting the crossover to produce only legal solutions may bias the search toward particular directions.

There are several variations to the simple genetic algorithm that have been used to enhance the search. Implementations with several crossovers, adaptively varying mutation/crossover probabilities, dynamically varying population sizes, and so forth, have been reported. We shall touch upon these aspects in some detail in a later section (Section 3.9).

Finally, as in other iterative algorithms of this type, the stopping criterion in GA can also be a function of solution quality, the available runtime, the number of generations, no improvement in solution quality for the last k generations, and so forth. In most engineering problems, the objective is to obtain a reasonable solution that satisfies all constraints. In that case, the termination condition will depend on the solution obtained.

3.7   Applications of GAs

In addition to their application to classical optimization problems such as the knapsack problem [Spi95], TSP [T+94, WSF89], Steiner tree problem [HMS89], set covering problem [ASHN96], N-queens problem [HTA92], clustering problem [ASK96], graph partitioning [PR94], and so on, GAs have also been applied to several engineering problems. Some examples of these applications include job shop and multiprocessor scheduling [BS94, HAH94, WSF89], discovery of maximal distance codes for data communications [DJ90], bin-packing [FD92], design of telecommunication (mesh) networks [K+97], test sequence generation for digital system testing [RPGN94], VLSI design (cell placement [CP87, SM90, SM91, SY95], floorplanning [S+95], routing [H+95]), pattern matching [ACH90], technology mapping [KP93], printed circuit board (PCB) assembly planning [LWJ92], and high-level synthesis of digital systems [ASB94, RS96]. The books by Goldberg (1989) [Gol89c] and Davis (1991) [Dav91], and recent conference proceedings on evolutionary computation and on applications of genetic algorithms discuss in detail the various applications of GAs in science and engineering. These range from optimization of pipeline systems and medical imaging to applications such as "robot trajectory generation" and "parametric design of aircraft" [Dav91, Gol89c].

In the previous sections, we illustrated the basic operations of the algorithm with the help of two problems, namely, finding the maxima of a function, and the problem of scheduling tasks to processors. We also illustrated how GAs can be used to solve the classical assignment problem (or its variations, such as cell placement in VLSI). In the following sections we will discuss the applications of GAs to some of the problems mentioned in the previous paragraph. In detail, we present the application of this technique to two problems: (1) the traveling salesman problem (TSP) and (2) the module placement problem. We will also briefly touch upon several of the above problems, by presenting the size of the search space (complexity), chromosomal representation, and the fitness functions employed.

3.7.1   Traveling Salesman Problem

The traveling salesman problem (TSP) (a well-known NP-hard problem) involves finding the shortest Hamiltonian path or cycle in a complete graph of N nodes, each node representing a city (see page 7). All known methods of finding exact solution involve searching the entire solution space that grows exponentially with the number of cities. Formally, the TSP can be defined as follows.

> **Definition 14**   Let N be the number of cities and $D = [d_{ij}]$ be the distance matrix whose elements d_{ij} denote the distances between cities i and j. The problem is to find the shortest tour visiting all cities exactly once.

The solution space Ω can be represented by the set of all cyclic permutations $\pi = (\pi_1, \ldots, \pi_i, \ldots, \pi_N)$, where π_i, $i = 1, \ldots, N$, denotes the successor city of city i in the tour represented by π. Let π_i^- denote the predecessor of city i. The cost function, to be minimized can be expressed as

$$Cost(\pi) = \sum_{i=1}^{N} d_{i,\pi_i} \tag{3.19}$$

Classic Technique

In order to apply GAs to solve this problem we have to represent the solution as a chromosome. One obvious way is to represent the cities (nodes in the graph) as a list of length N. The order of cities indicates the sequence in which they are visited. Each list is then treated as a genotype (or a chromosome) to which the genetic operators are applied [G+85].

Chromosomes (representing tours) are simply crossed to produce offspring tours. Simple crossover will generate illegal tours, where, some cities are visited twice and some others are skipped. These can be later corrected and duplicated cities replaced by omitted ones. The procedure is referred to as "cross and correct."

Since we use a permutation representation for the solution, in order to avoid the generation of illegal tours, we can also use one of the crossovers suggested in Section 3.5.1, that is, Cycle crossover (CX), Order crossover (OX) or PMX. Oliver et al. suggested the use of "cycle crossover operator" to solve the TSP problem [OSH87]. A cycle contains a common subset of cities in the two parent tours that occupy a common subset of positions. This operator always produces legal solutions. As an example, consider the tours [E D C B A] and [E B A D C]. These tours contain two cycles: (1) "-E-C-A-" and "-E-A-C-", and (2) "-D-B-" and "-B-D-". The cycles "-E-C-A-" and "-E-A-C-" both contain the cities A, C, and E in the positions 1, 3, and 5 in the parent tours. Note that the order of cities in a cycle is *not* important. What is important is that cycles can be exchanged between parents without introducing any city duplicates (or omissions). The off-springs in this example are [E B C D A] and [E D A B C]. The resulting offspring is guaranteed to inherit all of its city positions from one of the two parents.

Genetic operators such as cycle, order, and PMX crossovers are useful for problems where *positions* in the sequence are critical. In the TSP problem, the positions of the cities is not important. And preserving city positions has the tendency to destroy critical links that existed between cities in the parent structures. Therefore, the above operators do not do well because what is inherited from parents is *not* subtours. For example, in the cycle crossover, cycles do not necessarily correspond to subtours.

For the TSP problem, Whitely et al. [WSF89] experimented with the above crossovers. Studies on a limited set of problems by Oliver et al. [OSH87] showed that the cycle crossover actually destroys more edges than the "cross and correct" operator. The order crossover [Dav85b, Dav91] produced best results (since it breaks fewer links than other crossovers), followed by PMX crossover of Goldberg [GL85].

Inversion

Instead of crossover, we can also use inversion. In this case new solutions can be generated by choosing two arbitrary cities p and q, and reversing the sequence in which the cities between them are traversed. That is, in the tour, the sublist between p and q is laterally inverted. One good thing about using inversion is that it is a known genetic operator and is expected to produce good results. Also, it does not produce illegal tours. The difference in cost due to reversal of tour sublist between p and q can be calculated incrementally from the following expression (see Exercise 3.23).

$$\Delta Cost = d_{p,\pi_q^-} + d_{\pi_p,q} - d_{p,\pi_p} - d_{\pi_q^-,q} \qquad (3.20)$$

However, similar to mutation, inversion works on only one parent and therefore there is no recombination of genetic information from two parents.

Experiments with inversion have produced results better than "cross and correct" operator [WSF89]. There can be extensions to this operator too. For example, one can select three or more break points and invert the sublists, swap the sublists, and so on. Again, since the operations are performed on only one parent, the resulting list always represents a legal tour. In case we swap substrings, then, every time a substring is swapped, edges are broken and new edges are introduced.

Edge Recombination Operator

In this section we present a new technique suggested by Whitley et al. [WSF89] to solve the TSP problem. Their work was motivated by the fact that all proposed crossovers for permutation representations preserve city positions, and this has the tendency to destroy edges that existed in parents. An operator that preserves edges will exploit a maximal amount of information from the parent structures. Since the goodness of an individual tour is a direct consequence of the number of good subtours (or edges), operators that break links introduce unwanted mutation. This mutation can be thought of as a "leak" in the search process due to random loss of edges. Therefore, since it is the edges that reflect the goodness of a solution, Whitley et al. propose a crossover (called edge-recombination crossover) that inherits edges. That is, it produces an offspring tour that exclusively contains links present in one of the two parent structures [WSF89]. We illustrate with the help of an example the application of the *"edge-recombination crossover"* operator.

Example 3.14 Consider two parent tours: $P_1 = $ [D E F A B C] and $P_2 = $ [B D C A E F]. The link information in the above two tours is "DE EF FA AB BC DC" and "BD DC CA AE EF FB", respectively. The tours are circular and the journey finishes in the initial city forming a Hamiltonian cycle. Also note that edge "CD" has the same value as "DC".

The edge recombination operator uses an *"edge map"* to construct an offspring. This edge map stores all the connections from the two parents that lead into and out of a city. There will be at least two and at most four edges associated with each city in the parent tours. For the above two parent tours the edge map is as follows.

City	Has Edges To
A	F B C E
B	A C D F
C	B D A
D	C E B
E	D F A
F	A E B

That is, city A has edges to cities F and B in the first tour and to C and E in the second.

The recombination process works as follows. First, a new child tour is initialized with one of the two initial cities from its parents. It does not matter which city is chosen to initialize the tour, since the tours are circular. In the above case D and B are two initial cities (D in P_1 and B in P_2). City D has three edges and B has four edges. As explained later, it is preferable to choose those cities which currently have the fewest number of unused edges. The algorithm therefore chooses city D. The candidates for the next city are C, E, and B.

City	Has Edges To
A	B F C E
B	A C F
C	B A
E	F A
F	A E B

In the above table, entry for city D is removed. From the set of cities {C, E, B} which city should be chosen as the next one? Cities C and E have 2 edges, and city B has 3 edges, so we randomly choose one between C and E, say C. Now C has edges to A and B.

City	Has Edges To
A	B F E
B	A F
E	F A
F	A E B

Next, we have to choose between A and B. B is chosen, since it has fewer edges.

City	Has Edges To
A	F E
E	F A
F	A E

B has edges to F and A, both of which have two edges each. Randomly we choose A.

City	Has Edges To
E	F
F	E

City F has edge to A and E, so we can choose A, and finally E. The resulting tour is the sequence in which cities were chosen from the edge map, that is, [D C B A E F]. Verify that this tour is composed entirely of edges taken from the two parents.   ■

One problem that occurs with edge recombination is that cities are often left without a continuing edge. Thus they may become isolated, so a new edge has to be reintroduced. This is the reason why higher priority is given to choosing those cities which currently have the fewest number of unused edges.

Whitley's experiments indicate that a thousand trial recombination on a 30-city problem resulted in only 278 new edges being introduced out of the 30,000 edges manipulated. This is an effective mutation rate of less than 1 percent. The same test when run on a 50 city problem introduced 753 new edges, (mutation rate this time being 1.5 percent). Reported edge transfer rates for Hamiltonian tours/cycles was higher than 96 percent.

3.7.2 Module Placement

Our second example of the application of GAs is module placement. This problem is similar to the assignment problem discussed in Section 3.5 (and formally defined on page 8). Depending on the application, the cost function used may vary. Our objective here is to show a different chromosomal representation and different crossovers that have been suggested for inheritance and creation of next generation individuals. The problem can be defined as follows:

> **Definition 15** Given are, a set **M** of circuit elements or *modules*, $\mathbf{M} = \{e_1, \ldots, e_m\}$, and a set $\mathcal{N}$ of n signals or nets, $N = \{s_1, s_2, \ldots, s_n\}$, where a net is a set of modules to be interconnected. Also given are a set of l locations or *slots*, $L = \{c_1, c_2, \ldots, c_l\}$, $l \geq m$. The slots are organized as a matrix with r rows and c columns. The objective is to assign each module to a slot such that interconnection lengths are reduced, while satisfying some constraints.

We restrict our discussion in this section to the chromosomal representation and crossovers that have been used by Cohoon and Paris in *Genie*, a genetic placement system for placing modules on a rectangular grid [CP87, Y+95].

2-D Chromosome

The chromosomal representation must be amenable to genetic operations. The solution to the problem can also be represented as a one-dimensional (1-D) string as explained in Example 3.7. Since we are talking about the problem of assigning modules to slots in a 2-D matrix, another way to represent the solution is in the form of a 2-D array. In the following paragraphs we illustrate two crossover operators used in Genie for the placement problem [CP87, Y+95].

Crossover 1

The first crossover operator selects a random module e_s and brings its four neighbors in parent 1 (P_1) to the location of the corresponding neighboring slots in P_2.

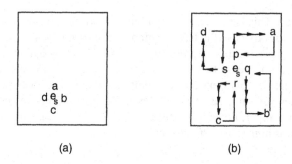

Figure 3.5: (a) A random module and its neighbors. (b) The neighbors in (a) of P_1 replace neighboring modules in P_2.

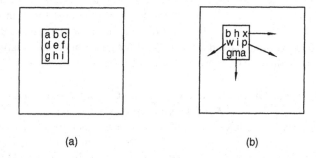

Figure 3.6: (a) A square is selected in P_1. (b) Modules of square in P_1 are copied to P_2 and duplicate modules are moved out.

Then, the modules that earlier occupied the neighboring locations in P_2 are shifted outward one location at a time in a chain move in the direction of the old locations of the four moved modules until a vacant location is found. This is shown in Figure 3.5(b). The result obviously is that a patch containing e_s and its four neighbors is copied from P_1 to P_2 and that other modules are shifted by at most one position.

Crossover 2

The second crossover operator selects a square consisting of $k \times k$ modules from P_1 and copies it to P_2, k is a random number with some mean and variance (say 3 and 1 respectively). Clearly, this method tends to duplicate some modules and leave out others. For example, referring to Figure 3.6, if modules in the square of P_1 are copied to the square of P_2, then those modules in the square of P_1 and not in the square of P_2 are duplicated. This problem is overcome as follows. Let $SP_2 - SP_1$ be the set of modules in the square of P_2 but not in the square of

P_1 ($SP_2 - SP_1 = \{x, w, p, m\}$). Similarly $SP_1 - SP_2$ is the set of modules in square of P_1 but not in square of P_2 ($SP_1 - SP_2 = \{c, d, e, f\}$). Each module in $SP_2 - SP_1$ is moved to a slot currently occupied by a module in $SP_1 - SP_2$. That is, in P_2, modules $\{x, w, p, m\}$ are moved to slots currently occupied by modules $\{c, d, e, f\}$. Then all the remaining modules in the square of P_1 are copied into the square of P_2 to yield a new offspring.

Experiments conducted by Cohoon and Paris indicate that both operators performed well, with crossover 2 consistently better than crossover 1.

The above two examples illustrate the variations that are available in applying GAs to solve practical engineering problems. It is not always required to represent the solution as a binary string. In fact, a representation that intuitively ensures inheritance and is closer to the actual problem most often leads to better results. However, in the absence of any information about the problem, one must resort to blind application of the classic genetic algorithm [CP87, Y+95].

2-D chromosomes have also been used for other problems such as TSP. Homaifar et al., used a binary matrix to represent edges. For an N city problem, the size of the matrix is $N \times N$. A 1 at any position of the matrix denotes the existence of an edge between the two cities. Homaifar et al. defined a new crossover called matrix crossover (MX) which is an extension of the one-point or two-point crossover and manipulates edges. It deals with column positions rather than bit positions. Using their representation, MX crossover and an inversion operator (2-opt) [WSF89] they obtained results competitive with the best known techniques. In their implementation, inversion, that is, cutting a string and reversing the order of cities in the substring is accepted only if the operation produces good results. They also presented schema and complexity analysis for their proposed technique [HGL92].

3.7.3   Applications of GAs to Other Problems

In this section we briefly look at some more applications of GA. We present only the definition of the problem, its application in engineering, the chromosomal representation, and the fitness measure suggested.

Steiner Tree Problem

The problem of finding an optimal Steiner tree appears in the design of telecommunication networks, power distribution, design of oil pipelines, and in layouts of PCBs and VLSI chips.

Given n nodes, a minimum spanning tree connecting the n nodes can be constructed in $O(n \log n)$ time. A minimum Steiner tree is a tree of smaller length than a minimum spanning tree, and is found if *additional* nodes are introduced, called Steiner points (see Figure 3.7).

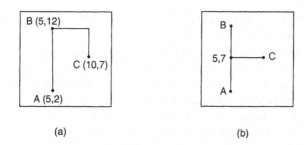

Figure 3.7: (a) A minimum spanning tree. (b) Steiner tree.

Therefore, to find a Steiner tree, one has to identify the number of Steiner points and their positions in the plane. This problem has been shown to be NP-complete [SG76].

Hesser et al. applied the GA for the construction of a minimal Steiner tree (MStT) [HMS89]. They represented each Steiner tree by a string (chromosome) of length l; each chromosome being an assembly of x, y-positions of a fixed number of Steiner points. For example, if a Steiner tree problem with 20 candidate Steiner points is to be solved, and b bits are used to represent x- and y-coordinates, the chromosome length l will be $2 \times b \times 20 = 40 \times b$ bits (240 bits for $b = 6$). Each chromosome represents one Steiner tree. The fitness of the individual belonging to the chromosome corresponds to the length of the MStT that can be constructed by using the original fixed points and the encoded Steiner points. Obviously, the length of the Steiner tree is a function of the positions of the Steiner points as specified by the chromosome [HMS89]. Hesser et al. experimented with the GA heuristic, simulated annealing, and other constructive techniques and found the results comparable.

Discovery of Maximal Distance Codes

The problem of discovering communication codes with properties useful for error corrections was presented by Dontas and De Jong (1990) [DJ90]. A code is represented by (n,M,d) where n denotes the code length (the number of bits in one code word), M the size of the code, that is, the number of distinct vectors in the code, and d is the Hamming distance of the code. The Hamming distance of a code is the number of bit positions in which *any* two vectors of the code differ. A good code has a small n (denoting less redundancy), a large M (large vocabulary) and large d (greater tolerance to error). Search spaces for these codes are large, for example, for a $(7,16,3)$ code the size of the search space is at least 10^{20}.

The solution method used by Dontas and De Jong was to represent the codes by a fixed length–binary strings. For example, for the $(7,16,3)$ code, the binary string of $7 \times 16 = 112$ bits was used to represent the code. Since the performance of the code is dependent on the collective composition of the words and is independent of the order in which the words are represented, the codes are sorted in decreasing order of the words. This sorting helps in reducing all equivalent codes to a single representation, thereby reducing the search space and the number of possible solutions by a large factor. For the (7,16,3) code, this factor is $16! \approx 20 \times 10^{12}$.

Dontas and De Jong experimented with two fitness functions $f_1(C)$ and $f_2(C)$ given below:

$$f_1(C) = \frac{1}{\sum_{i=1}^{\mathbf{M}} \min(\mathrm{d}_{ij})} \qquad j = 1, \ldots, 16; \quad j \neq i$$

$$f_2(C) = \sum_{i=1}^{\mathbf{M}} \sum_{j=1, j \neq i}^{\mathbf{M}} \frac{1}{\mathrm{d}_{ij}^2}$$

where d_{ij} represents the Hamming distance between words i and j in the code C. The above problem can also be visualized as that of placing **M** individuals in the corners of an n-dimensional hypercube so as to maximize the mutual distance between them. This situation is analogous to particles of equal charge trying to position themselves in the minimum energy configuration in a bounded space. $f_2(C)$ given in the above equation captures this idea and results in significantly better performance than $f_1(C)$.

N-Queens Problem

This is another complex combinatorial optimization problem that served as a benchmark to test AI search techniques. The problem consists of placing N-queens on an $N \times N$ chessboard so that no two queens can capture each other. This means, no two queens can be placed in the same row, same column, or the same diagonal. There are $\binom{N^2}{N}$ possibilities. Homaifar et al. applied GAs to solve this problem and presented results for $N \leq 200$ [HTA92]. The chromosome encoding consists of a permutation of N distinct numbers. For example, [8 6 1 4 3 5 7 2] is a chromosome for $N = 8$. The interpretation of this representation is as follows. Each column position in the string corresponds to a row number in which a queen is placed. That is, the first queen in column 1 is placed in row 8, the second queen in column 2 in row 6, and so on. Using this representation, no two queens can appear in the same row or the same column.

For each chromosome, its fitness value is a function of how many queens are being attacked. Since no two queens are placed in the same row or same column, we have to check only the diagonals. Let the two diagonals, one that goes up-right and down-left, and the other, that goes up-left and down-right, be called the positive and negative diagonals, respectively. Then, for each queen in every column, if it is not attacked by another queen on its positive diagonal, its fitness value is increased by $\frac{1}{2 \times N}$. A similar value is added if no queen is found on the negative diagonal.

Consider another string [3 5 1 7 8 4 6 2]. First the positive diagonal is checked for additional queens, and a queen is found in the third position of the string. Since there is an additional queen on this diagonal, the fitness value does not receive any type of reward. Next, the negative diagonal is examined. There are no additional queens, and thus the fitness value is increased by a factor $\frac{1}{2 \times 8}$. The procedure is repeated until the diagonals of each queen have been checked. A solution is feasible when its fitness value is one.

The initial population is generated at random. Experiments with edge recombination, inversion, uniform order-based crossover, and mutation operators were conducted. The application of the edge recombination operator requires an edge map. The edge map stores all the adjacencies of a queen that are in the row above and below it. Inversion is applied, and if improvement occurs then the move is accepted, else the substring is returned to its initial position. The uniform order-based crossover (page 136) was also used. Best performance occurred with the genetic edge recombination operator (see Section 3.7.1, page 149) [WSF89].

3.8   Parallelization of GA

The genetic algorithm is highly parallel. This is a direct consequence of the parallel nature of the genetic reproductive processes. Most GA parallelization techniques exploit the fact that GA works with a population of chromosomes (solutions) and proceed as follows. The population is partitioned into subpopulations which evolve independently using sequential GA. Interaction among the smaller communities is occasionally allowed. This strategy exposes the explicit parallelism of GA and makes it a suitable approach for running on a multiprocessor machine. This parallelization approach has been shown to converge faster to desirable solutions. This parallel execution model is a more realistic simulation of natural evolution in which communities are isolated but, occasionally interact through migration or cross-communities matings.

The reported parallelization strategies fall into three general categories: (1) the *island model*, (2) the *stepping-stone model*, and (3) the *neighborhood model*, also called the *cellular model*.

3.8.1   Island Model

In this variant, the population is divided among the available processors. Each processor runs sequential GA on its local subpopulation. Periodically, subsets of elements are migrated among subpopulations. Migration is allowed between

Algorithm ($Parallel\_GA$)
    Every processor will have one subpopulation of size p.
    Initialize.
    For $j = 1$ to **E Do**
        ParFor
            Run GA for a fixed number of iterations;
            Send a subset of local subpopulation to neighbors;
            Add the received subsets to local subpopulation;
            Select p elements from local subpopulation
        EndParFor
    EndFor;
    Return highest scoring element
End

Figure 3.8: Parallel GA using the stepping stone model.

all subpopulations. Examples of implementations of this model are reported in [SWM91, Tan89]. The island parallelization model is suitable for multiprocessor machines with a relatively small number of processors.

3.8.2 Stepping-Stone Model

This strategy is similar to the *island model* except that communication is restricted to neighboring populations only [GS91]. This model is inspired by the theory of punctuated equilibria which has been suggested to solve certain paleontological dilemmas in the geological record [EG72, Eld85]. The theory says that species tend to stay stable as long as the environment is steady but, when there is an environmental change, species undergo a rapid evolution to adapt to the new condition. In GA terminology, the model defines fitness of individuals relative to other individuals in the local subpopulation. This corresponds to having a steady environment. Each local community will stabilize after a number of generations. Then, by introducing new elements (new competitors) from neighboring communities, a change in the environment is simulated. The subpopulation elements will rapidly evolve to adapt to this new change. This parallelization approach is summarized in the algorithm of Figure 3.8. Examples of parallel implementations of this variant are reported in [CHMR87, CHMR91, GS91].

3.8.3 Neighborhood or Cellular Model

Although the above two models are reasonable parallel implementations, they are not suitable enough for massively parallel systems. Cellular genetic algorithms are

Algorithm $(Parallel\_GA)$
>   **Initialize.**
>   **For** j = 1 to **E Do**
> >   **ParFor** each processor
> > >   Send cost of element to all neighbors;
> > >   Select the neighbor with lowest cost;
> > >   Perform crossover between local element and selected element;
> > >   Replace local element with offspring according to some strategy
> >   **EndParFor**
>   **EndFor**;
>   Return highest scoring element
> **End**

Figure 3.9: Parallel GA using the neighborhood model.

designed to take advantage of massively parallel machines [GW94]. In this model, we throw away the local subpopulations boundaries and assume that communities are continuous. That is, every individual has its own neighborhood defined by some diameter. This model is more suitable for massively parallel systems, where each processor is assigned one element. The basic operations performed by each processor are summarized in the algorithm of Figure 3.9.

To reduce communication overhead, cellular GAs usually restrict mating based on distance. This form of restriction leads to what is called *isolation-by-distance* [GS89].

3.9   Other Issues and Recent Work

There are several additional GA issues that have not been mentioned or elaborated. In this section we briefly touch upon some of them. For details and other issues we refer the reader to the various references at the end of this chapter, especially [Dav91, Gol89c, Ree95b].

3.9.1   Performance Measurement

Our first concern in this section is the measurement of performance of the GA heuristic. Two commonly used performance measures were suggested by De Jong [Jon75]. One measure was devised to gauge the convergence (termed *off-line*) and the other to gauge the ongoing performance, termed *on-line*. Let the objective function value corresponding to the chromosome generated at step t be $f(t)$, and the best value found up to time t be $f^*(t)$. Then after T iterations (function evaluations) the on-line and off-line performances are defined as follows.

$$x = \frac{1}{T}\sum_{t=1}^{T} f(t) \tag{3.21}$$

where x is the on-line performance measure and relates to the average fitness of all strings generated. The off-line measure defined as x^* relates to the performance of the GA converging to the optimum and is defined as:

$$x^* = \frac{1}{T}\sum_{t=1}^{T} f^*(t) \tag{3.22}$$

where $f^*(t) = \text{best }\{f(1), f(2), \ldots, f(t)\}$. That is, the off-line performance is a running average of the best performance values up to a particular time [Gol89c].

Other performance measures that have been used are *best-so-far*, and the number of iterations required to reach the global optimum (if known).

3.9.2 Gray versus Binary Encoding

Most GA implementations use simple binary encoding. Is the binary encoding always the best? A problem that occurs when binary encoding is employed is that values which are close in the original space may be far apart in the binary mapped space. This results in adjacent genotypes having distant phenotypes, and vice versa. For example, in our optimization problem of Example 3.1 the optimum occurs at value 63 and the binary mapped value is 1 1 1 1 1 1. The binary number 0 1 1 1 1 1 with only one bit different represents a numerical value that is half the optimum, a large distance away in the original space. This led some researchers [CS88, ECS89] to advocate the use of Gray code mapping. The general characteristic of Gray code is that adjacent binary integers differ only in a single-bit position (a Hamming distance of 1).

3.9.3 Niches, Crowding, and Speciation

In previous sections we discussed several selection methods. We also mentioned that the result of crossover of two chromosomes does not necessarily yield a better offspring. The offspring may be worse than either parent. This is generally observed when we try to optimize multimodal functions. The result from the crossover of two chromosomes which are close to different optima may be much worse than either. Degraded performance of previous selection mechanisms, especially on multimodal functions, compelled the introduction of new reproductive plans. Ideas of *preselection, crowding,* and *speciation,* were introduced which, to some extent, overcome these problems.

Consider a multimodal function, that is, one which has several optima. For a randomly chosen initial population, we start with a relatively even spread of points across the function domain. If we run our simple genetic algorithm then the search converges to *one* of the peaks (assuming maximization) in the function, that is, most of the strings are distributed near the top of one of the hills. This ultimate convergence to one of the peaks is caused by what is known as *genetic drift*—stochastic errors in sampling caused by small population sizes. Somehow we would like to reduce the effect of these errors and enable *stable subpopulations* to form around each peak. In case of multimodal problems where the peaks are of varying magnitudes, we may like to allocate sub-populations to peaks in proportion to their magnitude. Inducement of niches and species will help achieve this [Gol89c, Mah94].

Niches and Species:

A niche can be viewed as an ecological role of an organism in a community, and species as a class of organisms with common characteristics. What is the role of inducement of niches and species in genetic search? In nature, similar individuals tend to occupy the same environmental niches. Competition for limited resources among similar members of a natural population results in what is known as *crowding*. On the other hand, dissimilar members occupy different environmental niches and therefore do not typically compete for resources. Increased competition for limited resources also decreases life expectancy and birthrates, whereas less crowded niches experience less pressure and achieve higher life expectancy and birthrates [Mah94].

Crowding:

One of the first studies to induce niche-like behavior in GA search was due to Cavicchio [Cav70]. He introduced a mechanism called *pre-selection*, where an offspring replaced the inferior of its parent. This was done only if the fitness of the offspring exceeded that of the replaced parent. In this way *diversity* was maintained in the population because strings tend to replace strings similar to themselves.

Motivated by the analogy of competition for limited resources among similar members (and poor results of simple GA on multimodal functions) De Jong proposed his "crowding factor (CF) model" [Jon75]. In this model, in the hope of maintaining more diversity in the population, De Jong forced newly generated offsprings to replace similar older adults [Mah94]. De Jong's crowding kills off a fixed percentage of the population at each generation. When an individual is born, one is selected to die. The dying individual is selected from a subset of CF members chosen at random from the population. In order to maintain diversity, the dying member chosen is one that closely resembles the new offspring.

For binary strings, resemblance may be measured in terms of Hamming distance. However, as mentioned earlier, numbers which are actually close may be mapped to string patterns which are far apart. Therefore, it is preferable to use actual values of parameters, that is, phenotype distances rather than genotype distances.

GAs which form and maintain niches by replacing population elements with *like* individuals, are called crowding methods. This definition also includes GAs which replace closely resembling parents with offsprings.

Speciation:

There have been several attempts to replicate the existence of species in nature. A scheme due to Goldberg and Richardson [GR87] relies on a *sharing function* to penalize or derate the fitness of similar chromosomes thereby limiting the uncontrolled growth of one species. The sharing function may take several forms. As an example, consider the following linear function:

$$s(d) = \begin{cases} 1 - \frac{d}{D} & d < D \\ 0 & d \geq D \end{cases} \qquad (3.23)$$

where d is the distance between chromosomes in the population (not necessarily Hamming distance), and D is a parameter. In this scheme, first the *sharing* function denoted by $s[d(x_i, x_j)]$ is evaluated for each pair (x_i, x_j) of chromosomes in the population. Then the sum denoted by σ_i is computed

$$\sigma_i = \sum_{j=1}^{n} s[d(x_i, x_j)] \quad j \neq i \qquad (3.24)$$

The distance measure is such that the closer an individual x_i is to another individual x_j, the lower is its $d(x_i, x_j)$ value, and the larger is the share value $s[d(x_i, x_j)]$. After accumulating the total number of shares in this manner, the fitness of chromosomes is adjusted (reduced) by taking the fitness and dividing it by the accumulated number of shares:

$$f_s(x_i) = \frac{f(x_i)}{\sigma_i} \qquad (3.25)$$

Thus, when many individuals are in the same neighborhood, they contribute to one another's share count, thereby reducing one another's fitness values. As a result, this mechanism limits the uncontrolled growth of particular species within a population.

3.9.4 Constant versus Dynamically Decreasing Population

Runtime requirements of genetic algorithms are larger than those of other iterative techniques described in this book. The size of population has a great effect on the total runtime of the algorithm. The smaller the population size, the smaller the runtime will be. Experiments conducted in [Y+95] indicated that the population fitness improves very rapidly during the early generations. The change in the population fitness is less rapid as the number of generations increases, until it becomes insignificant. The reason is that the improvements in the population are caused by crossovers and mutations involving high-scoring individuals. Therefore, toward the middle and later generations, the role of low-scoring individuals becomes insignificant as a source of new fit individuals for the next generations. Hence, it seems reasonable to allow the population size to progressively decrease (in a controlled manner) with the number of generations. Such a decrease will cause a sizable reduction in runtime without any noticeable change in solution quality.

To view the effect of this idea, experiments were conducted using two strategies [Y+95]. In the first strategy, the population size was fixed to 30 individuals. For the second strategy, the population was allowed to progressively decrease using the following reduction procedure. The performance of the best solution is checked periodically every *Reduction_Period*. If solution quality is found not to improve by at least 3 pecent during the last *Reduction_Period*, the population size is reduced by 20 percent. This reduction is allowed as long as the population size does not become less than half of the initial population size. The *Reduction_Period* parameter is also dynamically decreased. Initially it is assigned a large value. Then each time the population size is checked, the *Reduction_Period* is reduced by a *Period_Factor*. This is performed because the convergence rate in the early generations is higher than in the later ones. Thus, the reduction procedure monitors the performance after shorter periods in those generations where the improvement is too slow. Typical values for a 300,000-generation run were: *Reduction_Period* equal to 5,000 generations and the *Period_Factor* is equal to 5 percent.

The above idea bears some similarity to the cooling schedule of simulated annealing. Whereas in simulated annealing the cooling schedule does not have much influence on the runtime of the procedure, for the genetic algorithm a smaller *Reduction_Period* increases the rate at which the population size is reduced, thus leading to a much smaller runtime. In [Y+95] it was shown that the total runtime decreased by 46 percent when the population size was dynamically reduced. The quality of the results in both cases, that is, with fixed and dynamically decreasing populations, was comparable.

3.9.5   Multiobjective Optimization with GAs

What we have seen so far is the application of GAs to single-objective optimization problems. In case of single objective optimization we seek the best solution that maximizes (or minimizes) cost function. Most optimization problems have multiple objectives. In order to use GAs to solve multiobjective problems, the objective function should be combined into a scalar fitness function. The various techniques used to solve multiobjective problems include the use of ad hoc weights for each objective, the notion of Pareto optimality [HNG94], and goal-directed search [EK96]. Fuzzy logic can also be incorporated with genetic algorithms to produce an effective search heuristic that combines the parallel and robust search properties of GA with the expressive power of fuzzy logic [Zad65]. One possibility is to evaluate the fitness of individuals based on fuzzy logic rules expressed on linguistic variables modeling the desired objective criteria of the problem domain. The features that characterize good solutions can be expressed using fuzzy logic. Therefore, instead of rating solutions of a population on the basis of a scalar function of questionable origins, they can be ranked based on their degree of membership in the fuzzy subset *good solutions*. More details on use of fuzzy logic with GAs for multiobjective optimization are given in Chapter 7 (Section 7.4).

3.9.6 Other Related Material

There are several other concepts in the vast field of genetic algorithms that we consider beyond the scope of this book. Without any details, we shall refer to some of these.

The simple GA considers chromosomes as single stranded or haploids. Whereas in nature, at each locus there is a pair of genes. One of them is termed as dominant, and is always expressed. The other, known as recessive, and is expressed only when paired with another recessive gene [SG92]. The redundant memory of diploidy enables multiple solutions to be carried along, thus preserving useful information, which in the case of haploids may be lost forever. Although several attempts have been made to simulate this natural diploidy, and apply it to combinatorial optimization problems [GS87b], as yet it has not been found to be of much importance.

Recently, Walsh functions have been used in the analysis of GAs [Bet81]. They have been used in the introduction of what are known as *deceptive* problems [DHG93, Gol89a, Gol89b], and to derive the variance of schema fitness [PR92]. Deceptive problems are those where building block hypothesis (implicit parallelism property) fails [Bet81, Gol89b, Whi92]. Blind application of simple GAs to deceptive problems leads to poor results. These problems have led to another type of GAs called mGAs (messy genetic algorithms) [GKD89, GDK90].

In earlier sections we have seen how a schema defines subsets of chromosomes which have the same alleles at a specified locus. A *forma* also defines a subset of chromosomes, but in a more general way [Rad91]. With the concept of forma, it is possible to design operators which have certain properties. For example, in the case of the TSP problem, what is required is the inheritance of edges. Then, the defining characteristics of a forma may be that the chromosome possesses a certain edge [HGL92, Rad91, Ree95b].

While with schema analysis it is possible to explain why the simple crossover works, with forma it is possible to a priori design operators that have certain properties [Rad91, Ree95b]. Radcliffe defines two properties which he calls *respect* and *proper assortment*. Respect is defined as follows: When parents share a particular characteristic, their offsprings should always inherit it. Proper assortment, on the other hand implies that where parents have different characteristics, their offsprings should contain both the characteristics.

Another type of GA called problem space genetic algorithm was first proposed by Storer et al. [SWV92]. They realized that infeasible solutions occurred during the evolution process in each generation for conventional genetic algorithms. The infeasible solutions must be either corrected by a repairing mechanism or be discarded. They proposed an alternative to handle the occurrence of infeasible solutions by perturbing the problem space instead of the solution space. A fast heuristic algorithm is then used to map the problem space into the solution space, which guarantees that the solutions are always feasible. This approach was first adopted by Dhodhi et al. [D+95] to optimize the datapath in a high-level synthesis environment.

GAs may suffer from the problem of premature convergence. Their effectiveness can be increased by including some features of other heuristics. For example, GAs are combined with simulated annealing to introduce more diversity into the population thereby preventing premature convergence. A complete section in Chapter 7 (Section 7.3) is dedicated to this issue, where we discuss combination of GAs with other heuristics (such as tabu search and simulated annealing) discussed in this book.

3.10   Conclusions

In this chapter we have presented the basics of genetic algorithms. These algorithms emulate the natural process of evolution. Unlike other search heuristics, they conduct the search by operating on a set of solutions called the population. They work with chromosomal representations (encoded strings) of solutions, require only objective function values, and search from a set of points. The basic idea is to combine solutions called parents to produce new solutions called offsprings, with the objective that the offsprings will inherit some parental characteristics. To accomplish this, crossover is used. It is the crossover operator that distinguishes GAs from other optimization algorithms. We discussed several crossover operators. Mutation is another operator that is used to inject new characteristics in the individuals.

In this chapter, we also shed some light on the fundamental theorem of genetic algorithms, the schema theorem.

Several variations of the basic technique, convergence related issues, and practical considerations for implementation of GAs on a digital computer, were discussed. Implementation aspects of this powerful iterative heuristics were presented with applications and case studies. A brief survey of various problems to which GAs have been successfully applied was presented. We also touched upon techniques for parallelizing GAs, and summarized several recent related issues.

References

[ACH90] N. Ansari, M.-H. Chen, and E. S. H. Hou. Point pattern matching by genetic algorithm. *16th Annual Conference on IEEE Industrial electronics*, pages 1233–1238, 1990.

[Ack87] D. H. Ackley. An empirical study of bit vector function optimization. In L. Davis, editor, *Genetic Algorithms and Simulated Annealing*. Morgan Kauffmann, Los Altos, CA, 1987.

[AEH89] E. H. L. Aarts, A. H. Eiben, and K. M. Van Hee. A general theory of genetic algorithms. In *Computing Science Notes,*. Eindhoven University of Technology, 1989.

[Ala92] J. T. Alander. On optimal population size of genetic algorithms. *Proceedings of CompEuro'92, IEEE Computer Society Press*, pages 65–70, 1992.

[ASB94] S. Ali, S. M. Sait, and M. S. T. Benten. GSA: Scheduling and allocation using genetic algorithms. *Proceeding of EURO-DAC'94: IEEE European Design Automation Conference*, pages 84–89, September 1994.

[ASHN96] K. S. Al-Sultan, M. F. Hussain, and J. S. Nizami. A genetic algorithm for the set covering problem. *Journal of the Operational Research Society*, 47:702–709, 1996.

[ASK96] K. S. Al-Sultan and M. M. Khan. Computational experience on four algorithms for the hard clustering problem. *Pattern Recognition Letters*, 17:295–308, 1996.

[Bak85] J. E. Baker. Adaptive Selection Methods for Genetic Algorithms. *Proceeding of Genetic Algorithms and their Applications*, pages 101–111, 1985.

[Bet81] A. D. Bethke. *Genetic Algorithms as Function Optimizers*, Vol. 41 (9). Doctoral dissertation, University of Michigan, Ann Arbor, 1981.

[BS94] M. S. T. Benten and S. M. Sait. Genetic scheduling of task graphs. *International Journal of Electronics*, 77(4):401–415, 1994.

[Cav70]   D. J. Cavicchio. *Adaptive Search Using Simulated Evolution*. Doctoral dissertation, University of Michigan, 1970.

[CHMR87] J. P. Cohoon, S. U. Hegde, W. N. Martin, and D. S. Richards. Punctuated equilibria: A parallel genetic algorithm. *Proceedings of the Second International Conference on Genetic Algorithms*, pages 148–154, 1987.

[CHMR91] J. P. Cohoon, S. U. Hegde, W. N. Martin, and D. S. Richards. Distributed genetic algorithms for the floorplan design problem. *IEEE Transactions on Computer-Aided Design*, CAD-10:483–492, April 1991.

[CP87]   J. P. Cohoon and W. D. Paris. Genetic placement. *IEEE Transactions on Computer-Aided Design*, CAD-6:956–964, November 1987.

[CS88]   R. A. Caruana and J. D. Schaffer. Representation and hidden bias: Gray vs binary coding for genetic algorithms. *Proceedings of 5th International Conference on Machine Learning*, 1988.

[D+95]   M. K. Dhodhi et al. Data path synthesis using problem-space genetic algorithm. *IEEE Transactions on Computer-Aided Design*, CAD-14(8):934–943, 1995.

[Dav85a]   L. Davis. Applying Adaptive Algorithms to Epistatic Domains. *Proceedings of the 9th Joint Conference on Artificial Intelligence*, pages 162–164, 1985.

[Dav85b]   L. Davis. Job shop scheduling with genetic algorithms. *Proceeding of Genetic Algorithms and their Applications*, pages 136–140, 1985.

[Dav91]   L. Davis, editor. *Handbook of Genetic Algorithms*. Van Nostrand Reinhold, NY, 1991.

[DHG93]   K. Deb, J. Horn, and D. E. Goldberg. Multimodal deceptive functions. *Complex systems*, 7:131–153, 1993.

[DJ90]   K. Dontas and K. De Jong. Discovery of maximal distance codes using genetic algorithms. *Proceedings of the 2nd International IEEE Conference on Tools for Artificial Intelligence*, pages 805–811, 1990.

[DP91]   T. E. Davis and J. C. Principe. A Simulated Annealing Like Convergence Theory for the Simple Genetic Algorithm. *Proceedings of the 4th International Conference on Genetic Algorithm*, pages 174–181, 1991.

[DP93]   T. E. Davis and J. C. Principe. A Markov Chain Framework for the Simple Genetic Algorithm. *Proceedings of the 4th International Conference on Genetic Algorithm*, 13:269–288, 1993.

[EAH90]   A. H. Eiben, E. H. L. Aarts, and K. M. Van Hee. Global convergence of genetic algorithms: A markov chain analysis. In H. P. Schwefel and Männer, editors, *In Parallel Problem Solving from Nature*, pages 4–12. Springer-Verlag, Berlin, 1990.

[ECS89]   L. J. Eshelman, R. A. Caruana, and J. D. Schaffer. Biases in the crossover landscape. *Proceedings of 3rd International Conference on GAs*, pages 10–19, 1989.

[EG72]   N. Eldredge and S. J. Gould. Punctuated Equilibria: An alternative to phyletic gradualism. In T. J. M. Schopf, Ed., *Models of Paleobiology*, Freeman, Cooper and Co., San Francisco, 1972.

[EK96]   H. Esbensen and E. S. Kuh. Design Space Exploration Using The Genetic Algorithm. *ISCAS '96. IEEE International Symposium on Circuits and Systems*, pages 500–503, 1996.

[Eld85]   N. Eldredge. *Time Frames*. Simon and Schuster, New York, 1985.

[FD92]   E. Falkenauer and A. Delchambre. A genetic algorithm for bin packing and line balancing. *Proceedings of International Conference on Robotics and Automation*, pages 1186–1192, May 1992.

[Fog95]   D. B. Fogel. *Evolutionary Computation: Toward a New Philosophy of Machine Intelligence*. IEEE Press, 1995.

[For85]   S. Forrest. Documentation for PRISONERS DILEMMA and NORMS programs that use genetic algorithm. Unpublished Manuscript, University of Michigan, Ann Arbor, 1985.

[Fre94]   J. A. Freeman. *Simulating Neural Networks: with Mathematica*. Addison-Wesley, 1994.

[FW93]   H. Freund and R. Wolter. Evolution of bit strings II: A simple model of co-evolution. *Complex Systems*, 7:25–42, 1993.

[G+85]   J. Grefenstette et al. Genetic algorithm for traveling salesman problem. *Proceedings of International Conference of Genetic Algorithms and Their Applications*, pages 160–165. Lawrence Erlbaum, Hillsdale, NJ, 1985.

[GD91]   D. E. Goldberg and K. Deb. A comparative analysis of selection schemes used in genetic algorithms. In G. Rawlins, editor, *Foundations of Genetic Algorithms and Classifier Systems*, pages 69–93. Morgan Kaufmann, San Mateo, CA, 1991.

[GDC92]   D. E. Goldberg, K. Deb, and J. H. Clark. Genetic algorithms, noise, and the sizing of populations. *Complex Systems*, 6:333–362, 1992.

[GDK90]   D. E. Goldberg, K. Deb, and B. Korb. Messy genetic algorithms revisited: studies in mixed size and scale. *Complex Systems*, 5:183–205, 1990.

[Gil85]   A. M. Gillies. *Machine Learning Procedures for Generating Image Domain Feature Detectors*. Doctoral dissertation, University of Michigan, Ann Arbor, 1985.

[GKD89]   D. E. Goldberg, B. Korb, and K. Deb. Messy genetic algorithms: Motivation, analysis and first results. *Complex Systems*, 3:493–530, 1989.

[GL85]   D. E. Goldberg and R. Lingle. Alleles, loci and the traveling salesman problem. *Proceedings of the International Conference on Genetic Algorithms and their Applications*, 1985.

[Gol85]   D. E. Goldberg. Optimal initial population size for binary coded genetic algorithm. TGCA Rep # 85001, University of Alabama, AL, 1985.

[Gol89a]   D. E. Goldberg. Genetic algorithms and Walsh functions: Part I, A gentle introduction. *Complex systems*, 3:129–152, 1989.

[Gol89b]   D. E. Goldberg. Genetic algorithms and Walsh functions: Part II, A gentle introduction. *Complex Systems*, 3:153–171, 1989.

[Gol89c]   D. E. Goldberg. *Genetic Algorithms in Search, Optimization and Machine Learning*. Addison-Wesley, 1989.

[Gol90]   D. E. Goldberg. A note on Boltzmann tournament selection for genetic algorithms and population-oriented simulated annealing. *Complex Systems*, 4:445–460, 1990.

[Goo88]   R. Goodman, editor. *Introduction to Stochastic Models*. Benjamin/Cummings, Reading, MA, 1988.

[GR87]   D. E. Goldberg and R. Richardson. Genetic algorithms with sharing for multimodal function optimization. *Proceedings of 2nd International Conference on GAs*, pages 41–49, 1987.

[GS87a] D. E. Goldberg and P. Segrest. Finite markov chain analysis of genetic algorithms. *Genetic Algorithms and Their Applications: Proceedings of 2nd International Conference on GAs*, pages 1–8, 1987.

[GS87b] D. E. Goldberg and R. E. Smith. Nonstationary function optimization using genetic algorithms with dominance and diploidy. *Proceedings of 2nd International Conference on GAs*, pages 59–68, 1987.

[GS89] M. Gorges-Schleuter. ASPARAGOS—An asynchronous parallel genetic optimization strategy. In J. D. Schaffer, editor, *Proceedings of the 3rd International Conference on Genetic Algorithms and their Applications*, pages 422–427. Morgan-Kaufmann, San Mateo, CA, 1989.

[GS91] M. Gorges-Schleuter. Explicit parallelism of genetic algorithms through population structures. In H. P. Schwefel and R. Männer, editors, *Problem Solving from Nature*, pages 150–159. Springer Verlag, New York, 1991.

[GW94] V. Scott Gordon and Darrell Whitley. A machine-independent analysis of parallel genetic algorithms. *Complex Systems*, 8:181–214, 1994.

[H+95] H. I. Han et al. GenRouter: a genetic algorithm for channel routing problems. *Proceeding of TENCON 95, IEEE Region 10 International Conference on M. roelectronics and VLSI*, pages 151–154, November 1995.

[HAH94] E. S. H. Hou, N. Ans.ri, and R. Hong. genetic algorithm for multiprocessor scheduling. *?E Transactions on Parallel and Distributed Systems*, 5(2):113–120, uary 1994.

[HGL92] A. Homaifar, S. Guan, and G. E. Liepins. Schema analysis of the traveling salesman problem using genetic algorithms. *Complex Systems*, 6:533–552, 1992.

[HMS89] J. Hesser, R. Männer, and ?. Stucky. Optimization of steiner trees using genetic algorithms. In *ICGA'89*, pages 231–236, 1989.

[HNG94] J. Horn, N. Nafpliotis, and D. E. Goldberg. Niched Pareto genetic algorithm for multiobjective optimization. *Proceedings of 1st International Conference on Evolutionary Computation*, pages 82–87, 1994.

[Hol75] J. H. Holland. *Adaptation in Natural and Artificial Systems*. University of Michigan Press, Ann Arbor, 19?5.

[HTA92]   A. Homaifar, J. Turner, and S. Ali. The N-queens problem and ge-
          netic algorithms. *IEEE Proceedings of Southeastcon'92*, pages 262–
          267, April 1992.

[Jon75]   K. A. De Jong. An analysis of the behavior of a class of genetic adap-
          tive systems. Doctoral dissertation, University of Michigan. Univer-
          sity Microfilms No. 76-9381, 36(10), 1975.

[K+97]   K.-T. Ko et al. Using genetic algorithms to design mesh networks.
          Computer, pages 56–60, 1997.

[KP93]   V. Kommu and I. Pomeranz. GAFPGA: Genetic algorithms for
          FPGA technology mapping. *Proceeding of EURO-DAC'93: IEEE
          European Design Automation Conference*, pages 300–305, Septem-
          ber 1993.

[LWJ92]   M. C. Leu, H. Wong, and Z. Ji. Genetic algorithm for solving printed
          circuit board assembly planning problems. *Proceedings of Japan-
          USA Symposium on Flexible Automation*, pages 1579–1586, July
          1992.

[Mah93]   S. W. Mahfoud. Finite markov chain models of an alternative selec-
          tion strategy for the genetic algorithm. *Complex Systems*, 7:155–170,
          1993.

[Mah94]   S. W. Mahfoud. Crossover interactions among niches. *Proceedings
          of the First IEEE Conference on Evolutionary Computation*, pages
          188–193, 1994.

[NV93]   A. E. Nix and M. D. Vose. Modeling genetic algorithms with markov
          chains. *Annals of Mathematics and Artificial Intelligence*, pages 79–
          88, 1993.

[OSH87]   I. Oliver, D. Smith, and J. R. Holland. A study of permutation
          crossover operators on the traveling salesman problem. In John
          Grefenstette, editor, *Genetic Algorithms and their Applications: Pro-
          ceedings of the 2nd International Conference on Genetic Algorithms*,
          pages 224–230. Lawrence Erlbaum, Hillsdale, NJ, 1987.

[PR92]   S. E. Page and D. W. Richardson. Walsh functions, schema variance
          and deception. *Complex Systems*, 6:533–552, 1992.

[PR94]   H. Pirkul and E. Rolland. New heuristic solution procedures for uni-
          form graph partitioning problem: Extensions and evaluation. *Com-
          puters & Operations Research*, 21(8):895–907, October 1994.

[Rad91]   N. J. Radcliffe. Equivalence class analysis of genetic algorithms. *Complex Systems*, 5:183–205, 1991.

[Ree95a]   C. R. Reeves. A genetic algorithm for flowshop sequencing. *Computers & Operations Research*, 22(1):5–14, January 1995.

[Ree95b]   C. R. Reeves. Genetic algorithms. In C. R. Reeves, editor, *Modern Heuristic Techniques for Combinatorial Problems*. McGraw-Hill Book Co., Europe, 1995.

[RPGN94] E. M. Rudnick, J. H. Patel, G. S. Greenstein, and T. M. Niermann. Sequential circuit test generation in a genetic algorithm framework. *Proceedings of the 31st Design Automation Conference*, pages 698–704, 1994.

[RS96]   C. P. Ravikumar and V. Saxena. TOGAPS: A testability oriented genetic algorithm for pipeline synthesis. *VLSI Design*, 5(1):77–87, 1996.

[Rud94]   G. Rudolph. Convergence analysis of canonical genetic algorithms. *IEEE Transactions on Neural Networks*, 5:1:96–101, 1994.

[S+89]   J. D. Schaffer et al. A study of control parameters affecting online performance of genetic algorithms for function optimization. *Proceedings of 3rd International Conference on GAs*, 1989.

[S+95]   S. M. Sait et al. Timing influenced general-cell genetic floorplanner. In *ASP-DAC'95: Asia and South-Pacific Design Automation Conference*, pages 135–140, 1995.

[SG76]   S. Sahni and T. Gonzalez. P-complete approximation problems. *Journal of the ACM*, 23:555–565, 1976.

[SG92]   R. E. Smith and D. E. Goldberg. Diploidy and dominance in artificial genetic search. *Complex Systems*, 6:251–285, 1992.

[SM90]   K. Shahookar and P. Mazumder. A genetic approach to standard cell placement using meta-genetic parameter optimization. *IEEE Transactions on Computer-Aided Design*, 9(5):500–511, May 1990.

[SM91]   K. Shahookar and P. Mazumder. VLSI cell placement techniques. *ACM Computing Surveys*, 23(2):143–220, June 1991.

[Spi95]   R. Spillman. Solving large knapsack problems with a genetic algorithm. *International Conference on Systems, Man and Cybernetics*, pages 632–637, 1995.

[SWM91]   T. Starkweather, D. Whitley, and K. Mathias. Optimization using distributed genetic algorithm. In *Parallel Problem Solving from Nature*, 1991.

[SWV92]   R. H. Storer, D. S. Wu, and R. Vaccari. New search spaces for sequencing problems with application to job shop scheduling. *Management Science*, 38(10):1495–1509, 1992.

[SY95]   S. M. Sait and H. Youssef. *VLSI Design Automation: Theory and Practice*. McGraw-Hill Book Co., Europe, 1995.

[Sys89]   G. Syswerda. Uniform crossover in genetic algorithms. *Proceedings of 3rd International Conference on GAs*, pages 2–9, 1989.

[T+94]   H. Tamaki et al. A comparison study of genetic codings for the traveling salesman problem. *Proceedings of the Ist IEEE Conference on Evolutionary Computation*, pages 1–6, 1994.

[Tan89]   M. Tanese. Distributed genetic algorithms. In J. D. Schaffer, editor, *Proceedings of the 3rd International Conference on Genetic Algorithms*, pages 434–439. Morgan-Kaufmann, San Mateo, CA, 1989.

[Whi92]   D. Whitley. Deception, dominance and implicit parallelism in genetic search. *Annals of Mathematic and Artificial Intelligence*, 5:49–78, 1992.

[Whi94]   D. Whitley. A genetic algorithm tutorial. *Statistics and Computing*, 4:65–85, 1994.

[WSF89]   D. Whitley, T. Starkweather, and D. Fuquay. Scheduling problems and traveling salesmen: The genetic edge recombination operator. *Proceedings of the 3rd International Conference on Genetic Algorithms and their Applications*, pages 133–140, 1989.

[Y+95]   H. Youssef et al. Performance driven standard-cell placement using genetic algorithm. *GLSVLSI'95: Fifth Great Lakes Symposium on VLSI*, pages 124–127, March 1995.

[Yao97]   X. Yao. Global optimization by evolutionary algorithms. *Proceedings of IEEE International Symposium on Parallel Algorithms Architecture Synthesis*, pages 282–291, 1997.

[Zad65]   L. A. Zadeh. Fuzzy sets. *Information Control*, 8:338–353, 1965.

Exercises

Exercise 3.1
Enumerate and briefly discuss the main features of GAs that distinguish them from other combinatorial optimization algorithms.

Exercise 3.2
With respect to GAs, briefly answer the following questions.

1. What do you understand by the term "survival of the fittest" and how and where is it applied?

2. What is the main purpose of the crossover operator?

3. What are the various points in the algorithm where nondeterminism is introduced (give at least three)?

Exercise 3.3
If we choose to adopt "survival of the fittest" strategy, that is, the new population is made of the best individuals chosen from the current population and new offsprings, would GA still be able to climb out of local minima? Justify your answer.

Exercise 3.4
In the context of genetic algorithms, explain briefly what you understand by the following terms:

1. Generation gap

2. Elitist GA

3. Steady-state GA

4. Operator probabilities

5. Scramble list mutation

6. Uniform crossovers

7. Crowding

Exercise 3.5
1. Provide an intuitive description of the effect of PMX crossover, order crossover, and cycle crossover.

2. Compare these crossovers with respect to (a) their inheritance properties of good genes, and (b) their disruptions of the population schemata.

Exercise 3.6
Consider the function given below.

$$f(x) = 2x^3 - 240x^2 + 7200x + 2000 \qquad 0 \leq x \leq 63$$

It is required to find the value of x that maximizes $f(x)$. Represent x as a 6-bit binary string. Let $f(x)$ itself represent the fitness value. You are required to implement a genetic algorithm to find the maximum value of x. Choose a population size of 6, the probability of crossover $p_c = 1.0$, and the probability of mutation $p_\mu = 0.03$. Implement the roulette wheel method for parent selection (see Exercise 3.8). Choose the best strings from offsprings and parents to survive for the next generation. Use the simple cut-catenate operator for crossover and complementing of a bit for mutation. Run the program for 10 generations and observe the following.

1. That the average fitness of the entire population increases with every generation.

2. The fitness value of the best individual increases in every generation.

3. Verify that $f(x)$ has a maximum at $x = 20$ and a minimum at $x = 60$. This can be done by equating the first derivative to zero and finding the roots. Since the value of x that maximizes the function is $x=20$, the number of copies of schema $0\ 1\ 0\ *\ *\ *$ must therefore increase from generation to generation. Similarly, since the value of x that minimizes the function is 60, the number of copies of the schema $1\ 1\ *\ *\ *\ *$ must decrease with number of generations. How many copies of each of the two schemata are found in your population after 10 generations?

4. Repeat for a larger number of generations (greater than 100) and plot for each generation the best and the average fitness. Compare the results for (a) different mutation probabilities; (b) different selection schemes (including ranking).

Exercise 3.7
Suggest a chromosomal representation to the scheduling problem of Example 3.2 which includes both the assignment of tasks to processors, and their order of execution on each processor.

Exercise 3.8
Write a program to implement the procedure below that emulates the selection of individuals based on the roulette wheel method. The steps are:

1. Construct a list of the fitness values of all individuals that comprise the population.

2. Create another list by replacing each fitness value by adding to it the fitness values of all elements prior to it in the list (that is, the running total of fitness values).

3. Generate a uniformly distributed random number between 0 and the total of all of the fitnesses in the population.

4. Return the first individual from the list whose fitness value is equal to or greater than the random number generated.

Run your program for the population in Example 3.4 (page 115), where the list of the fitness values of individuals that comprise the population is [625, 1,936, 2,809, 3,136] and the new list of running totals is [625, 2,561, 5,370, 8,506]. Note that in this list, the total of all fitnesses is the last element.

Chromosome	1	2	3	4
Fitness	625	1,936	2,809	3,136
Running total of fitness	625	2,561	5,370	8,506

(a). In Example 3.4, to select a parent, a random number should be generated between what range?

(b). If we generated the random number 3,371, then which individual from the population of four will be selected?

Exercise 3.9

For the problem in Exercise 3.6, let H_1, H_2 and H_3 be three schemata represented by the following strings: $H_1 = [1 * 1 * * *]$, $H_2 = [0\,0\,1 * * *]$, and $H_3 = [1 * 0 * 1 *]$. Let the population in a certain generation be given by: $s_1 = [0\,0\,1\,0\,0\,1]$, $s_2 = [1\,0\,1\,1\,0\,0]$, $s_3 = [1\,1\,0\,1\,0\,1]$, $s_4 = [1\,1\,1\,0\,0\,0]$, $s_5 = [1\,0\,0\,0\,1\,0]$, and $s_6 = [1\,1\,0\,1\,1\,1]$. Answer the following:

1. How many strings in the population does each schema match?

2. What is the *order* and *defining length* of each schema?

3. How many chromosome does each schema represent?

4. What is the average fitness $f(H)$ of each schema?

5. What is the probability of survival and destruction of each schema?

Exercise 3.10

1. Determine the expected number of offsprings generated in terms of the probability of crossover and population size.

2. Determine the expected number of individuals mutated in terms of mutation probability P_μ.

3. What is the probability that a gene never gets mutated?

Exercise 3.11

Show that, for a population of n strings of length l each, the state space has $\frac{(n+x)!}{n!x!}$ states, where $x = 2^l - 1$.

Exercise 3.12

1. In case of problems that use permutation representation for their solutions, for what type of applications will the order crossover be more suitable than the cycle crossover?

2. List one advantage and one disadvantage of the cycle crossover.

3. A pairwise swap is a common mutation strategy. Another strategy could be to select two elements and move the second in the position before the first. With what crossover operator will this mutation strategy fit well? What are the disadvantages of this mutation strategy in terms of computing the fitness of the mutated chromosome and the amount of new characteristics introduced?

Exercise 3.13

Devise an experiment to study the various selection strategies discussed in this chapter (see page 139). Compare the selection procedures with *Ranking* in terms of quality of solution, ease of implementation, runtime, and so forth.

Exercise 3.14

You are required to obtain a balanced bipartition of an undirected graph containing $2n$ nodes. The weight of the node represents its size. Generate random graphs as explained in Exercise 1.6. Assume that all the nodes have equal weight. Explain how you will do the following?

a. Design a suitable solution encoding (chromosomal representation).

b. The basic operations one performs to generate new offsprings are crossover and mutation. Suggest at least two crossovers that will ensure inheritance and two mutation operations that will always result in valid solutions.

c. Write a program to implement the GA, and plot the best cost and average cost versus generation number (iteration). Use simple crossover and mutation operators. Use suitable values for probabilities of crossover and mutation, size of population, number of generations, and so forth. For cost of the solution use the number of edges cut.

    d. Propose a suitable technique to convert cost values to fitness values (see Section 3.5.2).

    e. What will be the encoding of your chromosome, if you are to obtain a balanced partition of a graph where nodes have varying weights (or sizes)?

Exercise 3.15
For the problem in Exercise 3.14, if the graph contains elements of the same size, and if you are required to partition a circuit into two unequal halves, one containing at least n_1 nodes and the other at most n_2 nodes ($n \times 2 = n_1 + n_2$, $n_1 < n_2$), how will your crossover ensure that this requirement is not violated.

Exercise 3.16
Nodes of the graph given in Figure 3.10 are to be placed in the 12 slots of a 3×4 grid. Genetic algorithm is to be used for placement. The different slots can be labeled as shown in Figure 3.10(b).

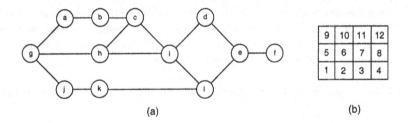

(a)   (b)

Figure 3.10: Graph for Exercise 3.16.

A placement (or assignment) of nodes of the graph to the given grid can be represented in the form of a string using the encoding scheme explained in Example 3.7. For example, in the string given below,

$$c \; e \; a \; g \; b \; h \; d \; k \; f \; j \; l \; i$$

node c is assigned to slot 1 of Figure 3.10(b), node e to slot 2, node a to slot 3, and so on.

Answer the following questions:

1. What is the cost of the above assignment in terms of wire-length if "Manhattan measure" (see page 365 for definition) is used for wire-length estimation?

2. Assuming the point of crossover to be after the 5th gene, what will be the resulting placement if the initial configuration is crossed with the configuration (second parent) below using the PMX crossover?

$$i \; j \; l \; c \; g \; a \; k \; b \; f \; d \; e \; h$$

3. Repeat the above for order and cycle crossovers.

Exercise 3.17
For the placement problem of Exercise 3.16, write a function that will take the chromosome and return the cost of the placement. Use the expression given in Section 3.5.2 to translate cost to fitness.

Exercise 3.18
Write a program to implement the GA for placement. Use the graph of Exercise 3.16 as input. Use the function designed in Exercise 3.17 to compute the cost. Convert cost to fitness using one of the strategies explained in Section 3.5.2. Plot the best cost and average cost versus generation number (iteration). Use partially mapped crossover (PMX), pairwise exchange for mutation, $p_c = 0.9$, $p_\mu = 0.05$, and population size of 10.

What is the effect of scaling on the quality of solution (see Section 3.5.3)?

Exercise 3.19
Repeat Exercise 3.18 by replacing the PMX by (a) order crossover and (b) cycle crossover.

Exercise 3.20
An alternate implementation of PMX is given on page 132. For the two parents $P_1 = $ badefgchi and $P_2 = $ aghcbidef, apply the procedure assuming the crossover position to be after 5 and show that the offspring obtained is bachg|idef.

Exercise 3.21
Compare the performance of the three permutation crossovers, PMX, OX, and CX, for the 1-D and 2-D placement problems in terms of solution quality and runtime. You will have to repeat the same experiments in Exercises 3.18 and 3.19 on larger graphs for comparison (see Exercise 1.6).

Exercise 3.22
Suggest a mechanism to prevent premature convergence of GA by making the mutation probability a function of population diversity. How will you determine the population diversity? What ranges of mutation probabilities can be allowed?

Exercise 3.23
Verify expression 3.20.

Exercise 3.24
Write a program to solve the TSP problem using GAs.

1. Suggest a suitable encoding that uses edge information to store the tours (you can use a 2-D matrix to represent your solution).

2. Propose a suitable crossover operator that will ensure inheritance, and a suitable mutation operator.

3. Compare your implementation with the representation that stores a tour as a string of cities. Use as input test cases whose optimal solution is known.

Exercise 3.25

1. How important is it to select a suitable populations size? How is the performance of GA influenced by the choice of the size of population?

2. What data or information would you use in selecting the size of the population?

3. In the classic GA, the size of the population is fixed for all generations. Population size can be made dynamic by starting with a fairly large number of individuals and then reducing the size by discarding useless individuals as the search progresses. What are the benefits and disadvantages of starting with a large population and decreasing it in later generations?

4. Suggest a scheme to dynamically reduce the size of the population with generations. What criteria will you use to determine when to apply reduction, and by how much?

Exercise 3.26
Consider the *vehicle routing problem* described in Chapter 1, page 7.

1. Devise an efficient chromosomal encoding for this problem.

2. Design and implement a genetic algorithm for the *vehicle routing problem*.

3. Derive an equation expressing the relationship between the algorithm time complexity, the problem size, the complexity of the fitness function, and the complexity of the genetic operators such as crossover and mutation.

Exercise 3.27
Repeat the previous exercise (Exercise 3.26) considering the *flowshop scheduling problem* described in Chapter 2 (Exercise 2.16).

Exercise 3.28
Repeat Exercise 3.26 for the *terminal assignment problem* described in Chapter 2 (Exercise 2.17).

Exercise 3.29
Repeat Exercise 3.26 for the *concentrator location problem* described in Chapter 2 (Exercise 2.18).

Exercise 3.30
Repeat Exercise 3.26 for the *constrained minimum spanning tree problem* described in Chapter 2 (Exercise 2.19).

Exercise 3.31
Repeat Exercise 3.26 for the *mesh topology design problem* described in Chapter 2 (Exercise 2.20).

Exercise 3.32
Repeat Exercise 3.26 for the *weighted matching problem* described in Chapter 2 (Exercise 2.21).

Exercise 3.33
Repeat Exercise 3.26 for the *plant location problem* described in Chapter 2 (Exercise 2.22).

Exercise 3.34
Repeat Exercise 3.26 for the *bandwidth packing problem* described in Chapter 4 (Section 4.7.2).

Exercise 3.35
What schemes will you use to evaluate GAs performance for a certain combinatorial optimization problem? On your GA implementations apply the two performance measures mentioned in this chapter and comment on your observations.

Exercise 3.36

For problems given in Exercises 3.26 to 3.34, and the various combinatorial optimization problems discussed in Chapter 1 (pages 6–8), experiment with the following and comment on the change in solution quality, ease of implementation, convergence, and runtime:

1. Single-point versus multipoint crossover.

2. Different selection strategies.

3. Change in mutation probability.

4. Ranking versus nonranking based implementation.

5. The various scaling procedure described to prevent premature convergence.

6. Static versus dynamically decreasing population.

7. Various schemes that translate cost to fitness.

Exercise 3.37

Compared to other iterative heuristics discussed in this book, is GA more suitable for solving multiobjective optimization problems? Justify your answer.

Exercise 3.38

Programming Exercise:

A GA formulation to solve the Steiner tree problem is given in this chapter. How would you quickly estimate the fitness of the offsprings? What is your opinion about the chromosomal representation presented? Can it be improved? What type of crossovers can you use for the given chromosomes to ensure inheritance? Suggest a suitable mutation strategy.

CHAPTER 4

Tabu Search (TS)

4.1 Introduction

In the previous chapters we discussed simulated annealing, which was inspired by the cooling of metals, and genetic algorithms, which imitate the biological phenomena of evolutionary reproduction. In this chapter we present a more recent optimization method called tabu search (TS) which is based on selected concepts of artificial intelligence (AI).

Tabu search was introduced by Fred Glover [GL97, Glo89b, Glo90b, GTdW93] as a general iterative heuristic for solving combinatorial optimization problems. Initial ideas of the technique were also proposed by Hansen [Han86] in his *steepest ascent mildest descent* heuristic.

Tabu search is conceptually simple and elegant. It is a form of local neighborhood search. Each solution $S \in \Omega$ has an associated set of neighbors $\aleph(S) \subseteq \Omega$. A solution $S' \in \aleph(S)$ can be reached from S by an operation called a *move* to S'. Normally, the neighborhood relation is assumed symmetric. That is, if S' is a neighbor of S then S is a neighbor of S'.

Tabu search is a generalization of local search (see Chapter 1, page 11). At each step, the local neighborhood of the current solution is explored and the best solution in that neighborhood is selected as the new current solution. Unlike local search which stops when no improved new solution is found in the current neighborhood, tabu search continues the search from the best solution in the neighborhood even if it is worse than the current solution. To prevent cycling, information pertaining to the most recently visited solutions are inserted in a list called *tabu list*. Moves to tabu solutions are not allowed. The tabu status of a solution is overridden when certain criteria (aspiration criteria) are satisfied. One example of an aspiration criterion is when the cost of the selected solution is better than the best seen so far, which is an indication that the search is actually not cycling back, but rather moving to a new solution not encountered before.

Tabu search is a *metaheuristic*, which can be used not only to guide search in complex solution spaces, but also to direct the operations of *other* heuristic procedures. It can be superimposed on any heuristic whose operations are characterized as performing a sequence of *moves* that lead the procedure from one trial solution to another. In addition to several other characteristics, the attractiveness of tabu search comes from its ability to escape local optima.

Tabu search differs from simulated annealing (Chapter 2) or genetic algorithm (Chapter 3) which are "memoryless," and also from branch-and-bound, A* search, and so on, which are rigid memory approaches. One of its features is its systematic use of *adaptive* (flexible) memory. It is based on simple ideas with a clever combination of components, namely, [Glo90a, SM93]:

1. a short-term memory component; this component is the core of the tabu search algorithm,

2. an intermediate-term memory component; this component is used for regionally **intensifying** the search, and,

3. a long-term memory component; this component is used for globally **diversifying** the search.

As will be elaborated in this chapter, the central idea underlying tabu search is the exploitation of the above three memory components. Using the short-term memory, a *selective history* **H** of the states encountered is maintained to guide the search process. Neighborhood $\aleph(S)$ is replaced by a modified neighborhood which is a function of the history **H**, and is denoted by $\aleph(\mathbf{H}, S)$. History determines which solutions may be reached by a move from S, since the next state S is selected from $\aleph(\mathbf{H}, S)$. The short-term memory component is implemented through a set of *tabu* conditions and the associated *aspiration criterion*.

The major idea of the short-term memory component is to classify certain search directions as tabu (or *forbidden*). By doing so we avoid returning to previously visited solutions. Search is therefore forced away from recently visited solutions, with the help of a memory known as *tabu list* **T**. This memory contains *attributes* of some k most recent moves. The size of the tabu list denoted by k is the number of iterations for which a move containing that attribute is forbidden after it has been made. The tabu list can be visualized as a window on accepted moves as shown in Figure 4.1. The moves which tend to undo previous moves within this window are forbidden.

Cycling back to previously visited solutions is prevented by the tabu list(s). However, since only move attributes (not complete solutions) are stored in tabu lists, these tabu moves may also prevent the consideration of some solutions which were *not* visited earlier. To relax the actions of tabu lists, aspiration criteria are introduced. Then, solutions that are the result of moves having attributes found in the tabu list are also considered *if* they satisfy the aspiration criteria. A flowchart illustrating the basic short-term memory tabu search algorithm is given in Figure 4.2. Intermediate-term and long-term memory processes are used to intensify and diversify the search respectively, and have been found to be effective in increasing both quality and efficiency [DV93, Glo95, Glo96].

In this chapter, we first introduce the basic tabu search algorithm based on the short-term memory component (Section 4.2). Then we will build the necessary background and the required terminology. Following this we present some practical issues of the tabu search algorithm for implementation on a digital computer (Section 4.3). Limitations of short-term memory, uses of intermediate- and long-term memories, and strategies for diversifying the search are explained in Sections 4.4 and 4.5. Convergence related issues are discussed in Section 4.6. In Section 4.7 we discuss some engineering applications, with case studies and examples, that further illustrate the implementation aspects of this powerful iterative technique. Parallelization related issues are discussed in Section 4.8. Other important and neglected issues such as target analysis, candidate list strategies, strategic oscillation, path relinking, and so forth, are discussed in Section 4.9.

4.2   Tabu Search Algorithm

An algorithmic description of a simple implementation of the tabu search is given in Figure 4.3. The procedure starts from an initial feasible solution S (current solution) in the search space Ω. A neighborhood $\aleph(S)$ is defined for each S. A sample of neighbor solutions $\mathbf{V}^* \subset \aleph(S)$ is generated. An extreme case is to generate the entire neighborhood, that is to take $\mathbf{V}^* = \aleph(S)$. Since this is generally impractical (computationally expensive), a small sample of neighbors $(\mathbf{V}^* \subset \aleph(S))$ is generated called *trial* solutions $(|\mathbf{V}^*| = n \ll |\aleph(S)|)$. From these trial solutions the best solution, say $S^* \in \mathbf{V}^*$, is chosen for consideration as the next solution. The move to S^* is considered even if S^* is worse than S, that is, $Cost(S^*) > Cost(S)$. A move from S to S^* is made provided certain conditions are satisfied.

Selecting the best move in $\mathbf{V}^*$ is based on the assumption that good moves are more likely to reach optimal or near-optimal solutions. As mentioned above, the best candidate solution $S^* \in \mathbf{V}^*$ *may* or *may not* improve the current solution,

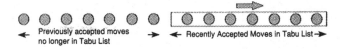

Previously accepted moves
no longer in Tabu List   ← Recently Accepted Moves in Tabu List →

Figure 4.1: The tabu list can be visualized as a window over accepted moves.

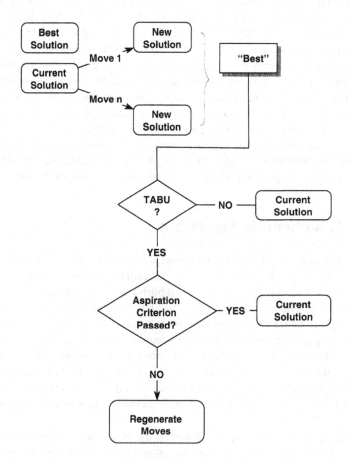

Figure 4.2: Flowchart of the tabu search algorithm.

Algorithm $Tabu\_Search()$;
Ω :   Set of feasible solutions.
S :   Current solution.
S^* :   Best admissible solution.
$Cost$:   Objective function.
$\aleph(S)$:   Neighborhood of $S \in \Omega$.
$\mathbf{V}^*$:   Sample of neighborhood solutions.
$\mathbf{T}$:   Tabu list.
$\mathbf{AL}$:   Aspiration Level.

       Begin
1.   Start with an initial feasible solution $S \in \Omega$;
2.   Initialize tabu lists and aspiration level;
3.   **For** fixed number of iterations **Do**
4.   Generate neighbor solutions $\mathbf{V}^* \subset \aleph(S)$;
5.   Find best $S^* \in \mathbf{V}^*$;
6.   **If** move S to S^* is not in $\mathbf{T}$ **Then**
7.   Accept move and update best solution;
8.   Update tabu list and aspiration level;
9.   Increment iteration number;
10.   **Else**
11.   **If** $Cost(S^*) < \mathbf{AL}$ **Then**
12.   Accept move and update best solution;
13.   Update tabu list and aspiration level;
14.   Increment iteration number;
15.   **EndIf**
16.   **EndIf**
17.   **EndFor**
       End.

Figure 4.3: Algorithmic description of short-term tabu search (TS).

but is still considered. It is this feature that enables *escaping* from local optima. However, even with this strategy, it is possible to reach a local optimum, ascend (in case of a minimization problem) since moves with $Cost(S^*) > Cost(S)$ are accepted, and then in a later iteration return back to the same local optimum. That is, there is a possibility of *cycling* by returning back to previously visited solutions. This may cause the search to go through the same subset of solutions for ever.

A tabu list is maintained to prevent returning to previously visited solutions. This list contains information that to some extent forbids the search from returning to a previously visited solution. It is *not* a list of solutions, since storing previously visited solutions, even a small number of them, and comparing them with newly generated ones would be expensive both in terms of computation time and memory requirement. Instead, selected move attributes are stored in the tabu list. Tabu restrictions therefore may also forbid moves to attractive *unvisited* solutions. For example, if a move is made tabu in iteration i and its reversal comes in iteration j, where $j = i + l$ and $1 < l < |\mathbf{T}|$, then it is possible that the reverse move, although tabu, may take the search into a new region because of the effects of $l - 1$ intermediate (previous) moves. It is therefore necessary to relax the actions of the tabu list and overrule the tabu status of moves in certain situations. This is done with the help of the notion of *aspiration criterion*.

Aspiration criterion is a device used to override the tabu status of moves whenever appropriate. It temporarily overrides the tabu status if the move is sufficiently good. The aspiration criterion must make sure that the reversal of a recently made move (that is, a move in the tabu list) leads the search to an unvisited solution, generally a better one.

Several aspiration criteria have been suggested and used in the literature. The customary one, also the simplest and most commonly used, overrides the tabu status if the reversal of a move in the tabu list produces a solution better than the best obtained thus far during the search. This is also known as *best solution* aspiration criterion. Other aspiration criteria will be discussed later (see Section 4.3.4).

Referring again to the algorithmic description in Figure 4.3, initially the current solution is the best solution. Copies of the current solution are perturbed with moves to get a set of new solutions. The best among these is selected and if it is not tabu then it becomes the current solution. If the move is tabu its aspiration criterion is checked. If it passes the aspiration criterion then it becomes the current solution. If the move to the next solution is accepted, then the move or some of its attributes are stored in the tabu list. Otherwise moves are regenerated to get another set of new solutions. If the current solution is better than the best seen thus far, then the best solution is updated. Whenever a move is accepted the iteration number is incremented. The procedure continues for a fixed number of iterations, or until some prespecified stopping criterion is satisfied.

Tabu restrictions and aspiration criterion have a symmetric role. The order of checking for tabu status and aspiration criterion may be reversed, though most applications check if a move is tabu before checking for aspiration criterion [Glo90c].

Below we explain some phrases and terms frequently used in this chapter. We will illustrate the working of the basic tabu search algorithm with the help of an example. Following this, we discuss various implementation-related issues.

Definitions

Trial solution: A solution generated from current solution S as a result of a move (denoted by S^{trial}).

Tabu restriction: A device to avoid cycling back to previously visited solutions by making selected attributes of moves tabu (forbidden). They allow the search to go beyond the points of local optimality.

Aspiration criterion: A device used to override the tabu status of a move whenever possible.

Candidate list: The list containing the subset of neighborhood moves examined.

Admissible neighborhood solutions: Those neighborhood solutions that are either nontabu or pass the aspiration criterion.

Attribute of a move: Any aspect (feature or component of a solution) that changes as a result of a move from S to S^{trial} can be an attribute of that move. A single move can have several attributes.

Recency based memory: A memory structure used to show how recently solutions have been visited, or how recently attributes of moves have changed. Generally a queue (FIFO) or an array is used.

Tabu tenure: The duration for which a move containing the particular tabu attribute is forbidden.

Move Evaluator: A composite function of cost and history of the search that is used to determine the "goodness" of a move.

Move_value: "Move_value" is the decrease in the cost function, or, more generally, a decrease in the move evaluator function.

Example 4.1 Consider the graph of five nodes and eight edges (e_1 to e_8) given in Figure 4.4. The problem is to find a minimal spanning tree subject to the following two constraints: (1) only one of the three edges e_3, e_7, or e_8 can appear in the tree, and (2) edge e_8 can appear in the tree only if edge e_6 appears in the tree. Since we have five nodes, the minimum cost tree will have exactly four edges. The edge names can be assigned 0-1 variables, $x_j, j = 1, \ldots, 8$, with the following meaning,

$$x_j = \begin{cases} 1 & \text{if edge } e_j \text{ is in the tree} \\ 0 & \text{if edge } e_j \text{ is not in the tree} \end{cases}$$

Then the constraints on the tree edges can be simply expressed as

$$x_3 + x_7 + x_8 \leq 1; \quad \text{and} \quad x_8 \leq x_6$$

The cost of each edge is given below.

Edges	e_1	e_2	e_3	e_4	e_5	e_6	e_7	e_8
Cost	13	7	9	1	3	19	10	7

To allow evaluations of trees that violate constraints, use an arbitrary penalty of 100 for each violation. Use the standard "edge swap" move to transform the current tree to a new tree. For tabu restriction, *prevent the dropping of three most recently added edges.* Override this tabu restriction (aspiration criterion) if the move produces a solution better than the best seen. Choose the size of the candidate list $|\mathbf{V}^*| = 4$ and tabu tenure $k = |\mathbf{T}| = 3$.

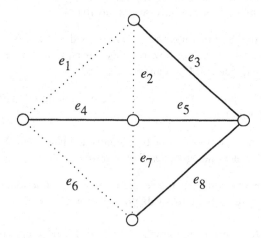

Figure 4.4: Graph for problem in Example 4.1. Cost of tree $= 9 + 1 + 3 + 7 + 2 \times 100 = 220$.

Solution Initially the tabu list is empty. Let the current solution consist of edges e_3, e_4, e_5, and e_8 (as shown by thick lines in Figure 4.4). The tree can be represented in a tabular form as shown below. Blank entries correspond to missing edges, nonblank entries are the costs of edges in the tree.

Current Solution

e_1	e_2	e_3	e_4	e_5	e_6	e_7	e_8
		9	1	3			7

Cost=220
Best Cost=220

In this tree both constraints are violated, that is, edges e_3 and e_8 exist in the tree when only one of them can appear (constraint 1), and, e_8 has appeared without e_6 (constraint 2). The cost of this tree therefore is 220 (sum of cost of edges + cost of two violations).

Iteration #1: Each iteration begins by generating a set $\mathbf{V}^*$ of neighboring solutions. Four neighboring solutions, called trial solutions, of the initial configuration are generated. They correspond to the following four trial swaps: (e_6,e_5), (e_6,e_8), (e_7,e_8), and (e_1,e_4). Each of these swaps corresponds to adding a missing edge and removing an existing edge to produce a new spanning tree. No move that creates a cycle in the graph is allowed. As shown in the table below, from the list of candidates, the swap (e_6,e_8) marked with an "$\ll$" corresponds to the best move, and is therefore chosen as the move to a new solution.

Four Neighbors of
Current Solution

Add	Drop	New Cost
e_6	e_5	136
e_6	e_8	32
e_7	e_8	123
e_1	e_4	232

$\ll$ (for the e_6, e_8 row)

Tabu Queue

e_6	ϕ	ϕ

Current Solution

e_1	e_2	e_3	e_4	e_5	e_6	e_7	e_8
		9	1	3	19		

Cost=32
Best Cost=32

The new solution produced by the accepted move is given in the table above. Since the tabu restriction is to prevent the dropping of the recently added edges, edge e_6 is added to the tabu list. We use a queue data structure to store the tabu attribute which consists in this case of the edge added. The cost of the current solution is 32.

Iteration #2: As in the previous case, once again four new neighbors are generated by swapping edges (e_1,e_5), (e_7,e_4), (e_8,e_4), and (e_8,e_5). Since our move attribute that is to be assigned a tabu status is the edge that has been added, that is edge e_6, and none of our swaps in the candidate list consist of dropping this tabu edge, none of the generated moves are tabu.

Four Neighbors of
Current Solution

Add	Drop	New Cost
e_1	e_5	42	≪
e_7	e_4	141
e_8	e_4	138
e_8	e_5	136

Tabu Queue

e_1	e_6	ϕ

Current Solution

e_1	e_2	e_3	e_4	e_5	e_6	e_7	e_8
13		9	1		19		

Cost=42
Best Cost=32

The best neighboring move is the swap (e_1,e_5), consisting of the inclusion of edge e_1 and the removal of edge e_5. This move increases the cost to 42 (an uphill move). Edge e_1 is now added to the tabu queue, and edge e_6 is shifted in by one position.

Iteration #3: The four moves of the next iteration and the cost of the corresponding new solution are shown below. Once again none of the moves in the candidate list is tabu.

Four Neighbors of
Current Solution

Add	Drop	New Cost
e_8	e_3	40
e_2	e_4	48
e_5	e_3	36	≪
e_5	e_4	44

Tabu Queue

e_5	e_1	e_6

Current Solution

e_1	e_2	e_3	e_4	e_5	e_6	e_7	e_8
13			1	3	19		

Cost=36
Best Cost=32

As before, the best move is accepted, edge e_5 is inserted into the tabu queue, and the cost is updated to 36.

Iteration #4: The same steps as above are repeated. A new situation is seen in this iteration. Observe in the table below that the best neighbor move consists of swap (e_7,e_6), that is, adding of edge e_7 and dropping of edge e_6. But dropping edge e_6 is forbidden (tabu), since it is still in the tabu queue. However, the cost of the solution generated as a result of this move is only 27, better than the best cost seen until now. Since this move satisfies our aspiration criterion, the tabu status is overruled, and the move is accepted. Note that the swap (e_7,e_6) is better than the other tabu move (e_2,e_1), which also satisfies the aspiration criterion.

Four Neighbors of
Current Solution

Add	Drop	New Cost	
e_3	e_4	44	
e_7	e_6	27	T≪
e_2	e_1	30	T
e_8	e_4	42	

Tabu Queue

e_7	e_5	e_1

Current Solution

e_1	e_2	e_3	e_4	e_5	e_6	e_7	e_8
13			1	3		10	

Cost=27
Best Cost=27

The new solution is shown above. The cost is 27, and the tabu queue is updated by inserting edge e_7. Since the size of the tabu queue is only 3, edge e_6 is thrown out and therefore is no longer tabu.

Iteration #5: A situation similar to that encountered in the previous iteration is seen once again. A tabu move takes us to a solution with a new best cost of 21.

Four Neighbors of
Current Solution

Add	Drop	New Cost	
e_6	e_4	45	
e_2	e_1	21	T≪
e_3	e_4	135	
e_3	e_5	133	T

Tabu Queue

e_2	e_7	e_5

Current Solution

e_1	e_2	e_3	e_4	e_5	e_6	e_7	e_8
	7		1	3		10	

Cost=21
Best Cost=21

The new set of moves is shown above. Observe, that a new best solution (with $Cost = 21$) is generated by the swap (e_2, e_1). Although this swap is tabu, the aspiration criteria is once again satisfied. The move is accepted, and the above procedure continues for a given fixed number of iterations, or until any specified stopping criterion is met.

∎

4.3 Implementation-Related Issues

In the previous example we illustrated some basic characteristics of the short-term tabu search heuristic. There are several variations of the above method that can be incorporated. Below we give a flavor of some of these variations which are related to moves and their attributes, tabu lists and their sizes, possible data structures, aspiration criteria, and so forth [GL95].

4.3.1 Move Attributes

To prevent the reversal of moves, we may store the move, the reverse move, or some attributes of the move. Any aspect that changes as a result of the move from S to S^{trial} can be an attribute of that move. If the reversal of the move is stored then it is prevented, but if only the move attributes are stored then all moves with those attributes are prevented (if made within the next k iterations). Different attributes restrict the search of the state space differently. A move can be thought of as consisting of several components. In our previous example, we used a *swap* of edges to move from one solution to another. This move consists of at least two attributes, an *added edge* and a *dropped edge*. Other possible attributes could be, the change in cost, the change in a function (independent of cost) that depends on the search strategy, and so on.

In many combinatorial optimization problems we can encode our solution S as a bit vector. For example, the initial solution to the MST problem in Example 4.1 can be represented by the following 8-bit vector [0 0 1 1 1 0 0 1]; a 1/0 corresponds to the presence/absence of edge in the tree, the left-most bit corresponds to index 1 or edge e_1, and the rightmost bit (bit 8) corresponds to edge e_8.

If we assume a binary encoding of solutions, some possible attributes that can be stored in the tabu memory are [GL95]:

1. Changing a selected variable x_j from 0 to 1 (corresponds to the added edge e_j).

2. Changing a selected variable x_k from 1 to 0 (corresponds to the dropped edge e_k).

3. Both of the above, that is, the change of x_j from 0 to 1, and of x_k from 1 to 0, is another attribute.

4. Another aspect that changes as a result of the move and can be used as a move attribute is the change in cost or the objective function value from $Cost(S)$ to $Cost(S^{\text{trial}})$.

5. Instead of relying on the cost, a function say $\mathcal{G}(S)$ that depends on the problem formulation or the search strategy may be used. Then the attribute stored could be the change of the function $\mathcal{G}(S)$ to $\mathcal{G}(S^{\text{trial}})$, or the change represented by the difference $\mathcal{G}(S) - \mathcal{G}(S^{\text{trial}})$. The function $\mathcal{G}(S)$ chosen may be independent of the objective function. For example, it may be a measure of the difference between the solution S and some reference solution. An example of a reference solution may be the best solution seen so far ($BestS$).

6. Any combination of the above may also be used as an attribute of the move.

4.3.2 Tabu List and Tabu Restrictions

Move attributes are used to impose tabu restrictions to prevent reversal of changes represented by these attributes. A tabu restriction is imposed only when the attributes satisfy certain thresholds of recency (or sometimes frequency). Generally, if a move contains attribute m, then the reverse attribute $\overline{m}$ is stored in the tabu list.

Sometimes, the entire move (or the reverse move) is stored. For example, in the swap move, an ordered pair of elements that are swapped is stored. Using ordered pairs of combinations in tabu restrictions does not prevent cycling. For example, a sequence of two or more swaps can result in a cycle. To avoid this, the ordered pairs are broken into $from\_attributes$ and $to\_attributes$. For example, the swap (e_2, e_3) (e_2 added to the tree and e_3 deleted) can be thought of as x_2 changing $from$ 0 to 1, and x_3 changing from 1 to 0. Then, the attribute that corresponds to preventing an added edge from being deleted will be changing x_2 $from$ 1 to 0, or simply $from[x_2] = 0$. That is, for the move attribute $from[x_2] = 0$ the corresponding tabu attribute will be $to[x_2] = 0$. Now if we impose the condition that the $to\_attribute$ of a current move is not a $from\_attribute$ of a previous move, cycling can be avoided [DV93, GL95].

In addition to preventing cycling, clearly, tabu restrictions also play the role of inducing vigor in the search. It should also be mentioned here, that cycle avoidance is not the ultimate goal of the search process since sometimes it may be better to backtrack to previously visited solutions and start again in another direction. Below we enumerate some examples of tabu restrictions. A move is tabu if [GL95]:

1. A variable x_j changes from 0 to 1 (assuming that earlier this value changed from 1 to 0).

2. A variable x_k changes from 1 to 0 (assuming that earlier this value changed from 0 to 1).

3. At least one of the above restrictions in (1) and (2) occurs (this makes more moves tabu).

4. Both of the above restrictions in (1) and (2) occur (this makes fewer moves tabu).

5. A function $\mathcal{H}(S)$ receives a value v that it received in a previous iteration, that is, $v = \mathcal{H}(S')$ for some previously visited solution S'. $\mathcal{H}(S)$ changes from v'' to v' where $\mathcal{H}(S)$ changed from v' to v'' on a previous iteration. That is, $v' = \mathcal{H}(S')$ and $v'' = \mathcal{H}(S'')$ for some pair of solutions S' and S'' previously visited in sequence.

Tabu List Size

One of the parameters of the algorithm is the size of the tabu list. In our example we used a tabu list of fixed size (3). Generally tabu list size is small. This corresponds to the short-term memory tabu search.

Early experiments on practical problems reported good performance with list sizes varying between 5 and 12. The magic number 7 is also used in many applications. Results of recent experiments show that tabu list size must be a function of the search/solution space, and the type of tabu restrictions used [Glo90c]. As a general rule, the more stringent the tabu restriction is the smaller should be the size of the tabu list [GL95]. The size can be determined by experimental runs, watching for occurrence of cycling when the size is too small, and the deterioration of solution quality when the size is too large [GTdW93]. Several rules have been proposed in the literature to determine this value. For static tabu lists, suggested values of k include 7, $\sqrt{N}$, N, and so on (where N is related to the problem size, for example, number of modules to be assigned in the quadratic assignment problem (QAP), or the number of cities to be visited in the TSP, and so on) [Glo86, Osm93].

In Example 4.1 (see page 189) we had only one tabu restriction, and we used a single tabu list. Multiple tabu lists, one for each attribute are recommended and have also been used, where the size of each list depends on the tabu restriction [Glo90c]. In addition to different tabu tenures used for different attributes, a variety of aspiration criteria may also be associated with each tabu list.

Example 4.2 In Example 4.1, the tabu restriction was to prevent the dropping of a recently added edge. Another tabu restriction could be the reverse of this, that is, *"to prevent adding of a recently dropped edge."* In this case our move attribute will be to store the dropped edge in the first in, first out (FIFO) tabu list. In applications where the number of elements to be dropped from a solution are *fewer* than those to be added, a tabu restriction that prevents previously dropped edges from being added back to the solution allows a greater degree of flexibility in the search. A general recommendation is to select those attributes whose tabu status imposes lesser restriction on the choice (or number) of available moves [Glo90c]. For example, in the problem of finding the minimal-cost spanning tree, preventing the addition of recently dropped edges gives more flexibility than preventing the dropping of added ones. This is because for a graph with n vertices, there are approximately $O(n)$ edges ($n - 1$ precisely in our case) from which one should be chosen to be dropped while there are approximately $O(n^2)$ edges from which one can be chosen to be added.

■

Dynamic Lists

A small tabu list size is preferred for exploring the solution near a local optimum, and a larger tabu list size is preferable for breaking free of the vicinity of a local minimum. Varying the tabu list size during the search process provides one way to take advantage of this effect.

Dynamic rules have been found to be more robust than static rules [DV93, GL95, GTdW93, Glo90b, LG93a] (see Section 4.7.2). When using a dynamic tabu list, its size will be varied between some bounds t_{min} and t_{max}, for example 5 (t_{min}) and 12 (t_{max}).

In the solution of the quadratic assignment problem (QAP) using tabu search [Tai91] the size of the tabu list is selected randomly from an interval ranging from $t_{min} = \lfloor 0.9N \rfloor$ to the value $t_{max} = \lceil 1.1N \rceil$ where N is the dimension of the problem (see page 196). The size of the list is changed approximately every $2 \times k$ iterations from its current value to one that is randomly selected between the minimum and maximum allowed size. Other variations of dynamic tabu lists have also been reported. Some of these will be discussed in Section 4.7 related to case studies.

Based on the problem characteristics, an appropriate size of the tabu list can also be estimated. For the vehicle routing [Osm93] problem (see Chapter 1, page 7) where the parameters are n, v, and ρ (n the number of customers, v the number of vehicles, and $\rho = \frac{q_i}{Q}$ is the ratio of the required demands q_i, and the available vehicle capacities Q) experimental data had been used to estimate a good size (k) for tabu list values. Regression is employed on data from experimental runs with various problem sizes (that is, values, of n, v, ρ, and so on). For one particular heuristic, the size k was estimated to be [Osm93]

$$k = 8 + (0.078 - 0.076 \times \rho) \times n \times v \tag{4.1}$$

For another heuristic to solve the same problem, [Osm93], the value of k was estimated to be

$$k = \max\{7, -40 + 9.6 \times \ln(n \times v)\} \tag{4.2}$$

Since k is statistically estimated, an error might occur. Therefore, its value is varied to take in a systematic order each of the three values $0.9k$, k, and, $1.1k$. The size of the tabu list is changed every $2 \times k$ iterations.

4.3.3   Data Structure to Handle Tabu Lists

Arrays are convenient data structures to store moves or their attributes. Two arrays tabu_start(m) and tabu_end(m) may be used, where m represents the move attributes. The size of the array depends on the problem. The array tabu_start(m) stores the iteration number when the attribute m becomes tabu and tabu_end(m) stores the iteration number when the attribute m loses its tabu status. In each iteration, attributes that are components of the current move are used to update the above arrays.

As an example, if element e_3 is the attribute of a current move (say a dropped edge from a tree) in iteration i, and tabu_start(m) and tabu_end(m) represent the arrays that indicate the iteration numbers between which the addition of the dropped edge is forbidden, then tabu_start(e_3), or simply tabu_start(3) is set to $(i + 1)$ and tabu_end(3) is set to $(i + k)$ where k is the tabu tenure (size of the tabu list). To check if any attribute is tabu_active, we just have to check if tabu_end(m)$\geq$ *current_iteration number*. It is sufficient to only maintain array tabu_start since the value tabu_end(m) can be derived from the value of tabu_start(m), that is, tabu_end(m)= tabu_start(m) + $k - 1$.

Move attributes can also be stored in a queue as was done in Example 4.1. Every time a move to a new state is accepted, its attribute is inserted into the tabu queue, and the oldest attribute in the queue is deleted. A circular queue initialized to null values can be used to implement such a tabu list. The size of the memory required to implement a queue is much lesser than that required by array tabu_start. When queues are used, an additional array denoted by tabu_status(m) can be used to help quickly check if the attribute under consideration is tabu_active or not. Whenever an attribute (denoted by new_attribute) is inserted in the queue, and the old attribute (denoted by old_attribute) deleted from it, the tabu_status array can be updated as follows:

tabu_status(old_attribute)=0   old_attribute no longer tabu
tabu_status(new_attribute)=1   new_attribute becomes tabu

Queues can also be used to store swaps. For permutation problems, another convenient data structure to store swaps is a 2-D matrix of size $n \times n$ (n represents

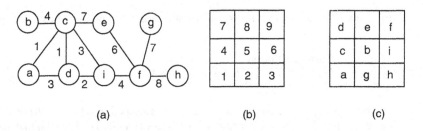

(a)   (b)   (c)

Figure 4.5: (a) Graph whose nodes are to be assigned. (b) Position definition (labels of slots). (c) One possible assignment.

the number of elements in the problem). Only the upper diagonal matrix is sufficient to store the tabu tenure of each swap. Every time swap (i, j) is made, element $M(i, j)$ is assigned a value k, and the remaining nonzero entries are decremented by 1 (that is, $M(p, q) = M(p, q) - 1$, $p \neq i, q \neq j$). We shall illustrate the use of this data structure in the example below (Example 4.3) and also show how the lower diagonal matrix can be used to store the frequency of swaps which are useful in diversifying the search.

Example 4.3 Consider the graph of Figure 4.5(a). The illustration is repeated here from Chapter 3 for convenience. The nine vertices represent modules and the numbers on the edges represent their weighted interconnections. The problem is to use tabu search to assign the nine modules to the nine slots in a way that requires the smallest amount of wire to interconnect them.

The nine modules can be assigned to the nine slots as shown in Figure 4.5(c). We can also represent the solution as a 1-D array. For example, the solution in Figure 4.5(c) can be represented as shown below.

Solution of Figure 4.5(c)

Location	1	2	3	4	5	6	7	8	9
Cell	a	g	h	c	b	i	d	e	f

It can also be represented as a string "aghcbidef," where the leftmost slot index of the string corresponds to slot "1" of Figure 4.5(b) and the rightmost to slot 9.

Use standard "module swap" as a move to transform the current assignment to a new one. For tabu restriction, prevent the reversal of the four most recent swaps ($k = 4$). Override this tabu restriction (aspiration criterion) if the tabu swap produces a solution better than the best seen. Choose size of the candidate list $|V^*| = 3$. Illustrate the first six iterations of tabu search.

Solution We can begin with the initial solution given below whose cost is 85.

Current Solution

| a | b | c | d | e | f | g | h | i | Cost=85

A tabu list can be used to store pairs of swapped modules. Another way to keep track of recently made moves is to use a matrix. The tabu matrix is initialized to zero. During each iteration, location (i, j) of the matrix will hold an integer that represents the number of iterations for which the swap of pair (i, j) is tabu. Only the upper half of the tabu matrix is sufficient. Such a matrix structure is convenient if we are to use it later to store not only tabu swaps, but also frequencies of swaps.

Iteration #1: The three neighbors of the initial solution and the gain of each are tabulated below.

Three Neighbors of
Current Solution

Swap	Gain
b↔d	- 6	≪
a↔c	-10
c↔i	-10

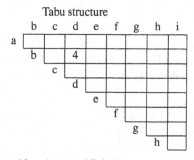

Tabu structure

New Accepted Solution

| a | d | c | b | e | f | g | h | i | Cost=91
Best Cost=85

The best solution from the candidate list is the swap (b, d). Although all moves lead to a solution poorer than the current one, the best among these is chosen. The entry in location $(b, d) = 4$ indicates that this swap will remain tabu for the next four consecutive iterations. The new accepted solution has a cost of 91 and is shown above.

Iteration #2: Three new neighbors of the above solution are generated. This time we have a solution better than the current solution resulting from the swap (e, i). A new entry in location (e, i) is made, and entry in the other location (b, d) is reduced to 3.

Three Neighbors of
Current Solution

Swap	Gain	
e↔i	4	≪
d↔f	-10	
a↔g	-8	

Tabu structure

	b	c	d	e	f	g	h	i
a								
b			3					
c								
d								
e								4
f								
g								
h								

New Accepted Solution

a	d	c	b	i	f	g	h	e

Cost=87
Best Cost=85

Iteration #3: The same procedure is repeated and the best among them [swap (c, i)] is chosen. No tabu moves have yet appeared. Observe the new entry made and the previous entries decremented by one. The cost of the new solution is 79 (which is also the best solution seen so far).

Three Neighbors of
Current Solution

Swap	Gain	
c↔i	8	≪
a↔g	-8	
c↔d	-4	

Tabu structure

	b	c	d	e	f	g	h	i
a								
b		2						
c								4
d								
e								3
f								
g								
h								

New Accepted Solution

a	d	i	b	c	f	g	h	e

Cost=79
Best Cost=79

Iteration #4: In this iteration, another good move [swap (b, g)] is made and the cost further reduces by 3 units. This is the last iteration in which the first move, swap (b, d), is tabu. It loses its tabu status after this iteration.

Three Neighbors of
Current Solution

Swap	Gain
a↔h	-10
b↔g	3	≪
f↔i	-20

Tabu structure

	b	c	d	e	f	g	h	i
a								
b		1			4			
c								3
d								
e								2
f								
g								
h								

New Accepted Solution

a	d	i	g	c	f	b	h	e

Cost=76
Best Cost=76

Iteration #5: In this iteration we see that two of the three moves made are tabu, since they have nonzero entries in our tabu matrix. We therefore select an alternative swap (b, f) which yields a decrease in cost of wire-length by one unit.

Three Neighbors of
Current Solution

Swap	Gain	
e↔i	-4	T
b↔f	1	≪
b↔d	-6	T

Tabu structure

	b	c	d	e	f	g	h	i
a								
b		0		4	3			
c								2
d								
e								1
f								
g								
h								

New Accepted Solution

a	d	i	g	c	b	f	h	e

Cost=75
Best Cost=75

Iteration #6: In this final iteration, once again we see two of the three moves tabu. The best move $[(c, i)]$ has a tabu tenure of 2, but satisfies our aspiration criterion, and is therefore accepted. The tabu matrix is updated, entry (c, i) is made 4, and other nonzero entries are decremented by one. The solution resulting after the first six iterations is shown below.

Three Neighbors of
Current Solution

Swap	Gain	
b↔g	-14	T
c↔i	8	T≪
a↔f	-26	

Tabu structure

	b	c	d	e	f	g	h	i
a								
b		0		3	2			
c								4
d								
e								0
f								
g								
h								

New Accepted Solution

a	d	c	g	i	b	f	h	e

Cost=67
Best Cost=67

∎

4.3.4 Other Aspiration Criteria

As discussed above, a simple type of aspiration criterion consists of overriding the tabu status when the move yields a solution that is better than the best seen so far, that is, $Cost(S^{\text{trial}}) < Cost(BestS)$. This is also known as *Global Aspiration by Objective* and is most widely used. A variation of this method is the *Regional Aspiration by Objective* which consists of subdividing the search space into regions $\Omega_r \in \Omega$. As a special case of regional aspiration by objective, a hashing function $g(S)$ may be defined to distinguish between different solutions. The region Ω_r can then be identified by placing bounds on values of $g(S)$ [GL95, LZ93]. For example, $\Omega_r = \{S : g(S) = r\}$. Then, if $BestCost(\Omega_r)$ is the minimum $Cost(S)$ for $S \in \Omega_r$, a move aspiration is satisfied if $Cost(S^{\text{trial}}) < best\_Cost(\Omega_r)$ [GL95, LZ93].

Another aspiration criterion is based on the direction of the search and is known as *Aspiration by Search Direction*. Here, if an improving move m is made, then the reverse move $\overline{m}$ in the tabu list is accepted if it is also an improving move. A vector "direction" similar to tabu_end is used where $direction(m)$ is set to a value *improving* or *nonimproving* depending on the move; $direction(m) = improving$ (*nonimproving*) if the most recent move containing $\overline{m}$ was an improving (nonimproving) move. An attribute aspiration for m is satisfied making it tabu-inactive if $direction(m) = improving$ and the current trial move is an improving move, that is if $Cost(S^{\text{trial}}) < Cost(S)$. In other words, aspiration of a move m is satisfied if the move leads to a solution with a lower cost and its reversal also leads to a solution with a lower cost than that of the current solution.

As an example consider the swap (c, i) in iteration #3 of Example 4.3 (page 201). This is an improving move, since it leads to a new solution with a gain of 8. The tabu tenure chosen was 4. In iteration #6 the swap of the same pair reverses the move (page 203). This move is tabu, however, the move may be accepted since the reversal is also an improving move. Swap (c, i) in iteration #6 results in gain=8. (Note that we have used the iterations of Example 4.3 only as an illustration; the aspiration criterion used there is different.)

A degree of change in the solution structure or quality called *"influence"* can also be used to define an aspiration criterion called *Aspiration By Move Influence*. The greater the change in the structure or solution quality due to a move, the larger we say is its influence. Influence can also be thought of as associated with distance. A high-influence move takes the solution farther away from the current solution. Therefore, if a low-influence move is made, its reversal can be accepted provided a high influence move is made prior to the reversal [GTdW93]. The reason for this is that if a high-influence move is made between two low-influence moves, and if these low-influence moves are the reverse of one another, then the reversal of the low-influence move will most likely not be a previously visited solution.

To further understand the notion of move "influence," consider the graph bisection problem (see Chapter 1, page 7) where it is required to bisect a graph with vertices having varying weights, into two subgraphs, each subgraph having approximately the same weight. A high-influence move, which significantly changes the structure of the current solution can be a swap of two vertices of dissimilar sizes (or weights). High-influence moves may or may not improve the current solution, but are important especially when it is required to break away from local optima. This is because a series of moves that is confined to making only small changes is unlikely to discover good solutions [GL95].

The strategy when employing *aspiration by move influence* may be as follows. Moves of lower influence are applied until any further gain from them appears unlikely. At this point, and in the absence of improving moves, aspiration criteria can shift to give influential moves more importance. And once an influential move is made, tabu restrictions previously determined for less influential moves may be dropped.

Let us assume that moves are classified into two categories based on their influence L; "0" for low-influence moves, and "1" for high-influence moves; $influence(m) = 0/1$ depending on whether the move m is a low- or high-influence move. Let $latest(L)$, $L=0$ or 1, be the most recent iteration where a move of influence level L was made. Then an aspiration attribute for m is satisfied if $influence(m) = 0$ and $tabu\_start(m) < latest(1)$, that is, m is associated with a low-influence move, and a high-influence move has been performed since establishing the tabu status for m. In general, for multiple levels of influence, $L = 0, 1, 2, \ldots$, the aspiration by influence for m is satisfied if there is an $L > influence(m)$ and $tabu\_start(m) < latest(L)$.

In situations when all available moves are classified tabu, and are not admissible by any aspiration criteria, then the least tabu move may be selected. This criterion is also known as *Aspiration by Default*. An example of least tabu move may be the move that is least recent in the tabu queue.

Another approach is to employ the same attribute of the move that is used to identify the tabu status and associate an aspiration level value with it. The reversal has to do better than this historical aspiration level. In some applications, it has been found useful to give aspiration level a *tenure* that parallels the tenure of the tabu list. This means that the aspiration level of the selected attribute is updated whenever that move is made tabu and whenever the aspiration level criterion is passed. More details on above and other proposals for aspiration criterion are suggested in [GL95].

4.4   Limitations of Short-Term Memory

In many applications, the short-term memory component by itself has produced solutions superior to those found by alternative procedures, and usually the use of intermediate-term and long-term memory is bypassed. However, several studies have shown that intermediate and long-term memory components can improve solution quality and/or performance [DV93, IE94, MGPO89, Rya89].

Below we illustrate with the help of an example, how the short-term memory component based on tabu restrictions and aspiration criteria alone will not direct the search toward an optimal solution. Once again we will use the example of finding a minimal cost spanning tree with constraints [Glo90c].

> **Example 4.4**   A graph with five nodes and nine edges (e_1 to e_9) is shown in Figure 4.6(a). As in the previous example we would like to find a minimal-cost spanning tree subject to the following constraints:
>
> $$x_5 + x_6 \leq 2x_9 \quad \text{and} \quad x_7 \leq x_6$$
>
> The cost of each edge is given in the table below.

Edge	e_1	e_2	e_3	e_4	e_5	e_6	e_7	e_8	e_9
Cost	20	18	19	18	9	8	10	17	29

> To allow evaluations of trees that violate the constraints, as before, let us use an arbitrarily chosen penalty of 100 for each violation.
>
> Figure 4.6(b) shows the minimum cost optimal tree that satisfies both constraints. Our objective in this example is to intuitively argue, that starting from the tree given in Figure 4.6(a), the use of short-term memory component alone will not drive the search to the optimal tree [Glo90c].

Solution   The cost of the initial solution [Figure 4.6(a)] is the sum of the cost of edges plus the cost of two violations since edges e_5 and e_6 can appear in the tree only when edge e_9 appears. Since the first constraint is violated by two units, the cost of the initial tree is 54 + 200= 254. Now as we proceed in the search, in order to satisfy constraint $x_5 + x_6 \leq 2x_9$, moves that lead us from this initial solution will tend to drop edges e_5 and e_6 rather than add the high-cost edge e_9, $Cost(e_9) = 29$. Further, once a feasible solution is obtained from which edge e_9 is excluded, the chances that it will be reintroduced are low. For example, if we reach the solution with edges e_2, e_3, e_4, and e_8 (with $Cost = 72$), then we cannot add edge e_7 until we add edge e_6, (constraint 2), and edges e_6 and e_5 cannot be added until we add edge e_9

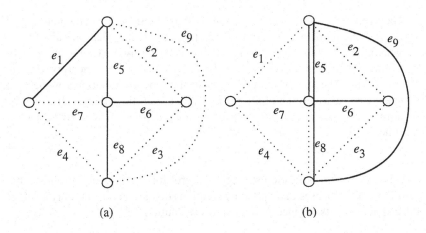

(a)   (b)

Figure 4.6: (a) Tree of initial solution of Example 4.4. (b) Optimal solution of Example 4.4.

which is an expensive edge. Therefore it is not likely that we will reach the optimal solution shown.

Increasing the size of the tabu list will also not remedy the situation. Clearly, there are situations where the short-term memory component alone fails to discover the right move to drive the solution into new regions (diversify).
∎

Having studied the short-term memory component and seen its limitation, we now proceed to look at the intermediate-term and long-term memory functions. As will be illustrated, these components can be added modularly to the basic TS technique based on a short-term criteria.

4.4.1   Intermediate-Term Memory (Search Intensification)

The basic role of the intermediate-term memory component is to *intensify* the search. By its incorporation, the search becomes more aggressive. As the name suggests, memory is used to intensify the search.

Intermediate-term memory component operates as follows. A selected number $m \gg |\mathbf{T}|$ (recall that $|\mathbf{T}|$ is the size of tabu list) of best trial solutions generated during a particular period of search are chosen and their features are recorded and compared. These solutions may be m consecutive best ones, or m local optimal solutions reached during the search. Features common to most of these are then taken and new solutions that contain these features are sought. One way to accomplish this is to restrict/penalize moves that remove such attributes.

Example 4.5 For example, in the TSP problem with moderately dense graphs, the number of different edges that can be included into any tour is generally a fraction of the total available edges (Why?). After some number of initial iterations, the method can discard all edges not yet incorporated into some tour. The size of the problem and the time per iteration now become smaller. The search therefore can focus on possibilities that are likely to be attractive, and can also examine many more alternatives in a given span of time.

∎

This type of intensification strategy is useful for solving large problems because the search focuses on generating solutions that are good, and only a subset of decision elements are incorporated in these solutions.

4.4.2 Long-Term Memory (Search Diversification)

The goal of long-term memory component is to *diversify* the search. The principles involved here are just the *opposite* of those used by the intermediate-term memory function. Instead of more intensively focusing the search with regions that contain previously found good solutions, the function of this component is to drive the search process into new regions that are different from those examined thus far.

Diversification is used to explore new regions of the solution space. Most heuristic search techniques use or have a built in mechanism for diversifying the search. Without diversification, the search can become localized in a small area of the solution space, eliminating the possibility of finding a global optimum.

The introduction of randomization to achieve diversification is common among search procedures such as simulated annealing and genetic algorithms. Simulated annealing incorporates randomization to make diversification a function of temperature (see Chapter 2). Genetic algorithms (Chapter 3) also use randomization in crossover, mutation, and, selection, to diversify the search. Diversification strategies in tabu search are designed and used in a number of ways. The long-term memory component is used to incorporate diversification. Generally there appears to be a hidden assumption that diversification must tantamount to randomization [KLG94]. However, in tabu search deterministic diversification is employed with the help of short- and long-term memories.

Diversification using long-term memory in tabu search can be accomplished by creating an evaluator whose task is to take the search to new starting points [Glo89b]. For example, in the TSP, a simple form of long-term memory is to keep a count of the number of times each edge has appeared in the tours previously generated. Then, an evaluator can be used to penalize each edge on the basis of this count, thereby favoring the generation of "other hopefully good" starting tours that tend to avoid those edges most commonly used in the past. This sort of approach is viewed as a **frequency**-based tabu criterion in contrast to the **recency**-based (tabu list) illustrated above. Such a long-term strategy can be employed by means of a long-term tabu list (or any other appropriate data structure) which is periodically activated to employ tabu conditions of increased stringency, thereby forcing the search process into new territory.

It is easy to create and test the short-term memory component first, and then incorporate the intermediate/long components for additional refinements. Below we illustrate this by two examples. One is an optimization problem based on the short-term memory component. The other example illustrates how frequency can be accommodated in the previous example to diversify the search. Examples of other techniques used for diversification are discussed in Section 4.5.

Penalizing Frequent Moves

We now illustrate how the long-term memory can be incorporated to diversify the search process. To do this, we use the same matrix data structure used in our earlier example (Example 4.3, page 199). Recall that the upper diagonal matrix was used to store the recency information. We will use the lower diagonal matrix to store the frequency of moves made. That is, each entry (i, j) in the lower diagonal matrix stores the number of times the swap (i, j) was made. We can then use this information to define a move evaluator $\mathcal{E}(\mathbf{H}, S)$, which is a function of both the cost of the solution, and the frequency of the swaps stored. Our objective is to diversify the search by giving more consideration to those swaps that have not been made yet, and to penalize those that frequently occurred [LG93a]. Therefore, the design of the evaluator must be such that moves that most frequently occurred in the past are given less consideration. For example, if a swap (i, j) was made to take the solution from current state S to a new state S^*, and the term $\text{Freq}(i, j)$ is the number of times swap (i, j) was made, then the evaluation of the move can be expressed as follows:

$$\mathcal{E}(\mathbf{H}, S^*) = \begin{cases} Cost(S^*) & Cost(S^*) \leq Cost(S) \\ Cost(S^*) + \alpha \times \text{Freq}(i, j) & Cost(S^*) > Cost(S) \end{cases}$$

α is constant which depends on the range of the objective function values, the number of iterations, the span of history considered, etc. Its value (α's) is such that cost and frequency are appropriately balanced.

Example 4.6 For the problem in Example 4.3 (page 199), the solution after 30 moves is given below.

Solution After 30 Moves   Cost=95

a	g	e	f	d	h	b	i	c

Best Cost=67

The number of times each move has been made is given in the lower diagonal matrix. We will illustrate how this information can be used to diversify the search.

Tabu structure

(Recency)

Solution	a	b	c	d	e	f	g	h	i
a	■						2		
b		■						3	
c		1	■						4
d	2	1	1	■					
e			2		■				1
f		3		1		■			
g	3	1	1				■		
h		3		1				■	
i		1	4	3	1		1		■

(Frequency)

For the sake of illustration, let us use a candidate list of size 5. The five neighbors of the current solution are given in the table below:

Five Neighbors of
Current Solution

Swap	Gain	Penalized Gain	$\mathcal{E}(\mathbf{H}, S)$	
a↔g	11	11	84	T
f↔b	-21	-36	131	
i↔g	-6	-6	101	≪
a↔d	-4	-14	109	
c↔b	-12	-17	112	

In the table above, the first move, swap (a, g) is the only move with a positive gain (see column 2), but this move is tabu, does not satisfy our aspiration criterion, and is therefore not considered. For the remaining moves, those with negative gains, we will resort to our evaluator.

$$\mathcal{E}(\mathbf{H}, S^*) = Cost(S^*) + \text{Penalty-term}$$
$$= Cost(S^*) + 5 \times \text{Freq}(i, j)$$

The "Penalized Gain" is obtained by adding the "penalty term" to the gain of the move. We use a value of $\alpha=5$ since for our cost values between 60 and 120, this value seems reasonable. In our case, we chose to diversify once every 30 iterations, In a later section (Section 4.9.2), we explain how the values of parameters such as α, are determined.

From the table above, the swap (i, g) has the smallest value of $\mathcal{E}(\mathbf{H}, S)$, hence it becomes the accepted move. Observe that of all the moves with negative gains, the swap (a, d) has the largest nonpenalized value (of -4). However, the penalty incurred because Freq(a, d) is high since this swap has been made two times, whereas swap (i, g) has not yet been made. Thus accepting the swap (i, g) will hopefully take the search into new regions.

■

4.5 Examples of Diversifying Search

In this section we will illustrate how *deterministic* diversification is employed in tabu search using two examples, the quadratic assignment problem (QAP) and the processor scheduling problem.

4.5.1 Diversification in Quadratic Assignment (QAP)

The diversification strategy presented here was studied by Kelly et al. [KLG94] for the quadratic assignment problem. The technique suggested can be extended to other permutation problems, and can be integrated with other heuristics.

The QAP can be viewed as a permutation problem with the following objective function:

$$\text{Minimize} \sum_{i=1}^{n-1} \sum_{j=i+1}^{n} f_{ij} d_{\pi(i)\pi(j)} \tag{4.3}$$

In this function, f_{ij} is the flow between objects i and j, $d_{\pi(i)\pi(j)}$ is the distance between the locations where objects i and j are placed, and n is the total number of objects or locations. A feasible solution is then given by $\Pi = \{\pi(1), \pi(2), \ldots, \pi(n)\}$, where $\pi(i)$ is the index of the location that contains object i.

The method to solve the QAP problem proposed in [KLG94] starts by using the local search procedure with pairwise swap as a move strategy. This procedure is extremely fast but rarely finds the optimal solution. Tabu search based on short-term memory can also be used. Then, a completely deterministic diversification approach with no reliance on randomization is used to move away from the local minimum. When the current solution is determined to be sufficiently far away from the previous local minimum, or, if a new best solution is found during this stage, the diversification restrictions are lifted and the local search procedure is activated once again [KLG94]. As will be explained below, the approach uses two simple memory devices. Following the generation of a starting solution, memory is used to store the recent local optimum to achieve what is called "first-order form of diversification." A frequency-based memory is also used to achieve a second-order form of diversification.

Generating a Starting Solution

The initial solution is generated by solving a linear placement problem which assigns objects to locations to minimize a linear cost function. Cost coefficients c_{ij}, which are lower bounds on the cost of assigning objects i to location j, are first generated. These c_{ij} provide a lower bound on the optimal solution.

To determine the cost coefficients for the linear assignment problem, the flow matrix is defined as $F = (f_{ij}) = (f_1, f_2, \ldots, f_i, \ldots, f_n)$, and the distance matrix as $D = (d_{ij}) = (d_1, d_2, \ldots, d_i, \ldots, d_n)$, f_i and d_j are vectors of n non-negative integers. Column f_i consists of the flows between object i and the n objects in the problem. Similarly, column d_j consists of distances between locations j and the n locations in the problem. Let f_i' be the vector formed by removing the ith element (zero) from f_i and reordering the remaining elements in ascending order. Similarly, let d_j' be formed by removing the jth element (zero) from d_j and reordering the remaining elements in descending order. The cost of assigning object i to location j can be bounded from below by $c_{ij} = f_i' * d_j'^T$.

First-Order Diversification

Following the construction of the initial solution, and the succeeding series of pair-wise exchanges that lead to a local optimum, the algorithm enters this stage. This first order diversification stage is designed to take the search to a solution that is "maximally diverse" with respect to the local minimum most recently visited. The notion of diversity in this context employs two concepts. One is the distance concept that characterizes two solutions as being increasingly diverse as their separation increases. The separation is defined to be the minimum number of moves to get from one to the other. The second concept concerns the "difficulty" of getting from one solution to the next. Starting from a local optimum, another solution is said to be *diverse* in relation to this point if it is distantly separated (relative to the minimum number of moves to reach it) and has an objective function value close to or better than that of the first.

The first-order diversification strategy takes the following form. Let the most recent local minimum be denoted by the permutation $\Pi_{\min} = \{\pi_{\min}(1), \pi_{\min}(2), \ldots, \pi_{\min}(n)\}$ and the current solution by permutation $\Pi_{\text{cur}} = \{\pi_{\text{cur}}(1), \pi_{\text{cur}}(2), \ldots, \pi_{\text{cur}}(n)\}$. Consider all swaps $\pi_{\text{cur}}(x) \leftrightarrow \pi_{\text{cur}}(y)$ such that $\pi_{\text{cur}}(x) = \pi_{\min}(x)$ or $\pi_{\text{cur}}(y) = \pi_{\min}(y)$. That is, if module x or module y in the current solution is in the same location as in the most recent local minimum, then modules x and y are considered for swap. Swaps of this type will always increase the separation from the local minimum. Then, from the swaps in the indicated category, we choose one that degrades the objective function the least (or improves it the most if improving moves are available since the move may increase, decrease, or keep the objective value constant).

Diversifying moves are made until no moves exist that belong to the above-indicated set. At this point the algorithm switches back to local search heuristic, and then the procedure is repeated.

The above procedure of first-order diversification may be perceived as a form of tabu search, in the sense that the restriction imposed on the choice of swaps is equivalent to the tabu restriction that disallows the exchange of objects i and j if both are currently placed in locations different from the ones they occupied in the most recent local minimum. This restriction is not lifted until either no more moves are possible or a solution is found that is better than the best visited so far [KLG94].

Second-Order Diversification

For the second-order diversification, a frequency-based memory matrix M is maintained, where m_{ij} counts the number of times object i occupies location j in the local minima encountered throughout the search history. By keeping track of the total number m^* of local optima encountered, we get from M the matrix M^* whose entries $m_{ij}^* = m_{ij}/m^*$ represent the relative number of times an item i occurs in location j over the set of local optima. Two possible uses of matrices M and M^* in the application of second-order diversification are suggested [KLG94].

Restarting:

Here, a certain cutoff rule is used to terminate the first-order diversification, then a new starting solution is generated by solving a linear assignment problem with cost coefficients given by $c_{ij} = m_{ij}$. Once this new solution is generated, the first-order diversification resumes until again meeting the conditions of the cutoff rule.

Periodic Second-Order Evaluation:

After a selected number of local optima are generated during the first-order phase, the next sequence of moves replaces the objective function evaluation with an evaluation that minimizes $m_{iy} + m_{kx}$, (or more generally a convex combination of this term and $\text{Max}(m_{iy}, m_{kx})$), where $i = \pi_{\text{cur}}(x)$ and $k = \pi_{\text{cur}}(y)$. The idea is to move objects out of high-frequency locations. An incremental version of this rule replaces m_{iy} with $m_{iy} - m_{ky}$ and m_{kx} with $m_{kx} - m_{ix}$, thereby favoring exchanges that move objects out of high-frequency locations or into locations that have corresponding low frequencies [KLG94]. The contribution of the second-order evaluation can also be weighted by a penalty factor p (see Section 4.4.2 on page 209) and added to the objective function evaluation in the first-order process [KLG94].

4.5.2   Diversification in Multiprocessor Scheduling

The multiprocessor scheduling problem can be defined as follows. Let $L = \{q_1, q_2, \ldots, q_n\}$ denote a collection of n tasks to be executed on a collection of m identical processors say $P_1, P_2, \ldots, P_m$. The goal is to find an assignment that minimizes the makespan of the m parallel processors, that is, to find

$$\min \max_{1 \leq i \leq m} \sum_{q_j \in P_i} t(q_j) \qquad (4.4)$$

where $t(q_j)$ is the time taken to execute task q_j. The value $T_i = \sum_{q_j \in P_i} t(q_j)$ is the latest finishing time of processor i, and the goal may be expressed as that of distributing the tasks to $P_1, P_2, \ldots, P_m$ to minimize $\max_i T_i$ [HG94].

The scheduling problem can also be viewed as assigning n items $\{q_1, q_2, \ldots, q_n\}$ with weight $t(q_i)$ to m bins with the goal of minimizing the weight of the heaviest bin. In this case, T_i can be interpreted as the weight of bin i [HG94]. The problem is similar to the one discussed in Chapter 3 (Example 3.2) with the difference that communication times for passing messages between processors is ignored.

The application of tabu search to solve the above problem is discussed in detail in [HG94]. A dynamic tabu list and the associated tabu criteria have been used to avoid repetitions of long move sequences. However, they were not sufficient to guide the search to improve the best solution found. The search was trapped into regions of schedules with extremely unbalanced distribution of short and long tasks. Certain processors were assigned many small tasks, and other processors were assigned many big tasks. The simple exchange move was not powerful enough to modify the general form of such a structure. Based on this observation, whenever the search gave evidence of failing to improve the current best solution for a long period, Hübscher and Glover [HG94] proposed the following diversification scheme. Task sets that contain a relatively large or relatively small number of long tasks are redistributed by an *influential diversification move*. The diversification is called "influential" because it considerably modifies the solution structure.

Hübscher and Glover [HG94] introduced the notion of task distribution factor $f(i)$ for each processor i. Factor $f(i)$ is used to identify two processors that have the shortest and the longest tasks.

$$f(i) = \frac{1}{T_i^2} \sum_{q_j \in P_i} t^2(q_j)$$

where

$$T_i = \sum_{q_j \in P_i} t(q_j)$$

$f(i)$ is an approximate measure of the number of long tasks in P_i. The greater the value of $f(i)$, the greater the number of long tasks in P_i. Let i be such that $f(i) \leq f(k)$, $1 \leq k \leq m$, and let j be such that $f(j) \geq f(k)$, $1 \leq k \leq m$. That is, processor i has a deficiency and processor j has an excess of long tasks assigned. Now P_i and P_j are taken and tasks are redistributed to have a significant influence on the current solution. A new solution is created by reallocating their elements as follows.

Let S_i' and S_j' be two empty sets. First, take P_j (with an excess of long tasks) and successively assign its tasks, in order of decreasing task length on a best-fit basis to S_i' and S_j'. Then, assign the elements of P_i in the same way to S_i' and S_j'. Finally, assign all tasks of S_i' to P_i and of S_j' to P_j. The above procedure redistributes the longer tasks of P_j and shorter tasks of P_i on both processors. Elements of P_i and P_j are redistributed between S_i' and S_j' one after the other, because this results in assigning S_i' and S_j' about half of the tasks from P_i and the other half from P_j . This is especially useful if m, the number of processors, is small.

When is the influential diversification step executed? For test cases used in [HG94], experiments have shown that executing such a step after 3,000 non-improving moves is all that is needed. Smaller number of iterations, generally, will not allow the search procedure adequate time to settle in on a better (local) minimum, especially considering that an influential diversification step results in a significantly altered state for continuing the search [HG94].

4.6   TS Convergence Aspects

Simulated annealing (Chapter 2) is seen as a probabilistic version of *local search*. For ordinary local search the acceptance probabilities of uphill moves are equal to zero. For simulated annealing the acceptance probabilities of uphill moves depend on the magnitude of the cost increase and the value of a control parameter called temperature. This nondeterministic behavior causes the simulated annealing algorithm to converge in the limit to a global minimum (see Chapter 2, Section 2.3).

The tabu search algorithm as described in previous sections is known as *ordinary* or *deterministic tabu search*. Ordinary TS is a generalization of deterministic local search. The main differences between tabu search and local search are:

1. Local search is completely memoryless while in tabu search move decisions are made based on past moves (short-term, intermediate-term, or long-term memory).

2. In local search, only moves to lower cost states are accepted. The search stops as soon as a minimum state (local or global) is reached. On the other hand, for tabu search, we move to the state with the lowest cost in the neighborhood of the current state (subject to tabu criteria). The cost of the new

state may be larger than that of the current state. Hence, tabu search can escape local minima.

Because of its deterministic nature, ordinary tabu search may never converge to a global optimum state. The incorporation of a nondeterministic element within tabu search allows the algorithm to lend itself to mathematical analysis similar to that developed for simulated annealing, making it possible to establish corresponding convergence properties. Tabu search with nondeterministic elements is called *probabilistic tabu search* [FK92, Glo89b].

Simulated annealing is a special generalization of local search. On the other hand, probabilistic tabu search is a general framework for a variety of local search strategies. Probabilistic tabu search relies on appropriately designed probabilities to guide the search process. The probabilities are designed based on the following principles [Glo89b]:

1. More attractive moves yielding lower-cost states have higher status and thus should receive higher acceptance probabilities

2. The status of a move is diminished (entailing a lower probability of acceptance) if it reverses or repeats a recently made move

3. Thresholds of aspiration, based on previous performance, can override an otherwise diminished status, yielding a reinforced or even a preemptive basis for selection (acceptance with probability 1)

Let S be the current state and $\aleph(S)$ be its local neighborhood. Following the first principle, a positive weight function is used to assign a weight w_i to each state $S_i \in \aleph(S)$. The lower the cost of state S_i, the more attractive is the move to S_i. Hence, the lower the cost of a state, the higher is its weight. For example one may choose the following weight function:

$$w_i = \frac{1}{Cost_i}$$

Let p_i be the probability of accepting the move from S to $S_i \in \aleph(S)$. The p_i's can be computed as follows:

$$p_i = \frac{w_i}{\sum_{S_j \in \aleph(S)} w_j}$$

Following the second principle, tabu moves with shorter residence time in the tabu list should receive a lower acceptance probability than those of longer residence. One may achieve this by reducing the weights of tabu states in proportion to their residence in the tabu list. For example, for a tabu list of size 10 one may assign a reduction factor r of 0.1 to the most recent tabu move, 0.2 to the 2nd most recent, ..., 1 to the least recent tabu move. Let S-to-S_i be a tabu move and

r_i be its reduction factor,[1] then the acceptance probability of this move is equal to $r_i \times p_i$.

According to the third principle, aspiration levels should override the tabu status of the move. For example, if S-to-S_i is a tabu move which satisfies the aspiration criteria, then its acceptance probability is set to p_i, that is, r_i is set to 1. Another alternative strategy is to set to 1 the acceptance probability of such a move.

Probabilistic tabu search has been shown to converge in the limit to a global optimum state. The proof consists of showing that the state transitions of the algorithm correspond to an ergodic Markov chain. The proof is analogous to that of simulated annealing and therefore will not be reproduced here. The interested reader is referred to Chapter 2 of this book and to [FK92]. Below, we provide a brief informal proof due to Fred Glover [Glo89b].

The configuration graph of the solution space is finite. Given that the assigned probabilities are positive (a condition not too difficult to satisfy), a directed path of finite length exists from each node (state or solution) of the configuration graph to each other node of the graph. Each time a state is visited, there is a nonzero probability of leaving that state and reaching another feasible state. Following this argument, starting from any state, there must exist a finite sequence of transitions with positive probabilities leading to a global optimum state. Hence, probabilistic TS will have a nonzero probability of visiting a global optimum state if allowed to run infinitely long.

4.7 TS Applications

Tabu search has been applied to solve combinatorial optimization problems appearing in various fields of science, engineering, and business. Results reported indicate superior performance to other previous techniques. Examples of some hard problems to which tabu search has been applied with success include graph partitioning [LC91], clustering [AS95], traveling salesman problem (TSP) [MHKM89], maximum independent set problem [FHdW90], graph coloring [DdW93, HdW87], maximum clique problem [GSS93], and quadratic assignment problem [SK90, Tai91] to name a few. In the area of engineering, tabu search has been applied to machine sequencing [Ree93], scheduling [BC95, DT93, IE94, MR93, WH89, Wid91], fuzzy clustering [ASF98], multiprocessor scheduling [HG94], vehicle routing [Osm93, RLB96, ST93], general fixed-charge problem [SM93], bin-packing [GH91], bandwidth packing [LG93a], very-large-scale integration (VLSI) placement [SV92], circuit partitioning [AV93], global routing [YS98], high-level synthesis of digital systems [AK94, SAB96], and so on.

---

[1] If the move is nontabu $r_i = 1$.

A good summary of most recent applications of tabu search can be found in [GL95, Glo96]. Below we present in some detail how tabu search has been adapted to solve two hard problems: (1) the classical QAP, and (2) the bandwidth packing problem that occurs in telecommunication.

4.7.1 QAP Problem

Most methods to solve the QAP consist of two phases, construction and improvement [SK90, Tai91]. One way to improve the search is to use pairwise exchange. Tabu search can be incorporated in this improvement phase in order to continue the search when local optima are reached. The procedure described in this section is due to Skorin-Kapov and is referred to as tabu-navigation. In this procedure, the user can interact during the execution (navigate through the search space) by using new parameter values and by invoking long-term memory [SK90].

A move in tabu-navigation procedure is a pairwise swap. The attribute of a move is an unordered pair (i, j) of the objects that exchange their locations. The Move_value is the difference between the objective function after and before the move. If Move_value<0 than the swap is an improving move. The best swap is the one that identifies a pair $(i_{\text{best}}, j_{\text{best}})$ for which the Move_value is the smallest. The subset of *all* pairs (i, j) is the domain of admissible moves.

Tabu list of length tabu_size is a circular list that is updated during the improvement phase of the algorithm, and stores (i, j) pairs that represent the modules that have been swapped. The "best solution" aspiration criterion is used (see page 188). Length of the tabu list and the maximum number of iterations are user specified parameters. The procedure runs for a certain number of iterations with a given tabu_size. Then the user is given the following four choices to *restart the procedure with new values for tabu_size and maximum number of iterations*, or to end the procedure and return the best solution found.

1. Restart from the *beginning* of the improvement phase.

2. Restart from the *best* solution obtained thus far.

3. Restart from the beginning of the construction phase, penalizing the move performed thus far in order to diversify the search.

4. End the procedure.

When user choice is (3), the short-term tabu is terminated and the long-term tabu is invoked. The long-term memory is a function that records moves taken in the past in order to penalize them. The goal is to diversify, by compelling the search to explore unvisited regions. As discussed above, one form of long-term memory function for permutation problems of size n is an $n \times n$ matrix (let this be denoted by **LTM**, see Example 4.6). When pairs of objects (i, j) exchange locations, **LTM**$_{ij}$ is replaced by **LTM**$_{ij} + 1$.

In this procedure, at the end of the short-term memory phase, and before starting the construction of the new initial permutation, the matrix $\mu \times \textbf{LTM}$ is added to the distance matrix D, where μ is a penalty parameter. That is, the distance between two locations i, j is increased by μk, where k is the number of times the pair (i, j) was swapped. This way the search can be directed closer to or farther from the explored regions by changing μ.

Also in this procedure, following the construction of the new initial solution, the value of the objective function for that solution is computed without penalties and the improvement phase is restarted. The short-term memory is reinitialized, in contrast to the long-term memory which restarts with values from the end of the previous phase. The description of the tabu-navigation algorithm is given in Figure 4.7.

Algorithm $Tabu\_Navigation$
Begin

Step 1. Read the "flow" matrix **F** and the "distance" matrix **D**.
Initiate long-term memory.
Step 2. Construct the initial permutation using a constructive algorithm.
Step 3. Initiate short-term memory by reading the values for parameters tabu_size and max_iter (i.e., maximal number of iterations).

For $K = 1$ to max_iter **Do**
Begin
(a) examine all possible pair-wise exchanges and perform the best admissible move
(b) update tabu list
(c) update long-term memory
End

Step 4. Perform one of the following:
i) Restart from the solution given by the construction phase.
Read new value for tabu_size and/or max_iter and **Goto** Step 3.
ii) Restart from the *best* solution generated thus far.
Read new values for tabu_size and/or max_iter and **Goto** Step 3.
iii) Invoke long-term memory.
Replace the original matrix **D** by **D+LTM** and **Goto** Step 2 .
iv) End the procedure. Display best solution and the CPU time used.
End

Figure 4.7: Tabu-navigation algorithm.

The above tabu-navigation algorithm was tested on a standard set of problems of varying sizes [SK90]. By incorporating TS into the simple pairwise exchange algorithm, the best-known solutions or better were obtained in record CPU time. For each of the problems, a number of runs were performed to assess good parameter values and the use of aspiration criteria and long-term memory. For some problems (n=15 and 20 from [NVR68]), the best-known solutions were obtained without the use of long-term memory and aspiration criteria, and for others (n=30 [NVR68]) best solutions were obtained without the aspiration criterion, and by invoking the long-term memory.

Tabu-navigation was executed [SK90] using different values of the parameter tabu_size. The best value of $tabu\_size$ was observed to be an increasing function of the size of a problem. When the algorithm was used without aspiration criteria, the best tabu sizes were integers between $n/2$ and $n/3$. It was also observed that the use of aspiration criteria caused good values of parameter tabu_size to become larger.

Different strategies were tested for changing tabu sizes when choosing alternative ii) in Step 4 of Figure 4.7 [SK90]. For the QAP problem, it was found that if the aspiration level criterion is *not* used, then decreasing tabu list sizes in a stepwise manner produces the best results. The intuitive justification given for this behavior was that smaller tabu sizes enable more careful examination of the state space (provided that no cycling occurs). In the experiments conducted, the tabu size was decreased every 50 iterations in steps of 30,15,10,8, and so on.

For the same QAP problem, if an aspiration level criterion is used, the restrictions imposed by larger tabu sizes are balanced by the possibility of overriding the tabu status of a move. In that case, it seems that the strategy to increase the tabu size works better. The tabu size was increased every 50 iterations in steps of 6,8,10,20, and so on.

Note that all possible pairwise exchanges are examined at Step 3 of Figure 4.7. This becomes extremely expensive as the problem size increases. Candidate list strategies (discussed in Section 4.9.3) suggest ways of avoiding this extensive computational effort without sacrificing solution quality.

4.7.2   Bandwidth Packing Problem (BWP)

In this section we present the adaptation of the tabu search algorithm to another problem known as the *bandwidth packing problem* (BWP). This practical problem occurs in the area of telecommunications. The demand requirements of calls to be routed through a given telecommunication network may exceed the network's installed capacity. It is then required to select a subset of calls and assign them to feasible paths, with the objective of maximizing profit.

In this section we present the tabu search implementation for the *static* version of the BWP problem, where the demand is given in the form of a table of calls, and the bandwidth (BW) requirements are fixed and known [LG93a].

Laguna and Glover define the BWP by reference to a graph with capacitated edges [LG93a]. Each call has a known revenue and a non-negative BW requirement, and can be assigned to a path in the graph. Associated with each link in the graph is a capacity (or BW) and a unit cost. The demand of the calls exceed the total capacity of the network. The problem is to find an optimal assignment of a feasible subset of calls to paths. The notation used is as follows.

n, p, and q : number of *nodes*, *links*, and *calls*, respectively.
For each link j : b_j is its capacity, c_j the unit cost and f_j the flow.
For each call i : r_i is the capacity requirement, v_i the revenue, s_i the source node, and t_i the terminal node.

Links represent undirected arcs or edges. Let A denote the set of assigned calls, that is, those calls with an assigned path. Mathematically, the problem may be expressed as follows [LG93a]:

$$\text{Maximize Profit} = \sum_{i \in A} v_i - \sum_{j=1}^{p} c_j \times f_j \qquad (4.5)$$

subject to

$$f_j \leq b_j, \qquad j = 1, \ldots, p, \qquad \text{where } f_j = \sum_{i \in A_j} r_i \qquad (4.6)$$

and A_j is the set of calls routed through link j.

In Equation 4.5, the first term identifies the total revenue from all assigned calls. The second term identifies the cost of using links to which the calls are assigned. Only those links with positive flow f_j contribute to the total cost. In Equation 4.6, the inequality constraint ensures that the capacity of each link is not violated. Flow of each link equals the sum of the BW requirements for each call routed through the link.

The procedure is initiated by first computing a prespecified number of profitable paths for each call i ($i = 1, \ldots, q$), up to a maximum of $k_{\max}$ paths. A path π is profitable for call i if

$$v_i - r_i \times \sum_{j \in L_\pi} c_j > 0 \qquad (4.7)$$

where L_π is the set of links in path π. The total cost of routing a call through any of its profitable paths is known (since these costs are calculated when the paths are generated).

Now given q calls, and k_i profitable paths for each call i, the problem consists of assigning calls to paths (upto a maximum of $k_{\max}$ paths), in order to increase profit [LG93a]. A move (i, h), for $i = 1, \ldots, q$ and $h = 0, \ldots, k_i$ is an operation that changes the assignment of call i from its current path g to path h. After a move, tabu list forbids call i from being assigned to path g for tabu_size iterations where tabu_size is the current size of the tabu list.

At each iteration the method performs the best move available and the tabu information is updated. The definition of "best move" is a function of the search state and the information contained in the different memory structures discussed below.

Frequency information is used in BWP for diversification based on long-term memory. The idea behind using frequency information, as discussed in Section 4.4.2, is to direct local choices by exploiting the knowledge of how often the same choice has been made in the past (see Example 4.6). The long-term memory function embedded in this method consists of q lists of the from $\mathrm{Freq}(i, h)$ for $i = 1, \ldots, q$ and $h = 0, \ldots, k_i$. The (i, h) element identifies the number of times that call i has been moved to path h during the search. The best move at any iteration is the nontabu move with the largest penalized Move_value (pmv). If call i is currently assigned to path g, then the pmv for the move (i, h) is given by:

$$\mathrm{pmv}(i, h) = \mathrm{Move\_value}(i, h) - \alpha \times \mathrm{Freq}(i, h) \tag{4.8}$$

where

$$\alpha = \begin{cases} 0 & \text{if } \mathrm{Move\_value}(i, h) > 0, \\ 10 & \text{otherwise} \end{cases} \tag{4.9}$$

$$\mathrm{Move\_value}(i, h) = r_i \cdot \left(\sum_{j \in L_g} c_j - \sum_{j \in L_h} c_j \right) \tag{4.10}$$

The parameter α can be made to depend on the problem class and solution history. The choice of 10 was based on experimentation.

Multiple dynamic lists whose sizes change systematically are used. Specifically, each call i has its own tabu list size, denoted by tabu_size(i). This size is allowed to take three possible values that are a linear function of the number of profitable paths k_i for each call i. For any call i, small (S), medium (M), and large (L) sizes are set equal to k_i, $1.5 \times k_i$, and $2.0 \times k_i$, respectively. The value of tabu_size(i), for $i = 1, \ldots, q$ is initially set to S (that is, k_i), and then systematically changed every $2\times$ tabu_size(i) iterations following the sequence {S,M,S,L,M,L}. The sequence is repeated until the end of the search [LG93a]. Tabu status is overridden if cost is better than the best.

4.8   Parallelization of TS

General iterative heuristics such as tabu search are getting more widely adopted to obtain near-optimal solutions to numerous hard problems. For small problems, all these techniques have reasonable runtime requirements. For example, for a placement problem with few hundred modules, all iterative heuristics described in this book were able to find good solutions in less than an hour on an Ultra I Sun station. However, most practical problems are extremely large and require several hours of computer time to solve by iterative heuristics. Application-specific constructive heuristics always lead to solutions that are far from optimal. In many instances they fail to find even a feasible solution. One way to adapt iterative techniques to solve large problems in reasonable time is to resort to parallelization strategies. In Chapters 2 and 3 we have seen various parallelization strategies of simulated annealing and genetic algorithms, which resulted in remarkable speedups. In this section we shall briefly survey parallelization of the TS heuristic.

Let T be a random variable representing the time to find a desired solution by tabu search heuristic. For many problems solved by tabu search with short-term memory, empirical evidence showed that the random variable T is exponentially distributed [Tai91] (the sample distribution of T approximates the exponential distribution). That is,

$$Prob(T < t) = 1 - e^{-\lambda t}$$

with $\lambda > 0$. The parameter λ is equal to $1/\overline{T}$, where $\overline{T}$ is the average time required to obtain a desired solution observed over a large number of runs of the algorithm. This observation is equivalent (in probability) to saying that, if the search of a desired solution over a single computer takes t units, then the same solution will be found in t/k units by k parallel searches on k independent computers. Hence, ideal linear speed-up is achieved by concurrent searches. Furthermore, because of the properties of the exponential distribution (namely, the memoryless property), there will be no advantage in restarting the tabu search.

The most straightforward and widely adopted parallelization approach is based on the above observation [FBTV94, GPR94, Tai90]. In this approach, k tabu search processes are spawned and run concurrently on k processors. Each process has the task of exploring a subset of the neighborhood of current solution. Two approaches are followed: *synchronous* and *asynchronous*. In the synchronous approach the various processes are always working with the same solution, but exploring different partitions of the current local neighborhood. A *master* process orchestrates the activities of the *slave* processes [GPR94, Tai90]. In the asynchronous approach, all processes are peer and usually are not all working with the same current solution [FBTV94, Tai93]. Furthermore, sometimes each process is seeking a partial solution and then a global solution to the original problem is constructed by merging the partial solutions [Tai93]. Both approaches require that the set of possible moves be partitioned among the available processors so that each processor will be exploring a distinct subregion of the current solutions neighborhood.

Synchronous Parallel Implementation:

In this implementation a master process and one of the slave processes are running on one machine. The remaining slave processes are running on distinct machines. All slave processes are started with the same initial solution. After searching its part of the current neighborhood, each slave process reports its best move back

Algorithm MasterProcess;
Begin
       Initialize parameters and data structures;
       $S_0 =$ Initial solution;
       $BestS = S_0$;
       $CurS = S_0$; /* Current solution */
       Send $CurS$ to all slave processes;
       While *not-time-to-stop*
           Begin
               Wait for best moves from all slaves;
               Select the best move subject to tabu restrictions;
               Send the selected move to all slaves;
           End
       Force all slaves to *stop*;
       Return $(BestS)$ /* of slave running on same machine */
End. /* MasterProcess */

Figure 4.8: Synchronous parallel implementation: The master process.

to the master. The master process selects the best among the received best moves (subject to tabu conditions). If the stopping criteria are met the search stops; otherwise the master broadcasts the selected move back to the slaves and the search continues. The pseudo code of the master and slave processes are given in Figures 4.8 and 4.9.

A number of synchronous parallel implementations have been reported in the literature [GPR94, Tai90]. For example, in [GPR94] a parallel implementation of the tabu search algorithm for the vehicle routing problem is described. The approach reported is a slight variation of the aforementioned master-slave strategy. The main steps of the reported parallel algorithm are outlined in Figure 4.10. For a more detailed description of this parallel implementation the reader is referred to [GPR94] where a noticeable improvement in solution quality over one of the best constructive algorithms for vehicle routing problem, with substantial reduction in runtime, is reported.

Another possible parallel implementation of this class is as follows. Divide the neighborhood into k parts of approximately the same size and evaluate these parts in parallel on k distinct processors. At each iteration, every processor evaluates the moves attributed to it. It then broadcasts to the other $k - 1$ processors the best move it has found in its region of the current neighborhood. Finally, each processor will select the best among its proposed move and the $k - 1$ moves proposed by the other processors, executes the move, and performs the necessary updates to its data structures. In case of a tie among several good moves, the move proposed by

Algorithm SlaveProcess;
Begin

      Initialize parameters and data structures;
      Wait for initial solution S_0 from master process;
      $BestS = S_0$;
      $CurS = S_0$; /* Current solution */
      Repeat
            Wait for selected move from the master;
            Perform the move;
            Update *tabu_list*;
            Update $BestS$ and $CurS$;
            Try all moves in partial neighborhood;
            Select best move and send it to the master;
      Until *stop*;
End. /* SlaveProcess */

Figure 4.9: Synchronous parallel implementation: The slave process.

Algorithm ParallelTabuSearch;
Begin

1.   Construct initial solution and broadcast it to all slaves;
2.   Each slave process explores its own neighborhood and
        sends its best move to the master;
3.   The master identifies a subset of moves that improve the
        objective function (subject to tabu restrictions);
4.   **If** there is no such move **Then** the master randomly selects
        one uphill move;
5.   The master broadcasts to all the slaves the selected move(s);
6.   Each slave performs the received move(s) and makes necessary updates;
7.   **If** *time-to-stop* **Then Return** $BestS$;
8.   **Goto** Step 2
End.

Figure 4.10: Synchronous parallel implementation of tabu search.

Algorithm PeerProcess;
Begin
1.   Construct initial solution and initialize parameters;
2.   Explore own neighborhood;
3.   Select best move subject to tabu restrictions;
4.   Update tabu list;
5.   Exchange current best solution with neighbors;
6.   Update current solution based on received neighbor solutions;
7.   **If** *time-to-stop* **Then Return** best solution;
8.   **Goto**step 2
End.

Figure 4.11: Asynchronous parallel implementation of tabu search.

the processor with the least recently accepted move is executed. Such parallel implementation has been reported in [Tai91] for the quadratic assignment problem. The author reported a linear speedup with respect to a sequential implementation of the tabu search algorithm.

Asynchronous Parallel Implementation:

In this approach, each processor is exploring a subset of the neighborhood of its current solution. Each processor is competing with its neighbors (its adjacent processors) in finding a superior solution. When the stopping criteria are met, every processor reports its best solution. The general outline of this parallelization approach is given in Figure 4.11.

Similar asynchronous parallel tabu search implementations for the traveling salesman and quadratic assignment problems have been reported in [FBTV94]. The results reported indicate a marked improvement in solution quality as well as convergence speedup. In [FBTV94], the time between successive solution exchanges is called *diffusion interval*. The authors stated that the best results were obtained by performing this exchange and updating current solution at each iteration as indicated in steps 5 and 6 of Figure 4.11.

Other Parallel Implementations:

In [MGPO89] the following synchronous parallelization approach is described. A parent process initiates several child tabu search processes, one on each processor. Each child process is started with different conditions and parameters. Running each tabu process with different parameters allows the exploration of distinct subregions of the search space. Periodically, the parent process stops the child processes. The best solutions from all tabu search processes are compared and the search is restarted with the current best solution. Each child process explores (as much as possible) a distinct part of the search space. The child processes are restarted with empty tabu lists as it is counterproductive to apply past restrictions to the new solution. This parallel implementation was tested on several instances of the traveling salesman problem. The authors reported that the solution obtained with their parallel implementation were of lower cost than those obtained with other algorithms reported in earlier literature. For most instances, the parallel tabu program was able to obtain an optimal tour in a relatively short time. For example, for a 75-city tour, the average runtime was about 150 seconds on a Sequent Balance 8000 multiprocessor machine.

A massively parallel implementation of tabu search for the quadratic assignment problem (QAP) is reported in [CSK93]. A move consists of a pairwise exchange of the locations of two elements. For an $n \times n$ QAP the examination of the whole neighborhood requires $O(n^2)$ pairwise trial exchanges. $O(n^2)$ processors are used to explore the entire pairwise exchange neighborhood in constant time. The effect of each pairwise exchange on the objective function is evaluated and communicated to a *master* process, which selects the best exchange (subject to tabu restrictions) and sends it back to all the slaves. This parallelization strategy has been implemented on the Connection Machine CM-2, a massively parallel SIMD machine [CM-89]. A sizable reduction in the runtime per iteration was achieved when compared to other sequential and parallel implementations [CSK93, Tai91]. Furthermore, this parallel implementation produced for some of the benchmark QAP test cases better solutions than the earlier reported sequential TS implementations [CSK93]. It was also observed that the increase in the runtime per iteration is a logarithmic function of the problem size.

The use of move decomposition as a basis for creating candidate lists can also offer opportunities of parallel processing. To do this, it is necessary to identify restrictions on the move available in each component of the decomposition so that the outcome of treating each component independently does not damage objective function measures. Restrictions of this type can sometimes be simple, for example, fixing the end points of subsequences in certain permutation problems, such as TSP and flow scheduling problems [MHKM89, ROS89].

The approaches discussed above exhaust neither all possible avenues nor all opportunities to parallelize the tabu search algorithm. Surveys of several other parallel implementations are given in [Glo90b] and [Glo96].

Parallel Tabu Search Taxonomy:

Recently Crainic, Toulouse, and Gendreau [CTG97, GL97] suggested a taxonomy for the classification of TS parallelization approaches. Three dimensions are recommended: (1) *control cardinality*, (2) *control and communication type*, and (3) *search differentiation*.

Control cardinality: A parallel search procedure can be *1-control* or *p-control*. In the *1-control* case, one processor has the distinctive role of running the algorithm and distributing the search tasks (such as move evaluations) among other processors. For the *p-control* case, each processor is in control of its own search and the communication with other processors.

Control and communication type: This dimension relates to how the parallel search is controlled, how processes communicate, and what information is communicated. With respect to this dimension, a parallel tabu search procedure can have *rigid synchronization, knowledge synchronization, collegial,* or *knowledge collegial. Rigid synchronization* refers to a synchronous mode of operation, where processes will be exchanging information at specific points of the search. *Knowledge synchronization* also refers to synchronous operational mode. Processes will be required to periodically stop and exchange information. The difference between *knowledge* and *rigid* synchronization is in the amount of information exchanged among the processors. *Collegial communication* falls in the category of asynchronous approaches. In a *collegial* parallel TS procedure, processes will be asynchronously making different searches, and broadcasting (globally or selectively) to each other improving solutions. *Knowledge collegial communication* also refers to an asynchronous operational mode. However, parallel approaches of this type rely on a more complex form of communication, where findings of the processors are used to influence each other search strategies.

Search differentiation: This dimension is indicative of the number of initial solutions and the search strategies followed by the parallel tabu search procedure. Two letters are used to indicate whether the search starts from a single point (SP) or multiple points (MP), and two letters indicate whether a single strategy (SS) or different strategies (DS) are employed by the processors.

Many of the reported parallel tabu search procedures can be classified according to this taxonomy. For example, the two tabu search parallel implementations for the quadratic assignment problem earlier reviewed in this section [CSK93, Tai91] are *1-control, rigid synchronization, single point, single strategy (1-RS-SPSS).*

4.9   Other Issues and Related Work

4.9.1   Neighborhood, Evaluator Functions, Stopping Criteria

Neighborhood:

In most combinatorial optimization problems, the number of available moves increases very rapidly with the size of the problem. For example, the number of simple swap moves grows as the square of the size of the problem. In case of more complex moves, the number of moves may grow at an even faster rate. Clearly, for most problems, the entire neighborhood of S, $\aleph(S)$, may be too large and costly to examine. For this reason, only a candidate subset of neighborhood, denoted by V^*, is examined [Glo89a]. The size of the neighborhood examined is a trade-off between quality and performance. Generally this size is fixed, as was done in our previous examples. We shall address this issue in more detail in Section 4.9.3.

Evaluator Functions:

As mentioned in the introduction, from any current solution, a reasonably sized subset of neighborhood is explored. And the best move among these is chosen. The use of the "best move criterion" is based on the supposition that moves with higher evaluations have a higher probability of leading to an optimal solution (or leading to an optimal solution in fewer number of steps).

In order to select the best move from the candidate list, one needs an evaluator function to rate each candidate move. In memoryless algorithms such as simulated annealing, the function to evaluate the merit of a move is generally the objective function itself. In such a case we say that the move evaluator is a function of the solution state, as was in our previous example (Example 4.1). There are situations where the standard cost function evaluator may not be very effective. An important principle in tabu search is that the evaluator chosen should be a function of the search path and search state. That is, the evaluator must implicitly reference the *history* H of the search process. As will become evident, this has several advantages, for example in breaking of ties, in diversifying the search, and so on. If two moves are equally good, history can be used to decide which search direction to choose. Similarly, moves that have more frequently occurred in the past can be given less consideration in the future, thereby diversifying the search.

As an example, the evaluation of a move can be expressed as the sum of the cost of the new solution and a function g that depends on the search history (memory). History here not only refers to the tabu list but also to some previous record of moves.

$$\mathcal{E}(\mathbf{H}, S) = Cost(S) + g(\mathbf{H}) \tag{4.11}$$

For example, $g(\mathbf{H})$ can be a function of the frequency of some previous moves. One can also think of more complex evaluation functions.

The interpretation of the evaluator can depend on the region searched. In some situations, after reaching a local optimum, it may be preferable to move a distance away (see Section 4.5) before considering moves with higher evaluations. That is, the evaluator should apply a different standard of comparison in this region. An approach for developing evaluators that support intensification and diversification for a class of problems, referred to as "target analysis" (TA) is discussed in the following section (Section 4.9.2). Target analysis provides a means of uncovering and exploiting information that leads to the determination of such evaluators in a systematic fashion.

Stopping Criteria:

The algorithm given in Figure 4.3 (page 187) is executed for a fixed number of iterations. Another stopping criterion is to continue until no improvement on the best solution is obtained over a fixed number of successive iterations. An *estimate* $Cost^*$ of the minimum value of the cost function can also be used to decide when to stop. The search can stop as soon as we reach close enough to $Cost^*$. For example, we know that the cost of the tree in Example 4.1 cannot be less than the sum of the four least cost edges, that is, edges e_2, e_4, e_5, and e_8 ($c(e_2) + c(e_4) + c(e_5) + c(e_8) = 18$). Of course, this tree violates our constraints, but we are sure that the cost of the optimal tree will not be less than this. In case we do not get close to $Cost^*$, then we stop after a certain maximum number of iterations. In some problem instances we do not seek to minimize, but would like to have a solution within a certain cost range. In this case, the moment a feasible solution with the desired cost is found the search can stop.

4.9.2 Target Analysis (TA)

As mentioned above, tabu search works by making the "best" admissible move at each iteration. The move evaluator generally chosen is the objective function where the "Move_value" is given by the decrease in the cost, or a function of cost and how frequently that particular move was made. However, this strategy does not always guarantee that the selected move will take the search in the direction of an optimal solution. It has actually been observed that its merit diminishes as the number of iterations during a solution attempt increases [Glo90a, LG93b].

Improved problem solving methods can be created by incorporating a learning component in the search. Target analysis (TA) is one such procedure that has been described by Glover and Greenberg [GG89]. It helps in creating dynamic evaluation functions thereby providing a systematic process for diversifying the search over a longer term. Its main features have been sketched by Laguna and Glover by viewing the approach as a five-phase procedure [LG93b]:

Phase 1:

This phase consists of applying existing methods to determine optimal or exceptionally high-quality solutions to representative problems of a given class. It is a straightforward phase where extensive effort is involved.

Phase 2:

This phase uses solutions produced by Phase 1 as *targets*, and each problem is solved again, with the following purpose:

1. to evaluate the ability of the current decision rule in order to (a) identify "good" moves, and (b) determine regions where these rules are operating effectively,

2. to score available moves at each iteration and to bias choices in order to select moves with high scores, thereby leading to the target solutions more quickly than the customary decision rule, and,

3. to generate information that can be used to infer the scores.

Phase 3:

This phase is concerned with the construction of a parameterized function of the information recorded in the previous phase. The goal of this phase is to find values of the parameters to create what is known as a *master decision rule* (MDR).

Phase 4:

This phase generates a mathematical or statistical model to determine effective parameter values for the MDR.

Phase 5:

This phase consists of applying the MDR to the original representative problems and to other problems from the chosen solution class to confirm its merit.

TA can be useful in integrating effective diversification in the search. When TA is used as a tool for diversification within tabu search, some of the functions that integrate the MDR may depend on long-term memory structure. For the machine scheduling problem, Laguna and Glover have shown how TA methodology can be embedded within the heuristic solution framework provided by TS to create a more effective form of diversification [LG93b]. Laguna and Glover's implementation focussed on a specific class for scheduling problems, however, the concepts are general and are capable of being adopted to many other scheduling settings and other combinatorial optimization problems. Below we present the application of target analysis to the machine sequencing problem.

Application of TA to Machine Sequencing Problem

Consider the problem of scheduling N jobs, each arriving at time 0 on a continuously available machine. The goal is to minimize the sum of the setup costs and linear delay penalties. Each job i, $(i = 1, 2, \ldots N)$, requires t_i units of time on the machine, and a penalty p_i is charged for each unit of time when the job commencement is delayed; s_{ij} is the setup cost of scheduling job j immediately after job i. Two dummy jobs, 0 and $N + 1$, are included in every schedule, where $t_0 = t_{N+1} = 0$, and $p_0 = p_{N+1} = 0$. The costs $s_{0,j}$ and $s_{i,N+1}$ are considered to be an initial setup cost and a cleanup cost, respectively. A schedule has the form:

$$\Pi = \{0, \pi(1), \pi(2), \ldots, \pi(N), N + 1\}$$

where $\pi(i)$ is the index of the job in position i of the schedule. No precedence constraints are enforced and no preemption is allowed, therefore, any permutation of the N jobs is a feasible schedule. The objective is to minimize the sum of penalty (delay) and setup costs for all jobs [LG93b].

Two classes of moves were used to solve the above problem. The first is the common pairwise exchange (or swap) of two jobs, called the *swap move*. The second class of moves consists of taking a job out of its current position and inserting it somewhere else in the schedule, which is referred to as the *insert* move (see Exercise 4.5).

Let the transfer of job $\pi(i)$ to a position between jobs $\pi(j)$ and $\pi(j-1)$ be denoted by $Insert(\pi(i), j)$ and the swap of the jobs in positions i and j be denoted by $Swap(\pi(i), \pi(j))$, where $i < j$. In both cases, the attribute of the move chosen to classify tabu is the job $\pi(i)$. In addition to $tabu\_list$, another array called $tabu\_state$ is used as a counter of the number of times each job appears in the $tabu\_list$.

During Phase 2, to measure the goodness of a move, Laguna and Glover use a *scoring procedure* based on the knowledge gained in the first phase. To do this, *solution scores* are constructed to measure the extent to which any given solution deviated from the target solution. From this, *move scores* are derived as the difference between the solution scores obtained before and after the application of the move.

Two different solution scores are defined for the job sequencing problem, namely, the *absolute position score* and the *relative position score*. The absolute position score is simply a count of the number of jobs that occupy their targeted optimal positions. Therefore, N is the highest value that can be obtained by any solution. Similarly, the relative position score is a count of the number of jobs that are scheduled immediately after their targeted predecessor jobs. Again, N is the highest value that can be obtained. Both the above scores are combined into a single composite solution score (by summing them). The resulting maximum targeted value is $2 \times N$.

From the composite solution score determined, the score attributable to each move is computed as the score of the schedule after the move minus the score of the schedule before the move. Therefore, moves with positive scores have the ability to move the schedule "closer" to its target, and higher scoring moves generally produce a faster convergence than lower scoring moves.

Using the above approach, each problem in the sample is solved again in order to measure the effectiveness of the current choice rule. Also, scores are kept separate for the two categories of moves: improving (Move_value < 0) and non-improving (Move_value ≥ 0).

Laguna and Glover chose a class of machine sequencing problems (scheduling problem) comprising between 20 and 35 jobs. The average move score per iteration was calculated every 50 iterations for a solution attempt of 500 iterations. From the experimental results the following was observed: *the average quality of the decisions made in nonimproving situations tends to decrease as the number of moves increases*, while *the average quality of the decisions made in improving situations tends to increase as the number of moves increases* [LG93b]. Based on these observations, they used frequency counts to bias the selection of moves in TS solution states where no improving moves are available. The frequency count is multiplied by a penalty parameter and added to the move value of every nonimproving move. This procedure is used to successfully avoid long-term cycling and allows the procedure to find improved solutions during later stages of the search process. During the search, the move with the least penalty is selected [LG93b].

The information chosen to be examined as a basis for diversification utilizes a simple count of the number of times the particular moves are selected for execution. Two arrays are defined for this purpose; *Swap_count* and *Insert_count*. Swap_count(i, j) contains the number of times that job i has exchanged positions with job j; and Insert_count(i, j) contains the number of times that job i has been moved to a positions immediately before job j.

This information is used in Phase 3 to design evaluation functions capable of diversifying the search. The MDR then combines these functions, including the one currently in use (that is, Move_value), to provide a device to further focus the search procedure on good target solutions. Since the merit of the current evaluation function in improving regions does not seem to decrease as the execution time progresses, the focus then was to design functions for diversification in those regions in which nonimproving moves are available. A simple form of a diversification function was created for this purpose. If the admissible move $Swap(\pi(i), \pi(j))$ is being considered for the best move at the current iteration, then its relative attractiveness (Move_appeal) is evaluated as follows:

> **If** Move_value($\pi(i), \pi(j)$) < 0
>   Move_appeal=Move_value($\pi(i), \pi(j)$)
> **Else**
>   Move_appeal=Move_value($\pi(i), \pi(j)$)
> $+ \alpha \times$ Swap_count($(\pi(i), \pi(j))^{\beta}$

Recall that an improving move has a Move_value<0. Similarly, the more negative the value of Move_appeal, the more appealing is the move. Hence the strategy is to make more frequent moves less appealing.

A similar function for admissible *Insert* moves is obtained by substituting Swap_count by Insert_count in the expression above. This function has the characteristic of allowing different levels of diversity within the search. These levels are controlled by the selection of α and β. For example, for large values of β, the method reduces rapidly the likelihood for selecting moves that have been frequently preferred earlier in the search. On the other hand, α is used to assure only a minimal diversification. This is especially important in early search stages, when the *count* values are relatively small.

The values of α and β are determined via experimentation (Phase 4). The values α and β are varied to identify the combination that produces the highest average scores for the move selected, applied to the initial representative set of trial problem. The best parameter setting found was a linear Move_appeal function for which $\alpha=10$ and $\beta=1$.

Finally, (Phase 5) the modified tabu search procedure is applied. In the experiments conducted, optimal solutions to all 20 job problems were found within 30 CPU seconds. For all cases tested, the combination TS/TA was found to be superior than tabu search alone.

4.9.3   Candidate List Strategies

A common phenomenon in most combinatorial optimization problems is that $\aleph(S)$, the neighborhood of solution S, is large. Complete examination of all alternatives then becomes computationally expensive, especially as problem sizes become large. In such cases, the number of solutions examined can be restricted using what is known as candidate list strategies [Glo89a, Glo95, HG94].

A trivial candidate list strategy is similar to what was employed in our earlier examples. A small number of *random* moves are made that constitute the candidate list, and the "best" among them is chosen. Instead of choosing a random sample, strategies can be used for example to restrict the search to a certain region, thereby intensifying the search. Below we highlight some of the candidate list approaches suggested by Glover, that can been used to create improved solution approaches [Glo89a, Glo95].

Decomposition of Moves:

One candidate list strategy known as *subdivision strategy* decomposes moves into components [Glo89a, Glo95]. Here, compound moves are decomposed with the aim of isolating good "components" that will most likely be part of the best compound move [Glo95]. The motivation for this approach is that components are much fewer and are often evaluated much faster than the compound moves. For example, the swap move, a compound move, is composed of "add moves" and "drop moves." The total number of swap moves generally equals the product of the numbers of their add and drop components [Glo95]. Permutation problems are particularly suited to the use of move decomposition strategies. In permutation problems, it is convenient to divide the permutation into successive subsequences, and then examine only moves that involve changes within these subsequences [LBG89].

Candidate lists can also be created by decomposing moves into subsets based on structural attributes of the problem or of the current solution. In many applications, moves can be subdivided according to a natural classification of their components. For example, moves can be segregated based on different regions, machines (as in the case of the scheduling problem), products, activities, due dates, and so on [Glo89a, Glo95].

As mentioned above, candidate list strategies can also be seen to be related in function to intensification strategies proposed in connection with the use of intermediate-term memory (Section 4.4.1) in tabu search [Glo89a, Glo89b]. The goal in intensification is to concentrate the search effort in areas expected to yield highest rewards. From this point of view, decomposition itself constitutes a form of intensification which is determined by features of position or classification. The idea is to focus on a particular subregion of the search space. Advanced types of intensification strategies may make use of learning to determine good ways to focus the search (see Section 4.9.2).

Simple learning strategies have been found to be very effective. For example, in the application of tabu search to the TSP, in order to learn which subclasses of edges are most likely to appear in good tours, the method saves information during early stages of the search process. A large weight is assigned to each node of an edge meeting that node in successive local optima. Another version of the same problem records the actual identities of edges incorporated into each successive solution beginning with the first local optimum (see also Example 4.5). After a certain fixed number of iterations gathering such information, candidate lists based on examining only the edges whose weights or identities lie within a specified range may be employed to guide the search in subsequent iterations. Both of the above intensification-based candidate list strategies have led to reduced solution times without sacrificing solution quality [Glo89a, Glo89b, Kno89].

Layered Evaluations:

This strategy is based on weeding out moves by applying evaluations in successive layers. Moves that pass the evaluation criteria in one layer are subjected to evaluation criteria in the next. Specifically, a list of moves associated with each layer, list i for layer i is derived by applying criterion i to evaluate the moves of list $i - 1$. List 1 is created from the set of all available moves, and it contains the best b_1 of these moves according to criterion 1. List 2 then contains the b_2 best moves from list 1 according to criterion 2, and so on. More generally, subsequent lists may not merely contain moves that are members of earlier lists, but may contain moves derived from these earlier moves. The values b_i may be fixed or determined adaptively. As with the move decomposition procedures, the layered evaluations procedures can be embedded within a more advanced candidate list method [Fox83, Glo89a, Low76].

Sequential Fan Strategy:

This strategy is highly exploitable in parallel processing and is known as the *sequential fan* candidate list strategy [Fox83, Glo95, Low76]. Here p best alternative moves at any given step are generated. Then, a fan of solution streams is created, one stream for each alternative. The best moves for each stream are again examined, and p best overall moves are used for the p new streams at the next step. This method is sometimes called *beam* search. Refinements to this method (called *filtered beam search*) have been proposed by Glover [Glo89b] and by Ow and Morton [OM88].

Aspiration Plus Strategy:

Another kind of candidate list strategy called *aspiration plus* strategy is based on an aspiration threshold for the quality of move to be selected. Based on the history of search patterns, moves are examined until finding one that satisfies this threshold. At this point, an additional fixed number of moves (denoted by *Plus*) is examined, and the best overall move is selected. *Min* and *Max* values may be used to avoid too many or too few moves from being examined. The aspiration threshold can be determined in several ways. One trivial way is to choose a threshold based on the quality of the initial *Min* moves examined during the current iteration. Another strategy called *first improving* strategy results by setting *Plus=0* [Glo95].

Elite Candidate List Strategy:

Yet another approach called *elite candidate list* strategy consists of first building a *master list* of a relatively large number of moves, and selecting from it a certain fixed number of k best moves. Then at subsequent iterations the current best move from the master list is chosen, and this continues until a move that falls below a given quality threshold is obtained, or the total number of iterations have elapsed. Then a new master list is constructed and the process repeated [Glo95].

Bounded Change Strategy:

In this strategy, only moves that do not cause a change of the solution cost by more than a limited amount are accepted [Glo95].

According to Glover, in constructing candidate lists such as those described above, the concept of *move influence* is important for long-term considerations.

Therefore, evaluation criteria should be periodically modified to create significant structural changes, especially when no improving moves are found [Glo95].

4.9.4   Strategic Oscillation

This is another diversification approach of tabu search, where the idea is to drive the search toward and away from selected boundaries of feasibility. It operates by moving until hitting a boundary that would represent a point where the search would normally stop, also known as the *critical level*. Then, instead of stopping, the neighborhood definition is extended, or, the evaluation criteria modified, to permit crossing the boundary. The approach proceeds for a certain depth, and then the boundary is crossed again in the opposite direction proceeding to a new entry point. This process of crossing the boundary from different directions creates a form of *oscillation*. Control over this oscillation is established by generating modified evaluations and rules of movement, depending on the region navigated and the direction of the search. This process is also known as *strategic oscillation*.

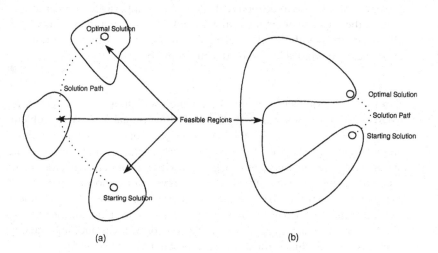

Figure 4.12: Topologies that can benefit from strategic oscillation [KGA93]. (a) Disjoint feasible regions; (b) Nonconvex feasible region.

There are several reasons for considering the use of strategic oscillation when solving optimization problems [KGA93]. One of them is that if the feasible solution space of the problem is disjoint, then strategic oscillation provides a mechanism for crossing regions of infeasibility in the course of search for optimal solution. As illustrated in Figure 4.12(a), maintaining feasibility at all times will not result in reaching an optimal solution, unless the starting solution is located in the

·feasible region that contains one of the optimal solutions. In some problems the feasible region may be connected; however, reaching the optimal solution may require a long path through the feasible state space, whereas if a solution path is allowed to enter infeasible regions, the optimal solution may be found easily [see Figure 4.12(b)].

Recent applications of strategic oscillation have proved effective in solving graph partitioning, scheduling and other hard problems [KGA93, MR93, RP91]. A common implementation of strategic oscillation is to alternate a series of constructive moves with a series of destructive moves as explained in the following examples.

Example 4.7 Consider the problem of finding an optimal spanning tree subject to inequality constraints (see Examples 4.1 and 4.4). Strategic oscillation for this problem results from a constructive process of adding edges to a growing tree until it is spanning, and then continuing to add edges to cross the boundary defined by the tree construction (more than $n - 1$ edges). A different graph structure results, which is no longer a tree, therefore rules for selecting moves have to be modified. The rules again change in order to proceed in the opposite direction, removing edges until again recovering a tree. Of course, the possibility of retracing a prior trajectory which may result in cycling can be avoided by standard tabu list mechanism.

■

Example 4.8 Another example of strategic oscillation that uses constructive/destructive moves arises in the multidimensional knapsack problem. Here values of zero-one variables are changed from 0 to 1 until reaching the boundary of feasibility. The method then continues into the infeasible region using the same type of change, but with a modified evaluator. After a selected number of steps, the direction is reversed by choosing moves that change variables from 1 to 0. Evaluation criteria to drive toward improvement vary according to whether the movement occurs inside or outside the feasible region. Recently, such an approach has been reported to produce high-quality solutions for multidimensional knapsack problems [FP86, GK95]

■

The boundary incorporated in strategic oscillation need not be defined in terms of feasibility or structure alone. It can also be defined in terms of a region where the search appears to settle around local optima. The oscillation then consists of compelling the search to move out of this region and allowing it to return. When applying strategic oscillation, it is recommended that more time be spent in searching regions close to the critical level [GL95, Glo95].

A desirable attribute of strategic oscillation is that it ensures sufficient diversity in the search by emphasizing different parts of the problem over time. The importance of feasibility is emphasized and deemphasized according to a prescribed pattern.[2] This diversifying effect of strategic oscillation increases the search power of the method by using a dynamic objective evaluation criteria that emphasizes and deemphasizes various parts of the problem, thereby making the search procedure more robust.

4.9.5 Path Relinking

Path relinking in tabu search consists of generating new solutions by exploring trajectories that connect *elite* solutions produced by other approaches, or elite solutions produced in previous iterations.

In path relinking, one of the elite solutions is selected as an *initiating* solution S', and another as the *guiding* solution S''. The procedure works as follows. The two solutions generate a path from S'-to-S'', producing a sequence of intermediate solutions $S' = S'(1), S'(2), \ldots, S'(r) = S''$. $S'(i + 1)$ is generated from $S'(i)$ a the result of a move. This move is chosen such that the number of moves remaining to reach S'' is minimized. This is accomplished by selecting moves that introduce attributes contained in the guiding solution, or reduce the distance between attributes in the initiating and those in the guiding solution. Once the path is complete, one or more of the solutions in the $S' - to - S''$ path is selected as a solution to initiate a new search phase [GL95].

A *set* of elite solutions can also be used as guiding solutions. Attributes provided by this set can be assigned weights. Larger weights are assigned to attributes that occur in greater numbers in the guiding solutions. This allows giving more emphasis to solutions with higher quality and/or special features [Glo96]. By modifying these assigned weights, promising regions in the search space can be searched more thoroughly.

The generation of paths "relinks" previous points in ways not achieved by previous search history. The initiating (guiding) solutions can also be 'null' solutions. In this case constructive (destructive) methods are used to reach the guiding solution. The initiating and guiding solutions can have interchangeable roles, therefore they are collectively called as reference solutions. For appropriate choices of reference solutions and neighborhoods for generating paths from them, additional elite points are likely to be found in the regions traversed by the paths (proximate optimality principle [Glo95]). It has been observed that combinatorial solution spaces often have topologies that may be usefully exploited by such an approach [Mos93, NS93].

Path relinking has similarities to a population-based approach called *scatter search* [Glo77]. In scatter search, new solutions are generated by creating modified *linear* combinations of the reference points [Glo77]. In both, path relinking

---

[2]This type of diversification is substantially different from the traditional types of diversification schemes based on long-term memory functions discussed in Section 4.5.

and scatter search, the reference points are elite solutions, and the best combined solutions are used to reinitiate the search processes which is executed repetitively. However, the modified linear combinations in scatter search can be viewed as generating paths in Euclidean vector space, whereas in path relinking, the combination is in neighborhood space [Glo96].

Since the solutions produced by path relinking may be viewed as combinations of their reference solutions, there is also a connection between tabu search and genetic algorithms (Chapter 3). According to Glover [Glo95], many recently developed crossover operators in genetic algorithms (see Chapter 3) can be shown to arise as instances of path relinking, by restricting attention to two reference points (which represent parents in GAs), except that strategic selection replaces randomization (frequently used in GAs). Path relinking automatically provides solution combination procedures that suit specific contexts. This is different from GAs where each new class of problems requires the design of new crossovers [Glo96].

Intensification and diversification can also be incorporated in path relinking. With reference to path relinking, intensification approaches typically choose reference solutions S' and S'' to be elite solutions that lie in a *common* region, or those which share common features. Diversification strategies based on path relinking select reference solutions that come from *different* regions or those that exhibit contrasting features. Diversification strategies may also place emphasis on paths that go beyond the reference solutions.

The basic path relinking process can be summarized as follows. First a neighborhood structure and associated solution attributes are identified. Neighborhoods for path relinking process may differ from those used in other search phases. For example, they may be chosen to tunnel through infeasible regions. Then, a collection of two or more reference solutions are chosen to serve as initiating and guiding solutions. Intermediate solutions are generated with the help of moves that connect initiating and guiding solutions. These moves may also take the generated solutions beyond the guiding solutions. These intermediate solutions serve as initial solutions in subsequent search iterations.

4.10 Conclusions

In this chapter we presented the basics of tabu search heuristic. Several implementation issues such as moves and their attributes, tabu lists (static/dynamic) and tabu restrictions, data structures to handle tabu lists, and various aspiration criteria were presented with examples (Section 4.3).

Tabu search is different from other search techniques in several respects. One, of course, is the use of memory. In addition, reasonably sized subset of neighborhood is explored and the best move among these is chosen. Further, unlike other search techniques where "best" generally refers to the best cost of the solution, in tabu search best refers to change in the evaluation function which depends not only on the objective/cost function, but also on the search history, region being searched, and so forth.

The core of the tabu search algorithm is the short-term memory component, implemented with the help of tabu_list(s) and aspiration criterion. Intermediate and long-term memory components are also used for intensification and diversification (Sections 4.4.1 and 4.4.2). Diversification techniques that penalize frequently occurring moves, and others that are suitable for permutation problems, were discussed in Section 4.5.

Convergence aspects were discussed in Section 4.6. Deterministic tabu search is not guaranteed to converge; on the other hand, probabilistic tabu search would converge if run for a large amount of time.

In the section on tabu search applications (Section 4.7) we illustrated how tabu search can be engineered to solve several hard combinatorial optimization problems. Two such applications have been discussed in detail.

Tabu search has been able to find optimal solutions for many relatively small problems instances in a reasonably small time. The runtime can grow to unacceptable proportion for large problem size. Several parallelization strategies have been proposed for TS. All of them resulted in significant speed-up (Section 4.8).

Other important, recent, and often neglected issues were discussed in Section 4.9. Target analysis, presented in Section 4.9.2, helps in designing suitable evaluators useful when applying diversification strategies. The term "neighborhood" has a different meaning in tabu search than in other search methods. Often, the term "neighboring solution" refers to a solution that is obtained by means of a small perturbation to the current solution. However, in TS, when intensification and diversification are applied using intermediate- and long-term memory processes, $\aleph(\mathbf{H}, S)$ may contain solutions not in $\aleph(S)$. For example, these may include high-quality local optima (elite solutions) encountered at various points during the search process.

A common phenomenon in most combinatorial optimization problems is that the amount of computational effort needed to generate all the available moves grows faster than linearly with increase in the problem dimension. Complete examination of all alternatives then becomes computationally expensive. In such cases, the number of solutions examined can be restricted using what is known as "candidate list strategies." Various proposed candidate list strategies that help increase the efficiency of search were discussed (Section 4.9.3). Using such strategies, search can also be restricted to certain regions, thereby causing intensification.

Strategic oscillation is a critical component in some tabu search applications [KGA93]. The general concept (see Section 4.9.4) is one of varying the weights applied to different parts of the problem when evaluating moves [Glo77, Glo89b]. In the study presented in [KGA93], the importance of *feasibility* during the search procedure is dynamically varied. In tabu search, sometimes infeasible neighboring solutions are also considered. By allowing feasible as well as *infeasible* solutions to occur, the search is able to traverse more of the solution space and locate better solutions in the process.

In order to generate new starting solutions, path relinking is employed (see Section 4.9.5). In path relinking, some elite solutions are selected, one of them serves as an initiating solution. Then, smallest number of moves are made that take the initiating solution to the remaining solutions (guiding solutions). The intermediate points (or solutions) can be used as new starting solutions. New elite solutions may also be found in this process, since the process is similar to that of combining good characteristics of various solutions.

References

[AK94]   S. Amellal and B. Kaminska. Functional synthesis of digital systems with TASS. *IEEE Transactions on Computer-Aided Design*, 13(5):537–552, May 1994.

[AS95]   K. S. Al-Sultan. A tabu search approach to the clustering problem. *Pattern Recognition*, 28(9):1443–1451, 1995.

[ASF98]   K. S. Al-Sultan and C. A. Fedjki. A tabu search based algorithm for the fuzzy clustering problem. *Pattern Recognition*, 1998 (in press).

[AV93]   S. Areibi and A. Vannelli. Circuit partitioning using a tabu search approach. In *1993 IEEE International Symposium on Circuits and Systems*, pages 1643–1646, 1993.

[BC95]   J. W. Barnes and J. B. Chambers. Solving the job shop scheduling problem with tabu search. *IIE Transactions*, 27:257–263, 1995.

[CM-89]   *Connection Machine Model CM-2, Technical Summary Version 5.1*. Thinking Machines Corporation, Cambridge, MA, May 1989.

[CSK93]   J. Chakrapani and J. Skorin-Kapov. Massively parallel tabu search for the quadratic assignment problem. *Annals of Operations Research*, 41:327–341, 1993.

[CTG97]   T. G. Crainic, M. Toulouse, and M. Gendreau. Toward a taxonomy of parallel tabu search heuristics. *INFORMS Journal of Computing*, 9(1):61–72, 1997.

[DdW93]   N. Dubois and D. de Werra. EPCOT: An efficient procedure for coloring optimally with tabu search. *Computers Math Applications*, 25(10/11):35–45, 1993.

[DT93]   M. Dell'Amico and M. Trubian. Applying tabu search to the job-shop scheduling problem. *Annals of Operations Research*, 41:231–252, 1993.

[DV93]   F. Dammeyer and Stefan Voß. Dynamic tabu list management using the reverse elimination method. *Annals of Operations Research*, 41:31–46, 1993.

[FBTV94]   I. De Falco, R. Del Balio, E. Tarantino, and R. Vaccaro. Improving search by incorporating evolution principles in parallel tabu search. *Proceedings of the First IEEE Conference on Evolutionary Computation- ICEC'94*, pages 823–828, June 1994.

[FHdW90]   C. Friden, A. Hertz, and D. de Werra. TABARIS: An exact algorithm based on tabu search for finding a maximum independent set in a graph. *Computers and Operations Research*, 19(1–4):81–91, 1990.

[FK92]   U. Faigle and W. Kern. Some convergence results for probabilistic Tabu Search. *ORSA Journal on Computing*, 4(1):32–37, Winter 1992.

[Fox83]   M. S. Fox. Constraint-directed search. Doctoral dissertation, Carnegie-Mellon University, 1983.

[FP86]   A. Freville and G. Plateau. Heuristics and reduction methods for multiple constraint 0-1 linear programming problems. *European Journal of Operational Research*, 24:206–215, 1986.

[GG89]   F. Glover and H. J. Greenberg. New approaches for heuristic search: A bilateral linkage with artificial intelligence. *European Journal of Operational Research*, 39:119–130, 1989.

[GH91]   F. Glover and R. Hübscher. Binpacking with a tabu search. Technical Report, Graduate School of Business Administration, University of Colorado, Boulder, 1991.

[GK95]   F. Glover and G. Kochenberger. Critical event tabu search for multi-dimensional knapsack problems. Technical Report, Graduate School of Business Administration, University of Colorado, Boulder, 1995.

[GL95]   F. Glover and M. Laguna. Tabu search. In C. Reeves, editor, *Modern Heuristic Techniques for Combinatorial Problems*. McGraw-Hill Book Co., Europe, 1995.

[GL97]   F. Glover and M. Laguna. *Tabu Search*. Kluwer, MA, 1997.

[Glo77]   F. Glover. Heuristics for integer programming using surrogate con-
            straints. *Decision Sciences*, 8:156–166, 1977.

[Glo86]   F. Glover. Future paths for integer programming and links to arti-
            ficial intelligence. *Computers & Operations Research*, 13(5):533–
            549, 1986.

[Glo89a]   F. Glover. Candidate list strategies and tabu search. Technical Re-
            port, Graduate School of Business Administration, University of
            Colorado, Boulder, 1989.

[Glo89b]   F. Glover. Tabu search—Part I. *ORSA Journal on Computing*,
            1(3):190–206, 1989.

[Glo90a]   F. Glover. Artificial intelligence, heuristic frameworks and tabu
            search. *Managerial and Decision Economics*, 11:365–375, 1990.

[Glo90b]   F. Glover. Tabu search—Part II. *ORSA Journal on Computing*,
            2(1):4–32, 1990.

[Glo90c]   F. Glover. Tabu search: A tutorial. Technical Report, University of
            Colorado, Boulder, February 1990.

[Glo95]   F. Glover. Tabu search fundamentals and uses. Technical Report,
            Graduate School of Business Administration, University of Col-
            orado, Boulder, June 1995.

[Glo96]   F. Glover. Tabu search and adaptive memory programming—
            advances, applications and challenges. Technical Report, College
            of Business, University of Colorado, Boulder, 1996.

[GPR94]   Bruno-Laurent Garica, Jean-Yves Potvin, and Jean-Marc Rousseau.
            A parallel implementation of the tabu search heuristic for vehicle
            routing problems with time window constraints. *Computers & Op-
            erations Research*, 21(9):1025–1033, November 1994.

[GSS93]   M. Gendreau, P. Soriano, and L. Salvail. Solving the maximum
            clique problem using a tabu search approach. *Annals of Operations
            Research*, 41:385–404, 1993.

[GTdW93]   F. Glover, E. Taillard, and D. de Werra. A user's guide to tabu search.
            Annals of Operations Research, 41:3–28, 1993.

[Han86]   P. Hansen. The steepest ascent mildest descent heuristic for combi-
            natorial programming. *Congress on Numerical Methods in Combi-
            natorial Optimization*, 1986.

[HdW87]   A. Hertz and D. de Werra. Using tabu search techniques for graph coloring. *Computing*, 39:345–351, 1987.

[HG94]   R. Hübscher and F. Glover. Applying tabu search with influential diversification to multiprocessor scheduling. *Computers & Operations Research*, 21(8):877–884, 1994.

[IE94]   O. Icmeil and S. Selcuk Erenguc. A tabu search procedure for the resource constrained project scheduling problem with discounted cash flows. *Computers & Operations Research*, 21(8):841–853, 1994.

[KGA93]   J. P. Kelly, B. L. Golden, and A. A. Assad. Large-scale controlled rounding using tabu search with strategic oscillation. *Annals of Operations Research*, 41:69–84, 1993.

[KLG94]   J. P. Kelly, M. Laguna, and F. Glover. A study of diversification strategies for the quadratic assignment problem. *Computers and Operations Research*, 21(8):885–893, 1994.

[Kno89]   J. Knox. The application of tabu search to symmetric traveling salesman problem. Doctoral dissertation, Graduate School of Business Administration, University of Colorado, Boulder, July 1989.

[LBG89]   M. Laguna, J. W. Barnes, and F. Glover. Scheduling jobs with linear delay penalties and sequence dependent setup costs using tabu search. Research Report, Department of Mechanical Engineering, The University of Texas, Austin, April 1989.

[LC91]   A. Lim and Yeow-Meng Chee. Graph partitioning using tabu search. *1991 IEEE International Symposium on Circuits and Systems*, pages 1164–1167, 1991.

[LG93a]   M. Laguna and F. Glover. Bandwidth packing; a tabu search approach. *Management Science*, 39(4):492–500, 1993.

[LG93b]   M. Laguna and F. Glover. Integrating target analysis and tabu search for improved scheduling systems. *Expert Systems with Applications*, 6:287–297, 1993.

[Low76]   B. T. Lowerre. The HARPY speech recognition system. Doctoral dissertation, Carnegie-Mellon University, September 1976.

[LZ93]   D. L. Woodruff and E. Zemel. Hashing vectors for tabu search. *Annals of Operations Research*, 41:123–137, 1993.

[MGPO89] M. Malek, M. Guruswamy, M. Pandya, and H. Owens. Serial and parallel simulated annealing and tabu search algorithms for the traveling salesman problem. *Annals of Operations Research*, 21:59–84, 1989.

[MHKM89] M. Malek, M. Heap, R. Kapur, and A. Mourad. A fault tolerant implementation of the traveling salesman problem. Research Report, Department of Electrical Engineering and Computer Engineering, The University of Texas, Austin, May 1989.

[Mos93]   P. Moscatto. An introduction to population approaches for optimization and hierarchical objective functions: A discussion on the role of tabu search. *Annals of Operations Research*, 41:85–122, 1993.

[MR93]   E. L. Mooney and R. L. Rardin. Tabu search for a class of scheduling problems. *Annals of Operations Research*, 41:253–278, 1993.

[NS93]   E. Nowicki and C. Smutnicki. A fast taboo search algorithm for the job shop problem. Technical Report 8/93, Institute of Engineering Cybernetics, Technical University of Wroclaw, 1993.

[NVR68]   C. E. Nugent, T. E. Vollmann, and R. Ruml. An experimental comparison of techniques for the assignment of facilities to locations. *Operations Research*, 16:150–173, 1968.

[OM88]   P. S. Ow and T. E. Morton. Filtered beam search in scheduling. *International Journal of Production Research*, 26(1):35–62, 1988.

[Osm93]   I. H. Osman. Metastrategy simulated annealing and tabu search algorithms for the vehicle routing problem. *Annals of Operations Research*, 41:421–451, 1993.

[Ree93]   C. R. Reeves. Improving the efficiency of tabu search for machine sequencing problems. *Journal of Operational Research Society*, 44:375–382, 1993.

[RLB96]   J. Renaud, G. Laporte, and F. F. Boctor. A tabu search heuristic for the multi-depot vehicle routing problem. *Computers and Operations Research*, 23:229–235, 1996.

[ROS89]   J. Ryan, S. Oliveira, and G. Stroud. A parallel version of tabu search and the path assignment problem. *Heuristics for Combinatorial Optimization*, pages 1–24, 1989.

[RP91]   E. Rolland and H. Pirkul. Heuristic search for graph partitioning. 31st Joint National TIMS/ORSA Meeting, Nashville, TN, 1991.

[Rya89]   J. Ryan, editor. *Heuristics for Combinatorial Optimization*. June 1989.

[SAB96]   S. M. Sait, S. Ali, and M. S. T. Benten. Scheduling and allocation in high-level synthesis using stochastic techniques. *Microelectronics Journal*, 27(8):693–712, October 1996.

[SK90]   J. Skorin-Kapov. Tabu search applied to the quadratic assignment problem. *ORSA Journal on Computing*, 2(1):33–45, 1990.

[SM93]   M. Sun and P. G. McKeown. Tabu search applied to the general fixed charge problem. *Annals of Operations Research*, 41:405–420, 1993.

[ST93]   F. Semet and E. Taillard. Solving real-life vehicle routing problems efficiently using tabu search. *Annals of Operations Research*, 41:469–488, 1993.

[SV92]   L. Song and A. Vannelli. VLSI placement using tabu search. *Microelectronics Journal*, 17(5):437–445, 1992.

[Tai90]   E. Taillard. Some efficient heuristic methods for the flow shop sequencing problem. *European Journal of Operational Research*, 417:65–74, 1990.

[Tai91]   E. Taillard. Robust tabu search for the quadratic assignment problem. *Parallel Computing*, 17:443–455, 1991.

[Tai93]   E. Taillard. Parallel iterative search methods for the vehicle routing problem. *Networks*, 23:661–673, 1993.

[WH89]   M. Widmer and A. Hertz. A new heuristic method for the flow shop sequencing problem. *European Journal of Operational Research*, 41:186–193, 1989.

[Wid91]   M. Widmer. Job shop scheduling with tooling constraints: A tabu search approach. *Journal of Operational Research Society*, 42(1):75–82, 1991.

[YS98]   H. Youssef and S. M. Sait. Timing driven global router for standard cell design. *International Journal of Computer Systems Science and Engineering*, 1998 (in press).

Exercises

Exercise 4.1
Describe the key features of the tabu search heuristic and enumerate the key differences with other search heuristics discussed in the book.

Exercise 4.2
Write a program to solve the problem discussed in Example 4.1, page 189. Experiment with: (1) different tabu list sizes, (2) different move attributes, and (3) different candidate list sizes.

Exercise 4.3

1. Explain how you will determine a good size for the tabu list. What output will you need to observe and what range of sizes will you experiment with?

2. Should the size of the list be a function of the problem size, type of moves, or both? Justify your answer.

3. What are the benefits of using dynamic tabu lists?

Exercise 4.4
What experiments must be designed to determine a suitable value of tabu list size and candidate list size, and suitable move attributes?

Exercise 4.5
Show that the swap move for the scheduling problem discussed in Section 4.9.2 examines $N \times (N - 1)/2$ neighbor solutions, and the *insert* move is able to examine $N \times (N - 3) + 2$ additional neighbors.

Exercise 4.6

1. Write a tabu search program to solve the problem discussed in Example 4.3, page 199, using tabu search.

2. Compare the performance of the heuristic if the move attribute stored is one of the elements that has been swapped, and the tabu condition is any swap that involves this element in the tabu list. Is this condition more or less stringent than the one used in Example 4.3? How will this change in move attribute affect the change in the size of the tabu list?

3. Repeat the above if the *swap* move is replaced by the *insert* move. How does this small change affect the execution time of the program?

Exercise 4.7
The multiprocessor scheduling problem in Section 4.5 is defined as follows:

let $L = \{q_1, q_2, \ldots, q_n\}$ denote a collection of n tasks which must be assigned to m processors say $P_1, P_2, \ldots, P_m$. The goal is to find an assignment that minimizes the makespan of the m parallel processors. Show that on an average there are about n/m tasks assigned to each processor, which allows $(n/m)^2 \times m^2/2 = n^2/2$ possible exchange moves.

Exercise 4.8
What are the limitations of short-term memory tabu search? How can memory be used to intensify/diversify the search? For some combinatorial optimization problems discussed in this chapter, explain what type of information you will need to intensify/diversify the search. How will you use this information? Illustrate your suggestions using the problems discussed in Examples 4.1 and 4.3.

Exercise 4.9
Write a program to show that using only short-term memory component it is not possible to go from the initial solution given in Figure 4.6(a) to the optimal solution given in Figure 4.6(b).

Exercise 4.10
Explain how you will use recent local minima solutions encountered to diversify your search from current solutions (see page 212).

Exercise 4.11
In the context of tabu search explain briefly what do you understand by the following terms:

1. Aspiration by move influence
2. Candidate list strategies
3. Dynamic tabu lists
4. Evaluator functions
5. Frequency-based and recency-based tabu criterion
6. Multiple tabu lists
7. Strategic oscillation
8. Target analysis

Exercise 4.12
Repeat Exercise 4.6 by including information on frequency of moves to penalize them. Suggest an evaluation function. Explain when and how often you will switch to this evaluation function to diversify the search. Use the data structure given in Example 4.6 and explain how you will determine the value of α in the Equations on page 209.

Exercise 4.13
Consider the *vehicle routing problem* described in Chapter 1, page 7.

1. What type of moves and what memory structure will you use to transform one solution to another?

2. Suggest at least two attributes of moves that can be used.

3. What memory structure would you use for storing recency and frequency information?

4. Solve the problem using short-term tabu search. Choose suitable values for sizes of tabu list(s) and candidate list.

5. Experiment with different tabu list sizes, and different attributes of moves.

6. Describe how you will use elite solutions to incorporate their good attributes during intensification.

7. Store frequencies of moves and elite solution and devise a suitable scheme based on memory to diversify the search. Use target analysis to develop evaluators to support intensification and diversification for this problem. Incorporate this strategy in your short-term tabu implementation and compare the quality of solution and runtime.

8. Propose criteria that you would use to determine when to apply intensification and when to apply diversification.

9. Finally, if strategic oscillation is to be allowed by crossing boundaries of feasible solutions, explain how you will accept moves that violate constraints. Discuss the effect of inclusion of strategic oscillation in your program.

Exercise 4.14
Repeat the previous exercise (Exercise 4.13) considering the *flowshop scheduling problem* described in Chapter 2 (Exercise 2.16).

Exercise 4.15
Repeat Exercise 4.13 for the *terminal assignment problem* described in Chapter 2 (Exercise 2.17).

Exercise 4.16
Repeat Exercise 4.13 for the *concentrator location problem* described in Chapter 2 (Exercise 2.18).

Exercise 4.17
Repeat Exercise 4.13 for the *constrained minimum spanning tree problem* described in Chapter 2 (Exercise 2.19).

Exercise 4.18
Repeat Exercise 4.13 for the *mesh topology design problem* described in Chapter 2 (Exercise 2.20).

Exercise 4.19
Repeat Exercise 4.13 for the *weighted matching problem* described in Chapter 2 (Exercise 2.21).

Exercise 4.20
Repeat Exercise 4.13 for the *plant location problem* described in Chapter 2 (Exercise 2.22).

Exercise 4.21
Repeat Exercise 4.13 for the *bandwidth packing problem* described in Chapter 4 (Section 4.7.2).

Exercise 4.22
For problems given in Exercises 4.13 to 4.21, and the various combinatorial optimization problems discussed in Chapter 1 (pages 6–8), experiment with the following and comment on change in solution quality, ease of implementation, convergence, and runtime:

1. With change in candidate list size

2. With change in tabu list size

3. With dynamic tabu lists

4. With multiple tabu lists (if applicable)

5. Different move strategies

6. Different move attributes

7. Different candidate list strategies (some types are more suitable for one type of problem than others)

CHAPTER 5

Simulated Evolution (SimE)

5.1 Introduction

Ever since Kirkpatrick and colleagues [KCGV83] suggested the use of the simulated annealing (SA) paradigm to tackle hard combinatorial optimization problems, much research work has been conducted on its use and improvement. Concurrently, efforts were made to design other randomized iterative optimization algorithms that are based on somehow more elaborate heuristic knowledge, which should allow the newly designed algorithm to exhibit superior performance to that of simulated annealing with respect to runtime requirements and/or quality of solution. One of those heuristics is *simulated evolution* (SimE) which was proposed by Kling and Banerjee in 1987 [KB87b]. Simulated evolution is based on an analogy with the principles of natural selection thought to be followed by various species in their biological environments.

During the process of biological evolution, organisms tend to develop features that allow them to adapt to the peculiarities of their environment. The more an organism adapts to its environment, the better are its chances of survival. In other words, by adapting, an organism optimizes its chances of surviving in its environment. Hence, adaptation is seen as a form of optimization. This similarity has given rise to a new class of randomized iterative algorithms which consists of *genetic algorithms* (GAs), *simulated evolution*, and *stochastic evolution* (StocE). *Genetic algorithms* have been discussed in Chapter 3, *stochastic evolution* will be discussed in the next chapter, and *simulated evolution* will be the subject of this chapter. All three algorithms of this class are general randomized search heuristics that are based on concepts learned from biological evolution. For all three algorithms, the cost function is an estimation of the degree of adaptation of a particular solution to the target objective. For a maximization problem, the higher the value of the objective function is, the more that particular solution is adapted to

253

its environment.

In this chapter, we start in Section 5.2 with a brief narration of the fairly recent history of *simulated evolution* (SimE). Then Section 5.3 describes the basic SimE algorithm. SimE operators and parameters are addressed in Section 5.4. A qualitative comparison of SimE, SA, and GA algorithms is provided in Section 5.5. In Section 5.6 we look into the convergence aspects of SimE. Examples of SimE applications are given in Section 5.7. Parallelization strategies of SimE are presented in Section 5.8. Finally, in Section 5.9, we briefly present other issues and recent development related to SimE.

5.2   Historical Background

The first paper describing simulated evolution (SimE) appeared in 1987 [KB87b]. The paper was authored by Ralph Kling (working then on his Ph.D.) and Prithviraj Banerjee (his dissertation chairman). Other papers by the same authors followed [KB89, KB90, KB91]. Since all of the work of Kling and Banerjee appeared in design automation conferences and journals, applications of simulated evolution by other researchers were mostly to solve hard design automation problems [LHT89, LM93, Mao94, MH94, MH96]. Very few other applications were in other areas of engineering [C.V94, G.M94].

Simulated evolution is a powerful general iterative heuristic for solving combinatorial optimization problems. It is an instance of the class of general iterative heuristics discussed in [NSS85]. It is stochastic because the selection of which components of a solution to change is done according to a stochastic rule. Already well-located components have a high probability to remain where they are. The probabilistic feature gives SimE hill-climbing property.

Like SA and GA, SimE is conceptually simple and elegant. Actually, all algorithms discussed in this book are similar in several aspects: (1) they are general in the sense that they can be tailored to solve most known combinatorial optimization problems; (2) they have the capability of escaping local minima; and (3) they are blind, that is, they do not know the optimal solution and have to be told when to stop.

5.3   Simulated Evolution Algorithm

The simulated evolution algorithm (SimE) is a general search strategy for solving a variety of combinatorial optimization problems. It is usually confused with the stochastic evolution algorithm that will be the subject of a later chapter. However, as shall be seen, each algorithm has its own distinctive features. Distinctions among these two heuristics are the result of differences in the way they mimic the biological processes of evolution as well as in the way they adapt their parameters during the search.

Combinatorial optimization problems seek to find a global optimum of some real valued cost function $cost : \Omega \to R$ defined over a *discrete* set Ω. The set Ω is called the state space and its elements are referred to as states. A state space Ω together with an underlying neighborhood structure (the way one state can be reached from another state) form the solution space.

Combinatorial optimization problems can be modeled in a number of ways. A generic formulation suggested by Saab and Rao [SR90] is the following:

> *Given a finite set M of distinct movable elements and a finite set L of locations, a state is defined as an assignment function $S : M \to L$ satisfying certain constraints.*

Many of the combinatorial problems can be formulated according to this generic model. Below, we give few examples. Other examples are provided in the next chapter.

Example 5.1 *Quadratic assignment problem* (**QAP**) [SR90].

Problem: Given a set M of n modules and a set L of $|L|$ locations, $|L| \geq n$. Let $c_{i,j}$ be the number of connections between elements i and j, and $d_{k,l}$ be the distance between locations k and l.

Objective: Assign each module to a distinct location so as to minimize the wire-length needed to interconnect the modules.

To formulate QAP in terms of the above state model, choose $M = \{1, 2, \ldots, n\}$ and $L = \{1, 2, \ldots, |L|\}$. Then a state is defined as the *onto function* $S : M = \{1, 2, \ldots, n\} \to \{1, 2, \ldots, |L|\}$. In this case, one additional constraint is required, which can be stated as $S(i) \neq S(j) \ \forall \ i \neq j$, that is, no two elements are assigned to the same location. The cost of a state, $Cost(S)$ is the wire-length required to interconnect all the elements in their present locations. That is,

$$Cost(S) = \sum_{i=1}^{n} \sum_{j=1}^{n} c_{i,j} d_{S(i),S(j)}$$

∎

Example 5.2 *The graph bisection problem* (**GBP**) [SR90].

Problem: Given a graph $G = (V, E)$ where V is the set of vertices, E the set of edges, and $|V| = 2n$. Partition the graph into two subgraphs $G_1(V_1, E_1)$ and $G_2(V_2, E_2)$ such that (1) $|V_1| = |V_2| = n$, (2) $V_1 \cap V_2 = \emptyset$, and (3) $V_1 \cup V_2 = V$.

Objective: Minimize the number of edges with vertices in both V_1 and V_2.

To formulate GBP in terms of the proposed state model, choose $M = V$, the vertex set, and $L = \{1, 2\}$. Then a state is defined as the *onto function* $S : V \rightarrow \{1, 2\}$. In this case, there is one constraint which can be stated as $|S^{-1}(1)| = |S^{-1}(2)|$, that is, a state is a partition of the vertex set into two parts of equal cardinalities. Moreover, the cost of a state, $Cost(S)$, is the number of edges $(i, j) \in E$ with $S(i) \neq S(j)$.

■

Example 5.3 *The traveling salesman problem* **(TSP)** [SR90].

Problem: Given a complete graph $G = (V, E)$ with n vertices. Let $d_{u,v}$ be the length of the edge $(u, v) \in E$ and $d_{u,v} = d_{v,u}$. A path starting at some vertex $v \in V$, visiting every other vertex exactly once, and returning at vertex v is called a *tour*.

Objective: Find a *tour* of minimum length, where the length of a *tour* is equal to the sum of lengths of its defining edges.

To formulate TSP in terms of the suggested state model, choose the movable elements as the order in which the vertices are visited, that is, $M = \{1, 2, \ldots, n\}$ and choose $L = V$. Then a state is defined as the *one-to-one function* $S : \{1, 2, \ldots, n\}, \rightarrow V$, where $1 \leq S(i) \leq n$, $S(i) \neq S(j)$, $1 \leq i \leq n$, $1 \leq j \leq n$, and $i \neq j$. $S(1)$ is the vertex where the tour starts and ends, and $S(i)$ is the ith vertex visited during the tour, $1 \leq i \leq n$. A state is simply a permutation of the sequence $[1, 2, \ldots, n]$, The tour corresponding to state S is $[S(1), S(2), \ldots, S(i), S(i + 1), \ldots, S(n), S(1)]$. The cost of state S, $Cost(S)$, is the length of the corresponding tour, that is,

$$Cost(S) = d_{S(n),S(1)} + \sum_{i=1}^{n-1} d_{S(i),S(i+1)}$$

■

The SimE algorithm starts from an initial assignment, and then, following an evolution-based approach, it seeks to reach better assignments from one generation to the next. SimE assumes that there exists a population P of a set M of n (movable) elements. In addition, there is a cost function $Cost$ that is used to associate with each assignment of movable element m a cost C_m. The cost C_m is used to compute the goodness (fitness) g_m of element m, for each $m \in M$. Furthermore, there are usually additional constraints that must be satisfied by the population as a whole or by particular elements. A general outline of the SimE algorithm is given in Figure 5.1.

ALGORITHM *Simulated_Evolution(M, L)*;
/* M: Set of movable elements; */
/* L: Set of locations; */
/* B: Selection bias; */
/* Stopping criteria and selection bias can be automatically adjusted; */
INITIALIZATION;
Repeat
    EVALUATION:
        ForEach $m \in M$ **Do** $g_m = \frac{O_m}{C_m}$ **EndForEach**;

    SELECTION:
        ForEach $m \in M$ **Do**
           If *Selection(m,B)* **Then** $P_s = P_s \cup \{m\}$
             Else $P_r = P_r \cup \{m\}$
        EndIf;
        EndForEach;
    Sort the elements of P_s;

    ALLOCATION:
        ForEach $m \in P_s$ **Do** *Allocation*(m) **EndForEach**;
Until *Stopping-criteria are met*;
Return $(BestSolution)$;
End *Simulated_Evolution*.

Figure 5.1: Simulated evolution algorithm.

SimE algorithm proceeds as follows. Initially, a population[1] is created at random from all populations satisfying the environmental constraints of the problem. The algorithm has one main loop consisting of three basic steps, *Evaluation*, *Selection*, and *Allocation*. The three steps are executed in sequence until the population average *goodness* reaches a maximum value, or no noticeable improvement to the population *goodness* is observed after a number of iterations. Another possible stopping criterion could be to run the algorithm for a prefixed number of iterations (see Figure 5.1). We now look at each of the steps of the SimE algorithm in more details, and illustrate it with the help of some examples.

---

[1] In SimE terminology, a population refers to a single solution. Individuals of the population are components of the solution; they are the movable elements.

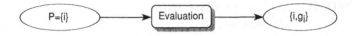

Figure 5.2: Evaluation.

5.3.1 Evaluation

The *Evaluation* step consists of evaluating the goodness of each individual i of the population P (see Figure 5.2). The *goodness* measure must be a single number expressible in the range $[0, 1]$. *Goodness* is defined as follows:

$$g_i = \frac{O_i}{C_i} \tag{5.1}$$

where O_i is an estimate of the optimal cost of individual i, and C_i is the actual cost of i in its current location. The above equation assumes a minimization problem (maximization of goodness). Notice that, according to the above definition, the O_i's **do not** change from generation to generation, and therefore, are computed only once during the initialization step. Hence only the C_i's have to be recomputed at each call to the *evaluation* function.

Empirical evidence [Kli90] shows that the accuracy of the estimation of O_i is not very crucial to the successful application of SimE. However, the *goodness* measure must be strongly related to the target objective of the given problem.

Let us illustrate how one might define *goodness* for two well-known combinatorial optimization problems: the *graph bisection problem (GBP)* and the *traveling salesman problem (TSP)*.

> **Example 5.4** *Graph bisection problem:*
> The population is equal to the set of vertices, that is, $P = V$. An individual is just a vertex. The edge $(u, v) \in E$ is said to be *cut* if and only if $u \in V_p$ and $v \in V_{3-p}$, $p = 1, 2$, that is, $S(u) \neq S(v)$. The cost of a state S is equal to the number of edges whose state is *cut*. Each edge (i, j) is assigned a weight $w_{i,j}$ as follows:
>
> $$w_{i,j} = \begin{cases} 0 & \text{if } S(i) = S(j) \\ 1 & \text{if } S(i) \neq S(j) \end{cases}$$
>
> That is, each edge whose state is cut is assigned a weight equal to 1 and 0 if its state is uncut.
>
> Then, for each vertex $i \in V$, we can define its *goodness* with respect to a particular partition as follows:
>
> $$g_i = \frac{d_i - w_i}{d_i} = 1 - \frac{w_i}{d_i}$$

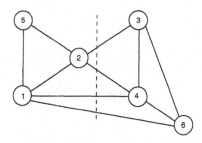

Figure 5.3: Example of graph bisection problem: $V = \{1, 2, 3, 4, 5, 6\}$, $E = \{(1, 2),$ $(1, 4)$, $(1, 5)$, $(1, 6)$, $(2, 3)$, $(2, 4)$, $(2, 5)\}$, $(3, 4)$, $(3, 6)$, $(4, 6)\}$, $S^{-1}(1) = \{1, 2, 5\}$, $S^{-1}(2) = \{3, 4, 6\}$, and $Cost(S) = 4$.

where d_i is equal to the degree of vertex i and w_i is the sum of the weights of the edges connected to vertex i. Hence, a vertex whose neighbor vertices are all located in the same partition $S(i)$ of vertex i will have a weight $w_i = 0$, thus giving a maximum goodness of 1. Such a vertex should remain in its current location.

∎

For the example in Figure 5.3, the weights of the various edges for this particular bipartition are $w_{1,2} = w_{1,5} = w_{2,5} = w_{3,4} = w_{3,6} = w_{4,6} = 0$ and $w_{1,4} = w_{1,6} = w_{2,3} = w_{2,4} = 1$. Then the degree, weight, and goodness of each of the six vertices are:

$$
\begin{array}{lll}
d_1 = 4 & w_1 = 2 & g_1 = 1 - \frac{2}{4} = 0.5 \\
d_2 = 4 & w_2 = 2 & g_2 = 1 - \frac{2}{4} = 0.5 \\
d_3 = 3 & w_3 = 1 & g_3 = 1 - \frac{1}{3} = 0.667 \\
d_4 = 4 & w_4 = 2 & g_4 = 1 - \frac{2}{4} = 0.5 \\
d_5 = 2 & w_5 = 0 & g_5 = 1 - \frac{0}{3} = 1 \\
d_6 = 3 & w_6 = 1 & g_6 = 1 - \frac{1}{3} = 0.667
\end{array}
$$

Example 5.5 *Traveling salesman problem:*
For each vertex $i \in V$, let $Nearest(i)$ and $NextNearest(i)$ be the closest and next closest vertices to i, and $d_i^{\min}$ be the distance of i to its two nearest neighbors. That is,

$$d_i^{\min} = d_{i,Nearest(i)} + d_{i,NextNearest(i)}$$

For any particular tour $[S(1), \ldots, S(i-1), S(i), S(i+1), \ldots, S(n), S(1)]$,

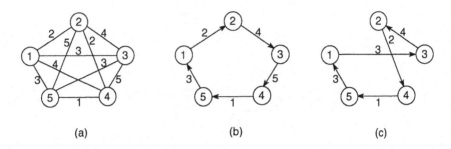

(a)   (b)   (c)

Figure 5.4: TSP example. (a) A complete graph on five vertices; weights on the edges represent distances between the corresponding vertices. (b) A tour with length 15. (c) A tour of length 13.

the goodness of vertex $S(i) \in V$, $1 \leq i \leq n$ is defined as follows:

$$g_{S(i)} = \frac{d_{S(i)}^{\min}}{d_{S(i)}}$$

where

$$d_{S(1)} = d_{S(1),S(2)} + d_{S(n),S(1)}$$

$$d_{S(n)} = d_{S(n-1),S(n)} + d_{S(n),S(1)}$$

$$d_{S(i)} = d_{S(i-1),S(i)} + d_{S(i),S(i+1)} \quad 2 \leq i \leq n-1$$

Figure 5.4 illustrates how the goodnesses are computed for a TSP instance with five vertices. For this graph, $d_1^{\min} = 2 + 3 = 5$, $d_2^{\min} = 2 + 2 = 4$, $d_3^{\min} = 3 + 3 = 6$, $d_4^{\min} = 1 + 2 = 3$, $d_5^{\min} = 1 + 3 = 4$. For the tour of Figure 5.4(b), $g_1 = \frac{5}{5} = 1$, $g_2 = \frac{4}{6} = 0.667$, $g_3 = \frac{6}{9} = 0.667$, $g_4 = \frac{3}{6} = 0.5$, $g_5 = \frac{4}{4} = 1$, and the average goodness in the population is $(1/5) \times \sum_{i=1}^{5} g_i = 0.7667$. For this tour $S(1) = 1$, $S(2) = 2$, $S(3) = 3$, $S(4) = 4$, and $S(5) = 5$. Similarly, for the shorter tour of Figure 5.4(c), the goodnesses will be $g_1 = \frac{5}{6} = 0.8333$, $g_2 = \frac{4}{6} = 0.6667$, $g_3 = \frac{6}{7} = 0.8571$, $g_4 = \frac{3}{3} = 1$, $g_5 = \frac{4}{4} = 1$, and the average goodness in the population is $(1/5) \times \sum_{i=1}^{5} g_i = 0.8714$. For this tour $S(1) = 1$, $S(2) = 3$, $S(3) = 2$, $S(4) = 4$, and $S(5) = 5$.

Notice, that after a particular perturbation, only the goodnesses of those vertices affected by the perturbation need to be updated.

Function *Selection(m,B)*;
/* m: is a particular movable element; */
/* B: Selection Bias; */
        If $Random \leq 1 - g_m + B$ **Then** **Return** True
            Else **Return** False
        EndIf
End*Selection*;

Figure 5.5: Selection function employed in the SimE algorithm of Figure 5.1.

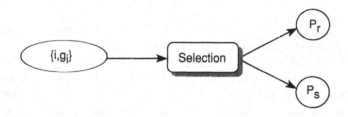

Figure 5.6: Selection.

5.3.2 Selection

The second step of the SimE algorithm is *Selection* (see Figure 5.5). *Selection* takes as input the population P together with the estimated *goodness* of each individual, and partitions P into two disjoint sets, a selection set P_s and a set P_r of the remaining members of the population (see Figure 5.6). Each member of the population is considered separately from all other individuals. The decision whether to assign individual i to the set P_s or set P_r is based solely on its *goodness* g_i. The *Selection* operator uses a selection function $Selection$, which takes as input g_i and a parameter B, which is a *selection bias*. Values of B are recommended to be in the range $[-0.2, 0.2]$. In many cases a value of $B = 0$ would be a reasonable choice.

The *Selection* function returns *true* or *false*. The higher is the *goodness* value of the element, the higher is its chance of staying in its current location, that is, unaltered in the next generation. On the other hand, the lower is the *goodness* value, the more likely the corresponding element will be selected for alteration (mutation) in the next generation (will be assigned to the selection set P_s).

The *Selection* operator has a nondeterministic nature. An individual with a high *fitness* (*goodness* close to one) still has a nonzero probability of being assigned to the selected set P_s. It is this element of nondeterminism that gives SimE the capability of escaping local minima.

5.3.3 Sorting

For most problems, it is always beneficial to alter the elements of the population according to a deterministic order that is correlated with the objective function being optimized. Hence, in SimE, prior to the *Allocation* step, the elements in the selection set P_s are sorted. The sorting criterion is problem-specific. Usually there are several criteria to choose from. For example, for the graph bisection problem (GBP), one may sort the elements of P_s in ascending order of their goodnesses. Another possible criterion would be to sort the elements of P_s in descending order of their D-values, where D_v, the D-value of vertex $v \in V$ is defined as follows [KL70]:

$$D_v = E_v - I_v$$

where E_v and I_v are the number of edges having v as one of their ends and whose states are cut and uncut, respectively. Refering to Figure 5.3, $D_1 = 2 - 2 = 0$, $D_2 = 2 - 2 = 0$, $D_3 = 1 - 2 = -1$, $D_4 = 2 - 2 = 0$, $D_5 = 0 - 2 = -2$, and $D_6 = 1 - 2 = -1$. In descending order of their D-values, the sequence of these six vertices would be [1, 2, 4, 3, 6, 5]. This is the same order that would have been obtained if the vertices were sorted in ascending order of the goodness values (see Example 5.4 on page 258).

5.3.4 Allocation

Allocation is the SimE operator that has most impact on the quality of solution. *Allocation* takes as input the two sets P_s and P_r and generates a new population P' which contains all the members of the previous population P, with the elements of P_s mutated according to an allocation function, *allocation* (Figure 5.7).

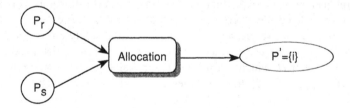

Figure 5.7: Allocation.

The choice of a suitable *allocation* function is problem-specific. The decision of the *allocation* strategy usually requires more ingenuity on the part of the designer than the *selection* scheme. The *allocation* function may be a nondeterministic function which involves a choice among a number of possible mutations (moves) for each element of P_s. Usually, a number of *trial-mutations* are performed and rated with respect to their *goodnesses*. Based on the resulting goodnesses, a final configuration of the population P' is decided. The goal of *allocation* is to favor improvements over the previous generation, without being too greedy.

Allocation functions can be *local* or *global*. With *local allocation*, a selected individual is altered on the basis of local information so that only local alterations within the immediate neighborhood of that individual are allowed. On the other hand, *global allocation* uses global information about all the individuals of the population so that it may affect any of the individuals in the entire population. For example, in the quadratic assignment problem a local alteration would attempt to swap the selected module with another module in its local neighborhood, whereas a global alteration would seek a swap with any of the modules of the population.

The *allocation* operation is a complex form of genetic *mutation* which is one of the genetic operations thought to be responsible for the evolution of the various species in biological environments. The *allocation* function mutates the population P by altering the locations of the elements of the selected set P_s. The population P is regarded as the parent and the population after mutation is P' and is regarded as the *offspring*. There is no need for a *crossover* operation as in GA since only one parent is maintained in all generations. However, since *mutation* is the only mechanism used by SimE for inheritance and evolution, it must be more sophisticated than the one used in GA.

Allocation alters (mutates) all the elements in the selected set P_s one after the other in a predetermined order. The order as well as the type of mutation are problem specific. For example, for the case of the quadratic assignment problem, alteration of a module may consist of swapping the location of a selected module with the location of another module. For each individual e_i of the selected set P_s, W distinct trial alterations are attempted. The trial that leads to the best configuration (population) with respect to the objective being optimized is accepted and made permanent. Since the *goodness* of each individual element is also tightly coupled with the target objective, superior alterations are supposed to gradually improve the individual goodnesses as well. Hence, *allocation* allows the search to progressively converge toward an optimal configuration where each individual is optimally located. As shall be seen later, depending on the problem being solved, it is sometimes beneficial to make the parameter W decrease with increasing number of iterations (generations). Hence, as SimE progresses from generation to generation, *allocation* changes gradually from being near-global to local. The reason is that, after a number of generations, more and more elements are assigned to their optimal locations. A large value of W would waste too much time making *bad trial-moves*, that is, trial-moves that cause a large decrease of the population fitness.

5.3.5 Initialization Phase

This step precedes the iterative phase. In this step, the various parameters of the algorithm are set to their desired values, namely, the maximum number of iterations required to run the main loop, the selection bias B, and the number of trial alterations W per individual. Furthermore, like any iterative algorithm, SimE requires that an initial solution be given. The convergence aspects of SimE are not affected by the quality of the initial solution. However, starting from a randomly generated solution usually increases the number of iterations required to converge to a near-optimal solution.

The magnitude of the selection bias B is less than one. A negative value for B will increase the number of elements selected at each iteration, which allows the algorithm to work and search harder at each iteration. This may lead to better solutions, but at the expense of higher runtime requirement. On the other hand, a positive value of B will have the effect of inflating the fitness of the elements, thus causing a reduction in the number of cells selected for relocation (mutation). This will speed up the algorithm, but at the risk of an early convergence to a suboptimal structure (local optimum). Experiments on several placement problems suggest that the *selection bias* B must be in the range $[-0.2; 0.2]$ for best results. However, the value of B is a function of how realistic is our estimate of the optimal cost O_i of individual i. In case O_i is a tight lower bound on the actual cost C_i of element i, then a value of $B = 0$ is a reasonable choice. On the other hand, if O_i is a loose lower bound for C_i, that is, if O_i cannot possibly be achieved, then one should choose a negative value for B to compensate for the lack of an accurate estimate of O_i.

The number of trial alterations (moves) per individual is problem-specific. For example, for the TSP problem a move of a vertex i may consist of a swap with any of the other vertices. Therefore, the maximum value of W would be in this case equal to $n - 1$. However, a smaller value for W would be more appropriate to keep the runtime under control. The parameter W does not have to be the same or constant for all individuals. W might be interpreted as defining a window of locations around a particular individual (a vertex in the case of TSP). For the case of TSP, a reasonable value for W would be a function of a radius constraint R around the vertex in question. That is, each vertex will be trial swapped with only those vertices that are at most R units of length away from it.

5.4 SimE Operators and Parameters

The operators used by SimE to evolve from generation to generation are *selection* and *allocation*. These have the most effect on the convergence speed of SimE algorithm as well as its runtime requirement. Other parameters seem to have marginal effect on the performance and runtime requirement of the algorithm.

Kling and Banerjee studied extensively various aspects of the SimE algorithm and their effect on its runtime requirement and performance. These aspects are [KB91]

1. *Selection* operator

2. *Allocation* operator

3. The number of iterations

4. The number of populations

5.4.1 Effect of Selection

The *selection* operator examines at each iteration the goodness of each element, and decides its chances of survival in its current state. *Selection* decides the survival of each element independent of all other elements of the population. Highly fit elements are rewarded with a high probability of survival. With such strategy, each element i has a probability $p_i = 1 - g_i$ of getting selected for alteration (assuming $B = 0$). Therefore, when $g_i \approx 1$, $p_i \approx 0$. Hence, following the SimE selection strategy, more and more elements are gradually assigned good locations. Kling and Banerjee compared SimE *selection* with a *random selection* strategy [KB91]. For a *random selection* strategy, the selection probability of element i will be $p_i = 1 - random$, where $random$ is a number uniformly distributed on the interval $[0, 1]$. Experimental results showed that SimE *selection* (according to fitness) allows the SimE algorithm to converge more rapidly to a slightly better solution. With a random selection, SimE algorithm was also able to converge reasonably fast to a good solution of much better quality than the best solution obtained with a completely *random walk* in the same amount of time.

5.4.2 Effect of Allocation

Among the SimE functions, *allocation* has most impact on the rate of convergence as well as the quality of solution. *Allocation*'s role is to perturb the current population by assigning the elements of the selected set P_s to new locations. In order for the offspring population to be fitter than its parent, the selected elements must be assigned to better locations. SimE *Allocation* performs for each element of P_s a number of *trial relocations*. The trial locations are within a window that is a function of a parameter W. For each trial relocation the objective function is evaluated and recorded. After performing all the trials of the current element, the best trial is made permanent, and the element is removed from the selection set P_s. This procedure is repeated until P_s becomes empty.

SimE *allocation* was compared with a *random allocation* strategy [KB91]. *Random allocation* assigns each element of the selected set to a **random** location within its trial window. Experimental results [KB91] showed that SimE Algorithm with a *random allocation* function exhibits a similar performance to that obtained with a complete *random search* heuristic. This illustrates the importance of the *allocation* function on the performance of SimE algorithm.

5.4.3   Effect of Number of Populations

Kling and Banerjee have experimented with several concurrent noninteracting populations.[2] N populations are used, where at each generation, N offsprings are generated, one from each population, leading to $2N$ populations. Then, out of the $2N$ populations N are selected based on their average goodnesses. As the number of populations N was increased, a less than linear improvement in solution quality was observed, but at the expense of a linear increase in space and runtime requirements. Also, when the number of populations was increased, improvement in quality of solution became less predictable [KB91].

5.4.4   Effect of Number of Iterations

The quality of solution obtained by SimE improves when the number of iterations is increased. The improvement is steep in the early iterations. It gets less steeper with later iterations until it becomes almost insignificant. The number of required iterations can be easily tuned via experimentations. This behavior is observed with all problems. One interesting observation though, is that doubling the number of iterations usually leads to less than a double of runtime requirement. The reason is that, as more and more iterations get executed, less and less cells get selected for alteration. Therefore, the algorithm works less and less harder in later generations. Hence, an increase in the number of iterations is an efficient way of improving the quality of solution obtained by SimE algorithm. This is a more efficient way than increasing the number of populations.

5.5   Comparison of SimE, SA, and GA

In this section, we look at the main differences between SimE and SA, then SimE and GA.

SA and SimE have the following fundamental differences:

1. In SA, a perturbation of current state (solution) is a single move, while for SimE it is a compound move.

---

[2]Recall that in SimE terminology, a population refers to a single solution as opposed to several solutions in the case of GA.

2. For SA the elements involved in the move are selected at random, while for SimE the elements (usually more than two) are selected based on their fitnesses;

3. for SA the iterative process is guided by a parameter called *temperature*, while for SimE the search process is guided by the individual fitnesses of the solution components.

As discussed in the previous chapter, GA is another evolution based randomized iterative algorithm. GA and SimE follow a similar strategy in exploiting evolution to move from one generation to the next. However, there are significant differences between the two algorithms:

1. SimE works with a single solution called *population*. The constituents of a solution are called individuals or elements. On the other hand, GA works with a set of solutions. A single solution is an individual (also called a chromosome), and an individual (solution) is made up of genes.

2. GA relies on genetic reproduction. The population of the next generation is selected among individuals of current generation and their offsprings. Fitter individuals have higher probabilities of surviving to the next generation. Offsprings are reproduced using crossover between selected pairs of parent individuals of current population. Also, a small fraction of the individuals may undergo mutation. In contrast, SimE maintains a single individual throughout the generations. Evolution from one generation to the next uses genetic mutation only whereby some elements of current solution are altered. SimE has no crossover since this operator requires two individuals.

3. In SimE, an individual is evaluated by estimating the fitness of each one of its genes. The single individual of the next generation is obtained by probabilistically altering some of the genes of the current individual (single parent of current generation). Genes with lower fitnesses have higher probabilities of getting altered. On the other hand, GA computes the fitnesses of complete solutions. In general, solutions with higher fitnesses have higher probabilities for mating. However, which substrings of mating parent solutions are inherited by the offspring are completely random. Usually the fittest among the parents and their offsprings survive to the next generation. Therefore, though both SimE and GA perform a stochastic evolutionary-based search of the state space, SimE is more greedy, and thus usually requires fewer iterations to converge toward desirable solutions.

Overall, SimE algorithms usually run much faster than SA and GA algorithms. The reason is that the concept of fitness helps the algorithm converge quickly to a near optimal solution. Furthermore, since a single solution is maintained at all times, it has much less time and space requirements than GA.

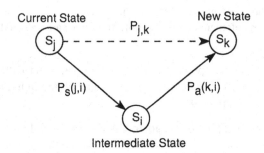

Current State

Intermediate State

Figure 5.8: Probability transition diagram of SimE algorithm.

5.6 SimE Convergence Aspects

The proof that SimE algorithm converges to a global optimum consists of showing that the SimE walk through the state space corresponds to an *ergodic Markov chain*. The proof described in this section is due to Kling and Banerjee [KB91]. Another proof has been reported in [MH96].

Recall that the SimE algorithm has three main steps: *evaluation, selection,* and *allocation*. Only the *selection* and *allocation* steps change the current state. The *selection* step changes the current state into an intermediate illegal state. The *allocation* step changes the incomplete intermediate state into a new legal state. The state space can be seen as a graph where the nodes correspond to states and edges correspond to transitions between states. The walk that is followed by the SimE algorithm consists of a path in the state space graph. Note that a transition to a new state depends only on the current state and not on any of the states that were visited prior to the current state. Hence, the search process is memoryless. Therefore, this allows us to describe the search state with a Markov chain. A state of the Markov chain models a particular valid solution configuration. Edges in the probability transition diagram of the Markov chain correspond to transitions between corresponding solution configurations (states). The transition from current state S_j to a new state S_k is labeled with the probability $p_{j,k}$ that such transition is executed.

Let S_j, S_i, and S_k be, respectively, the current, intermediate, and new states, and P_s^i be the set of elements selected for alteration by the *selection* operator. The *selection* operator changes the current state S_j into the intermediate state S_i with a selection probability $p_s(j, i)$.

Similarly, the *allocation* operator changes the intermediate state S_i into the new state S_k with probability $p_a(i, k)$. Each iteration of the SimE algorithm consists of a transition from some current state S_j to some new state S_k via some intermediate incomplete state S_i as illustrated in Figure 5.8.

The transition probability from state S_j to state S_k via intermediate state S_i can be expressed as follows:

$$p_{j,k}(i) = p_s(j, i) \times p_a(k, i) \tag{5.2}$$

To keep the Markovian analysis simple, the selection set S_i is restricted to consist of a single element. Let i refer to the only element in S_i.

Let $g_i(j)$ be the goodness of element i at current state S_j. Since the probability that a particular element i of current state S_j is selected for alteration is proportional to $1 - g_i(j)$, the selection probability $p_s(j, i)$ can be expressed as the ratio of a selection function $F_s(j, i)$ and a normalization function $N_s(j, i)$ to make the $p_s(j, i)$ a distribution.

$$p_s(j, i) = \frac{F_s(j, i)}{N_s(j, i)} \tag{5.3}$$

where,

$$F_s(j, i) = 1 - g_i(j) \tag{5.4}$$

and

$$N_s(j, i) = \sum_{k=1}^{n} (1 - g_k(j)) \tag{5.5}$$

where n is the number of elements in the population. Substituting Equations 5.4 and 5.5 into Equation 5.3, we get the following,

$$p_s(j, i) = \frac{1 - g_i(j)}{n(1 - G_j)} \tag{5.6}$$

where G_j refers to the average goodness of current state S_j.

Similarly, the allocation probability $p_a(k, i)$ can be expressed as the ratio of an allocation function $F_a(k, i)$ and a normalization function $N_a(k, i)$,

$$p_a(k, i) = \frac{F_a(k, i)}{N_a(k, i)} \tag{5.7}$$

where

$$F_a(k, i) = (1 - g_i(k))G_k \tag{5.8}$$

and

$$N_a(k, i) = \sum_{l \in \mathcal{N}_k} (1 - g_i(l))G_l \tag{5.9}$$

where $\mathcal{N}_k$ is the set of all reachable new states from intermediate state S_i (recall that the selection set consists of element i only). The term $[1 - g_i(k)]$ in Equation 5.8 compensates for the selection of element i, while the term G_k is responsible for choosing destination state S_k.

When the allocation sets $\mathcal{N}_l$ are disjoint, Equation 5.9 can be rewritten as follows [KB91]:

$$N_a(k, i) = N_a^*(i)(1 - G_k)^2 \qquad (5.10)$$

where the term $N_a^*(i)$ depends only on the selection set P_s^i. The disjointness of the $\mathcal{N}_i$'s can be guaranteed by a careful implementation of the allocation operator [Kli90].

Now, substituting the expressions of $p_s(j, i)$ and $p_a(k, i)$ in Equation 5.2, we get the following expression of the transition probability from current state S_j to new state S_k via intermediate state S_i:

$$p_{jk}(i) = \frac{(1 - g_i(j)) \times (1 - g_i(k))G_k}{n(1 - G_j) \times N_a^*(i)(1 - G_k)^2} \quad \forall P_s^i \ and \ j \neq k \qquad (5.11)$$

and,

$$p_{jj}(i) = 1 - \sum_k p_{jk}(i) \qquad (5.12)$$

The above equations show that all transition probabilities are strictly positive for goodness values $0 < g < 1$. Also, the transition probabilities do not depend on the iteration index. Therefore, the state transition diagram of the SimE algorithm is a time homogeneous irreducible Markov chain. The chain is obviously finite since the population is finite. Moreover, since each state is reachable from itself by a single transition, the chain is aperiodic, and hence, it is ergodic. Consequently, the steady-state probability vector of this Markov chain exists. Note however, that the transition probabilities are dependent on the selected set P_s^i, thus complicating the derivation of the stationary distribution. Fortunately, for the case of disjoint allocation sets, the term $N_a^*(i)$ depends only on the set P_s^i, and therefore, the dependency on P_s^i is canceled out in the local balance equations as illustrated in Equation 5.13 below,

$$\frac{p_{kj}}{p_{jk}} = \frac{\pi_j}{\pi_k} \quad \forall S_j, \forall S_k \qquad (5.13)$$

where π_j is the steady-state probability of state S_j.

Using Equation 5.11, the local balance equations (Equation 5.13) simplify to the following:

$$\frac{\pi_j}{\pi_k} = \frac{G_j(1 - G_k)}{G_k(1 - G_j)} \quad \forall S_j, \forall S_k \qquad (5.14)$$

Letting S_k be equal to S_0, the initial state, Equation 5.14 simplifies to the following:

$$\pi_j = \frac{G_j}{1 - G_j} \times \frac{1 - G_0}{G_0} \pi_0 \quad \forall S_j, \qquad (5.15)$$

The π_j's constitute a distribution, that is,

$$\sum_j \pi_j = 1 \qquad (5.16)$$

Therefore, using Equations 5.16 and 5.15, and solving for π_j, we get

$$\pi_j = \frac{1}{G} \times \frac{G_j}{1 - G_j} \; \forall \, j \qquad (5.17)$$

where G is a normalization constant used to force the π_j's to be a distribution. That is,

$$G = \sum_j \frac{G_j}{1 - G_j} \qquad (5.18)$$

Equation 5.17 states that, if given infinite time, the SimE algorithm will visit the global optimum state S_{opt} with probability

$$\pi_{opt} = \frac{1}{G} \times \frac{G_{opt}}{1 - G_{opt}} \qquad (5.19)$$

Also, the fraction of time (probability) spent by the algorithm in a state S_k of high goodness is proportionally higher than the proportion of time spent in a state of lower goodness. Furthermore, since the optimum state has the highest goodness, correspondingly, it will have the largest steady-state probability. In other words, the SimE algorithm will bias the search to drift toward high goodness states, and once it reaches such states, it has a high probability of remaining there.

5.7 SimE Applications

As mentioned above, the SimE algorithm can be used to solve a wide range of combinatorial optimization problems. The algorithm, however, has to be adapted to the type of problem under investigation. Specifically, (1) the solution space has to be defined, (2) a suitable state representation has to be adopted, and (3) the operators *evaluation*, *selection*, and *allocation* must be properly defined.

Kling and Banerjee published their results with respect to SimE in design automation conferences [KB87b, KB90] and journals [KB89, KB91]. This explains the fact that most published work on SimE has been originated by researchers in the area of design automation of VLSI circuits [LHT89, LM93, MH94, Mao94, MH96].

The first problem on which SimE was first applied is standard cell placement [KB87b, Kli90]. In this section we describe this SimE-based standard cell placement algorithm as reported in [KB87b].

5.7.1 Standard-Cell Design Style

In standard-cell design style, all cells have the same height but varying widths. The widths of the cells are usually a multiple of some grid unit. Cells are placed

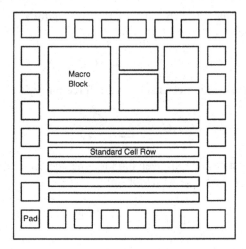

Figure 5.9: Example of standard-cell layout.

in an array of horizontal rows, and all interconnections of signal nets are made in the spaces between the adjacent rows. Usually, for each terminal on one side of a standard cell there is also an electrically equivalent terminal on the opposite side. The standard-cell layout model is shown in Figure 5.9. The four blocks surrounding the cell rows on the top, bottom, right and left are the external input/output (I/O) buffers. The rectangular areas in between the cell rows are the routing channels. Feed-through cells are inserted within the cell rows in order to provide interchannel routing. Feed-throughs are also available within some of the cells (wide cells). For the standard-cell design style, the channels do not have prefixed capacities.

The objective of standard-cell placement is to arrange the various cells of the design in rows so as to optimize a given cost function that is supposed to accurately characterize the quality of the placement. The cost function used in [KB89] is an estimate of the total wire-length. The placement program consists of two phases (see Figure 5.10): (1) an initialization phase where the various parameters and data structures are set, and (2) an iterative placement phase which consists of the SimE algorithm.

Initialization Phase

The initial placement solution is randomly generated. Optionally, the program can accept a previously generated good placement. The evolution process should maintain already well-placed cells in their current locations and try to improve the locations of the remaining cells.

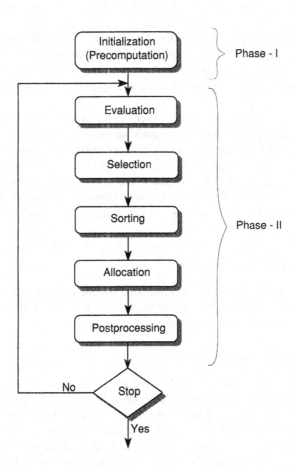

Figure 5.10: Flowchart of SimE-based standard-cell placement program.

As discussed in Section 5.3.1 on page 258, the goodness g_i of a cell i is equal
to

$$g_i = \frac{O_i}{C_i}$$

where O_i is a reference value (a lower bound on C_i) and C_i is the actual cost
of the cell in its current location. All reference values are computed during the
initialization phase.

Since placement quality is measured by the total wire-length, the goodness of
the current location of a particular cell i is a function of the length of all the nets
connected to that particular cell. Therefore, we need to establish a lower bound
on the length of each net, which will serve as a reference value for the quality of
placement.

The approach used to compute a lower bound on net length is illustrated in
Figure 5.11. The idea consists first of packing the cells connected by the net in
the smallest possible rectangle. Then, all cells are reshaped so that the enveloping
rectangle forms an approximate square. Row spacing is included in this computation. Next, half a cell height (equal to the maximal pin displacement in the
y-direction) is subtracted from each side of the square. Finally, half the perimeter of the resulting square is used as a lower bound on the length of the net (see
Figure 5.11).

Evaluation of Placed Cells

The goodness measure used by the evaluation routine must be highly correlated
with the overall objective of the placement problem. Kling and Banerjee [KB87b]
experimented with the following three goodness measures.

Concentric Circle Function.

The goodness function used is based on the assumption that good placement requires that most of the cells connected to the cell being evaluated be within its
immediate vicinity. For each cell i, the area a_i covered by all its neighboring
cells (cells connected to it) is computed. The cell is then enclosed by concentric
circles which cover integer multiples of a_i. The area of the innermost circle is
a_i, the area of the next innermost circle is $2a_i$, and so on. Let n_i be the number
of concentric circles of cell i. Then each concentric circle is assigned a weight
$\alpha_{i_j} = 1 - (j-1)\frac{1}{n_i}, 1 \le j \le n_i$. For example, for $n_i = 4$, the weights will be
$\alpha_{i_1} = 1, \alpha_{i_2} = 1 - 0.25 = 0.75, \alpha_{i_3} = 1 - 0.5 = 0.5$, and $\alpha_{i_4} = 1 - 0.75 = 0.25$,
from the innermost circle to the outermost circle. The area lying outside the out-
ermost circle has a weight of 0. Now, each pin is assigned the weight of the circle
it falls in. The goodness of the cell in its current location is equal to the average
weight of all the pins connected to it. The cost function evaluation is illustrated in
Figure 5.12.

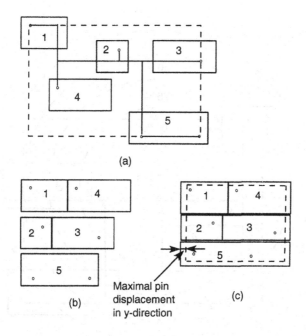

Figure 5.11: Computation of the smallest possible net length: (a) five cells connected by one net; (b) the five cells are packed in the smallest possible rectangle; (c) the cells are reshaped to fit in a square and half a cell height is subtracted from each side of that square; half of the resulting square (in dotted lines) is taken as an estimate of the net length.

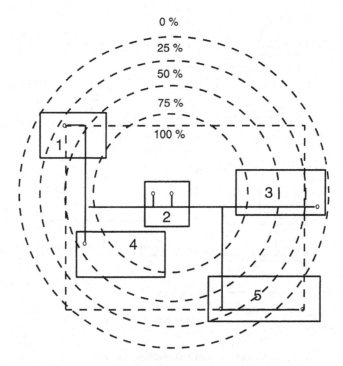

Figure 5.12: Concentric circle evaluation. Each circular region encloses an area equal to the total area of all the cells of the net. For this example, the goodness of cell 2 in the middle of the concentric circles is $g = \frac{1+1+0.75+0.5+0.5+0.25+0}{7} = 0.5714$.

Position-Oriented Function.

The second goodness function is based on the use of the reference net length values computed in the initialization phase (see Subsection 5.7.1 on page 272). The cells connected by a particular net cover a minimal area approximated by the area of the smallest rectangle that covers all the connected cells if they were located next to each other. All cells located inside that smallest bounding rectangle should not be penalized. On the other hand cells falling outside that rectangle contribute to some additional wiring cost and therefore should be penalized.

Initially the goodness values of all cells are set to zero. Then for each net n, the (x, y)-location of its gravity center is determined as follows.

Let E_n be the set of all the pins connected by net n. Then the gravity center $(x_n; y_n)$ of net n is computed as follows:

$$x_n = \frac{1}{|E_n|} \sum_{p \in E_n} x_p \;\; ; \;\; y_n = \frac{1}{|E_n|} \sum_{p \in E_n} y_p$$

Then, the smallest bounding rectangle of the net (determined during initialization) is drawn around the net gravity center. Each pin falling within the rectangle is assigned a goodness of 1. The goodness of a pin falling outside the rectangle is set equal to the ratio of the distance of the boundary of the net's smallest rectangle from the net's center over the distance of the nearest cell boundary of that pin from the net's center (Figure 5.13). After processing all nets, the goodness of a cell i is set equal to the average of the goodnesses of its pins. That is,

$$g_i = \frac{1}{|E_i|} \sum_{p \in E_i} g_{ip}$$

where $|E_i|$ is the set of pins of cell i and g_{ip} is the goodness of pin p of cell i. The cost function is illustrated in Figure 5.13.

Wire-Length–Based Function.

The last goodness function is based on the reference net length values precomputed during the initialization phase. Here, the goodness g_i of a cell i is equal to

$$g_i = \frac{O_i}{W_i}$$

where O_i is the reference wire-length value of cell i as precomputed during the initialization phase, and W_i is the actual wire-length of all the nets attached to the cell in its current location.

Let N_i be the nets connected to cell i, then, $\forall\, i$,

$$O_i = \sum_{n \in N_i} r_n$$

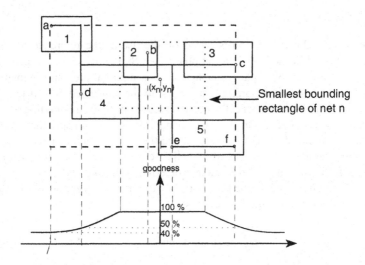

Figure 5.13: Position-oriented evaluation. (x_n, y_n) is the center of the net. The goodness of the pins a-to-f are $g_b = g_e = 1$, $g_c = g_d = g_f = 0.5$, and $g_a = 0.4$.

$$W_i = \sum_{n \in N_i} l_n$$

where r_n and l_n are, respectively, the reference length and actual length of net n. The reference length of each net n is computed as indicated in Subsection 5.7.1 on page 272. The actual length is estimated by half the perimeter of the smallest rectangle enclosing all the pins of the net in their current locations.

Selection of Cells for Relocation

This step determines which cells will retain their current locations and which should be assigned to new locations in the next generation. For each cell i, a random number in the range $[0, 1]$ is drawn and compared to the cell goodness g_i. If g_i is greater than the random number then cell i survives in its current location; otherwise it is stored in a *selection queue* for allocation. The selected cells are then removed from their current locations.

Allocation (Relocation of Selected Cells)

Recall that the *Allocation* function has the most impact on the quality of solution and the speed with which the search converges toward desirable solutions.

In early iterations (generations), the number of cells selected for alteration can be as much as 50 percent of the total number of cells. With increasing number of

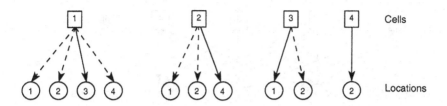

Figure 5.14: Sorted individual best fit allocation. Cell 1 is tried in all four available locations and assigned to its best location 3; then cell 2 is tried in the remaining three locations and assigned to location 4; next cell three is tried in the remaining two locations and assigned to location 2; and finally cell 4 is assigned to location 4, the only remaining available location.

generations, this number is decreased to lesser and lesser cells, reaching only few cells near convergence. Therefore, to save on runtime requirements, it is desirable to use a low complexity allocation function during the early generations, and then switch to a more complex and accurate allocation toward later generations when most cells are already optimally located.

Based on the above observation, three allocation functions are used, with increasing complexity. The least complex is used during early generations and relies on a simplified evaluation routine which ignores overlaps due to the swap of cells of unequal widths. For all three techniques, a windowing technique is applied to limit the number of trial locations per cell. From the least complex to the most complex, the three allocation schemes are [Kli90]: (1) sorted individual best-fit allocation, (2) weighted bipartite matching allocation, and (3) branch-and-bound search allocation.

Sorted Individual Best-Fit Allocation.

The cells in the selection queue are sorted such that the cell with the largest number of connections is at the head of the queue. Then the selected cells are removed from the queue one at a time in the sorted order and assigned to new locations as follows. Each selected cell is tried at all available locations. The number of trial locations decreases by one after the placement of each cell. Every trial location is evaluated using a simplified evaluation routine. The evaluation routine evaluates the wire-lengths taking into consideration already placed cells only. The allocation function assigns each selected cell to the available trial location of highest-goodness value. This allocation function is illustrated in Figure 5.14. It has a time complexity of $O(s^2)$, where s is the number of selected cells.

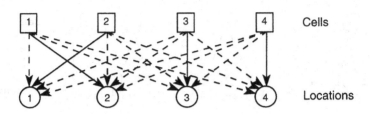

Figure 5.15: Weighted bipartite matching allocation. All four cells are tried in each of the four locations; then a matching algorithm is used to make the best possible assignment.

Weighted Bipartite Matching Allocation.

First, the goodness of each cell in the selection queue is evaluated in every possible trial location. A table $A[s, s]$ of size s^2 is constructed where $A[i, j]$ gives the goodness of assigning cell i to location j. Then a matching algorithm [AHU74] is used to identify the allocation of minimum overall wire-length cost (maximum average placement goodness). This allocation function is illustrated in Figure 5.15. It has a time complexity of $O(s^3)$. Here also, nets connected to unplaced cells are not considered during the evaluation of the trial locations.

Branch-and-Bound Search Allocation.

Branch-and-bound is an all state space search method [HS78]. The solution is constructed one element at a time. The branch-and-bound method builds a search tree, where each node of the tree is a partial solution. A path from the root to a leaf is a complete solution with all selected cells assigned to locations.

The root is at level 0. Children of the root are at level 1, and so on. A node at level 1 is a partial solution consisting of one element. A path from the root to a node at the kth level is a partial solution with k elements, $1 \leq k \leq s$. The root has s children $(1, 1)$, $(1, 2)$, ... $(1, i)$, ... $(1, s)$ corresponding to trial allocations of cell 1 to location 1, cell 2 to location 1, ..., cell i to location 1, ..., cell s to location 1, respectively. Each node is assigned a cost corresponding to the wiring incurred by that partial allocation. The node with the lowest cost is expanded next. It will have one less child than its parent. This process continues as long as there are live nodes. An unexpanded node remains alive as long as its cost is lower than any of the costs of the reached leaf nodes. Leaf nodes are at level s of the tree.

As an example, assume that the selected queue consists of $s = 4$ cells to be reassigned to four available locations (Figure 5.16). Level 1 will have the four nodes $(1; 1; 28)$, $(1; 2; 5)$, $(1; 3; 40)$, and $(1; 4; 30)$, corresponding to trial allocations of cells 1, 2, 3, and 4 to location 1 with wiring costs of 28, 5, 40, and 30, respectively. The assignment with minimum wiring cost is 5 and corresponds to assigning cell 2 to location 1 (node $(1; 2; 5)$) at level 1 of the branch-and-bound tree). That node is expanded next. It will have three children corresponding to trying out cells 1, 3, and 4 in location 2. The corresponding nodes have costs of 7, 10, and 50, respectively. These costs correspond to partial solutions with two cells already assigned, cell 2 to location 1 and cell 1, 3, or 4 to location 2. At this stage, the unexpanded alive nodes are $(1; 1; 28)$, $(1; 3; 40)$, and $(1; 4; 30)$ of level 1, and $(2; 1; 7)$, $(2; 3; 10)$, and $(2; 4; 50)$ of level 2. Node $(1; 2; 5)$ of level 1 has already been expanded. Among the unexpanded alive nodes, node $(2; 1; 7)$ of level 2 has the lowest cost of 7. That node is expanded next. Node $(2; 1; 7)$ will have two children corresponding to trying out cells 3 and 4 at location 3 and with costs of 30 and 17, respectively. The search process continues until the leaf node $(4; 3)$ is reached. The path from the root to that node corresponds to the assignment of cell 2 to location 1, cell 1 to location 2, cell 4 to location 3, and finally cell 3 to location 4. The cost of such assignment is 22. At this moment nodes $(1; 1; 28)$, $(1; 3; 40)$, and $(1; 4; 30)$ of level 1, node $(2; 4; 50)$ of level 2, and nodes $(3; 3; 30)$ and $(3; 4; 27)$ of the level 3 of the tree are pruned because their cost is higher than the cost of the leaf node $(4; 3; 22)$. The search continues by expanding node $(3; 1; 20)$ of level 3, which produces the child $(4; 4; 25)$ with cost 27. At this moment there are no more live nodes and the search stops. The best allocation is that corresponding to the path from the root to the leaf node $(4; 3; 22)$ with cost 22. In Figure 5.16, each edge has an integer label indicating when the trial allocation node at the end of that edge was performed. For example, the label of the edge from the root node to node $(1; 2; 5)$ is equal to 2, which means that the trial allocation of cell 2 to location 1 was performed second. Nodes enclosed in rectangles are those that have been expanded. Leaf nodes are enclosed in double rectangles. Remaining nodes are those at which the search was pruned.

It is well known that the branch-and-bound search approach has an exponential worst-time complexity. However, sorting of the selection queue can force pruning of large portions of the search space, thus reducing the required runtime of this allocation procedure. Furthermore, this allocation function is used only at later stages when the number of altered cells is small (usually less than 10).

Cell Realignment after Allocation.

The allocation function ignores mismatches among the sizes of the available trial locations and the selected cells. Therefore a postprocessing step is required to remove any cell overlaps or empty spaces that may result from such mismatches. The operations performed by this postprocessing step are illustrated in Figure 5.17.

Stopping Criteria

The iterative evolution-based search is stopped if a 100 consecutive iterations fail to improve the placement cost. The algorithm then outputs the best possible place-

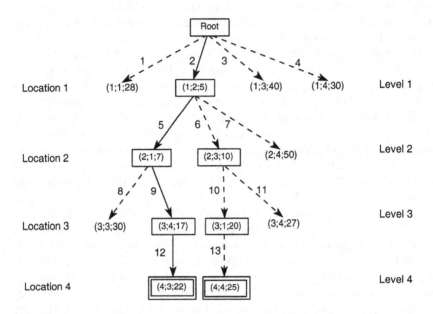

Figure 5.16: Branch-and-bound search allocation.

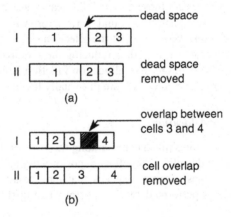

Figure 5.17: Operations of the realignment procedure. (I) Module positions after allocation and before realignment. (II) Module positions after realignment. (a) Removal of dead space. (b) Removal of cell overlap.

ment found. Optionally, at the user request, the algorithm invokes postprocessing routines which optimize the locations of the I/O pads and other aspects of the design such as the placement of macro blocks [Kli90].

Results and Discussion

Most of the research work on stochastic iterative algorithms has been sparked by simulated annealing (SA) and its many success stories on a large number of combinatorial optimization problems from a variety of disciplines. Since its invention, SA has enjoyed its status as being considered a sort of benchmark randomized iterative heuristic for all other heuristics in this class. It has become customary that every newly reported randomized search heuristic has to prove itself by performing better than SA on a number of (benchmark) test cases. Therefore, SimE was no exception, and its inventors had to compare their SimE-based standard cell placer with an SA-based placer.

The SimE-based placement program was compared to TimberWolf 5.4, a popular standard cell program implemented at the University of Berkeley [Sec88, SL87, SSV86]. Timberwolf follows the SA algorithm. The SimE-based placement program produced placements of similar quality (on some test cases marginally better), but in noticeably less time. For some of the test circuits, a 50 percent reduction in runtime with respect to TimberWolf was observed [Kli90]. Hence, SimE passed the test!

Furthermore, a comparison of the three proposed allocation schemes was conducted. The study indicated that the *sorted individual best-fit allocation* strategy was best during the initial stage. During the intermediate stage, the *weighted bipartite matching allocation* exhibited the best performance. The *branch-and-bound allocation* method gave the best results at the near convergence later stage [Kli90].

5.7.2 Other Applications of SimE

Simulated Evolution attracted a relatively low number of researchers. Furthermore, all reported SimE work has been exclusively in the area of electronic computer-aided design (ECAD). A number of papers described SimE-based heuristics to the routing of VLSI circuits [CLAHL95, CLH89, HHYLH91, LAH95, LHT88, LHT89, TSN93]. SimE was also successfully applied in high-level synthesis [KL92a, KL92b, TJ90]. Other reported SimE applications are in microcode compaction [IMK95] and the synthesis of cellular architecture field programmable gate arrays (FPGAs) [ANM93].

Another doctoral dissertation that was centered around the SimE algorithm was performed at the University of Wisconsin at Madison (USA) by C. Y. Mao [Mao94]. Mao applied SimE to perform the automatic synthesis of gate matrix layouts. He also performed theoretical analysis of SimE-based heuristics and elaborated general convergence proofs of SimE, where he modeled the SimE search process by an ergodic Markov chain [Mao94, MH94, MH96].

5.8 Parallelization of SimE

In previous sections, several aspects of the SimE algorithm were discussed. Similar to the simulated annealing algorithm, SimE is a sound approximation algorithm. It is a general algorithm that is relatively easy to apply to almost any combinatorial optimization problem. However, SimE seems to be more greedy than SA, thus allowing it to reach near-optimal solutions in less time than simulated annealing. This claim has been supported by experimental results [Kli90]. Nevertheless, SimE may still have large runtime requirements. The reason is that, like other stochastic iterative algorithms, SimE is blind. That is, it has to be told when to stop. Depending on which stopping criteria are used as well as the size of the problem, SimE may consume hours of CPU time before it stops. The most practical approach to speed up the execution of the SimE algorithm is to parallelize it.

Unlike SA, GAs, and TS, the parallelization of SimE has not been the subject of much research. The only effort at parallelizing simulated evolution is attributed to the inventors of the technique [KB87a, Kli90]. Kling and Banerjee suggested three ways of speeding up the SimE algorithm: (1) implementing the algorithm on a vector computer [Single Instruction, Multiple Datastream (SIMD) machine], (2) parallel acceleration where execution of the algorithm is distributed among a number of networked workstations, and (3) hardware acceleration which consists of implementing time consuming parts in hardware (namely, goodness computation) [Kli90].

Hardware acceleration is not a cost-effective approach. Therefore, in the remainder of this section we shall concentrate on the use of parallelization techniques to speed up SimE execution.

5.8.1 Implementation of SimE on Vector Processors

Vector processor computers are SIMD machines optimized for running scientific software programs that involve a large amount of numerical computations such as matrix multiplications. Besides involving symbolic manipulations, several design automation problems such as floorplanning and placement also require quite a bit of numeric computations. Such design automation programs can be designed to take advantage of the capabilities of vector processor machines. Kling and Banerjee ran an SimE-based placement program on several test circuits and reported that up to 50 percent of the program runtime was spent evaluating the goodnesses of cells [Kli90]. Therefore, a significant speed-up would be obtained if the computation of the goodness measure is accelerated. On the basis of this observation they

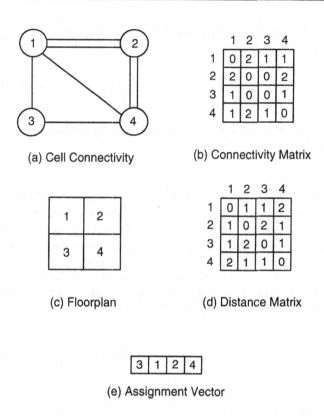

(a) Cell Connectivity   (b) Connectivity Matrix

(c) Floorplan   (d) Distance Matrix

(e) Assignment Vector

Figure 5.18: Example of quadratic assignment problem.

redesigned their placement program to take advantage of the vector processors architecture of an IBM 3090VF mainframe. They reported speed-ups in excess of 100 percent on all benchmark circuits used [Kli90]. Below, we briefly illustrate this parallelization approach on the *quadratic assignment problem* (QAP) (see Section 5.3 for a definition of QAP).

An instance of QAP is given in Figure 5.18. Connectivity among the cells is specified in the form of a matrix $C_{n \times n} = [\, c_{ij} \,]$, where c_{ij} is the number of connections between cells i and j, $1 \leq i \leq n$, $1 \leq j \leq n$, and n is the number of cells. The layout area is assumed to be a 2-D surface consisting of m locations, $m \geq n$. Assume that the distances between the various locations are specified in the form of a distance matrix $D_{m \times m} = [\, d_{kl} \,]$, where d_{kl} is the distance between locations k and l, $1 \leq k \leq m$, $1 \leq l \leq m$. A particular assignment of the cells to locations is represented as a vector $A = (a_1, a_2, \ldots, a_i, \ldots, a_n)$ where a_i is the current location of cell i, $1 \leq i \leq n$.

The objective is to seek an assignment A of minimum connection length. That is, the cost function to be minimized is

$$Cost(A) = \sum_{i=1}^{n} \sum_{j=1}^{n} c_{i,j} d_{a_i, a_j}$$

Hence, a possible measure of the goodness of the current location a_i of a particular cell i is

$$g_i = \frac{O_i}{W_i} \tag{5.20}$$

where O_i is the minimum length of all the connections to cell i, and W_i is the actual length of all the connections to cell i. O_i corresponds to the connection length if all the cells connected to cell i are packed in the smallest possible area around cell i (Figure 5.19). Let $i_1, i_2, \ldots, i_k$ be the k cells connected to cell i. Assume that the cells are sorted in nonincreasing order of the number of connections they have with cell i. That is, cell i_1 has the largest number of connections to i, then i_2 has the second largest, and finally i_k has the least number of connections to i. Then O_i is equal to the following (see Figure 5.19),

$$O_i = \sum_{j=1}^{k} \lceil \frac{k}{4} \rceil c_{i,i_j}, \quad 1 \le i \le n \tag{5.21}$$

Note that O_i, $1 \le i \le n$, are evaluated only once during the initialization phase of the algorithm.

The actual length of all connections to cell i is given by the following expression (see Figure 5.19):

$$W_i = \sum_{j=1}^{n} c_{i,j} d_{a_i, a_j} \quad 1 \le i \le n \tag{5.22}$$

Equation 5.22 is a dot product of the ith row vector of matrix C with a column vector of matrix D indexed by the assignment vector A. Such computation can be efficiently implemented on a vector processors machine such as the IBM 3090VF [Kli90].

5.8.2   Implementation of SimE on MISD and MIMD Machines

A straightforward parallelization of SimE on Multiple Instruction, Single Datastream (MISD) or Multiple Instruction, Multiple Datastream (MIMD) machines could be as follows. Each processor is assigned a particular initial population. Then each of the processors would be running sequential SimE starting from its assigned initial population. This simple approach would be good if the search

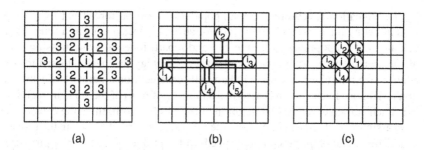

Figure 5.19: Illustration of the estimation of O_i and W_i for the quadratic assignment problem. (a) Locations of cells when packed in the smallest possible area around cell i: there are four locations at a distance of 1 from cell i, 8 at a distance of 2, 12 at a distance of 3, ..., $d \times 4$ at a distance of d. (b) Actual length of all connections to cell i according to Equation 5.22: $W_i = 2 \times 4 + 3 + 3 + 1 \times 2 + 4 = 20$. (c) Optimal length of all connections to cell i according to Equation 5.21: $O_i = 2 \times 1 + 1 + 1 + 2 \times 1 + 2 = 8$. Hence, $g_i = \frac{8}{20} = 0.4$.

subspaces of the various processors do not overlap (or have minimal overlap). In this case all processors would be concurrently searching distinct parts of the solution space. However, this would require that one has enough knowledge about the search space to partition it among the individual processors. In most cases this is an unrealistic assumption, and usually little is known about the search space. On the other hand, the subspace corresponding to the neighborhood of a particular solution is usually controlled by the algorithm designer (*allocation* operator and *windowing technique*), and can easily be searched in parallel by the available processors, with minimal overlap.

Another parallelization strategy would be to parallelize the execution of the simulated evolution operators. Unlike simulated annealing algorithm, which is inherently serial, most of the activities of the SimE algorithm can be executed in parallel. Recall that the SimE algorithm consists of three steps that must be executed in sequence: *evaluation*, then *selection*, and finally *allocation*. These steps are repeated until some stopping criteria are met. The activities of each of the first two steps can be performed concurrently without affecting the correctness of the algorithm. The elements of the population can be carefully partitioned among m processors. Each processor i, $1 \leq i \leq m$ would be assigned a subset P^i of the population P. Then, each processor i will evaluate the goodness of each element in P^i and run the *Selection* step to partition P^i into a selection subset P_s^i and a subset of remaining cells P_r^i. This will achieve a linear speed-up of the execution of the *evaluation* and *selection* steps of the algorithm.

The parallelization of the *allocation* function is more complex. For a carefully partitioned population and using a windowing technique, alterations performed by the allocation function on the subpopulations can be forced not to overlap, thus allowing the concurrent relocation of several selected cells at a time. Periodically, the subpopulations are merged and repartitioned to avoid missing parts of the search space. A similar parallelization strategy has been adopted to parallelize an SimE algorithm for standard-cell placement on a network of workstations [KB87a]. Each station is assigned a number of rows of the standard-cell layout. Each station executes one iteration of the SimE algorithm on the cells of the rows assigned to it. At each iteration, the rows are redistributed among the processors. The authors reported a linear speed-up for problems where each processor is assigned a fairly large number of cells (200–250 cells). For a large number of cells per processor, the processing time is more than one order of magnitude greater than the communication time among the processors [KB87a, Kli90].

In this parallelization strategy, one of the processors will have to be in charge of running SimE on a particular partition as well as performing the following tasks periodically (for example, at the end of each SimE iteration): (1) receive the subpopulations from all other processors and merge them into a new population, (2) partition the new population, and (3) finally distribute the resulting subpopulations among the processors.

5.9   Conclusions and Recent Work

In this chapter, we have examined an elegant and general randomized search heuristic. Like other heuristics of its class, it is suitable for solving hard combinatorial optimization problems, those with no known closed form solutions or polynomial time algorithms. SimE attempts to mimic natural selection processes of biological environments. A solution configuration is a population made of several elements. At each iteration, a *fitness measure* is evaluated for each element of current generation (population). Every element of current population has to prove its goodness in its current state. Unfit elements have proportionally high probability of being altered so as to gradually generate populations with higher overall fitness. The iterative process stops when no (significant) improvement is observed after a number of consecutive alterations. Hopefully, the search would have then converged to a global optimum.

Undoubtedly, the *simulated evolution* algorithm is a sound and robust randomized search heuristic. It is guaranteed to converge to a global optimum if given enough time. It is powerful, yet simple to tune to any particular combinatorial optimization problem. It has modest runtime and space requirements compared to *genetic algorithm*. It is built around the biological concept of *fitness*, a notion easier to digest and tune than the notion of *temperature* used in the *simulated annealing (SA) algorithm*. It is unfortunate though that SimE has not attracted as many researchers as simulated annealing, genetic algorithm, and tabu search did. We believe that this is due to two principal reasons: (1) SimE is fairly recent;

the first paper introducing the heuristic appeared in 1987 [KB87b]; and, most importantly, (2) Kling and Banerjee published most of their SimE-related papers in VLSI design automation conferences and journals. SimE would have attracted many more researchers from other engineering and scientific disciplines if it had been presented at events and journals of those disciplines. However, in the recent 2–4 years, SimE has seen a number of applications in domains other than computer-aided design (CAD) or very-large-scale integration (VLSI). Interested readers can consult references provided at the end of the chapter. It is our hope that this book will allow the randomized iterative heuristics herein described to reach a wider segment of the scientific and engineering communities.

References

[AHU74]   A. V. Aho, J. E. Hopcroft, and J. D. Ullman. *The Design and Analysis of Computer Algorithms*. Addison-Wesley, 1974.

[ANM93]   A. K. Dasari, N. Song, and M. Chrzanowska-Jeske. Layout-driven factorization and fitting for cellular-architecture fpgas. *Proceedings of NORTHCON'93 Electrical and Electronics Convention*, pages 106–111, Institute of Electrical and Electronics Engineers, New York, Oct. 1993.

[CLAHL95] C.-D. Chen, Y.-S. Lee, A.C.-H. Wu, and Y.-L. Lin. Tracer-fpga: A router for ram-based fpga's. *IEEE Transactions on Computer-Aided Design of Integrated Circuits and Systems*, 14(3):371–374, Mar. 1995.

[CLH89]   Y.-A. Chen, Y.-L. Lin, and Y.-C. Hsu. A new global router for ASIC design based on simulated evolution. *Proceedings of the 33rd Midwest Symposium on Circuits and Systems*, pages 261–265, IEEE, New York, May 1989.

[C.V94]   C. V. Buhusi. Learning by simulating evolution in automatic fuzzy systems synthesis. *Proceedings of 1994 IEEE 3rd International Fuzzy Systems Conference*, volume 2, pages 1308–1313, IEEE, New York, June 1994.

[G.M94]   G. M. Griner. A comparison of simulated evolution and genetic evolution performance. *Proceedings of the first IEEE Conference on Evolutionary Computation. IEEE World Congress on Computational Intelligence*, volume 1, pages 374–378, IEEE, New York, June 1994.

[HHYLH91] Y.-C. Hsich, C.-Y. Hwang, Y.-L Lin, and Yu-Chin Hsu. Lib: A CMOS cell compiler. *IEEE Transactions on Computer-Aided Design of Integrated Circuits and Systems*, 10(8):994–1005, Aug. 1991.

[HS78]   E. Horowitz and S. Sahni. *Fundamentals of Computer Algorithms*. Computer Science Press, 1978.

[IMK95]   I. Ahmad, M. K. Dhodhi, and K. A. Saleh. An evolutionary-based technique for local microcode compaction. *Proceedings of ASP-DAC'95/CHDL'95/VLSI with EDA Technofair*, pages 729–734, Nihon Gakkai Jimu Senta, Tokyo, Sep. 1995.

[KB87a]   R. M. Kling and P. Banerjee. Concurrent ESP: A placement algorithm for execution on distributed processors. *Proceedings of the IEEE International Conference on Computer-Aided Design*, pages 354–357, 1987.

[KB87b]   R. M. Kling and P. Banerjee. ESP: A new standard cell placement package using simulated evolution . *Proceedings of 24th Design Automation Conference*, pages 60–66, 1987.

[KB89]   R. M. Kling and P. Banerjee. ESP: Placement by Simulated Evolution. *IEEE Transactions on Computer-Aided Design*, 8(3):245–255, Mar. 1989.

[KB90]   R. M. Kling and P. Banerjee. Optimization by simulated evolution with applications to standard cell placement . *Proceedings of 27th Design Automation Conference*, pages 20–25, 1990.

[KB91]   R. M. Kling and P. Banerjee. Empirical and theoretical studies of the simulated evolution method applied to standard cell placement. *IEEE Transactions on Computer-Aided Design*, 10(10):1303–1315, Oct. 1991.

[KCGV83] S. Kirkpatrick, Jr., C. Gelatt, and M. Vecchi. Optimization by simulated annealing. *Science*, 220(4598):498–516, May 1983.

[KL70]   B. W. Kernighan and S. Lin. An efficient heuristic procedure to partition graphs. *Bell System Technical Journal*, 49(2):291–307, Feb. 1970.

[KL92a]   Y.-H. Kuo and S.-P. Lo. Automated synthesis of asynchronous pipelines. *Custom Integrated Circuits Conference, Proceedings of the IEEE 1992*, volume 2, pages 685–688, IEEE, New York, May 1992.

[KL92b]   Y.-H. Kuo and S.-P. Lo.   Partitioning and scheduling of asynchronous pipelines. *Computer Systems and Software Engineering, CompEuro 1992 Proceedings.*, pages 574–579, IEEE Computer Society Press, Los Alamitos, CA, May 1992.

[Kli90]   R. M. Kling. Optimization by simulated evolution and its application to cell placement. Doctoral dissertation, University of Illinois, Urbana, 1990.

[LAH95]   Y.-S. Lee and A. C.-H. Wu A performance and routability driven router for FPGAs considering path delays. *ANSI/IEEE Std 802.lb-1995*, pages 557–561, Mar. 1995.

[LHT88]   Y.-L. Lin, Y.-C. Hsu, and F.-S. Tsai. A detailed router based on simulated evolution. *Proceedings of the 33rd Midwest Symposium on Circuits and Systems*, pages 38–41, IEEE Computer Society Press, New York, Nov. 1988.

[LHT89]   Y. L. Lin, Y. C. Hsu, and F. H. S. Tsai. SILK: A simulated evolution router. *IEEE Transactions on Computer-Aided Design*, 8(10):1108–1114, Oct. 1989.

[LM93]   T. A. Ly and J. T. Mowchenko. Applying simulated evolution to high level-synthesis. *IEEE Transactions on Computer-Aided Design*, 12(3):389–409, Mar. 1993.

[Mao94]   C. Y. Mao. Simulated evolution algorithms for gate matrix layouts. Doctoral dissertation, University of Wisconsin, Madison, 1994.

[MH94]   C. Y. Mao and Y. H. Hu. SEGMA: A simulated evolution gate matrix layout algorithm. *VLSI Design*, 2(3):241–257, 1994.

[MH96]   C. Y. Mao and Y. H. Hu. Analysis of convergence properties of stochastic evolution algorithm. *IEEE Transactions on Computer-Aided Design*, 15(7):826–831, July 1996.

[NSS85]   S. Nahar, S. Sahni, and E. Shragowitz. Experiments with simulated annealing. *Proceedings of 22nd Design Automation Conference*, pages 748–752, 1985.

[Sec88]   C. Sechen. *VLSI Placement and Global Routing using Simulated Annealing*. Kluwer, Boston, 1988.

[SL87]   C. Sechen and K. W. Lee. An improved simulated annealing algorithm for row-based placement. *Proceedings of IEEE International Conference on Computer Aided Design*, pages 478–819, Nov. 1987.

[SR90]   Y. Saab and V. Rao. Stochastic evolution: A fast effective heuristic
           for some generic layout problems. *27th ACM/IEEE Design Automa-
           tion Conference*, pages 26–31, 1990.

[SSV86]   C. Sechen and A. L. Sangiovanni-Vincentelli. Timberwolf3.2: A
           new standard cell placement and global routing package. *Proceed-
           ings of 23rd Design Automation Conference*, pages 432–439, 1986.

[TJ90]   T. A. Ly and J. T. Mowchenko. Applying simulated evolution to
           scheduling in high level synthesis. *Proceedings of the 33rd Mid-
           west Symposium on Circuits and Systems*, volume 1, pages 172–
           175, IEEE Computer Society Press, New York, Aug. 1990.

[TSN93]   T. Koide, S. Wakabayashi, and N. Yoshida. An integrated approach
           to pin assignment and global routing for VLSI building-block lay-
           out. *1993 European Conference on Design Automation with the
           European Event in ASIC Design*, pages 24–28, IEEE Computer So-
           ciety Press, Los Alamitos, CA, Feb. 1993.

Exercises

Exercise 5.1
Discuss and compare similarities and differences between SimE, GA, and
SA.

Exercise 5.2
Based on your understanding of the SimE algorithm, rank the following according to their impact on the algorithm performance:

1. Accuracy of the estimation of the goodness measure.

2. Quality of initial solution.

3. Value of the selection bias parameter.

4. The Allocation step.

5. Sorting of the elements of the selection set.

Exercise 5.3
In the text, it was stated that, generally, it is beneficial to allocate the selected
elements according to a specific order which is problem specific. Argue in
favor or disfavor of such claim. Discuss the effect of sorted allocation on
runtime, quality of solution, rate of convergence, and so forth.

Exercise 5.4
Discuss the effect of the *selection bias* parameter on the runtime and quality of solution of the algorithm.

Exercise 5.5
The *selection bias* parameter has a large impact on the size of the selection set. This usually has major consequences on the quality of the search as well as the runtime requirement of the algorithm.

1. Why is the selection bias needed?

2. Suggest methods of setting the value of this parameter other than the trial and error approach proposed by Kling and Banerjee.

3. One approach that relieves the user from using the selection bias is to normalize the goodness values so as to force them to fall in the interval [0,1]. Provide a normalization formula that will force the goodnesses of elements to fall in the range [0.1,0.9].

Exercise 5.6
If one decides to limit the size of the selection set not to exceed a particular small value (say 10 percent of the number of movable elements), would that have any effect on the convergence of the algorithm? Justify your answer.

Exercise 5.7
For the random selection strategy discussed in the text (see Section 5.4.1 page 265), what would be the average size of the selection set?

Exercise 5.8
As the search progresses, the average fitness of the population keeps increasing. Let G_i be the average goodness of the population at the ith iteration. Derive an equation that would give an estimate of the percent reduction in runtime between two consecutive iterations, i and $i + 1$, as a function of G_i, G_{i+1}, and the number of elements n.

Exercise 5.9
1. Given a set of n distinct positive integers $X = \{x_1, x_2, \ldots, x_n\}$. The objective is to partition the set into two subsets X_1 of size k and X_2 of size $n - k$ $(1 \le k \le \frac{n}{2})$ such that the difference between the sums of the two subsets is minimized. This problem is known as the set partitioning problem. One of the best heuristics proposed for this problem for the case $k = \frac{n}{2}$ is the Karmarkar and Karp algorithm (given below).

Algorithm Karmarkar_and_Karp

Step 0. Initialize sets A and B to empty;

Step 1. Sort the numbers in descending order and put them in list L;

Step 2. Replace the largest two numbers in L by their difference;
   Repeat this step until there are only two numbers in the list;

Step 3. Put one number into set A and the other number into set B;
   (note that the difference between the two numbers is the
   difference of the final solution)

Step 4. Replace the numbers in the sets which are not in the original
   list as follows:
   Suppose x is in A and $x = y - z$, then
   remove x from A
   add y to A
   add z to B
   Repeat this step until only numbers in the original list are
   present in both sets

End.

2. Run the above algorithm on the following set of elements $\{12, 4, 7, 10, 8, 9, 25, 6, 18, 14\}$.

3. Find the time complexity of the Karmarkar and Karp algorithm.

4. Implement Karmarkar and Karp set partitioning heuristic and experiment with it on several instances of this problem.

5. Suggest a suitable goodness measure for this problem and illustrate it on the above problem instance.

6. Suggest a suitable allocation strategy for this problem.

7. Design and implement a Simulated Evolution algorithm to solve this problem. Run your SimE algorithm and compare quality of results with those obtained by Karmarkar and Karp. Discuss your results.

Exercise 5.10
Prove the result of Equation 5.14.

Exercise 5.11
Prove the result of Equation 5.17.

Exercise 5.12
Consider an instance of the quadratic assignment problem consisting of six modules to be assigned to locations in a 2×3-layout surface. The objective is to assign the modules so as to minimize the Manhattan length of the module

connections. Assume that the distance between two consecutive locations in the same row or the same column is equal to one unit. The connectivity matrix is as follows:

$$C = \begin{pmatrix} 0 & 1 & 0 & 1 & 1 & 0 \\ 1 & 0 & 1 & 1 & 1 & 0 \\ 0 & 1 & 0 & 0 & 1 & 1 \\ 1 & 1 & 0 & 0 & 0 & 0 \\ 1 & 1 & 1 & 0 & 0 & 1 \\ 0 & 1 & 1 & 0 & 1 & 0 \end{pmatrix}$$

where $c_{ij} = 1$ indicating that modules i and j are connected and $c_{ij} = 0$ otherwise.

1. Determine O_i, C_i, and g_i of each of the six cells as discussed in Example 5.1 on page 255. Assume that current state is as shown below. Find the goodness of this state.

6	5	4
1	2	3

Table 5.1: Assignment example for Exercise 5.12.

2. Assume that the selection set consists of module 1 and module swap is used by the allocation operator.

   (a) Find the goodness of the states resulting from the swap of module 1 with each of the other 5 modules.

   (b) Determine the transition probabilities (selection probabilities) from the current state to each of the possible intermediate states.

   (c) Determine the allocation probabilities from each of the intermediate states to each of the possible next feasible states.

Exercise 5.13
Consider the following instance of the two-way partitioning problem. There are six nodes numbered 1–6. Connectivity between these nodes is as indicated in the following connectivity matrix.

$$C = \begin{pmatrix} 0 & 1 & 0 & 0 & 0 & 0 \\ 1 & 0 & 1 & 1 & 0 & 0 \\ 0 & 1 & 0 & 0 & 0 & 0 \\ 0 & 1 & 0 & 0 & 1 & 1 \\ 0 & 0 & 0 & 1 & 0 & 1 \\ 0 & 0 & 0 & 1 & 1 & 0 \end{pmatrix}$$

The objective is to divide the above six nodes among two partitions so as to minimize the number of connections with ends in distinct partitions.

1. Propose a goodness measure and evaluate it for each node of the population. Assume that the current solution consists of nodes 1, 2, and 5 in one partition, and the remaining nodes in the other partition.

2. Suggest suitable cost function and allocation strategy and illustrate it on this problem instance.

Exercise 5.14
Consider the *vehicle routing problem* described in Chapter 1, page 7.

1. Devise suitable solution encoding and fitness measure (*evaluation* function).

2. Design appropriate *allocation* function for this *vehicle routing problem*.

3. Derive an equation expressing the time complexity of the algorithm as a function of the problem size, the complexity of the fitness function, and the complexity of the *allocation* operator.

4. Implement a simulated evolution-based program for the *vehicle routing problem*.

Exercise 5.15
Repeat the previous exercise (Exercise 5.14) considering the *flowshop scheduling problem* described in Chapter 2 (Exercise 2.16).

Exercise 5.16
Repeat Exercise 5.14 for the *terminal assignment problem* described in Chapter 2 (Exercise 2.17).

Exercise 5.17
Repeat Exercise 5.14 for the *concentrator location problem* described in Chapter 2 (Exercise 2.18).

Exercise 5.18
Repeat Exercise 5.14 for the *constrained minimum spanning tree problem* described in Chapter 2 (Exercise 2.19).

Exercise 5.19
Repeat Exercise 5.14 for the *mesh topology design problem* described in Chapter 2 (Exercise 2.20).

Exercise 5.20
Repeat Exercise 5.14 for the *weighted matching problem* described in Chapter 2 (Exercise 2.21).

Exercise 5.21
Repeat Exercise 5.14 for the *plant location problem* described in Chapter 2 (Exercise 2.22).

CHAPTER 6

Stochastic Evolution (StocE)

6.1 Introduction

In the search to develop new efficient procedures for combinatorial optimization, researchers have adapted ideas from other disciplines. Simulated annealing [KJV83] was inspired by the annealing of metals. Genetic algorithm [Gol89] and simulated evolution [KB91] were based on an analogy with the Darwinian theory of natural selection. In this chapter, we describe *stochastic evolution* (StocE), another randomized iterative search algorithm, inspired also by the alleged behavior of biological processes [Saa90, SR89, SR90].

Among the possible stochastic iterative algorithms for combinatorial optimization, those that rely on a random walk always perform worst. Nevertheless, many authors usually compare their iterative algorithms with results obtained by random walk search algorithms! When given limited CPU time, random walk undoubtedly leads to poor-quality solutions.

As discussed in Chapter 2, in the high-temperature regime, the *simulated annealing* (SA) algorithm follows almost a random search path. As temperature is lowered down, SA starts behaving like a classic gradient descent-method algorithm. An interesting question then comes to mind: If a random walk is the worse of search methods, why would SA or any other algorithm ever follows such a strategy? For the case of SA algorithm there are several answers: (1) SA was designed to start from any randomly selected initial solution. Therefore, in the early iterations, even large uphill moves should have a relatively high acceptance probability, thus breaking any possible nonoptimal clusters of elements within the early solution configurations, which may entrap the search in undesirable local minima. (2) SA was designed to ape the process of metal annealing, and therefore the initial temperature must be set high (as in the annealing of metals) and then cooled (lowered) gradually, forcing the algorithm to accept most of the uphill moves in this early hot regime. Would such strategy be suitable for combinatorial optimization? Many researchers do not agree with such search strategy and blame it for the excessive runtime requirements of SA. The reader can consult [KB87, KB89, Kli90, NSS85, Saa90, SR89, SR91] to cite a few. This partly explains the wealth of other iterative and constructive algorithms proposed in the literature. Several researchers rightfully object to the cooling paradigm adopted by SA. Why would someone have to always start with a random walk and slowly move toward a gradient-descent method? The subject of this chapter is to describe a relatively recent technique called *stochastic evolution* which prides itself by avoiding the random walk strategy altogether.

In this chapter, we start with a brief narration of the fairly recent history of *stochastic evolution*. We then describe the basic StocE algorithm; and give a brief qualitative comparison of *stochastic evolution* (StocE) with *simulated annealing* (SA) and *simulated evolution* (SimE). In Section 6.4 we address the convergence aspects of StocE. In Section 6.5 we illustrate its use on several hard combinatorial optimization problems. In Section 6.6 we present possible strategies to parallelize this algorithm. Finally, in Section 6.7, we briefly present other work and recent development related to stochastic evolution.

6.2 Historical Background

Stochastic evolution is a powerful general and randomized iterative heuristic for solving combinatorial optimization problems. The first paper describing StocE appeared in 1989 [SR89]. The paper was authored by Youssef Saab (working then on his Ph.D.) and Vasant Rao (his dissertation chairman). Other papers by the same authors followed [SR90, SR91].

Stochastic evolution algorithm is an instance of the class of general iterative heuristics discussed in [NSS85]. It is stochastic because the decision to accept a move is a probabilistic decision. *Good moves*, that is, moves which improve the cost function are accepted with probability one, and bad moves may also get accepted with a nonzero probability. This feature gives StocE hill-climbing property. The word *evolution* is used in reference to the alleged evolution processes of biological species. Like SA and SimE, StocE is conceptually simple and elegant. Actually StocE is somehow inspired in part by both SA (Chapter 2) and SimE (Chapter 5).

As pointed out above, *simulated evolution* and *stochastic evolution* are usually thought to be similar algorithms. Stochastic evolution is also seen as a generalization of simulated evolution. The confusion is mainly due to several historical facts. *Simulated evolution* was the fruit of the master's (M.S.), then Ph.D. work of Ralph Kling [Kli90], while *stochastic evolution* was the fruit of the Ph.D. work of Youssef Saab [Saa90]. Both were working concurrently at the University of Illinois at Urbana-Champaign. Both were awarded their degrees around the same time, Kling in July 1990 and Saab in August 1990. Furthermore, to add to the confusion, both Kling and Saab refer to their algorithms by the abbreviation SE. To remove some of the confusion, throughout the remainder of this book, we shall refer to Kling's *simulated evolution* with the acronym SimE and to Saab's *Stochastic Evolution* as StocE. This short historical account should convince the reader that SimE and StocE must be two different algorithms (after all, two Ph.D. degrees can't possibly be awarded for the same work!). Indeed, as we shall see, the two algorithms have several fundamental differences. They diverge in the way they mimic the biological processes of evolution, as well as the way they adapt their parameters during the search. Later in this chapter, we shall provide a thorough comparison of *stochastic evolution* (StocE) and *simulated evolution* (SimE). We will also contrast StocE with *simulated annealing* (SA).

6.3   Stochastic Evolution Algorithm

Stochastic evolution (StocE) is a general search strategy for solving a variety of combinatorial optimization problems.

Combinatorial optimization problems are problems that seek a global minimum of some real valued cost function $Cost : \Omega \rightarrow R$ defined over a *discrete state space* Ω. The elements of the discrete set Ω are referred to as states. A state space Ω together with an underlying neighborhood structure (the way one state can be reached from another state) form the solution space.

Combinatorial optimization problems can be modeled in a number of ways. StocE adopts the following generic model [SR90]:

> *Given a finite set M of movable elements and a finite set L of locations, a state is defined as a function $S : M \rightarrow L$ satisfying certain constraints.*

Many of the combinatorial optimization problems can be formulated according to this model. In [Saa90] the author illustrates the use of StocE on eight NP-hard problems: network bisection, vertex cover, set partition, Hamiltonian circuit, traveling salesman, linear ordering, standard cell placement, and multiway circuit partitioning. Below we recall some of these formulations.

The Network Bisection Problem (NBP)

Problem: Given a hypergraph $H = (V, E)$ where, V is the set of vertices and E the set of hyperedges. Each hyperedge $e \in E$ is a subset of V, that is, $e \subseteq V$.

Objective: Partition V into two sets V_1 and V_2 so as to minimize the number of hyperedges cut and such that, $|V_1| = |V_2| = n$, $V_1 \cap V_2 = \emptyset$, and

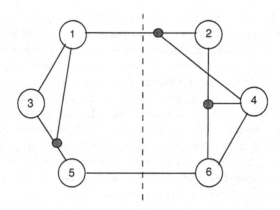

Figure 6.1: Network bisection example: $V = \{1, 2, 3, 4, 5, 6\}$, $E = \{(1, 2, 4),$ $(1, 3), (1, 3, 5), (2, 4, 6), (4, 6), (5, 6)\}$, $S^{-1}(1) = \{1, 3, 5\}$, $S^{-1}(2) = \{2, 4, 6\}$, and $Cost(S) = 2$.

$$V_1 \cup V_2 = V.$$

Let $V(e)$ be the vertices connected by hyperedge e. Hyperedge e is cut if and only if $\exists\, u \in V(e)$ and $\exists\, v \in V(e)$ such that $u \in V_1$ and $v \in V_2$. To formulate NBP in terms of the above state model, choose $M = V$ and $L = \{1, 2\}$. Then, a state is defined as the *onto function* $S : V \to \{1, 2\}$. In this case, there is one constraint which can be stated as $|S^{-1}(1)| = |S^{-1}(2)|$, that is, a state is a partition of the vertex set into two parts of equal cardinalities. Moreover, the cost of a state, $Cost(S)$, is the number of edges cut, that is,

$$Cost(S) = |E_{cut}|$$

where E_{cut}, the set of hyperedges cut, is defined below,

$$E_{cut} = \{e \in E : e \cap S^{-1}(1) \neq \emptyset \ and \ e \cap S^{-1}(2) \neq \emptyset\}$$

An instance of the network bisection problem is illustrated in Figure 6.1.

Hamiltonian Circuit Problem (HCP)

Problem: Given a graph $G(V, E)$ on n vertices.

Objective: Find a Hamiltonian cycle on the n vertices of the graph.

A *Hamiltonian cycle* is a simple cycle which includes all the n vertices in V. A graph containing at least one *Hamiltonian cycle* is called a *Hamiltonian graph*. A

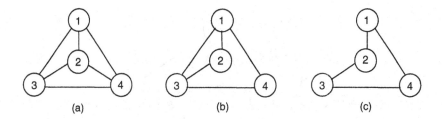

Figure 6.2: Hamiltonian circuit example: (a) $n = 4$, $V = \{1, 2, 3, 4\}$, and $E = \{(1, 2), (1, 3), (1, 4), (2, 3), (2, 4), (3, 4)\}$. E is not a chain-set since it violates condition (1) (for example, vertex 1 is in three edges), and it contains a cycle of length $3 \leq n - 1 = 4 - 1 = 3$ (violation of condition (2)). (b) $E' = \{(1, 2), (1, 3), (1, 4), (2, 3), (3, 4)\}$ is not a chain-set; it violates conditions (1) and (2). (c) $E' = \{(1, 2), (1, 4), (2, 3), (3, 4)\}$ is a chain-set since the graph induced by E' has no cycle of length ≤ 3 and each vertex is in at most two edges. Also, E' induces a Hamiltonian cycle since $\mid E' \mid = 4$.

complete graph on n vertices contains $n!$ Hamiltonian cycles. In general, checking whether a graph has a Hamiltonian cycle or not is NP-complete [GJ79].

A subset $E' \subseteq E$ of edges is a *chain-set* in $G(V, E)$ if,

1. each vertex in V is at most in two edges of E' and

2. the subgraph induced by E' in G contains no cycle of length $\leq n - 1$.

Clearly, if E' is a chain-set in G, then $\mid E' \mid \leq n$, and $\mid E' \mid = n$ if and only if E' induces a Hamiltonian cycle on G. Therefore, a chain-set E' induces either a collection of vertex-disjoint paths or a Hamiltonian cycle in the graph [Saa90] (Figure 6.2).

HCP can be formulated as a partitioning problem as follows [Saa90]. A state is defined as the *onto function* $S : E \rightarrow \{1, 2\}$, satisfying the condition that the set of edges in $S^{-1}(1)$ form a chain-set of G. The cost of a state S is computed as follows,

$$Cost(S) = n - |S^{-1}(1)|$$

Obviously, $Cost(S) \geq 0$, and $Cost(S) = 0$ if and only if the chain set $S^{-1}(1)$ induces a Hamiltonian cycle in G. The objective is to find a state with $Cost$ equal to zero, if such a state exists.

The Traveling Salesman Problem (TSP)

Problem: Given a complete graph $G = (V, E)$ with n vertices. Let d_{ij} be the length of the edge $(i, j) \in E$ and $d_{ij} = d_{ji}$. A path starting at some vertex s, visiting every other vertex exactly once, and returning to vertex s is called a *tour*.

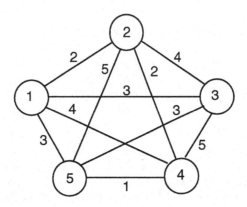

Figure 6.3: Traveling salesman example with five cities. Weights on edges represent distances, for example, $d_{1,2} = 2$, $d_{1,3} = 3$, $d_{1,4} = 4$, $d_{1,5} = 3$, and so on. The tour $[1, 2, 3, 4, 5, 1]$ has a length equal to $d_{1,2}+d_{2,3}+d_{3,4}+d_{4,5}+d_{5,1} = 2+4+5+1+3 = 15$. Hence for this tour $S^{-1}(1) = \{(1,2),(2,3),(3,4),(4,5),(5,1)\}$ and $Cost(S) = 15$.

Objective: Find a *tour* of minimum length, where the length of a *tour* is equal to the sum of lengths of its defining edges.

In the previous chapter, TSP was modeled as a permutation problem and here we model it as a partitioning problem [Saa90]. To formulate TSP as a partitioning problem in terms of the above state model, choose $M = E$, that is, the movable elements are the edges, and choose $L = \{1, 2\}$. Then a state is defined as the *onto function* $S : E \rightarrow \{1, 2\}$, satisfying the condition that the set of edges in $S^{-1}(1)$ forms a Hamiltonian cycle in G. The cost of a state S, $Cost(S)$, is the sum of the lengths of the edges included in the set $S^{-1}(1)$, that is,

$$Cost(S) = \sum_{(i,j)\in S^{-1}(1)} d_{i,j}$$

An instance of the TSP problem with five cities is given in Figure 6.3.

6.3.1   StocE Algorithm

The stochastic evolution (StocE) algorithm seeks to find a suitable location $S(m)$ for each movable element $m \in M$, which eventually leads to a lower cost of the whole state $S \in \Omega$, where Ω is the state space. A general outline of the StocE algorithm is given in Figure 6.4. The inputs to the StocE algorithm are:

1. an initial state (solution) S_0,

2. an initial value p_0 of the control parameter p, and

Algorithm StocE(S_0, p_0, R);
Begin
    $BestS = S = S_0$;
    $BestCost = CurCost = Cost(S)$;
    $p = p_0$;
    $\rho = 0$;
    Repeat
        $PrevCost = CurCost$;
        $S = PERTURB(S, p)$; /* perform a search in the neighborhood of S */
        $CurCost = Cost(S)$;
        $UPDATE(p, PrevCost, CurCost)$; /* update p if needed */
        If ($CurCost < BestCost$) **Then**
            $BestS = S$;
            $BestCost = CurCost$;
            $\rho = \rho - R$; /* Reward the search with R more generations */
        Else
            $\rho = \rho + 1$;
        EndIf
    Until $\rho > R$
    Return ($BestS$);
End

Figure 6.4: The stochastic evolution algorithm.

3. a stopping criterion parameter R.

Throughout the search, S holds *the current state (solution)*, while $BestS$ holds *the best state*. If the algorithm generates *a worse state*, a uniformly distributed random number in the range $[-p, 0]$ is drawn. The new uphill state is accepted if the magnitude of the loss is greater than the random number, otherwise the current state is maintained. Therefore, p is a function of the average magnitude of the uphill moves that the algorithm will tolerate. The parameter R represents the expected number of iterations the StocE algorithm needs until an improvement in the cost with respect to the best solution seen so far takes place, that is, until $CurCost \leq BestCost$. If R is too small, the algorithm will not have enough time to improve the initial solution, and if R is too large, the algorithm may waste too much time during the later generations. Experimental studies indicate that a value of R between 10 and 20 gives good results [Saa90].

Finally, the variable ρ is a counter used to decide when to stop the search. ρ is initialized to zero, and $R - \rho$ is equal to the number of remaining generations before the algorithm stops.

FUNCTION PERTURB(S, p);
Begin
   ForEach $(m \in M)$ **Do**   /* according to some apriori ordering */
     $S' = MOVE(S, m)$;
     $Gain(m) = Cost(S) - Cost(S')$;
     If $(Gain(m) > RANDINT(-p, 0))$ **Then**
        $S = S'$
   EndIf
   EndFor;
   $S =$ MAKE_STATE(S); /* make sure S satisfies constraints */
   Return (S)
End

Figure 6.5: The PERTURB function.

After initialization, the algorithm enters a **Repeat** loop **Until** the counter ρ exceeds R. Inside the **Repeat** body, the cost of the current state is first calculated and stored in $PrevCost$. Then, the **PERTURB** function (Figure 6.5) is invoked to make a compound move from the current state S. **PERTURB** scans the set of movable elements M according to some apriori ordering and attempts to move every $m \in M$ to a new location $l \in L$. For each trial move, a new state S' is generated, which is *a unique* function $S' : M \rightarrow L$ such that $S'(m) \neq S(m)$ for some movable object $m \in M$. To evaluate the move, the gain function $Gain(m) = Cost(S) - Cost(S')$ is calculated. If the calculated gain is greater than some randomly generated integer number in the range $[-p, 0]$, the move is accepted and S' replaces S as the current state.[1] Since the random number is ≤ 0, moves with positive gains are always accepted. After scanning all the movable elements $m \in M$, the **MAKE_STATE** routine makes sure that the final state satisfies the state constraints. If the state constraints are not satisfied then **MAKE_STATE** *reverses* the fewest number of latest moves until the state constraints are satisfied. This procedure is required when perturbation moves that violate the state constraints are accepted.

The new state generated by **PERTURB** is returned to the main procedure as the current state, and its cost is assigned to the variable $CurCost$. Then the routine **UPDATE** (Figure 6.6) is invoked to compare the previous cost ($PrevCost$) to the current cost ($CurCost$). If $PrevCost = CurCost$, there is a good chance that the algorithm has reached a local minimum and therefore, p is increased by p_{incr} to tolerate larger uphill moves, thus giving the search the possibility of escaping from local minima. Otherwise, p is reset to its initial value p_0.

---

[1] Here, we assume that we are dealing with a minimization problem.

PROCEDURE UPDATE(p, $PrevCost$, $CurCost$);
Begin
    If ($PrevCost = CurCost$) **Then** /* possibility of a local minimum */
        $p = p + p_{incr}$; /* increment p to allow larger uphill moves */
    Else
        $p = p_0$; /* re-initialize p */
    EndIf;
End

Figure 6.6: The UPDATE procedure.

At the end of the loop, the cost of the *current state* S is compared with the cost of the *best state* $BestS$. If S has a lower cost, then the algorithm keeps S as the best solution ($BestS$) and decrements R by ρ, thereby rewarding itself by increasing the number of iterations (allowing the search to live R generations more). This allows a more detailed investigation of the neighborhood of the newly found best solution. If S, however, has a higher cost, ρ is incremented, which is an indication of no improvements.

6.3.2 StocE versus SA

Simulated annealing and stochastic evolution are similar in several aspects:

1. like simulated annealing [KJV83], the StocE algorithm is general in the sense that it can be tailored to solve most known combinatorial optimization problems;

2. they both have the capability of escaping local minima; and

3. they both are blind, that is, they do not know the optimal solution and have to be told when to stop.

However, SA and StocE have several fundamental differences:

1. In SA, a perturbation of current state (solution) is a single move, while for StocE it is a compound move;

2. in StocE there is no hot or cold regime;

3. for SA the acceptance probability of an uphill move keeps decreasing with decreasing values of the temperature, whereas in StocE such probability gets increased whenever the search is suspected to have reached some local optimum, and reset to its initial value otherwise; and

4. the fourth fundamental difference is that StocE introduces the concept of a reward whereby the search algorithm cleverly rewards itself whenever it makes a good move.

We believe that StocE algorithms always run much faster than other stochastic iterative algorithms such as SA. The reason is that, for StocE, the parameter p, which controls how steep of a hill the algorithm can climb, may be relatively large only when there is evidence of the search getting stuck at a local minimum. Otherwise p is such that only small uphill moves are allowed. Therefore, StocE does not have a hot regime like simulated annealing where the algorithm will be performing almost a random walk, thus wasting runtime resources. This observation has been supported by experimental data [AM96, SR91].

6.3.3 StocE versus SimE

Because of its name, *stochastic evolution* (StocE) is often thought to be similar to *simulated evolution* (SimE, see Chapter 5). However, by now, it should be clear to the reader that StocE is fundamentally different from SimE. Below, we enumerate some of their similarities and differences.

1. Both StocE and SimE use a compound move to transit from current state to next state. For SimE, the intermediate states are incomplete states where some of the selected elements have not yet been relocated. For StocE, each intermediate state is a complete state, but which may violate some of the environmental constraints that characterize feasible solutions.

2. SimE selects a number of individuals, removes them from their current locations, and finally assigns them one at a time to new locations. Each of the selected individuals is assigned to a new location of highest goodness among all possible locations tried for that particular element. It is also possible to seek to allocate all the selected elements all at once and to choose the allocation that leads to the highest cost improvement. Such a strategy has been adopted in the *branch-and-bound allocation* scheme of the simulated evolution standard-cell placer (Section 5.7.1) [Kli90].

   In contrast, StocE usually examines each element of the current solution in a predetermined order, and attempts to alter the location of the element. If the new location has a positive gain (improves the goodness of the solution) then the alteration is accepted; alteration with negative gains are also accepted with a probability that is a function of the magnitude of the gain decrease and a user-specified parameter. After reaching a decision with the current element, the algorithm selects the next element.

3. For both algorithms each compound move is counted as one iteration (one generation). However, SimE stops the search after a user-specified maxi-

mum number of iterations or when no noticeable improvement is observed over a number of successive generations.

In contrast, StocE uses the notion of reward and penalty whereby a compound move is rewarded whenever the move takes us to a state better than the current best, and is otherwise penalized. The reward consists of increasing the number of generations (thus extending the life of the search) by a user-specified parameter R. The penalty consists of decrementing the number of generations by 1.

4. SimE decides on each move on the basis of the fitness (goodness) of the selected individual, which is a local information with respect to that individual. An element $m \in M$ is moved to a new location if and only if $Random(0, 1) \leq (1 - g_m)$ where g_m is the goodness of element m, a quantity in the interval $[0, 1]$. The new location is the one that leads to the maximum cost improvement among a window of locations.

On the other hand, StocE attempts to move each element. It decides on each move on the basis of the gain of that move. An element $m \in M$ is moved to a new location if and only if $Gain(S, S') = Cost(S) - Cost(S') \geq Random(-p, 0)$ where $S' = Move(S, m)$. $Gain$ is a global information about the new state and can have any real value.

5. Both SimE and StocE attempt to allocate the movable elements in a predetermined order. Also, usually, for each movable element only a window of trial locations are tried.

We believe that the notion of reward and penalty is useful in cleverly adjusting the number of required iterations to the nature of the search space. This has been confirmed by experiments conducted by various researchers [AM96, Saa90, SR91].

6.4 Stochastic Evolution Convergence Aspects

Saab stated in the conclusion of his doctoral dissertation that the stochastic evolution algorithm may never converge [Saa90]. He attributes that to the way the parameter p is updated.

In this section, we shall show that the behavior of the stochastic evolution algorithm can be modeled by a nonhomogeneous Markov chain. The nonhomogeneity is due to the fact that the transition probabilities between neighboring states depend on the parameter p, which gets updated during the course of the search. Were the parameter p fixed, the algorithm would be guaranteed to converge to a global optimum state since the behavior of the algorithm could in that case be modeled by a homogeneous ergodic Markov chain (see Section 1.8).

Similar to simulated evolution, the stochastic evolution algorithm consists of two phases, an initialization phase where all the parameters and data structures of the algorithm are set, and a randomized iterative search phase. The iterative phase consists of two main steps, a *perturbation* step, also called *generalization*, and a *make-state* step, referred to as *specialization* [MH96]. The generalization step relocates some of the movable elements, thus generating an intermediate state that may violate some of the problem constraints. The specialization step performs some changes to force a transition from the intermediate state to a new feasible state satisfying all the problem constraints.

In order to keep the analysis simple, we shall assume that each move changes the current state to another valid state. Furthermore, we will assume that the cost of a state is an integer.

Let X_n be the random variable representing the cost of the state reached after n iterations. The sequence of random variables $X_0, X_1, \ldots, X_n, \ldots$ forms a discrete time Markov chain. That is,

$$P[X_n = j \mid X_0 = x_0, X_1 = x_1, \ldots, X_{n-1} = i] = P[X_n = j \mid X_{n-1} = i]$$
$$(6.1)$$

Here x_0 denotes the cost of the initial solution. Let $p_{i,j}^n$ be the transition probability from current state of cost i to a next state of cost j at the nth generation, that is,

$$P[X_n = j \mid X_{n-1} = i] = p_{i,j}^n$$

We can easily show that

$$p_{i,j}^n = \begin{cases} 0 & \text{if } j - i \geq p_{n-1} \\ p_s^{(n-1)}(i,j) & \text{if } j \leq i \\ p_s^{(n-1)}(i,j) \times (1 - \frac{i-j}{p_{n-1}}) & \text{otherwise} \end{cases} \qquad (6.2)$$

where p_{n-1} is the value of the parameter p after $n-1$ iterations and $p_s^{(n-1)}(i,j)$ is the probability of selecting state $j \in \aleph^{(n-1)}(i)$ when at state i at $n-1$st iteration. $\aleph^{(n-1)}(i)$ is the set of neighbor states of i at the nth iteration. Recall that the parameter p is initialized to p_0 and may get updated at the end of each iteration. Equation 6.2 assumes that we are seeking a state of minimum cost.

Let $P[X_n = j \mid X_m = i] = p_{i,j}(m,n)$ be the $(n-m)$-step transition probability, for all $m < n$. It can be shown that,

$$p_{i,j}(m,n) = \sum_k p_{i,k}(m,q) \times p_{k,j}(q,n) \quad m \leq q \leq n \qquad (6.3)$$

The above multistep transition probabilities are known as the Chapman-Kolmogorov equations [Kle75]. Let $P(n) = [p_{i,j}(n, n+1)]$ be the one-step transition probability matrix after n iterations. $P(n) = P$ if the chain is homogeneous. Let $H(m,n) = [p_{i,j}(m,n)]$ be the multistep transition probability matrix.

Note that $H(n, n + 1) = P(n)$. In matrix notation, the Chapman-Kolmogorov equations can be rewritten as follows:

$$H(m, n) = H(m, q)H(q, n) \quad \forall \, q \in [m, n] \tag{6.4}$$

By recurrence, it can be shown that [Kle75],

$$H(m, n) = P(m)P(m + 1) \ldots P(n - 1) \quad \forall \, m \leq n - 1 \tag{6.5}$$

Let $\Pi^{(n)}$ be the state transient probabilities after n iterations.

$$\Pi^{(n+1)} = \Pi^{(n)} P(n) = \Pi^{(0)} H(0, n + 1) \tag{6.6}$$

Hence, the steady-state probabilities Π, if they exist, are given by the following equation:

$$\Pi = \lim_{n \to \infty} \Pi^{(0)} H(0, n + 1) \tag{6.7}$$

Therefore, because of the dependence of the state transitions on the time-varying parameter p, the stochastic evolution algorithm is not always guaranteed to hit the optimal state.

The existence of the steady-state solution is strongly dependent on the initial value of the parameter p and on the parameter R. For example, if $p_0 > Cost_{max} - Cost_{min}$ where $Cost_{max}$ is the cost of the state with the largest cost and $Cost_{min}$ is the cost of the global minimum, then starting in any initial state S_0 with cost $Cost_0$, the probability of moving to the global optimum in just one transition is equal to the following:

$$p_{Cost_0, Cost_{min}}(1, 2) = p_s^{(1)}(Cost_0, Cost_{min}) \times (1 - \frac{Cost_0 - Cost_{min}}{p_0})$$

The above probability is strictly positive provided that $p_s^{(1)}(Cost_0, Cost_{min})$ is positive. But since at each generation all the elements are processed, the probability of reaching (selecting) any state of the state space from the current state is positive provided the perturbation function (the *move* operation) is probabilistic (nongreedy).

If both p and R are small, the algorithm may never converge. The reason is that for small p some of the transitions become impossible (have a zero probability), thus pruning portions of the search space. Furthermore, if R is too small, the algorithm will not have enough time to move to an optimal state. The value of p_0, R, and the cost of the various states are strongly related. The identification of the condition(s) that will guarantee the existence of the stationary probabilities remains an open problem.

6.5   Stochastic Evolution Applications

As mentioned above, the StocE algorithm can be used to solve a wide range of combinatorial optimization problems. Like previously described algorithms, it has to be adapted to the type of problem under investigation. Specifically, (1) the solution space has to be defined, (2) a suitable state representation be adopted, (3) the notion of cost and perturbation have to be appropriately identified, (4) an initial value of the control parameter p and a method to update it must be chosen, and finally (5) a value for the stopping criterion be selected.

In this section, we first briefly describe how StocE can be used to solve four widely cited hard combinatorial optimization problems, namely, network bisection, vertex cover, Hamiltonian circuit, and traveling salesman problems. These as well as other examples are provided in [Saa90]. We then use StocE to solve FPGA technology mapping problem, a hard combinatorial optimization problem encountered in FPGA design methodologies.

6.5.1   Network Bisection

The state model as well as the cost function for the network bisection problem were given on page 301. A *move* consists of transferring a vertex v from its current part to the complementary part. Let $S' = MOVE(S, v)$ be an *onto* function that associates a new state S' for each move of a vertex v at current state S, such that $S'(v) = 3 - S(v)$ and $S(u) = S'(u)$ for all $u \neq v$.

The vertices are numbered 1, 2, ..., $|V|$. The function *PERTURB* scans all the vertices in ascending order. Since each move consists of transferring some vertex v from $S(v)$ to $3 - S(v)$, the state that is returned by the $PERTURB$ function may correspond to an unbalanced partition, that is, $|S^{-1}(1)| \neq |S^{-1}(2)|$. Therefore, a *MAKE_STATE* function is required to reverse the fewest last moves that will make the partition balanced. The initial value of the parameter p is equal to $p_0 = 2$, the *UPDATE* of p consists of incrementing it by one, and the algorithm starts from a randomly generated bisection.

On all test problems, stochastic evolution produced better results than simulated annealing and in a much shorter time [Saa90]. The StocE runtime was at times an order of magnitude less than SA runtime, while the cost is 30 percent less.

6.5.2   Vertex Cover Problem

A *vertex cover* of a graph $G(V, E)$ is a subset $V_c \subseteq V$ such that, for each edge $(i, j) \in E$, at least one of i or $j \in V_c$ (see Figure 6.7). For the *vertex cover problem*, we seek to find a vertex cover of minimum cardinality.

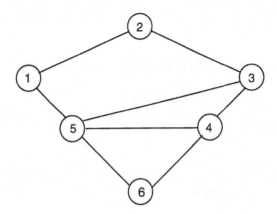

Figure 6.7: Vertex cover example: $V_c = \{1, 3, 4, 6\}$ is a vertex cover of size 4 and $V_c = \{1, 2, 4, 5\}$ is another vertex cover of size 4.

A matching of a graph $G(V, E)$ is a subset of edges $E_m \subseteq E$ such that no two edges in E_m share a common vertex. For example, $E_m = \{(1, 2), (5, 3)\}$ is a matching of the graph in Figure 6.7.

E_m is maximal if G has no matching E_m' such that $|E_m'| > |E_m|$. For the example in Figure 6.7 $E_m = \{(1, 2), (5, 3)\}$ is not maximal whereas $E_m = \{(1, 2), (5, 3), (6, 4)\}$ is maximal. If $(i, j) \in E_m$ then i is said to be matched with j. Observe that no vertex can be matched with two or more vertices. For any given graph, the size of a maximal matching is a lower bound on the size of any vertex cover in the graph.

To solve VCP by StocE the following state model is used [Saa90]: $M = V$, $L = \{1, 2\}$, and as a state the onto function $S : V \rightarrow L$ such that $S(i) = 1$ if vertex i is in the vertex cover, otherwise $S(i) = 2$. $\forall (i, j) \in E$, $S(i) = 1$ or $S(j) = 1$, that is, either or both of i and j are in the vertex cover.

Let $V = \{1, 2, \ldots, i, \ldots, n\}$ and $Adj(i) = \{j \in V : (i, j) \in E\}$ be the vertices adjacent to vertex i, $1 \leq i \leq n$. The initial state S_0 is generated by the constructive function given in Figure 6.8.

For example, for the VCP instance of Figure 6.7 the following initial vertex cover will be generated: $V_c = 1, 3, 6$. Vertex 2 will not be included in the initial vertex cover because vertex $1 \in Adj(2)$ and $S_0(1) = 1$. For similar reasons vertices 4 and 5 are not included in the initial vertex cover.

The **PERTURB** function scans the vertices in increasing order, that is, 1, 2, ..., n. The move strategy is as specified in Figure 6.9.

FUNCTION Construct_Initial_State(G);
Begin
    For $(i = 2)$ **To** n **Do** $S_0(i) = 2$ **EndFor**;
    $S_0(1) = 1$;
    For $(i = 2)$ **To** n **Do**
    Begin
      ForEach $j \in Adj(i)$ **Do**
      Begin
        If $S_0(j) = 2$ **Then**
          $S_0(i) = 1$;
          Exit /* from the **ForEach** loop */
        EndIf
      EndFor
    EndFor
    Return (S_0)
End

Figure 6.8: Construction of initial vertex cover.

FUNCTION MOVE(S, i);
/* S is current state and i vertex to move */
Begin
    If $S(i) = 1$ **Then** $S' = MOVE\_OUT(S, i)$
      Else $S' = MOVE\_IN(S, i)$
    EndIf
    Return (S')
End

Figure 6.9: Move strategy used in the PERTURB function of the vertex cover problem.

The functions **MOVE_IN** and **MOVE_OUT** proceed as follows. Let S be the current state and i be a vertex not in the vertex cover, that is, $i \notin S^{-1}(1)$ and $S(i) = 2$. Then a move to the next state S' can be made by putting i in the vertex cover and making the necessary adjustments to the vertices adjacent to i. Such steps are carried out by the following function.

FUNCTION MOVE_IN(S, i);
Begin
        For $j = 1$ **To** n **Do** $S'(j) = S(j)$ **EndFor**;
        $S'(i) = 1$;
        ForEach $j \in Adj(i)$ **Do**
            If $S'(k) = 1$ $\forall k \in Adj(j)$ **Then** $S'(j) = 2$ **EndIf**
        EndForEach
        Return (S')
End

Otherwise, if i is in the vertex cover, that is, $i \in S^{-1}(1)$ and $S(i) = 1$, then the following move strategy is adopted.

FUNCTION MOVE_OUT(S, i);
/* S is current state and i vertex to move */
Begin
        For $j = 1$ **To** n **Do** $S'(j) = S(j)$ **EndFor**;
        $S'(i) = 2$;
        ForEach $j \in Adj(i)$ **Do**
            If $S'(j) = 2$ **Then** $S' = MOVE\_IN(S', j)$ **EndIf**
        EndForEach
        Return (S')
End

MAKE_STATE is not required since all intermediate states are legal. The parameter p_0 is initialized to 2 and $p_{incr} = 1$.

On several random graphs varying in size from 100 vertices and 148 edges to 5,000 vertices and 11,508 edges, StocE produced smaller vertex covers than those obtained with SA in a fraction of the time required by simulated annealing (2 to 10 percent of the runtime of SA) [Saa90].

6.5.3 Hamiltonian Circuit Problem

Given a graph $G(V, E)$ on n vertices, the objective is to identify a Hamiltonian cycle if one exists. The following StocE-based HCP solution is due to Youssef Saab [Saa90] where the partitioning state model is adopted.

Recall from page 302, a state is defined as the *onto function* $S : E \rightarrow \{1, 2\}$, satisfying the condition that the set of edges in $S^{-1}(1)$ form a chain-set of G. The cost of a state S is $Cost(S) = n - |S^{-1}(1)|$. $Cost(S) = 0$ if and only if the chain set $S^{-1}(1)$ induces a Hamiltonian cycle in G. The objective is to find a state with $Cost$ equal to zero, if such a state exists.

The initial state S_0 is chosen such that $S_0^{-1}(1) = \emptyset$. Therefore, $S_0(e) = 2$, $\forall e \in E$.

Moves are only associated with edges of E that have at least one of their vertices as an end point of a path in the chain-set $S^{-1}(1)$. A linked list of all such edges is identified before each call to **PERTURB**. A vertex not belonging to any of the paths in $S^{-1}(1)$ is considered to be an end of an "*empty path.*" **PERTURB** scans the edges of L in their given order. The objective is to extend the chain-set $S^{-1}(1)$, which is initially empty, to a Hamiltonian cycle in the graph.

Let S be the current state and let (i, j) denote the current
edge being scanned
    If $Cost(S) = 0$ **Then** stop /* $S^{-1}(1)$ induces a HC in G */
    If $Cost(S) > 0$ **Then** the chain-set in $S^{-1}(1)$ is a
        collection of disjoint paths
        $S' = MOVE(S, (i, j)))$

The move function behaves as follows.

Case 1: $S((i, j)) = 2$ ((i, j) is not in the chain-set), and the vertices i and j are at the ends of two different paths (one path or both paths could be the "*empty path*") in the chain-set $S^{-1}(1)$. In that case, accept the move, that is, $S'((i, j)) = 1$ and $S'((k, l)) = S((k, l)) \forall (i, j) \neq (k, l), (k, l) \in E$.

Therefore, the chain-set is increased by one more edge which is (i, j), that is, the move has a gain of "+1".

> **Example 6.1** Referring to Figure 6.10(b), edge $(2, 3)$ of G belongs to two disjoint paths of the chain-set. Therefore $S((2, 3)) = 2$. Figure 6.10(c) is the chain-set after the addition of edge $(2, 3)$ to the chain-set of Figure 6.10(b). ∎

Case 2: $S((i, j)) = 2$ and i and j are the ends of the same path π of the chain-set $S^{-1}(1)$.

> **If** length $(\pi) = n - 1$ **Then** perform the move
> since that would create a Hamiltonian cycle
>   **Else** don't perform the move as that would violate
>   chain-set conditions.

> **Example 6.2** $(3, 5)$ would be rejected if current chain-set is the one given in Figure 6.10(b). However if current chain-set is the one given

in Figure 6.10(d) then $(4, 5)$ belongs to the path $\pi = [4, 1, 2, 3, 6, 5]$, where length$(\pi) = 5 = 6 - 1$ $(n = 6)$. Hence the addition of $(4, 5)$ would create a Hamiltonian circuit. Therefore, stop the search.

■

Case 3: $S((i, j)) = 2$ and i is at the end of one ("possibly empty") path and j is in the middle of another path in $S^{-1}(1)$ or vice versa. Assume that j is the vertex in the middle of another path.

Example 6.3 For the edge $(4, 6)$ in the chain-set of Figure 6.10(b), 6 is in the middle of the path [3,6,5] and 4 is the end of an empty path.

Let (k, j) and (j, l) be two edges in $S^{-1}(1)$ (for the example of Figure 6.10(b) $k = 3$, and $l = 5$).

In order to add the edge (i, j) (here $i = 4$ and $j = 6$) without violating Condition (1) (see page 303) of chain-set, one has to remove either the edge (k, j) or (j, l) from the current chain-set (Probability 1/2 for each choice). For the example of Figure 6.10(b) edge $(3, 6)$ or $(6, 5)$ must be removed and then edge $(4, 6)$ added to the chain-set. After such a move, the resulting chain-set will have the same number of edges, that is, the move has zero gain [see Figure 6.10(b) and Figure 6.10(e)].

■

Case 4: $S((i, j)) = 2$ and i is the end of a path in $S^{-1}(1)$ and j is in the middle of the same path, or vice versa.

Assume that i is in the end of a path and j is in the middle of the same path.

Example 6.4 In Figure 6.10(d), $i = 5$ and $j = 3$, $\pi = [4, 1, 2, 3, 6, 5]$, $n = 6$, and length$(\pi) = 5$.

■

If length $(\pi) = n - 2$ (that is, $Cost(s) > 1$) **Then** reject the move
    For example, $(5, 3)$ in Figure 6.10(c). $\pi = [1,2,3,6,5]$,
    length$(\pi) = 4 \leq 6 - 2 = 4$

Else Let k be a vertex in between i and j and is
    adjacent to j on $\pi \in S^{-1}(1)$
    Then remove (k, j) from $S^{-1}(1)$ and
        add (k, j) to $S^{-1}(1)$; $gain = 0$.
        For example, Figures 6.10(d) and (f): $i = 5$ and, $j = 3$, $k = 6$,
        remove $(3, 6)$ and add $(3, 5)$.

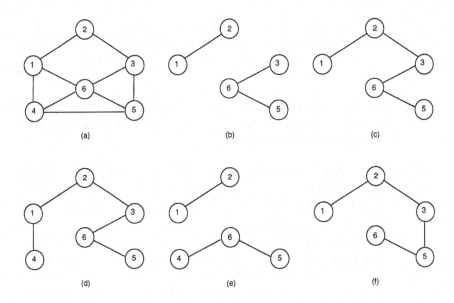

Figure 6.10: Examples of moves for the HCP problem. (a) Graph $G(V, E)$ where $V = \{1, 2, 3, 4, 5, 6\}$ and $E = \{(1, 2), (1, 4), (1, 6), (2, 3), (3, 5), (3, 6), (4, 5), (4, 6), (5, 6)\}$. (b) A chain-set. (c) Case 1: chain-set of (b) after the call to function Move[(2, 3)]. (d) Case 2: edge $(4, 5)$ extends the chain-set to become a Hamiltonian cycle. (e) Case 3: chain-set of (b) after removal of $(3, 6)$ and addition of $(4, 6)$. (f) Case 4: chain-set of (d) after removal of $(3, 6)$ and addition of $(3, 5)$.

Case 5: $S((ij)) = 2$ and both i and j are in the middle of the same path or different paths in $S^1(1)$. Then reject the move.

Case 6: $S(e) = 1$. Then reject the move.

    Whenever no move is made, the **PERTURB** function proceeds directly to scan the next edge in the list L. Since all states are legal, there is no need for function **MAKE_STATE**. The initial parameter $p_0 = 0$ and $p_{incr} = 1$. Notice that p will fluctuate between 0 and 1. Therefore, moves of negative gains (that is, strict uphill moves) are never performed by StocE in this HCP solution. However, the algorithm still has the capability of escaping local minima because of the acceptance of zero gain-moves.

    On experiments with random graphs of sizes varying between $n = 100$ vertices and 10,000 vertices ($|E|$=389 to 26,432)) StocE was able to find a Hamiltonian circuit (runtime varying between 100 seconds and 50 hours) where SA failed to locate a tour for all test cases.

6.5.4   Traveling Salesman Problem

Given a complete graph $G(V, E)$ and following the partitioning state model of the TSP problem (refer to the TSP formulation given in Section 6.3, page 303), $M = E$ and $L = \{1, 2\}$. A state is defined as the *onto function* $S : E \rightarrow \{1, 2\}$, satisfying the condition that the set of edges in $S^{-1}(1)$ forms a Hamiltonian cycle in G. The cost of a state S is the sum of the lengths of the edges included in the set $S^{-1}(1)$, i.e, $Cost(S) = \sum_{(i,j) \in S^{-1}(1)} d_{i,j}$ (see Figure 6.3).

The initial state (initial tour) S_0 is constructed using the *nearest-neighbor* heuristic. For example, for the TSP instance in Figure 6.3, $S_0 = [4, 5, 1, 2, 3, 4]$, and $Cost_0 = Cost(S_0) = 15$.

The parameters p_0 and p_{incr} are initialized as follows:

$$p_0 = \min_{\forall (i,j) \in E} d_{i,j}$$

$$p_{\text{incr}} = \max_{\forall (i,j) \in E} d_{i,j}$$

Let S be the current state and $(i, j) \in E$ not in the current tour, that is, $S((i, j)) = 2$. Let $i_1 = succ(i)$ and $j_1 = succ(j)$ in the current tour of $S^{-1}(1)$ (see Figure 6.11). The new state $S' = MOVE(S, (i, j))$ is formed so as to satisfy the following conditions (Figure 6.11):

$$S'((i, j)) = 1 = S'((i_1, j_1))$$

$$S'((i, i_1)) = 2 = S'((j, j_1))$$

$$\forall (k, l), \ S'((k, l)) = S((k, l))$$

For each vertex $i \in V$, a list Adj_i is constructed containing all other vertices in V in increasing order of their distance from i. That is, $Adj_i[k]$ is the kth closest vertex to i, $i \neq Adj_i[k]$, $1 \leq k \leq n - 1$. For example, for the TSP instance of Figure 6.3, $Adj_1 = [2, 3, 5, 4]$ and $Adj_2 = [1, 4, 3, 5]$. For large graphs, to save on storage requirements and processing time, only the first $\sqrt{n}$ entries are stored in Adj_i, $\forall i \in V$.

The **PERTURB** operator scans the edges as follows. Vertices are numbered 1 to n. Then starting at $i = 1$, **PERTURB** attempts to make the first legal move involving (i, j), $j = 1, 2, \ldots, \sqrt{n}$, $i \neq j$. The edges (i, j) are examined in the order in which they appear in the list Adj_i. Once a move of (i, j) has been attempted or the list Adj_i is exhausted, whichever occurs first, **PERTURB** attempts a move with $(i + 1, j)$ where $j \in Adj_{i+1}$ and $S((i + 1, j)) = 2$. Once $i = n$, **PERTURB** returns the final state reached (Figure 6.12).

The **MAKE_STATE** procedure is not required since all intermediate states are legal.

The above implementations was run on several randomly generated TSP instances and compared with results obtained with an efficient simulated annealing

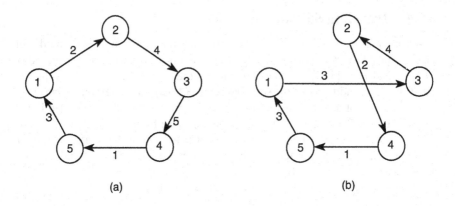

(a)   (b)

Figure 6.11: Perturbation on the TSP example given in Figure 6.3.   (a) $S^{-1}(1) = \{(1,2),(2,3),(3,4),(4,5),(5,1)\}$ and $Cost(S) = 15$. (b) $S'^{-1}(1) = \{(1,3),(3,2),(2,4),(4,5),(5,1)\}$ and $Cost(S') = 14$; $(1,3) \notin S^{-1}(1)$; $succ(1) = i_1 = 2$, $succ(3) = j_1 = 4$, and $(1,2)$ and $(3,4)$ are removed.

implementation [LD88]. On all instances StocE produced shorter tours in half the CPU time or less [Saa90].

6.5.5 StocE-Based Technology Mapping of FPGAs

Technology mapping is an important design problem of a typical CAD system of field programmable gate arrays (FPGAs) [BFRV92]. Among the widely used FPGA devices are island-based FPGAs which are devices consisting of universal programmable logic modules arranged according to a 2-D array topology (Figure 6.13).

A universal programmable module (UPM) is a logic cell that can be user-programmed to implement any Boolean function of its inputs. Typically, a K-input lookup table is used for each UPM. A K-input lookup table (K-LUT) is a universal logic block that can implement any Boolean function of its K inputs. Technology mapping for K-LUT-FPGAs consists of mapping a general combinational Boolean network into a functionally equivalent network of K-LUTs. The objective of such mapping can be a minimized number of LUTs (area minimization) [FRC90, FRV91a, FS94, Kar91, KP93, MNS+91], a minimized LUT depth (delay minimization) [CCD+92, CD94a, FRV91b], a combined area-delay minimization [CD94b], or easing routability [SKC94]. For $K \geq 5$, this problem has been shown to be NP-complete [FS94]. Figure 6.14 shows an example of a Boolean network and a possible mapping with LUTs of three inputs (3-LUTs).

FUNCTION PERTURB(S);
Begin
   For $(i = 1)$ **To** n **Do**
   Begin
      $done = FALSE; k = 1$;
      While $(k \leq \sqrt{n}$ **AND NOT**$(done)$ **Do**
      Begin
            $j = Adj_i(k); k = k + 1$;
            If $(i, j) \in S^{-1}(2)$ **Then**
                $S' =$MOVE$(S, (i, j))$;
                $Gain = Cost(S) - Cost(S')$;
                If $Gain > RANDOM(p, 0)$ **Then**
                    $S = S'$; /* accept move */
                    $done = TRUE$ /* exit the **While** loop*/
                EndIf
            EndIf
      EndWhile
   EndFor;
   Return (S) /* done with the compound move; return the new state */
End

Figure 6.12: Perturbation function for the TSP problem.

In this section, we illustrate how StocE can be used to solve the problem of technology mapping a Boolean network onto a K-LUT FPGA. This section is based on the work reported in [AM96].

Terminology and Background

A combinational logic circuit can be represented as a *directed acyclic graph* (DAG) $G(V, E)$ where each node $v \in V$ represents a Boolean function and each directed edge $(u, v) \in E$ represents a connection between the output of u and the input of v. Such a DAG representation is referred to as a *Boolean network*. A *primary input* (PI) is a node with no incoming edges, while a *primary output* (PO) is a node with no outgoing edges.

For node $v \in V$, *input(v)* is the set of nodes that supply inputs to v. In general, given a subset V_1 of V, *input*(V_1) is the set of nodes in $V - V_1$ that supply inputs to nodes in V_1. A node u is a *predecessor* of node v if there is a directed *path* from u to v in the Boolean network.

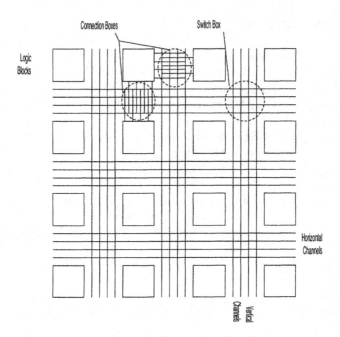

Figure 6.13: Architecture of an island-based FPGA.

Referring to Figure 6.14, nodes a to d are PIs and nodes i and j are POs. $input(j) = \{b, c, d\}$ and $input(\{g, h\}) = \{a, b, c, d, e\}$. Nodes a, b, c, d, f, g, and h are predecessor nodes of node i, while only nodes a and b are predecessors of nodes g.

Definition 16 *A K-feasible cone* at a node v, denoted by C_v, is defined as a subgraph consisting of v and a number of its predecessor nodes such that any path connecting v to any other node in C_v lies entirely in C_v, and $\mid input(C_v) \mid \leq K$ (see Figure 6.14).

Definition 17 The *depth* of a node v is defined as the maximum number of LUTs (K-feasible cones) along any path from any primary input to v. The depth of a primary input is taken as zero and the **depth** of a Boolean network is the largest node depth in the Boolean network.

For the example of Figure 6.14, $depth(g) = 1$, $depth(h) = 2$, and $depth(i) = depth(j) = 3$. The depth of the Boolean network of Figure 6.14 is equal to 3, assuming $K = 3$. Since each K-LUT is a programmable block with K inputs and one output, a K-LUT 4 can implement (or cover) any K-feasible cone in a Boolean network.

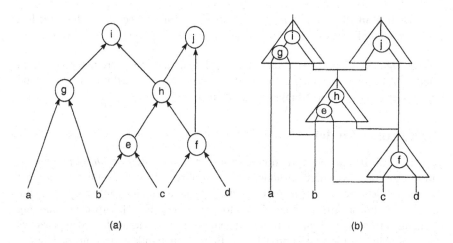

Figure 6.14: (a) A Boolean network example; (b) a covering of the Boolean network of (a) implemented with four 3-input look-up tables.

A node v with one outgoing edge is termed a *fanout-free* (FF) node. A node v with $n > 1$ outgoing edges is termed a *fanout* node. Such node can be replaced by n FF nodes without affecting the Boolean network functionality. This is accomplished by *replicating* the fanout node n times as illustrated in Figure 6.15. In Figure 6.15(a), node a with two outgoing edges ($n = 2$) can be replaced [Figure 6.15(b)] by two fanout-free nodes (a_1 and a_2) by replicating the original node functionality and connectivity twice. The replicated nodes (a_1 and a_2) are fanout-free [Figure 6.15(b)]. It should be noted that if a fanout node is replicated n times, the out-degree of its immediate predecessor nodes will increase by $n - 1$. If any of its immediate nodes is FF, it will turn into a fanout node.

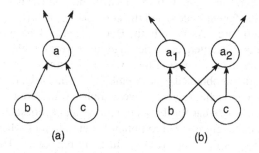

Figure 6.15: The effect of replicating a fanout node.

Definition 18 A *potential fanout node* is a fanout-free node which feeds a fanout node.

In Figure 6.15, node a is a fanout node while nodes b and c are potential fanout nodes. As shown in Figure 6.15(b), once node a is replicated into nodes a_1 and a_2, nodes b and c become fanout nodes themselves.

State Space Model

In a general Boolean network, nodes are either *fanout* nodes or *fanout-free* nodes. In the special case where all nodes of the Boolean network are fanout-free, that is, the Boolean network is actually a tree, optimal technology mapping of such a network in linear time has been shown to be possible [FS94]. However, mapping general networks is NP-hard. To map a general Boolean network, two approaches are possible. In the first approach, the Boolean network is decomposed into a forest of fanout-free trees by partitioning the network at every fanout node. In essence, breaking the Boolean network at a fanout node implies that this node is going to be the output of an LUT in the final mapping. The resulting trees are then individually mapped and the final solution is obtained by reassembling the individually mapped trees. In the second approach, the Boolean network is converted into a forest of fanout-free trees by *replicating* fanout nodes and the cones feeding them. This process is repeated until all nodes become fanout-free. In essence, a replicated node implies that the logic represented by this node will be implemented more than once in different LUTs. Again, the resulting trees are individually mapped and the final solution is obtained by reassembling the individually mapped trees. Figure 6.16 illustrates the two approaches. In this figure, the original Boolean network [Figure 6.16(a)] consists of one fanout node "a" and three cones C_1, C_2, and C_3. To map the Boolean network using the first approach, the Boolean network is partitioned by clipping the multiple fanout edges outgoing from "a" as shown by the dotted curved line in Figure 6.16(b). As a result, the Boolean network is transformed into a forest of three trees as shown by the dotted rectangles in Figure 6.16(b). To map the Boolean network using the second approach, the fanout node a and the cone that feeds it (C_1) are replicated as shown in Figure 6.16(c). As a result, the Boolean network becomes a forest of two trees as shown by the dotted rectangles in Figure 6.16(c). Following any of the above approaches results in a forest of trees where each tree is optimally mapped, and the overall solution is obtained by reassembling the individually mapped trees.

The above two approaches represent two extremes which are unlikely to yield good solutions. The search capability of an iterative algorithm such as stochastic evolution can be effectively utilized to obtain better solutions where only some fanout nodes and part of the cones feeding them are replicated. Thus, the replicated part of the Boolean network may include some, all, or none of the fanout nodes and their fanin cones. The mapping algorithm will partition the resulting

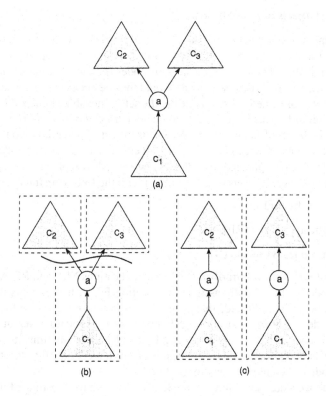

Figure 6.16: Alternatives for mapping networks with fanout nodes.

Boolean network at all nonreplicated fanout nodes. The resulting network is thus a forest of trees where each tree is mapped individually and the final solution is obtained by reassembling the mapped trees. With the proper choice of the cost function and the state model (solution space), the search capability of the iterative algorithm can be utilized to select the set of nodes in the Boolean network which should be replicated and the set of nodes which should be assigned to the outputs of LUTs in order to optimize some target criteria.

Movable Objects and Locations:

In mapping a Boolean network, the strategy adopted is to assign LUTs to some of the fanout nodes and to replicate some others. A replicated fanout node implies that its immediate fanout-free predecessor nodes (*potential fanout nodes*) would turn into fanout nodes themselves and would thus be either replicated or assigned to the outputs of some LUTs. Therefore, the set of movable element M is chosen to be the set of fanout (F) and potential fanout (PF) nodes, that is, $M = F \cup PF$, where F is the set of fanout nodes and PF is the set of potential fanout nodes.

In the final mapping, a node $m \in M$ will either be a fanout-free node, a fanout node which is not replicated, or a fanout node which is replicated. Accordingly, the set of possible locations is $L = \{1, 2, 3\}$ with the following interpretation:

1. fanout-free (FF),

2. replicated-fanout (RF), and

3. not-replicated-fanout (NRF).

Fanout nodes can arbitrarily move between locations NRF and RF. A potential fanout node (PF) is initially assigned to location FF. If, however, its immediate successor node is replicated, that is, moved from location NRF to location RF, the PF node is moved to location NRF. From there, a potential fanout node can move back and forth between locations NRF and RF. If, at any time, its immediate successor is unreplicated, that is, moved back from location RF to location NRF, the PF node is then moved back to location FF.

The above state model allows the StocE algorithm to investigate full, partial, or no replication of the nodes in cones that feed any fanout node in the network. The following example illustrates these concepts.

Example 6.5 Consider the network shown in Figure 6.17. The network has four primary inputs $PI = \{a, b, c, d\}$, two primary outputs $PO = \{i, j\}$, two fanout nodes $F = \{f, h\}$, and one potential fanout node $PF = \{e\}$. Note that the primary inputs are not classified as fanout nodes, for example, nodes b and c, or as potential fanout nodes, for example, node d.

According to our state model, the set of movable elements E is chosen to be the set of fanout and potential fanout nodes. Therefore, $E = \{e, f, h\}$.

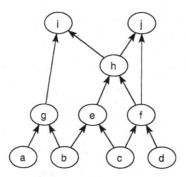

Figure 6.17: Example to illustrate the state model. PI={a,b,c,d}, PO={i,j}, F={f,h}, and PF={e}. The only fanout nodes are f and h and the only potential fanout node is e; therefore $E = \{e, f, h\}$.

Initially, f and h are in location NRF, and e is in location FF. As the algorithm proceeds in searching the solution space, those movable objects change their locations. Since f and h are fanout nodes, they can only move between locations NRF and RF. However, node e is a potential fanout node and will thus be in location FF unless h moves to location RF, in which case it will be automatically moved to location NRF from which it may move to location RF. If h moves back to location NRF, e automatically moves to location FF. Figure 6.18 shows some possible moves and valid states in the solution space and the locations of the movable objects in each case.

■

Ordering of the Movable Elements:

The **PERTURB** function of the StocE algorithm [SR91] scans the set of movable elements M according to some apriori ordering and moves every $m \in M$ to a new location $l \in L$. For this problem two orderings of movable elements are tried: (1) random ordering, where every movable element is randomly picked and perturbed. Each element is picked only once. This is a slight departure from the original StocE algorithm, where a deterministic order is followed; (2) depth first search (DFS) ordering, where nodes closer to primary outputs are perturbed first.

To illustrate, consider the previous example (see Figure 6.17). The set of movable elements E is $\{e, f, h\}$. For the random ordering, the order of objects can be any one of the possible six combinations, that is, $\{ehf, hef, hfe, feh, efh, fhe\}$. For the DFS ordering, the order of the objects can be one of two possible combinations, that is, $\{hef, hfe\}$. Both of the above orderings produced similar results [AM96].

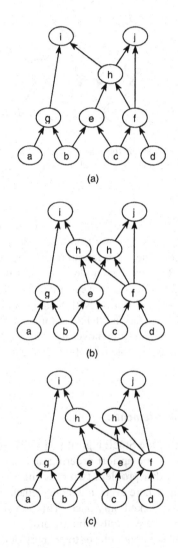

Figure 6.18: Example 6.5 continued. (a) S(e)=FF, S(f,h)=NRF. (b) S(e,f)=NRF, S(h)=RF. (c) S(f)=NRF.

ALGORITHM COST$(G(V, E), w_1, w_2)$;
    Perform a topological sort on $G(V, E)$;
    ForEach $v \in V$ **Do**
        compute d_v, z_v, and D_v;
        If $d_v > K$ **Then**
            (i) sort $ipred(v)$ in descending order of their weights,
                where **Weight(p)** = $w_1 \times z_p - w_2 \times D_p \times \frac{K}{D_v}$ $\forall p \in ipred(v)$
            (ii) keep assigning LUTs to each $p \in ipred(v)$ till $d_v \leq K$;
        EndIf
        If v is a primary output or at location NRF **Then**
            assign a LUT to v;
            set $z_v = 1$;
            update D_v;
        EndIf
    EndForEach
    Return ($\hat{w}_1 \times$ Mapping's no of LUTs + $\hat{w}_2 \times$ Mapping's Depth)
End /* of COST */;

Figure 6.19: The cost algorithm.

The Cost Function

The cost of a state is a weighted sum of the estimated area and delay of the resulting mapping. The total number of K-LUTs in the final mapping is used as an estimate of the required implementation area. Likewise, the **depth** of the final mapping is used as a measure for the resulting circuit delay.

To estimate the area and depth of a particular state, the corresponding Boolean network is mapped using a variation of the *level-map* algorithm reported in [FS94]. *Level-map* constructively maps in linear time an input Boolean network into a functionally equivalent network whose nodes represent K-LUTs. The optimization target of the mapping is controlled by two user-defined weight factors w_1 and w_2 which determine the desired relative weights assigned to area optimization and delay optimization respectively. These optimization weight factors are chosen such that $w_1 + w_2 = 1$. For example, if $w_1 = 1$ and $w_2 = 0$, the algorithm maps targeting area optimization only.

Level-map accepts a DAG representing the input Boolean network and the parameter K which is the number of inputs to a LUT. It performs a topological sort of all nodes starting from the primary inputs. Let $ipred(v)$ be the set of immediate predecessors of node v. The algorithm computes for each node v, its dependency d_v, its contribution z_v, and its depth D_v as follows (see algorithmic description given in Figure 6.19):

- Contribution z_v:
  (a) $z_v = 1$ if v is a primary input or v is assigned a LUT,
  (b) $z_v = \sum z_p \ \forall p \in ipred(v)$, otherwise.

- Dependency d_v:
  (a) $d_v = 1$ if v is a primary input,
  (b) $d_v = \sum z_p \ \forall p \in ipred(v)$, otherwise.

- Depth D_v:
  (a) $D_v = 0$ if v is a primary input,
  (b) $D_v = \max(D_p) \ \forall p \in ipred(v)$, if v is not assigned a LUT,
  (c) $D_v = \max(D_p) + 1 \ \forall p \in ipred(v)$, if v is assigned a LUT.

If the dependency d_v of any node v is found to be greater than K, its immediate predecessor nodes [$ipred(v)$] are sorted in a descending order according to the following weight function:

$$Weight(p) = w_1 \times z_p - w_2 \times D_p \times \frac{K}{D_v}$$

LUTs are assigned to the predecessor nodes of v with larger weights until $d_v \leq K$. Once a node is assigned to be the output of a LUT, its z value is set to 1, and the d and D values of its successor nodes are accordingly updated. The choice of the *weight* function is justified by the following argument. If the mapping objective is area minimization, that is, $w_1 = 1$ and $w_2 = 0$, then one should assign LUTs to nodes with larger contributions (z values) as this tends to reduce the number of LUTs. If the objective, however, is delay minimization, that is, $w_1 = 0$ and $w_2 = 1$, then one should assign LUTs to nodes with smaller depths (D values) as this tends to reduce the overall depth of the mapped network. The scale factor $\frac{K}{D_v}$ is used to limit the coefficient of w_2 to a maximum value of K which is also the maximum value of the contribution term z_p.

The cost function algorithm assigns a LUT to every primary output node and every node at location NRF. The z values of these nodes are set to 1 and their D values are updated. Upon completion, the returned cost value is a weighted sum of the number of LUTs and the depth of the resulting mapping. This value is used by the StocE algorithm to determine the cost gain of a new state. The control parameters $\hat{w}_1$ and $\hat{w}_2$ used in the weighted sum (Figure 6.19) are scaled versions of w_1 and w_2. The reason is that the number of LUTs and depth of the resulting mapping are not necessarily comparable in value. Therefore, there is a need to scale the control parameters w_1 and w_2 to reflect the target relative weights for area versus delay optimization [AM96].

Example 6.6 This example illustrates how the cost function is evaluated when the Boolean network shown in Figure 6.20(a) is mapped into a K-LUT

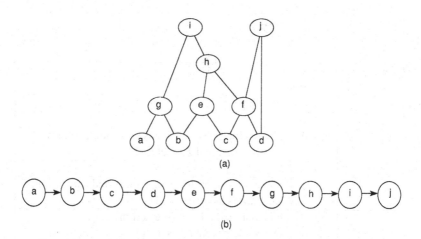

(a)

(b)

Figure 6.20: Example of a Boolean network. $K = 3$, $w_1 = 1$, $w_2 = 0$. (b) Topological order of the node of the Boolean network in (a).

network for $K = 3$. Let the mapping target area optimization only, that is, $w_1 = 1$, and $w_2 = 0$.

The network has four primary inputs, $PI = \{a, b, c, d\}$, two primary outputs, $PO = \{i, j\}$, one fanout node, $F = \{f\}$, and no potential fanout nodes. Accordingly, the set of movable objects $M = \{f\}$. Initially, f is in location NRF since it is not replicated. Level-map starts by topologically sorting the Boolean network. Figure 6.20 (b) shows a possible order. The algorithm proceeds by computing the d, z, and D values of every node in the Boolean network in the specified topological order. Table 6.1 lists the computed d, z, and D values for every node. In addition, the table shows the actions taken at some nodes. For example, node f is assigned a LUT since it is at location NRF (not-replicated fanout). Accordingly, its depth D is incremented by one and its contribution z is set to one. As another example, consider node i where the dependency d exceeds $K = 3$, and therefore, its immediate predecessors (nodes g and h) are sorted according to the *weight* function. Since node h has a higher weight, it is assigned a LUT, its D value is incremented by one, and its z value is set to one. Next, the d value of node i is updated. Finally, since node i is a primary output node, it is assigned a LUT, its D value is incremented by one, and its z value is set to one. ∎

The StocE-based technology mapper described in this section was tested on several benchmark circuits [Yan91] and compared with reported constructive technology mappers [CD94a, FRV91a, FRV91b, MNS+91, MSBSV91], as well as

Node	d	z	D	Actions
a	1	1	0	
b	1	1	0	
c	1	1	0	
d	1	1	0	
g	2	2	0	
e	2	2	0	
f	2	1	1	**f** is assigned a LUT because it is at location **NRF**. **D** is updated and **z** is set to **1**.
h	3	3	1	
i	5	1	3	Since $d_i > 3$, children of i are sorted and assigned LUTs, **h** is assigned a LUT.
h	3	1	2	**h** is assigned a LUT (see actions at **i**). **D** is updated and **z** is set to **1**.
i	3	1	3	**i** is assigned a LUT because it is a primary output.
j	3	1	3	**j** is assigned a LUT because it is a primary output.

Table 6.1: Execution of level-map on the Boolean network of Figure 6.20(a). $cost = w_1 \times No.\ of\ LUTs + w_2 \times Depth = 1 \times 4 + 0 \times 3 = 4$.

with a genetic-based mapper [KP93]. In general, it was observed that better solutions are obtained for several circuits, while for remaining circuits, solutions were of comparable quality [AM96]. The runtime of StocE mapper was found to be 25–70 times faster compared to that of the GA-based mapper [KP93]. The runtime varied between a fraction of a second (smallest test case) to less than an hour (largest test case).

6.6 Parallelization of Stochastic Evolution

Experimental results indicate that the stochastic evolution algorithm has been able to find near-optimal solutions in a relatively short time on all test problems. However, this behavior is preconditioned on the design skills and ingenuity of the designer who should cleverly decide several issues, namely, (1) a suitable state model, (2) appropriate move strategy, (3) an initial value for the parameter p and its update method, and (4) an adequate value of the stopping criterion parameter R. These issues have a large impact on both the runtime requirements and the quality of solution of the algorithm.

Because of its iterative and blind nature, stochastic evolution can require a large runtime, especially on large problems with thousands of movable elements and CPU-intensive cost functions. To speed up the execution of stochastic evolution on such problems we can resort to the acceleration techniques used with previous iterative algorithms, namely, (1) hardware acceleration, which consists of implementing time consuming parts in hardware, and (2) software acceleration, where execution of the algorithm is partitioned on several concurrently running processors.

The acceleration of the stochastic evolution algorithm did not receive any attention from the research community. This section is therefore necessarily tentative.

We believe that hardware acceleration does not offer a cost effective strategy, and therefore we rule it out. In the remainder of this section we shall concentrate on basic strategies to parallelize the stochastic evolution algorithm.

Unlike GA and SimE which are highly parallel, stochastic evolution is highly sequential. In that respect, it is similar to the SA algorithm. Recall that StocE has one main loop consisting of several steps. An iteration of StocE consists of the following tasks:

1. Perform a compound move on the current solution to create a new valid solution (call to the *PERTURB* function followed by a call to the *MAKE_STATE* function);

2. compute the difference in the cost between the new and current solution;

3. if the new solution has the same cost as the current solution then increment the parameter p; otherwise reset p to its initial value p_0;

4. if the new solution has the lowest cost among all previous solutions, then replace the current best solution with the new solution and decrement the counter ρ by R.

These tasks must be executed in sequence and repeated as long as the condition $\rho \leq R$ is satisfied. The most time consuming step is the *perturbation* step. This step is also highly sequential and consists of several tasks. In this step, the movable elements are processed one at a time in a predetermined order and each is tried in a number of candidate trial locations. After processing all elements, the routine *MAKE_STATE* is called to make sure that the new state is a valid one. This is achieved by reversing the fewest latest moves.

Because of the highly sequential nature of the StocE algorithm, the easiest parallelization approach would be to proceed as follows. Each processor is assigned a particular initial solution. Then each of the processors would be running sequential StocE starting from its assigned initial solution. This simple approach would be good if the search subspaces of the various processors do not overlap (or have minimal overlap). In this case all processors would be concurrently searching distinct parts of the solution space. However, this would require that one has enough knowledge about the search space in order to partition it among the individual processors. In some instances, this can be an unrealistic assumption, because little will be known about the search space.

For many problems, the subspace corresponding to the neighborhood of a particular solution is controlled by the algorithm designer (the state model, the parameter p, and the move operation). In many cases, it may be possible to tune the algorithm for a particular problem instance so that the state space is searched in parallel (with minimal overlap) by several processors.

Recall from Chapter 2 that SA is also highly sequential, where its parallelization is strongly related to the temperature parameter. To parallelize StocE, we can follow similar approaches to those adopted for the parallelization of simulated annealing, namely, (1) *move acceleration*, and (2) *parallel moves*. In move acceleration, a move is performed faster by distributing the various trial relocations on several processors working in parallel. The speed-up that can be achieved by *move acceleration* approach depends to a large extent on the problem instance. Recall that each simple move usually consists of several trial relocations of a particular movable element. The trial relocations can be performed in parallel without affecting the correctness of the algorithm. For problem instances where the window of trial relocations is large, sizable speed-up can be achieved. However, for problems with a state model having $|L| = 2$, such as the network bisection problem, this approach would be counterproductive.

For parallel moves, several moves are performed in parallel, where each move is executed on a single processor.[2] Figure 6.21 is a general description of a possible parallel stochastic evolution algorithm following this parallelization strategy.

In the description of Figure 6.21, it is assumed that one master processor is ordering the concurrent execution of p simple moves, where p is the number of processors. The master evaluates the outcome from all trials. In the case of no success, the master then orders the parallel evaluation of p new trials; otherwise, it selects the best new current solution among the accepted solutions, and updates the state of all processors. This process repeats until it is time to stop. At the end of the parallel execution of *PERTURB*, the master processor may be required to run the *MAKE_STATE* procedure to ensure a valid new state. The master processor is also in charge of updating the parameter p and the counter ρ.

The parallel algorithm given in Figure 6.21 is a synchronous parallelization where the processors are forced to communicate and synchronize after each trial. However, since the current solution will get updated only when a processor accepts a move and changes the state, the various processors should be allowed to proceed asynchronously with their trials until at least one of them accepts a simple move. Therefore, one can improve the parallel algorithm of Figure 6.21 by making the following change. The movable elements are distributed equally among the available processors. Each processor will be in charge of the trial relocations

---

[2]This approach assumes that the moves do not have to be performed in any specific order. This parallelization strategy will not work if the moves must be attempted in a fixed predetermined order.

Algorithm Parallel_StocE;
    /* S_0 is the initial solution */
Begin
        Initialize parameters;
        $BestS = S_0$; $CurS = S_0$; $p = p_0$;
            Repeat
                Communicate $CurS$ and a movable element m_i to each processor i;
                ParFor each processor i
                    $NewS^i = MOVE(CurS, m_i)$;
                    If Gain($CurS$, $NewS^i$) > $RANDOM(-p, 0)$
                        THEN A_i = TRUE;
                EndParFor
                If Success **Then**
                    /* Success = $(\bigvee_{i=1}^{p} A_i = True)$ */
                    Select($NewS$); /* $NewS$ is best solution among all $NewS^i$'s */
                    If Cost($NewS$) = Cost($CurS$) **Then** $p = p - 1$;
                    Else $p = p_0$;
                    EndIf
                    If Cost($NewS$) < Cost($BestS$) **Then**
                        $BestS = NewS$;
                        $\rho = \rho - R$
                        Else $\rho = \rho + 1$;
                    EndIf
                EndIf
            Until $\rho > R$;
            Return ($BestS$)
End. /*Parallel_StocE*/

Figure 6.21: General parallel stochastic evolution algorithm where synchronization is forced after each trial.

of its associated movable elements. Synchronization is forced only when one of the processors performs a successful trial. In this new variation communication will be less. Furthermore, it is a more efficient parallelization since no processor is forced to remain idle waiting for other processors with more elaborate trials to finish.

Both variations of this parallel algorithm can be implemented to run on a multicomputer or a multiprocessor machine. The parallel machine model assumed is an MISD or an MIMD machine. For both algorithms, it is assumed that each processor must be able to set a common variable to *True* whenever it accepts a simple move; then the solution accepted by the processor is communicated to a master processor which will force all other processors to halt and to properly update the current solution. The current solution together with the remaining unprocessed elements are again distributed among the available processors. Unfinished moves, that is, moves that were in progress when their processors were forced to halt, will be tried again in the next iteration. Another possibility is to allow the processors to complete the trials that are in progress when the request to stop was received. Then more than one solution could be accepted, and therefore the master processor has to arbitrate between them, select the best, and pass a copy to each processor. All moves tried during this iteration, whether accepted or rejected, are considered complete. During the following iteration only the remaining unprocessed movable elements will be tried.

Another possible approach would be to allow the processors to proceed concurrently with their search and to concurrently accept moves, with no interaction whatsoever. Algorithms following this strategy are known as *error algorithms*. The word error is used to highlight the fact that the processors have incorrect knowledge about the state of the parallel search. Few studies on such parallelization approach for the case of SA have indicated, that by limiting the number of concurrent moves or by ensuring that the moves are always *noninteracting*, error is minimized and convergence is maintained [IKB83, KR87, UKH83]. However, it is not always clear how one can go about restricting the moves to be of a particular type.

Another approach would be to use the notion of *serializable move set* introduced by Kravitz and Rutenbar [KR87] for the case of SA. The idea consists of restricting the set of concurrent moves to be *serializable*. Recall that a *serializable move set* is a set of moves that would produce the same reject/accept decisions whether executed in parallel or in some serial order. For example, any set of rejected moves is a serializable set. Also, moves that are completely noninteracting are also serializable. However, in general, the identification of the largest possible serializable subset of moves (to maximize speed-up) is a difficult problem. Kravitz and Rutenbar suggested instead a subclass of serializable move-sets that are easy to identify. They refer to this move-set as the *simplest serializable set*. A simplest serializable set is formed by taking a number of rejected moves and appending to them an accepted move. Such a move-set is always serializable. The expected size of the serializable move-set is a good estimation of the speed-up, since it is a measure of the average number of trials that are evaluated concurrently. The problem with this approach is that the size of the *simplest serializable* set is controlled by the parameter p, which is getting updated in an unpredictable way. This is unlike the case of SA where the size of this set is controlled by the value of the temperature which is steadily decreased in a predictable manner. For large p, the size of this set is extremely small (always close to 1) leading to unacceptably low speed-up (near 1). The reason is that a large p is equivalent to a hot regime in simulated annealing, where almost all moves are accepted, forcing the processors to communicate almost after each move. For small p, most simple moves are rejected, thus allowing the various processors to run in parallel most of the time. Because of the way the parameter p is updated, it is difficult to predict the speed-up that may result with such a parallelization strategy.

The above two strategies can also be carried at the level of a compound move (a call to the function *PERTURB*). Similarly, we will have two strategies: (1) *perturbation acceleration*, and (2) *parallel perturbations*. In perturbation acceleration, a compound move is performed faster by distributing the various simple moves on several processors working in parallel. This is actually the *parallel moves* approach discussed above.

For the *parallel perturbations* approach, several perturbations are conducted in parallel. To ensure that the various processors do not search the same subspaces, one can proceed as follows. Each processor runs sequential StocE with a different initial solution. Once all the processors have converged, the best solution among all processors is selected. Then each processor reruns sequential StocE on a mutated version of the current best solution. Obviously, each processor must be assigned a different mutated solution. These steps are repeated until no significant improvement is obtained in k (for example, $k = 2$) consecutive iterations.

The aforementioned strategies by no means exhaust all possible approaches to parallelizing stochastic evolution; they mainly illustrate how one might go about parallelizing a highly sequential algorithm such as StocE. Furthermore, the parallelization of a general algorithm such as StocE is usually highly influenced by the problem instance itself.

6.7 Conclusions and Recent Work

In this chapter we have described the StocE algorithm, a general randomized iterative heuristic for solving combinatorial optimization problems. Like all other iterative heuristics described in earlier chapters, StocE requires that it be adapted to the particular problem. There are four main issues a designer has to consider:

1. A suitable state model for the problem

2. Choice of an appropriate move operation to relocate movable elements

3. An initial value of the control parameter p and its update strategy

4. A value for the stopping criterion R

As we have discussed in Section 6.4, the above four issues are not independent. The move operation depends on the state model. Also, the initial value of the parameter p and the strategy of its update depend on the state model and the move set. Furthermore, the parameter R depends on the choice of the state model, the move operation, and the parameter p. Experimental studies have suggested that these parameters are not hard to design and tune to the particular problem in question.

Extensive experimental studies produced performance results better than the SA algorithm with respect to runtime and quality of solution [Saa90].

The main concern with the StocE algorithm is that its behavior corresponds to a nonhomogeneous Markov chain that may not have a stationary distribution, that is, the algorithm may miss hitting a global optimum even if given unlimited time. The reason for this behavior is that, unlike SA where an uphill move always has a nonzero probability of being accepted, for StocE a subset of the uphill moves are always discarded because of a parameter p that is updated during the course of the search. This issue is mainly of theoretical concern. On all practical test cases, StocE has been shown to produce better solutions than SA as well as GAs, and in much less time.

References

[AM96]   A. S. Al-Mulhem. SELF-MAP: Stochastic evolution LUT-FPGA technology mapper. M.S. thesis, Computer Engineering Department, King Fahd University of Petroleum and Minerals, Dhahran, Saudi Arabia, July 1996.

[BFRV92]   S. D. Brown, R. J. Francis, J. Rose, and Z. G. Vranesic. *Field-Programmable Gate Arrays*. Kluwer, 1992.

[CCD+92]   K. Chen, J. Cong, Y. Ding, A. B. Kahng, and P. Trajmar. Dag-Map: Graph-based FPGA technology mapping for delay optimization. *IEEE Design & Test of Computers*, pages 7–20, Sep. 1992.

[CD94a]   J. Cong and Y. Ding. FlowMap: An optimal technology mapping algorithm for delay optimization in lookup-table based FPGA designs. *IEEE Transactions on Computer-Aided Design of Integrated Circuits and Systems*, 13(1):1–12, Jan. 1994.

[CD94b]   J. Cong and Y. Ding. On area/depth trade-off in LUT-based FPGA technology mapping. *IEEE Transactions on VLSI Systems*, 2(2):137–148, June 1994.

[FRC90]   R. Francis, J. Rose, and K. Chung. Chortle: A technology mapping for lookup table-based FPGAs. *Proceedings of 27th Design Automation Conference*, pages 613–619, 1990.

[FRV91a]   R. Francis, J. Rose, and Z. Vranesic. Chortle-crf: Fast technology mapping for lookup table-based FPGAs. *Proceedings of 28th Design Automation Conference*, pages 227–233, 1991.

[FRV91b]   R. Francis, J. Rose, and Z. Vranesic. Technology mapping of lookup table-based FPGAs for performance. *International Conference on Computer-Aided Design (ICCAD)*, pages 568–571, Nov. 1991.

[FS94]   A. H. Farrahi and M. Sarrafzadeh. Complexity of the lookup-table minimization problem for FPGA technology mapping. *IEEE Transaction of Computer-Aided Design of Integrated Circuits and Systems*, 13(11):1319–1332, Nov. 1994.

[GJ79]   M. R. Garey and D. S. Johnson. *Computers and Intractability: A Guide to the Theory of NP-Completeness*. W. H. Freeman and Company, New York, 1979.

[Gol89]   D. E. Goldberg. *Genetic Algorithms in Search, Optimization and Machine Learning*. Addison-Wesley, 1989.

[IKB83]   A. Iosupovici, C. King, and M. Breuer. A module interchange placement machine. *Proceedings of 20th Design Automation Conference*, pages 171–174, 1983.

[Kar91]   K. Karplus. Xmap: A technology mapper for table-lookup field programmable gate arrays. *Proceedings of 28th Design Automation Conference*, pages 240–243, 1991.

[KJV83]   S. Kirkpatrick, C. Gelatt, Jr., and M. Vecchi. Optimization by simulated annealing. *Science*, 220(4598):498–516, May 1983.

[Kle75]   L. Kleinrock. *Queueing Systems, Volume I: Theory*. John Wiley & Sons, 1975.

[KB87]   R. M. Kling and P. Banerjee. ESP: A new standard cell placement package using simulated evolution . *Proceedings of 24th Design Automation Conference*, pages 60–66, 1987.

[KB89]   R. M. Kling and P. Banerjee. ESP: Placement by simulated evolution. *IEEE Transactions on Computer-Aided Design*, 8(3):245–255, Mar. 1989.

[KB91]   R. M. Kling and P. Banerjee. Empirical and theoretical studies of the simulated evolution method applied to standard cell placement. *IEEE Transactions on Computer-Aided Design*, 10(10):1303–1315, Oct. 1991.

[Kli90]   R. M. Kling. Optimization by simulated evolution and its application to cell placement. Doctoral dissertation, University of Illinois, Urbana, 1990.

[KP93]   V. Kommu and I. Pomeranz. GAFPGA: Genetic Algorithm for FPGA Technology Mapping. *Proceedings of IEEE EURO Design Automation Conference*, pages 300–305, 1993.

[KR87]   S. A. Kravitz and R. A. Rutenbar. Placement by simulated annealing on a multiprocessor. *IEEE Transactions on Computer-Aided Design of Circuits and Systems*, 6(4):534–549, July 1987.

[LD88]   J. Lam and J. Delosme. Simulated annealing: A fast heuristic for some generic layout problems. *Proceedings of the International Conference on Computer-Aided Design (ICCAD)*, pages 510–513, Nov. 1988.

[MH96]   C. Y. Mao and Y. H. Hu. Analysis of convergence properties of stochastic evolution algorithm. *IEEE Transactions on Computer-Aided Design*, 15(7):826–831, July 1996.

[MNS+91]   R. Murgai, Y. Nishizaki, N. Shenoy, R. K. Brayton, and A. Sangiovanni-Vincentelli. Logic synthesis for programmable gate arrays. *Proceedings of 28th Design Automation Conference*, pages 620–625, 1991.

[MSBSV91] R. Murgai, N. Shenoy, R. K. Brayton, and A. Sangiovanni-Vincentelli. Performance directed synthesis for look up programmable gate arrays. *Proceedings of the International Conference on Computer-Adided Design*, pages 572–575, 1991.

[NSS85]   S. Nahar, S. Sahni, and E. Shragowitz. Experiments with Simulated Annealing. *Proceedings of 22nd Design Automation Conference*, pages 748–752, 1985.

[Saa90]   Y. G. Saab. Combinatorial optimization by stochastic evolution with applications to the physical design of VLSI circuits. Doctoral dissertation, University of Illinois, Urbana, 1990.

[SKC94]   M. Schlag, J. Kong, and P. Chan. Routability-driven technology mapping for lookup table-based FPGA's. *IEEE Transactions on Computer-Aided Design of Circuits and Systems*, 13(1):13–26, Jan. 1994.

[SR89]   Y. Saab and V. Rao. An evolution-based approach to partitioning ASIC systems. *26th ACM/IEEE Design Automation Conference*, pages 767–770, 1989.

[SR90]   Y. Saab and V. Rao. Stochastic evolution: A fast effective heuristic for some generic layout problems. *27th ACM/IEEE Design Automation Conference*, pages 26–31, 1990.

[SR91]   Y. G. Saab and V. B. Rao. Combinatorial optimization by stochastic evolution. *IEEE Transactions on Computer-Aided Design*, 10(4):525–535, Apr. 1991.

[UKH83]   K. Ueda, T. Komatsubara, and T. Hosaka.   A parallel process-
            ing approach for logic module placement.   *IEEE Transactions
            on Computer-Aided Design of Circuits and Systems*, 2(1):39–47,
            Jan. 1983.

[Yan91]   S. Yang. *Logic Synthesis and Optimization Benchmarks User Guide
            Version 3.0*. Microelectronics Center of North Carolina, Research
            Triangle Park, NC, Jan. 1991.

Exercises

Exercise 6.1
Discuss similarities and differences between SA, SimE, and StocE.

Exercise 6.2
Stochastic evolution can be seen as a generalization of SA. Which aspects of
the StocE algorithm if modified would make it behave like the SA algorithm?

Exercise 6.3
1. What type of search would be performed by StocE if the parameter p is
   fixed to zero?

2. Repeat the previous question if p is fixed to a negative number of an
   extremely large magnitude?

3. Provide guidelines one should observe in deciding the initial value as
   well as the update strategy of the parameter p. Illustrate your suggestions using the *network bisection* instance given in Figure 6.1 and the
   traveling salesman problem instance given in Figure 6.3.

Exercise 6.4
For the simulated evolution algorithm, the function that has most effect on
the convergence of the algorithm is the *allocation* function. For the StocE
algorithm, which function do you think has the most effect on the convergence
of the algorithm to superior-quality solutions?

Exercise 6.5
According to your understanding of the StocE algorithm, rank, with justification, the following according to their impact on the algorithm performance:

1. Computation of the *Gain* of each move.

2. Quality of initial solution.

3. Initial value of the parameter p and the *UPDATE* function.

4. The *PERTURB* function.

5. The value of the reward parameter R.

Exercise 6.6
One of the important parameters of the StocE algorithm is the *reward* criteria R, which impacts both, the runtime requirement as well as the quality of the reported solution.

1. What effect would a low value of R have on the runtime and solution quality of the algorithm?

2. What effect would a large value of R have on the runtime and solution quality of the algorithm?

3. Which choice do you think will be more harmful, a low or a large R? Justify your answer.

4. What aspect(s) of the problem instance should dictate the choice of the adequate value of R? Illustrate your answers with some of the examples presented in the text, such as the *traveling salesman* and the *network bisection* problems.

Exercise 6.7
Several authors think that SimE and StocE are similar algorithms. Identify those distinctive features that are against such view. Are there any aspects of the algorithms that support such view?

Exercise 6.8
Suggest a heuristic approach that will select appropriate values for the parameters of the StocE algorithm, namely, R, and p.

Exercise 6.9
The behavior of the StocE algorithm is a nonhomogeneous Markov chain. Suggest the necessary changes to the algorithm that will turn its behavior into a homogeneous ergodic Markov chain.

Exercise 6.10
Show the result of Equation 6.2.

Exercise 6.11
Stochastic evolution uses the notion of *reward*, which consists of increasing the number of remaining iterations by R whenever the algorithm improves upon the current best solution, regardless of the magnitude of the improvement, or for how long the algorithm has been running. Suggest and experiment with alternative approaches to updating the algorithm parameters (p and ρ).

Exercise 6.12

In most experiments reported in the literature, StocE produced similar or better results than SA, and in a fraction of the time taken by SA. Identify those features of the StocE algorithm which in your opinion are the principal cause of this desirable behavior.

Exercise 6.13

Refer to the Hamiltonian circuit problem described in Section 6.5.3, page 315.

1. For the graph of Figure 6.10(b), which edges are movable elements?

2. Assume that edge $(1, 6)$ has been selected for movement from $S(2)$ to $S(1)$. Explain how will this be accomplished.

3. If instead edge $(4, 6)$ has been selected for movement, show the effect of this move on the chain-set.

Exercise 6.14

1. In Section 6.5.4 (page 319), a *partitioning* state model was adopted for the traveling salesman problem (TSP). Design a StocE algorithm for the TSP problem while adopting a *permutation* as a state model. That is, the set of movable elements as well as the set of locations are identified with the cities ($M = L = V$). Illustrate all your design decisions on the TSP instance given in Figure 6.3.

2. Which state model do you think is a more powerful model? Justify your answer.

Exercise 6.15

In the StocE-based implementation of technology mapping described in the text, the decision as to which fan-out node to replicate is random. There are more reasonable strategies which will take into consideration the depth of the node or the size of the cone rooted at that node.

1. Work out few examples by hand to argue in favor or against the usefulness of such strategies.

2. Design and implement a StocE-based technology mapper and compare strategies as the ones suggested above.

Exercise 6.16

Consider the *vehicle routing problem* described in Chapter 1, Page 7.

1. Devise a state model for this problem, that is, identify the set of movable elements M and the set of locations L.

2. Design suitable *Cost* and *PERTURB* functions for this problem.

3. Suggest suitable values for the parameters p_0 and R.

Exercise 6.17
Repeat the previous exercise (Exercise 6.16) considering the *flowshop scheduling problem* described in Chapter 2 (Exercise 2.16).

Exercise 6.18
Repeat Exercise 6.16 considering the *terminal assignment problem* described in Chapter 2 (Exercise 2.17).

Exercise 6.19
Repeat Exercise 6.16 considering the *concentrator location problem* described in Chapter 2 (Exercise 2.18).

Exercise 6.20
Repeat Exercise 6.16 considering the *constrained minimum spanning tree problem* described in Chapter 2 (Exercise 2.19).

Exercise 6.21
Repeat Exercise 6.16 considering the *mesh topology design problem* described in Chapter 2 (Exercise 2.20).

Exercise 6.22
Repeat Exercise 6.16 considering the *weighted matching problem* described in Chapter 2 (Exercise 2.21).

Exercise 6.23
Repeat Exercise 6.16 considering the *plant location problem* described in Chapter 2 (Exercise 2.22).

CHAPTER 7

Hybrids and Other Issues

7.1 Introduction

This book has introduced the reader to five effective heuristics that belong to the class of *general iterative algorithms*, namely, simulated annealing (SA), genetic algorithm (GA), tabu search (TS), simulated evolution (SimE), and stochastic evolution (StocE). From the immense literature that is available it is evident that for a large variety of applications, in certain settings, these heuristics produce excellent results. All these algorithms have several important properties in common, which are listed below:

1. They are blind, that is, they do not know when they reached an optimal solution. Therefore they must be told when to stop.

2. They have "hill climbing" property, that is, they occasionally accept uphill (bad) moves.

3. They are relatively easy to implement. All that is required is to have a suitable solution representation, a cost function, and a mechanism to traverse the search space.

4. They are all *"general,"* that is, practically they can be applied to solve any combinatorial optimization problem.

5. Under certain conditions, they asymptotically converge to an optimal solution. The rate of convergence is dependent on the choice of several parameters.

In each of the previous five chapters we illustrated how these techniques can be *individually* applied to solve several of the known NP-hard combinatorial optimization problems. Case studies and real problems in engineering were used as examples to explain the heuristics and clarify concepts. Effectiveness of each of these heuristics can be enhanced by *hybridization* where features of one heuristic are incorporated into another to search for optimal solutions. In this chapter (Section 7.3) we touch upon some work that has been reported in the area of hybridization.

All algorithms discussed in this book are iterative in nature, and operate on design solutions generated at each iteration. A value of the objective function is used to compare results of consecutive iterations and a solution is selected based on its value. If the problem being solved consists of multiple objectives to be optimized, then balancing different objectives by a weighted cost functions may not be sufficient to reach the desired solution. One convenient vehicle available for representing multiobjective cost functions is fuzzy logic. Fuzzy logic provides a required formal algebra to express and combine trade-off objective criteria. Functions for each objective are used (called membership functions) which map the numerical value of objectives to the interval [0,1]. Optimization of multiobjective functions is discussed in Section 7.4. Basics of fuzzy logic and its application in solving multiobjective optimization problems is presented in Section 7.5. In Section 7.6 we briefly discuss optimization using neural networks. Some points on how the quality of solution is gauged are also discussed in this chapter.

We begin with a brief overview of the heuristics discussed in this book, and highlight their strengths and weaknesses.

7.2   Overview of Algorithms

Before we go into discussion on some recently proposed hybrid techniques (hybrids), let us briefly recall the key characteristics of the various algorithms discussed in this book.

Simulated annealing (SA): This stochastic search procedure is based on the analogy of cooling of metals. The search proceeds step by step, choosing a *random* neighboring solution, always accepting good ones, and accepting bad ones with a nonzero probability. Initially the probability of accepting bad moves is high, and toward the end, when temperature tends to zero, it becomes less and less unlikely to accept bad moves. The acceptance of early bad moves is usually not profitable. Clearly, SA is a randomized nonaggressive search technique. Cycling in solution space is avoided due to randomness in neighborhood search. *One problem with simulated annealing is its slow convergence to optimal or near-optimal solution.*

Genetic algorithms (GAs): These algorithms emulate the natural process of evolution. Unlike other heuristics, search is conducted by operating on a population of solutions, where a solution is represented in the form of an encoded string. The basic idea is to obtain new solutions from the combinations of existing ones. For this, a crossover operator is used, which ensures that new solutions called offsprings inherit the characteristics of parents. Mutation is used to inject new characteristics in the individuals. Survival of solutions among parents and offsprings is based on their fitness. *The problem with genetic algorithms is that they may suffer from premature convergence to a suboptimal solution.*

Tabu search (TS): This is a more aggressive search technique based on the systematic exploration of memory functions. In this technique, for a given solution, a large number of neighbors are generated, from which the best is chosen. To determine which of the generated solutions is the best, an *evaluator* that is based on the objectives being optimized and the historical information that has been accumulated, is used. The trace of the current solution is controlled by the recent move history to avoid cycling in the solution space. Use of intensification and diversification in tabu search considerably helps in obtaining superior-quality solutions. This is accomplished with the help of additional memory structures that keep record of information such as frequencies of moves, elite solutions, and so forth.

Simulated evolution (SimE): Unlike in genetic algorithms, in SimE, a single solution is referred to as a population, and its elements as individuals. The procedure is best understood by comparing it with SA. In SA, a perturbation of the current state is a single move, while in SimE it is a compound move. Further, in SA, the elements involved in a move are selected randomly, whereas in SimE the elements selected are based on their *fitness*. A goodness function is required to determine the fitness of elements in the current solution. Highly fit elements have a high probability of remaining as they are. The individual fitnesses of the solution components guide the search, and there is no parameter such as temperature.

Stochastic evolution (StocE): This is another stochastic algorithm which, similar to SimE, operates by making compound moves. In addition to this, in this algorithm, the probability of acceptance of bad moves gets increased whenever the search is suspected to have reached a local optimum, and reset to its initial value otherwise. A parameter p is used which controls how steep a hill the algorithm can climb. The algorithm also cleverly rewards itself whenever it makes a good move. There are no hot/cold regimes as in SA.

7.3 Hybridization

Work on combining ideas from one heuristic into another has been around for
some time. In the previous section we briefly reviewed the key characteristics
of heuristics discussed in this book and highlighted some of their strengths and
weaknesses. The basic idea of hybridization is to enhance the strengths and compensate for the weaknesses of two or more complementary approaches [GKL95].
In the following paragraphs we describe several of the hybridization approached
attempts reported in the literature.

7.3.1 SA / TS Hybrid

We begin with a hybrid algorithm that combines ideas of SA and TS [Osm93].
The basic technique works as follows.

The general structure of this SA/TS hybrid is that of SA, with the following
major differences. First, the initial solution is not a random solution, but is generated heuristically. A cooling schedule is then determined by running the algorithm
(but without performing exchanges, as discussed in Section 2.4) and the parameters of the algorithm are determined. Parameters in this hybrid include the starting
temperature T_s, the final temperature T_f, and an additional parameter called *temperature reset variable* denoted by T_r. Initial value of T_r is set to T_s. Then, unlike
in SA where a single neighbor is generated randomly, in this hybrid, as in the case
of TS, the neighborhood is searched using a deterministic procedure and the best
amongst these is taken for consideration. The cost of this solution is determined,
and the new solution is accepted based on the Metropolis criterion. Every time a
solution better than the *best* seen so far is reached, the value of the temperature in
that iteration (say T_k, where k is the iteration number) is recorded as T_b.

The next major difference is the nonmonotonic cooling schedule used to update the value of temperature. Generally the normal decrement rule is applied and
the values of T and β are updated in each iteration. However, if a cycle of search
is completed without accepting any move, which may be due to freezing, or local
optima reached, then the value of T_r, the *temperature reset variable*, is updated as
shown below and the temperature at that iteration (T_k) is reset to the value of T_r.
The update rule used is:

$$T_r = \max\left\{\frac{T_r}{2}, T_b\right\} \text{ and set } T_k = T_r$$

The above heuristic was applied to the vehicle routing problem. Experimental
runs indicated that using the nonmonotonic cooling schedule to strategically manipulate the temperature, coupled with ordered search, gave superior performance
as compared to standard SA [Osm93].

7.3.2 GA / SA Hybrid

Recall that the performance of SA is often hindered by its slow convergence to optimal or near-optimal solution, while GAs may suffer from premature convergence [KHN95]. SA can be combined with GAs to: (1) introduce more diversity into the population, thereby preventing premature convergence, and (2) avoid the long computation time required by SA.

In some recent hybrids proposed, the convergence of genetic algorithms is improved by introducing the acceptance probability of SA as the criterion for accepting new trial solutions [KHN95, TWF95]. Tsoi et al. proposed two hybrid algorithms which they referred to as GAA and GAA2. These algorithms combine incremental GA (IGA) and SA. IGA is a variant of GA with the difference in processing newly generated chromosomes. Every new chromosome generated in IGA is evaluated immediately and replaces a selected chromosome in the existing population.

GAA and GAA2

In GAA, during each iteration of IGA, a newly generated chromosome will replace a selected chromosome from the existing population only when one of the following criteria is met:

1. if the offspring generated is the fittest among all those generated thus far, or

2. if the offspring is fitter than the selected chromosome, or

3. if the probability of replacement is greater than a number randomly generated between 0 and 1.

The probability of replacement for criterion (3) is equivalent to the acceptance probability used in fast SA [SH87], and is given by

$$\text{Prob}(\Delta) = \frac{1}{1 + e^{(\frac{\Delta}{T})}} \tag{7.1}$$

where Δ is the amount of decrease in the fitness value of the new individual and the individual selected for replacement. T is the temperature level of the current iteration, and is reduced in every iteration according to the rule $T_k = r^{k-1} \times T_0$, where T_0 is the initial temperature, T_k the temperature at the kth iteration, and r the temperature reduction factor ($r < 1$). Initially, some chromosomes in the population will be replaced by those with lower fitness values. However, as the temperature decreases, the probability of replacement is gradually decreased. Using this technique, sufficient diversity in the population is maintained and premature convergence avoided.

The second algorithm (GAA2) proposed in [TWF95] restricts the population size to two individuals, therefore no selection of parents is required. Time and memory requirements are reduced. Diversity is maintained by applying the replacement criterion of GAA. Criterion (1) is not required due to small population size. Elitist GA strategy is adopted where the fittest or the best individual is guaranteed to survive. The temperature level in each iteration is reduced when a predefined *pseudo population size* is reached.

GA / SA / TS Hybrid

This hybrid, proposed by Kim et al. [KHN95] is similar to the GAA hybrid discussed above [TWF95] with the difference that TS is also incorporated to escape from local optima. *The method is a reasonable combination of local search and global search.* The basic steps are as follows: (1) the solution region is globally searched using the GA; (2) the survival of newly produced offsprings and their acceptance in the population is decided by the acceptance probability of SA; and (3) the neighborhood of the accepted solution is searched by TS. Kim et al. applied this hybrid to solve the multiyear thermal unit maintenance scheduling problem. The quality of results obtained by the proposed hybrid was found to be better than GA or GA+SA [KHN95].

Glover explained the nature of connections between TS and GAs and showed that a variety of opportunities exist for creating hybrid approaches to take advantage of their complementary features. Glover also discussed another approach known as *scatter search* [Glo77] whose origins overlap with those of tabu search and roughly coincide with the emergence of GAs [GKL95, Glo94].

Hybrid SGA

Other techniques that combine local search with GAs have also been reported. One such work reports a hybrid elitist simple genetic algorithm (SGA) where steepest ascent technique (in case of the maximization problem) is repeatedly applied to every member of the population at each generation. A modification of this work is the *staged hybrid SGA*. In this algorithm, after the initial population has been improved by local search, a GA is allowed to continue uninterrupted for 10 generations. At the end of this genetic search stage, a single iteration of steepest ascent is applied to each individual in the population [MWSK94]. These proposed techniques were applied on seismic data interpretation problems and produced higher-quality solutions while using significantly less computational time.

TS / SimE Hybrid

Tabu search is a metaheuristic that can be used over other heuristics to control the search. As mentioned above, in case of TS, it is not possible to search the entire neighborhood, and only a subset of neighborhood is searched. This subset generally consists of some random solutions in the neighborhood. Candidate list strategies are also used (Section 4.9.3). Another possibility that will make the search more aggressive, and still work with a subset of neighbors, is to select the neighboring states as is done in the case of the simulated evolution (SimE) heuristic (Chapter 5). In order to implement this hybrid, a goodness function is required. Then, at the start of every iteration, from a given current solution, neighborhood states are generated by perturbing the individual elements of the solution, where the probability of perturbation is a function of the goodness of that element. Lower goodness maps to higher probability of the element leaving its current position.

A similar strategy can be followed to construct a SA/SimE hybrid. Here, unlike the original SA where the elements involved in the perturbation are selected at random, in the SA/SimE hybrid the elements will be selected on the basis of their fitnesses. Acceptance of particular perturbation would remain according to the Metropolis criterion.

7.3.3   Other Hybrids

Several other genetic algorithm hybrids that work on lines similar to the above have been summarized by Merkle and Gates [M+96]. Some of these include local search and others include SA. In one of the algorithms mentioned, (due to Judson et al.) individuals are always replaced by their locally optimized solutions [J+92]. Another similar hybrid (proposed by Unger and Moult) uses simulated annealing [UM93]. In this hybrid, each individual undergoes 20 steps of SA before selection is performed. Merkle et al. proposed a hybrid GA which incorporates efficient gradient based minimization in the fitness calculation. The algorithm also includes a *replacement frequency* parameter p_r which specifies the probability with which an individual is replaced by its minimized counterpart. The algorithm can implement Baldwinian ($p_r = 0$) or Lamarckian ($p_r = 1$) evolution, or more generally probabilistic Lamarckian ($0 \leq p_r \leq 1$) evolution [MM92, M+96]. The change in cost due to a move in SA is generally the objective function value, while in TS other factors of influence are taken into account such as the frequency of a move. Work on modifying SA to accept solutions based on *evaluators* instead of on objective function values has been found to yield better results [Kas92, Ree95]. For more on hybridization, and hybridizing the hybrids, and so forth, also see [Dav91, RB94, Ree95].

There are several other ways to hybridize heuristics, and as seen from above, it is easy to think of new combinations and experiment with them. Ideas of other heuristics can be incorporated not only at functional or higher levels but also at the operator level. As an example, ideas from SA have been incorporated in the design of new crossover operators [Ree95, SW87]. Below we describe a GA crossover whose characteristics and behavior change with the value of the SA temperature parameter T.

Example 7.1 In Chapter 3 we discussed the uniform crossover operator (Section 3.5.1). This crossover uses a binary string template. Then, for each bit position on the two selected parents, the value of the bit in the template will indicate which of the two parents will contribute its value in that position to the offspring. The template for the *simple crossover* can be represented as a binary string 1 1 1 1 0 0. According to this template, as in the case of the simple single point crossover, the first four elements are taken from one parent and the last two from the second. The binary elements in this string can also be generated stochastically, then, the string 1 0 1 0 1 1 will mean that the first, third, fifth, and sixth elements are taken from one parent and the remaining from the other. This latter method is also referred to as generalized uniform crossover.

Ideas from simulated annealing were used to modify the above basic operator [Ree95, SW87]. A threshold energy, referred to as θ_c, is used to influence the way in which the individual bits are chosen. The procedure can be briefly described as follows: As the offspring chromosome is being generated, bit $i + 1$ is favored for selection from the same parent as bit i, and bit $i + 1$ is taken from the other parent with a probability $e^{(-\theta_c/T)}$, where T is the temperature parameter of SA, which is slowly decreased according to a predefined cooling schedule. The effect of this is that at high temperature, since the number of switches is high, this operator behaves like the generalized uniform crossover operator. At medium temperature, the number of switches between parents decreases and it becomes like a simple crossover. And at extremely low values of T, the offspring actually is one of the parents. ∎

7.4   GA and Multiobjective Optimization

As discussed in Chapter 3, genetic algorithms (GAs) have been found to be effective in solving numerous optimization problems, especially those with many (possibly) conflicting and noisy objectives. However, there seems to be no consensus as to what fitness measure to use in such situations, and how to rank individuals in a population on the basis of several conflicting objectives [EK97]. In this section we present some recent work that uses GAs to solve multiobjective problems. Ideas discussed here can also be used with other heuristics explained in this book. In the following section we will discuss how fuzzy logic has been incorporated to address this issue.

In order to use GAs to solve multiobjective problems, the fitness function should be combined so as to reflect all objectives. Historically, multiple objectives have been combined into a scalar objective function, usually through a linear combination (weighted sum) of the multiple attributes, or by turning objectives into constraints. One way is to assign a constant weight to each of the multiple objective functions whose value will depend on the importance of that objective. For example, assuming that all objectives are to be maximized, the fitness of an individual 'x' (solution) in genetic algorithm can be expressed as

$$f(x) = w_1 \cdot f_1(x) + w_2 \cdot f_2(x) + \cdots + w_n \cdot f_n(x) \qquad (7.2)$$

where x is a string, n is the number of objective functions, $f(x)$ is a combined fitness function, $f_i(x)$ is the ith objective, and w_i is the weight of the ith objective. The problem with this weighted sum approach is the difficulty in determining suitable weights. Ad hoc methods are usually employed. For example, for the very-large-scale integration (VLSI) floorplan design problem [S+95, SY95], the cost function used consists of three terms, (1) the *area* or the size of the floorplan, (2) the overall interconnection *wire-length* and (3) *timing* performance or delay. Since the three terms are incompatible, they are normalized to fall in the same range. Then, weights depending on the designers preferences, are assigned to each term. Elitist preserve strategy is employed where the population of next generation, in addition to having the best overall fit solution, also contains the best solution with respect to each objective. That is, the solution with best *area*, with best *wire-length*, and a third solution that is best with respect to *timing*.

7.4.1 Pareto Optimality

A notion of optimality that respects the integrity of each of the separate criteria is the concept of Pareto optimality. Here, suppose we wish to *minimize* two objectives, expressed as f_1 and f_2. Let A, B, C, D, E, and F, be six possible solutions to a given optimization problem, with the following fitnesses [HNG94]:

A: (10, 90)   B: (20, 70)   C: (08, 75)
D: (15, 60)   E: (09, 65)   F: (14, 63)

That is, solution A has a value of $f_1=10$ and $f_2=90$. If we plot the six points f_1 versus f_2, obviously those that are lower and on the left are regarded as the best. Points C and D are good choices since there are no points better than these in both the criteria. C is best with respect to f_1, and D with respect to f_2. On the other hand, A and B are poor choices. Solution A(10,90) is dominated by solution C(08,75), since $10 > 8$ and $90 > 75$. (If any solution p is to the right and top of another solution q, then we say p is dominated by q.) A is also dominated by E. Similarly, B(20,70) is dominated by D(15,60), E(09,65) and F(15,60). The set of solutions that are not dominated by any other solution is {C, D, E, F}. In this problem, as in any other multiobjective optimization problem, such a set of solutions comprises the Pareto-optimal (P-optimal) set. It is from this set that the decision maker has to make a choice. The Pareto optimality concept does not assist in making a *single* choice.

7.4.2   VEGA

Let us now see how this concept of Pareto optimality has been applied to solve multiobjective optimization problems using GAs. One of the first works in applying genetic algorithms to multiobjective optimization problems was by Schaffer [Sch85]. Schaffer suggested a vector evaluated genetic algorithm (VEGA) for finding Pareto optimal solutions. In VEGA, the population is divided into equally sized, disjoint subpopulations, each governed by a different objective function. Selection is performed independently from each subpopulation; however crossover is performed across sub-population boundaries. The problem with this scheme is that independent selection of best solution in each criterion results in potential bias against middle solutions (such as E and F of Section 7.4.1)—that is, those which are good but not the best with respect to any single criterion.

VEGA mostly finds extreme solutions on the Pareto front. Schaffer suggested two approaches to improve VEGA. One is to provide a heuristic selection preference for nondominated individuals in each generation. The other is a cross-breeding among the "species" by adding some mate selection.

In another work, in order to spread the population out along the Pareto front, Horn et al. proposed the niched Pareto GA as an algorithm for finding the Pareto optimal set. In this algorithm they incorporate the concept of Pareto domination in the selection operator, and apply a niching pressure to spread its population out along the Pareto optimal trade-off surface [HNG94].

7.4.3   MOGA

Recently, Murata and Ishibuchi proposed a multiobjective GA (MOGA) [MI95] which uses a weighted sum of multiple objective functions to combine them into a scalar fitness function. The key feature of MOGA is that the weights attached to the multiple objective functions are *not* constant but randomly specified for each selection. Therefore, the direction of search in MOGA is not fixed. Weights are chosen as follows:

$$w_i = \frac{random_i(\cdot)}{\sum_{j=1}^{n} random_j(\cdot)} \tag{7.3}$$

where $random_j(\cdot)$ is a non-negative uniformly selected random number associated with objective j.

During the execution of MOGA, a tentative set of Pareto optimal solutions is stored and updated at every generation. A certain number (say N_{elite}) of individuals are randomly selected from the set at each generation and are used as elite individuals in MOGA. This elite preserve strategy has the effect of keeping the variety of each population.

The sequence of steps used in MOGA is as follows. Following the generation of initial population containing M strings, the values of the objective functions for the generated strings are calculated, and a tentative set of Pareto optimal solutions is updated. The fitness (Equation 7.2) of each string is then calculated using the random weights given in Equation 7.3. Next, pairs of strings are selected with a certain selection probability. The selection probability of string x in a population Ψ, denoted by $P(x)$, is specified as

$$P(x) = \frac{f(x) - f_{\min}(\Psi)}{\sum_{x \in \Psi} \{f(x) - f_{\min}(\Psi)\}} \qquad (7.4)$$

where $f_{\min}(\Psi) = \min\{f(x) | x \in \Psi\}$. This step is repeated until $\frac{M}{2}$ pairs of strings are selected from the current population. Then, following crossover and mutation, N_{elite} strings from the set of M strings generated by the previous operations are removed and replaced with N_{elite} strings randomly selected from a tentative set of P-optimal solutions. This process continues until a pre-specified set of stopping conditions is satisfied. MOGA returns a set of Pareto-optimal solutions to the decision maker. The best solution is then selected according to the decision maker's preference [MI95].

Murata and Ishibuchi [MI95] compared MOGA with VEGA and niched Pareto GA for a simple test problem called "unitation versus pairs" [HNG94]. This problem has two objectives to be maximized: "unitation," or Unit(x) refers to the number of 1's used in the fixed-length-bit string x, (Unit (00101011) = 4) and "pairs" denoted by Pairs(x) is the number of pairs of complementary adjacent bits (Pairs(00101011)= 5). The fitness function used was:

$$f(x) = w_{\text{unit}} \cdot \text{Unit}(x) + w_{\text{Pairs}} \cdot \text{Pairs}(x) \qquad (7.5)$$

where w_{unit} and w_{Pairs} are randomly specified non-negative weights.

In all three algorithms the one-point crossover was employed, with P_c =0.9, $N_{\text{pop}} = M = 100$. As expected, many individuals in VEGA were driven to the two extreme solutions (Pairs,Unitation)=(0,12) and (11,6). The niched Pareto GA succeeded in maintaining equal size subpopulations, but one Pareto-optimal solution, namely, (11,6) was not included in the final generation. Whereas MOGA found all Pareto-optimal solutions. The three algorithms were also run on other problems such as flowshop scheduling and fuzzy rule selection, and better solutions were obtained by MOGA. MOGA also was successful in finding all Pareto-optimal solutions for problems with concave Pareto fronts.

In another recent work, the authors of MOGA proposed a hybrid algorithm for finding a set of nondominated solutions of a multiobjective problem. The heuristic is similar to MOGA, with a local search procedure applied on each individual solution generated by genetic operations [IM96]. Similar to MOGA, this hybrid heuristic does not return a single final solution, but a set of solutions. The choice of the final solution is left to the decision maker. This hybrid heuristic produced high-quality results when applied to the flowshop scheduling problem [IM96].

7.5 Fuzzy Logic for Multiobjective Optimization

Most design problems that are encountered in science and engineering are NP-hard even in their simplest form. Moreover, in these problems designers usually seek to optimize several conflicting objectives. Solutions methods that are typically applied resort to heuristic knowledge acquired through experience and/or understanding of the problem domain. The natural language which is the basis of fuzzy logic is a suitable vehicle for expressing such knowledge. Another reason for resorting to fuzzy logic is the treatment of uncertainties. Fuzzy logic provides a natural framework for dealing with such imprecise knowledge.

Fuzzy logic is a branch of mathematics invented by Lotfi Zadeh to represent and manipulate fuzzy knowledge, and to infer from it crisp outcomes [Kar96, Zad65]. In this section we present a brief introduction to fuzzy logic, and show how it can be used to express heuristic knowledge and/or to combine conflicting objectives.

7.5.1 Fuzzy Set Theory

Unlike in ordinary set theory where an element is either in a set or not in a set, in fuzzy set theory, an element may *partially* belong to a set. Lotfi Zadeh defined a fuzzy set as a class of objects with a continuum of grades of membership. Formally, a fuzzy set A of a universe of discourse X is defined as $A = \{(x, \mu_A(x)) |$ all $x \in X\}$, where X is a space of points and $\mu_A(x)$ is a *membership function* of $x \in X$. The variable x is known as the base variable. For each value of x, $\mu_A(x)$ indicates the degree of membership of that value in the fuzzy subset A. In general the membership function $\mu_A(.)$ is a mapping from X to the interval [0,1]. If $\mu_A(x) = 1$, or 0, for all $x \in X$, the fuzzy set A becomes an ordinary set [Zad65].

> **Example 7.2** As an example, let h refer to height of an athlete, and "tall" considered as a particular fuzzy linguistic value of the linguistic variable "height." The linguistic value "tall" is a fuzzy subset that will be characterized by a particular membership function $\mu_{tall}(.)$ giving a meaning to the fuzzy linguistic value "tall." For each value of h, the base variable height, $\mu_{tall}(h)$ returns a number indicating the extent to which that height belongs to the fuzzy subset "tall."   ∎

> **Example 7.3** As another example, consider the possible heights of sportsmen in feet to be H={3.5,4.0,4.5,5.0,5.5,6.0,6.5}. Heights around 4.5 feet are considered short (S), around 5.5 feet are considered moderate (M), and heights around 6.0 feet are considered tall (T). Thus, short, moderate, and tall are **not** crisply defined. Fuzzy sets for short, moderate, and tall may be

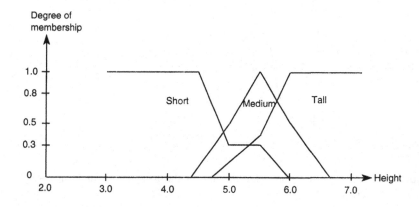

Figure 7.1: Membership functions for short, moderate, and tall.

expressed as sets of ordered pairs $\{(x, \mu_A(x)) \mid \forall x \in X\}$, where the first element of the pair is the height and the second is its membership in that set. From our previous knowledge we can define the fuzzy sets S, M, and T as follows:

S = {(3.5,1.0), (4.0,1.0), (4.5,1.0), (5.0,0.3), (5.5,0.3), (6.0,0.0), (6.5,0.0)}
M= {(3.5,0.0), (4.0,0.0), (4.5,0.1), (5.0,0.5), (5.5,1.0), (6.0,0.5), (6.5,0.1)}
T = {(3.5,0.0), (4.0,0.0), (4.5,0.0), (5.0,0.1), (5.5,0.4), (6.0,1.0), (6.5,1.0)}

Figure 7.1 illustrates the three membership functions. For simplicity we have used piecewise linear membership functions. Membership functions can also be continuous curves of many different shapes. For example, Figure 7.2 illustrates a continuous membership function of a fuzzy set: An individual's weight around 50 kilograms.Those thinking in Boolean terms may view the membership function as fuzzified variables of a multivariable logic. In our example of the sportsmen (Example 7.3), if the three crisp variables (trivalent logic) were defined as short=4.5 feet, moderate = 5.5 feet, and tall=6.0 feet, then heights between 4.5 and 5.5 and between 5.5 and 6.0 feet are not defined. Observe that the fuzzification of the three crisp variables, as in Figure 7.1, causes spreading of the variables with a distribution profile. This causes all heights in the given range to be included. If a sportsmen's height is 5.0 feet, this height belongs to variable short with degree of membership (or confidence) equal to 0.3, to variable moderate with degree of membership of 0.5, and, to tall with degree of membership of 0.1.

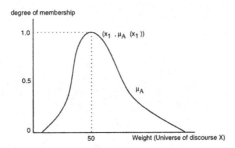

Figure 7.2: Continuous membership function for the fuzzy set: individual's weight around 50 kilograms.

7.5.2 Fuzzy Operators

As seen above, in fuzzy logic, the values are not crisp, and their fuzziness exhibits a distribution described by the membership function. In ordinary set theory, operations such as union ($\cup$), intersection ($\cap$), and complementation ($\neg$) are used. What is the result of these operations on fuzzy sets? This question has been addressed by various **fuzzy logics**. These are logics that have been defined for operations on fuzzy sets. One such logic defined by L. Zadeh is called the **min-max** logic [Zad65]. There are other fuzzy logics which we will discuss later. In **min-max** logic, the "union," "intersection," and "complementation" are defined as follows:

$$\mu_{A \cap B}(x) = \min(\mu_A(x), \mu_B(x))$$
$$\mu_{A \cup B}(x) = \max(\mu_A(x), \mu_B(x))$$
$$\mu_{\neg A}(x) = 1.0 - (\mu_A(x))$$

7.5.3 Fuzzy Rules

Approximate reasoning can be made based on linguistic variables and their values. Rules can be generated based on previous experience. The **rules** are expressed as **If ... Then** statements. Connectives such as **AND** and **OR** can be used in approximate reasoning to join two or more linguistic values. The **If** part (*antecedent*) is a fuzzy predicate defined in terms of linguistic values and fuzzy operators (**AND** and **OR**). The **Then** part is called the *consequent*. In optimization problems, the linguistic value used in the consequent part identifies the fuzzy subset of good solutions. Therefore, the result of evaluation of the antecedent part identifies the degree of membership in the fuzzy subset of good solutions according to the fuzzy rule in question.

As mentioned above, in **min-max** logic, the fuzzy **AND** is realized by the function **min**. If more than one rule is used to perform decision-making, each rule can be evaluated to generate a numerical value. Then, these numerical values from various evaluations of different rules can be combined to generate a crisp value on a higher level of hierarchy.

7.5.4 Example of Fuzzy Multiobjective Optimization

Consider the VLSI placement problem where it is required to pack a number of components (cells) while minimizing the circuit area, total interconnection length (wire-length), and the circuit delay. That is, we seek to find a solution optimized with respect to *area* (A), *wire-length* (L), and *delay* (D). Therefore, the objective function is not a scalar, but a vector-function

$$\bar{F}(x) = (f_a(x), f_l(x), f_d(x))$$

where $f_a(x)$ is the area of the design, $f_l(x)$ is the overall required wire-length, and $f_d(x)$ is the timing delay.

To obtain a fuzzy logic definition of the above multicriteria objective function one may proceed as follows. Three linguistic variables *area, length,* and *delay* are introduced for these functions. For each variable, several linguistic values can be defined. Let us define only one linguistic value for each variable. That is, *small* for area, *short* for wire-length, and *low* for delay. These linguistic values characterize the degree of satisfaction of the designer with the values of objectives $f_i(x)$, $(i = a, l, d)$. These degrees of satisfaction are described by membership functions $\mu_i(\cdot)$ on fuzzy sets of linguistic values.

Membership functions for *small area, short length,* and *low delay* are easy to build. They are nonincreasing functions, since the smaller the area $f_a(\cdot)$, shorter the length $f_l(\cdot)$, and lower the delay $f_d(\cdot)$, the higher is the degree of satisfaction $\mu_a(\cdot)$, $\mu_l(\cdot)$ and $\mu_d(\cdot)$ of the expert and, vice versa (Figure 7.3).

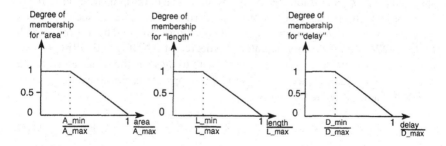

Figure 7.3: Normalized membership functions for *area, wire-length,* and *delay*.

To make the membership functions applicable to different designs, the base variables *area*, *length*, and *delay* are normalized to the interval [0,1]. The values A_{min}, L_{min}, and D_{min} are estimated lower bounds on the area, total wire-length, and timing delay of the circuit, respectively. The values of A_{max}, L_{max}, and D_{max} are upper-bound estimates for these variables. For example, if genetic algorithm is used, these values can be derived from the maximum among the several solutions of the initial population [SYSA97].

The most desirable solution is the one with the highest membership in the fuzzy subsets *small area*, *short wire-length*, and *low delay*. However, such a solution most likely does not exist since some of the criteria conflict with each other. Therefore, one has to trade off these individual criteria against each other. This trade-off is conveniently specified in linguistic terms in the form of one or several fuzzy logic rules illustrated below.

Let the fuzzy subset of good solutions be characterized by the following fuzzy rule:

R.0 **If** (small area) OR (short wire-length) OR (low delay)
        Then good solution.

We could implement the fuzzy OR above using the **max** operator. In that case, according to rule **R.0**, the membership function of the fuzzy subset of good solutions $\mu_{(S)}$ evaluates to the following:

$$\mu_{(S)}(x) = \max(\mu_a(x), \mu_l(x), \mu_d(x)) \qquad (7.6)$$

As mentioned above, in addition to the classical **min-max** logic, there are other fuzzy logics [DP80, Yag77, Zad65, Zim91].

The **max** (OR) and **min** (AND) operators are, respectively, s-norm and t-norm operators [Zim91]. Formulation of multiobjective functions does not favor pure ANDing and pure ORing. The reason is that these operators are noncompensatory. For the **max** operator the outcome of the fuzzy rule is dictated solely by the criterion with the highest membership value. Similarly, for the **min** operator the outcome of the fuzzy rule is dictated by the criterion with lowest membership value. This undesirable behavior has led to the development of other fuzzy operators which possess compensatory properties. Examples of such operators are the *ordered weighted averaging* (OWA) operators proposed by Yager [Yag88]. In these OWA compensatory operators the degree of ANDing and ORing is controlled by a parameter $\beta \in [0, 1]$. Yager refers to these as the *orlike* and *andlike* operators. For example, according to the *orlike* operation, the above fuzzy logic rule **R.0** evaluates to the following.

$$\mu_{(S)}(x) = \beta \times \max(\mu_a, \mu_l, \mu_d) + (1 - \beta) \times \frac{1}{3}(\mu_a + \mu_l + \mu_d) \qquad (7.7)$$

where β is a parameter between 0 and 1 indicating the degree of nearness of this *orlike* operator to the strict meaning of the **max** operator. When $\beta = 1$, the *orlike* operator behaves like a regular **max** operator, and for $\beta = 0$ it behaves like a weighted averaging operator.

In the previous fuzzification approach, each of the individual criteria is characterized by a fuzzy subset (membership function). The membership value in the fuzzy subset *good solution* results from the activation of a fuzzy rule (such as **R.0**) which combines the individual fuzzy subsets (criteria) using appropriate fuzzy operators. The solution with the highest membership value in the fuzzy subset *good solution* is returned as the best (optimum) solution. This approach got rid of the controversial weighted sum approach. However, it does not maintain the integrity of the individual criteria as in the case of Pareto-optimality.

Recently, a fuzzy goal directed search approach has been proposed [SyA99] which exploits the expressive power of fuzzy algebra as well as makes use of the notion of the Pareto-optimality. The approach has been applied in simulated evolution-based VLSI placement algorithm. Below we briefly describe this approach.

7.5.5 Fuzzy Goal Directed Optimization

Let there be Π solutions generated by the algorithm. Assume that we are optimizing a n-valued cost vector given by $C(x) = [C_1(x), C_2(x), ..., C_n(x)]$ where $x \in \Pi$. Assume that a vector $O = (O_1, O_2, ..., O_n)$ gives lower-bound estimates on individual objectives such that $O_i \leq C_i(x)$ $\forall i,$ $\forall x \in \Pi$. These are lower-bound estimates on each objective which are not necessarily achievable in practice. Further, assume that there is a user-specified goal vector $G = (g_1, g_2, ..., g_n)$ which indicates the relative *acceptable limits* for each objective. It means that x will be an acceptable solution if $C_i(x) \leq g_i \times O_i$ where $\forall i, g_i \geq 1.0$. The search algorithm seeks to find solutions that are nearest to each individual goal. The word *nearest* is a fuzzy linguistic value. Hence, the search objective can be conveniently expressed by the following rule:

R.1:   **IF** solution x is
          nearest goal 1 AND
          nearest goal 2 AND

          $\cdots$ $\cdots$ $\cdots$

          nearest goal i AND

          $\cdots$ $\cdots$ $\cdots$

          nearest goal n
          THEN x is a *good solution*.

In fuzzy algebra, and using the *andlike* compensatory operator of Yager, the above rule translates to the following:

$$\mu_{(S)}(x) = \beta \times \min(\mu_1(x), \mu_2(x), \dots, \mu_n(x)) + (1 - \beta) \times \frac{1}{n} \sum_{i=1}^{n} \mu_i(x) \quad (7.8)$$

where $\mu_{(S)}(x)$ is the membership value for solution x in fuzzy set *good solution*. Thus, the solution with the highest $\mu_{(S)}(x)$ in the fuzzy subset of good solution is the one that is nearest to all design goals. The solution which results in the maximum value for Equation 7.8 is reported as the best solution found by the algorithm. The membership function for a general objective "i" is shown in Figure 7.4. User preferences can be easily expressed in goal vector G. For example, by decreasing the goal value g_i to g_i^* in Figure 7.4, the subsequent membership value $\mu_i^*(x)$ for objective i will decrease. This might dictate the acceptance or rejection of solutions.

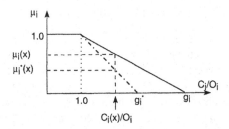

Figure 7.4: Membership function *within acceptable range*. By lowering the goal g_i to g_i^* the preference for objective "i" has been decreased.

The two approaches given above exhaust neither all possible factors to be considered in design nor their dependencies, but they demonstrate how a traditional definition of a multiobjective problem can be transformed into a fuzzy logic definition.

7.6   Artificial Neural Networks

In the recent past, a paradigm known as *neural computing* has become popular for applications such as machine vision, robot control, and so on. Traditional computing methods have not been very successful in attacking these applications, despite the fact that today's computers have achieved speeds of hundreds of million instructions per second (MIPS). On the other hand, the human nervous system routinely solves problems such as pattern recognition, and natural language understanding. Artificial Intelligence (AI) techniques, which were predominantly the theme of fifth-generation computers, have been only partially successful in solving problems such as machine vision. Recently, there has been a revival of interest in neural computing and natural intelligence techniques. These techniques revolve around the concept of an *artificial neural network*, which is an ensemble of a large number of *artificial neurons*. One can think of an artificial neural network as the analog of neural networks that are part of the human brain. It is believed by a large number of computer professionals that neural computing is the key to solving difficult problems like pattern recognition, computer vision, and hard optimization problems [Was89]. In this section we discuss the application of artificial neural networks to the two-dimensional (2-D) placement problem. We will focus our attention on a particular class of artificial neural networks introduced by Hopfield [HT85].

The main component of an artificial neural network (ANN) is an artificial neuron. An artificial neuron receives several analog inputs $X_1, X_2, \ldots, X_n$ and generates a single analog output OUT. The output is computed as follows. Each input is weighted down by the neuron; let W_i be the weight associated with input X_i. The net input, denoted *NET*, is given by

$$NET = \sum_{i=1}^{n} W_i \cdot X_i \qquad (7.9)$$

The output is a function F of *NET* (Figure 7.5). The function F is also known as the activation function of the neuron. A popularly used activation function is the sigmoid function $F(x) = 1/(1 + e^{-x})$. If x is a sufficiently large positive number, the sigmoid function approximates to unity. For sufficiently large negative values of x, the sigmoid function is close to 0. Another popular activation function is $F(x) = \tanh(x)$.

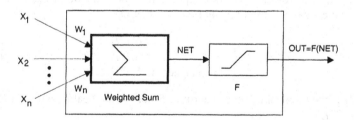

Figure 7.5: An artificial neuron. (Weights are not a part of the neuron. The weighting down is done along the connection between the input and the neuron.)

Several artificial neurons can be connected to form an artificial neural network. For example, a single layer *feed-forward* network consists of m neurons, each with n inputs. The principal inputs to the network are denoted $X_1, X_2, \ldots, X_n$. The weights associated with neuron i are denoted $W_{i1}, W_{i2}, \ldots, W_{in}$. The $m \cdot n$ weights of the network can be compactly represented by the $m \times n$ weight matrix $W = [W_{ij}]$. Figure 7.6(a) shows a feed-forward network with three neurons, each with three inputs. The output of neuron i is denoted by OUT_i. A single-layer *recurrent* network is similar to a feed-forward network, except that the outputs are fed back as inputs to the network. Figure 7.6(b) shows a recurrent network with three neurons, each with three forward inputs and one feedback input. Hopfield and Tank used recurrent neural networks to solve optimization problems [HT85].

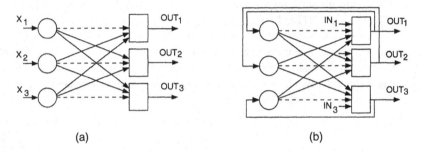

(a)   (b)

Figure 7.6: (a) A single-layer, feed-forward artificial neural network with three neurons. (b) A single-layer, recurrent artificial neural network with three neurons.

Energy Function and Stability

Just as temperature plays an important role in SA [KCGV83], energy plays an important role in Hopfield's neural networks. The set of all outputs OUT_i is known as the state of the network. Suppose that the activation function of each neuron in the network is a *threshold* function, that is,

$$OUT_i = \begin{cases} 1 & \text{if } NET_i > T_i \\ 0 & \text{if } NET_i < T_i \\ \text{unchanged} & \text{if } NET_i = T_i \end{cases} \qquad (7.10)$$

where T_i is the threshold level of neuron i. Since we are dealing with a recurrent network, NET_i is given by

$$NET_i = \left(\sum_{j \neq i} W_{ij} \cdot OUT_j \right) + IN_i \qquad (7.11)$$

It is clear that the network can be in 2^n different states, since each of the n neurons can output either 0 or 1. Each state is associated with an energy level. When the network changes state, there is a change in its energy level. It is known that the network will settle down to a state with minimal energy level if the weight matrix W is a symmetric matrix and all the diagonal entries of the matrix are 0. The network is said to *converge* to the state of minimal energy. By constructing a neural network whose energy function is the objective function of a minimization problem, one can hope to solve the minimization problem.

Example 7.4 Consider how an ANN can be set up to solve the simplest case of the placement problem. Given n circuit modules and a connectivity matrix $C = [C_{ij}]$, where C_{ij} denotes the connectivity between module i and module j; the objective is to put n interconnected objects into n slots of a 2-D array, such that the total Manhattan interconnection length is minimized. The *Manhattan distance* between the two pins is computed as follows. If the two pins are located at coordinates (x_1, y_1) and (x_2, y_2), the Manhattan distance between them is given by

$$d_{12} = |x_1 - x_2| + |y_1 - y_2| \qquad (7.12)$$

We shall use the circuit shown in Figure 7.7(a) to illustrate this approach. The slots to which these modules are to be assigned are shown in Figure 7.7(b).

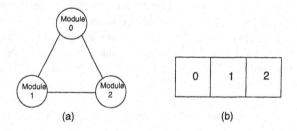

Figure 7.7: (a) Circuit for Example 7.4. (b) Position definitions.

Solution The solution to this problem presented below is due to Yu [Yu89], who used Hopfield's neural nets to solve the placement problem.

To solve this problem a network with n^2 neurons is set up. This network consists of an $n \times n$ matrix of neurons as seen in Figure 7.8 (a 2-D array NN). Neurons are numbered from 0 to $n^2 - 1$, left to right, and top to bottom. The value of element $NN_{i,j}$ represents the "chance" of module "i" being positioned at location "j". Each row corresponds to a circuit module. The n columns correspond to the n possible locations a circuit module can take. Therefore, in order to obtain a feasible solution, only one neuron in any row or any column can have its output 1. The output of the neuron is normalized and thus is always between 0 and 1.

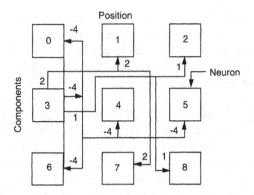

Figure 7.8: An artificial neural network for placement.

The next step is to define the synapse's (connection point's) parity and strength. First, the Manhattan distance between any two locations is computed. The value $T_{k_{i_1,j_1},l_{i_2,j_2}}$, between neurons k and l is defined as the connectivity between circuit modules i_1 and i_2 times $f(j_1, j_2)$, where f is a function of the distance between locations j_1 and j_2, $k = i_1 \times \sqrt{n} + j_1$ and $l = i_2 \times \sqrt{n} + j_2$. After some experimentation f was chosen to be the *offset* minus the Manhattan distance between j_1 and j_2, where the offset parameter is usually greater than $\sqrt{n}$. As an example, the synapse strengths between neurons 2 and 3 ($T_{2,3}$) can be found as follows. Neuron 2 has (i_1, j_1)=0,2; and neuron 3 has (i_2, j_2)=(1,0) (see Figure 7.8). Therefore $T_{2,3}$ by definition is equal to

$$C_{0,1} \times (\textit{offset} - \text{Manhattan distance between 2 and 0})$$
$$= 1 \times (3 - 2) = 1.$$

The partial synapse strength matrix is shown in Table 7.1 and the corresponding connections for neuron 3 are shown in Figure 7.8.   ■

In formalizing the above problem Yu [Yu89] modified the neural network solution to the traveling salesman problem (TSP) by Hopfield [HT85]. The energy function E used by Hopfield has several minima, some of which are local minima; the network can converge to any one of them. As a result, there is *no guarantee* that the solution obtained will correspond to a global minimum. Moreover, how does one determine the parameters of the network (the weight matrix, thresholds, the constants involved in the energy function, and the activation function)? How sensitive is the final solution to small variations in these parameters? How good is the final solution when compared to other known techniques for solving the same

T_{ij}	0	1	2	3	4	5	6	7	8
0	0	-4	-4	-4		-4			
1	-4	0	-4	2	-4		-4		
2	-4	-4	0	1		-4			-4
3	-4			0	-4	-4	-4		
4		-4		-4	0	-4		-4	
5			-4	-4	-4	0			-4
6	-4			-4			0	-4	-4
7		-4	0	2	-4		-4	0	-4
8			-4	1		-4	-4	-4	0

Table 7.1: Partial synapse strength matrix, offset=3, inhibit=-4.

optimization problem? And finally, how fast does the network converge to the final solution? Since neural computing is still an active research area, the answers to these questions are still being investigated.

Yu's results on applying Hopfield neural networks to the placement problem were not promising. Some of the difficulties Hopfield pointed out are long simulation times, poor solution quality, and high sensitivity of the solution to network parameters. At this stage, it can only be concluded that more research is required to understand the applicability of neural networks to hard optimization problems.

7.7 Quality of the Solution

It is natural to ask how good the solution generated by a heuristic really is. Assume that a heuristic algorithm A has been developed for a minimization problem. If S_A is the solution generated by the heuristic, and S^* is the optimum solution, a measure of the error (ϵ) made by the heuristic is the relative deviation of the heuristic solution from the optimal solution, that is,

$$\epsilon = \frac{S_A - S^*}{S^*} \tag{7.13}$$

Unfortunately, it is not easy to measure the error, since S^* is not known. Therefore, we have to resort to other techniques for judging the quality of solutions generated by heuristic algorithms.

One method to alleviate the above problem is to artificially generate test inputs for which the optimum solution is known apriori. For instance, in order to test a heuristic algorithm for floorplanning, we may generate the test input as follows. We start with a rectangle R and cut it into smaller rectangles. If these smaller rectangles are given as input to the floorplanner, we already know the best solution—a floorplan which resembles the rectangle R.

Example 7.5 We could also artificially generate test inputs for our assignment problem discussed in Chapter 3 (Example 3.2). What we are looking for is a scheme to generate task graphs whose optimal finish time is known a priori. To generate such task graphs we can apply the following procedure.

We assume that the number of processors and the time to completion are known. For each processor, the time interval between zero and the finish time is divided randomly into slices. That is, we have generated a random Gantt chart. Each slice in our randomly generated Gantt chart corresponds to a task and its width represents the time required to complete that particular task on the given processor. To generate random task graphs we have to generate nodes and edges. Each slice corresponds to a node (task) in the task graph. Next, edges are added between tasks (nodes) as follows. Several pairs of tasks (say T_i and T_j) are chosen randomly, and if the finish time of task T_i in our Gantt chart is before the starting time of task T_j, an edge is added in the task graph between them (from T_i to T_j). A communication cost must now be assigned to this edge. A value equal to or less than the separation between the finish time of task T_i and start time of T_j is assigned to the edge (i, j). If T_i and T_j are on the same processor, then any *reasonable* value of cost can be assigned to this edge.

Now that we know the best solution for our task graph, we use this task graph as input to our iterative heuristic.

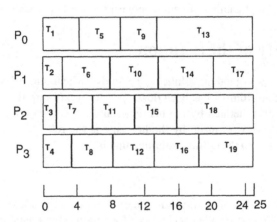

Figure 7.9: Random Gantt chart. P_0–P_3 indicate processors. Time to completion is 25.

An example of a Gantt chart is shown in Figure 7.9. The two tasks T_2 and T_6 are selected, and since they are assigned to the same processor, an edge with an arbitrary cost (18) is added between them. Whereas for tasks T_7 and T_{10} the difference in the finish time of T_7 and start time of T_{10} is 2 units, an edge with a cost of 2 units or less may be added between these nodes. The generated random graph corresponding to the above Gantt chart is given in Figure 7.10.

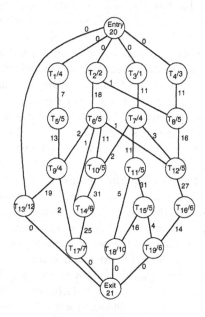

Figure 7.10: Random task graph corresponding to Gantt chart of Figure 7.9.

■

This method of testing, however, is not always feasible. It is difficult to generate such test inputs for several hard practical problems. Furthermore, a heuristic algorithm may perform well on artificial inputs but poorly on real inputs, and vice versa.

Test inputs comprising of real problem instances, called *benchmarks*, are used to compare the performance of heuristics. Generally, such benchmarks are universally recognized. Benchmarks are created by experts working in the field. For example, for VLSI layout problems [SY95], there are two widely used sets of benchmarks: the Microelectronics Center of North Carolina (MCNC) benchmarks and the International Symposium on Circuits and Systems (ISCAS) benchmarks. Then alternative heuristics are compared against the same benchmark tests [Brg93].

7.8 Conclusions

In this chapter we briefly reviewed the salient features of the five heuristics discussed in the book. All algorithms incorporate domain specific knowledge to dictate the search strategy. They also tolerate some element of nondeterminism that helps the search escape out of local minima. They all rely on the use of a suitable cost function which provides feedback to the algorithm as the search progresses. The principle difference among these heuristics is how and where domain-specific knowledge is used. For example, in SA such knowledge is mainly included in the cost function. Elements involved in a perturbation are selected randomly, and perturbations are accepted or rejected according to the Metropolis criterion which is a function of the cost. The cooling schedule has also a major impact on the algorithm performance and must be carefully crafted to the problem domain as well as the particular problem instance.

For the three evolutionary algorithms discussed in the book, genetic algorithms, simulated evolution, and stochastic evolution, domain-specific knowledge is exploited in all phases. In the case of GAs, the fitness of individual solutions incorporates domain specific knowledge. Selection for reproduction, the genetic operations, as well as generation of the new population also incorporate a great deal of heuristic knowledge about the problem domain. In SimE, each individual element of a solution is characterized by a goodness measure that is highly correlated with the objective function. The perturbation step (selection followed by allocation) affects mostly low-goodness elements. Therefore, domain-specific knowledge is included in every step of the SimE algorithm. In StocE, at each iteration the algorithm actually attempts to move each element. The acceptance or rejection of the move is based on a gain measure and a parameter p. Both the gain measure and p are tuned to the problem domain.

Tabu search is different from the above heuristics in that it has an explicit memory component. At each iteration the neighborhood of the current solution is partially explored, and a move is made to the best nontabu solution in that neighborhood. The neighborhood function as well as tabu list size and content are problem-specific. The direction of the search is also influenced by the memory structures (whether intensification or diversification is used).

It has not been our intention in this book to demonstrate the superiority of one algorithm over the other. Actually it would be unwise to rank such algorithms. Each one of them has its own merits. Recently, an interesting theoretical study has been reported by Wolpert and Macready in which they proved a number of theorems stating that the average performance of any pair of iterative (deterministic or nondeterministic) algorithms across all problems is identical. That is, if an algorithm performs well on a certain class of problems then it necessarily pays for that with degraded performance on the remaining set of problems [WM97]. However, it should be noted that the reported theorems assume that the algorithms do not include domain-specific knowledge of the problems being solved. Obviously, it would be expected that a well-engineered algorithm would exhibit superior performance to that of a poorly engineered one.

This chapter also addressed hybridization issues where desirable features of two or more algorithms are combined. In addition, we provided a brief introduction to fuzzy logic and illustrated how it can help deal with multiobjective optimization problems. The neural network is another legitimate soft computing paradigm that has been briefly described in this chapter.

The SimE algorithm discussed in this book should not be confused with the simulated evolution work of Fogel [FOW66]. Fogel's work operates on a population of algorithms to develop artificial intelligence. An algorithm's behavior is abstracted as a finite-state machine. An offspring machine is created by applying mutation to the parent machine. A machine that demonstrates the greatest ability (that is, one which provides the greatest payoff with respect to a certain cost measure) is retained for the next generation [Fog95, FOW66]. Evolution thus proceeds to find better and better programs for solving a given problem.

Genetic programming (GP) is another branch of genetic algorithms not discussed in this book [Koz92]. Genetic programming is considered more powerful than GAs primarily because its output is a computer program. It is useful in finding solutions where the variables are constantly changing. The main difference between GP and GAs is in the representation of the solution. GP creates computer programs as the solution whereas GAs create chromosomes (strings) that represent possible solutions. Operators such as crossover and mutation used in GAs are also used in GP. In GP, unlike in the case of GAs, identical parents can crossover to yield a different offspring. Fitness is assigned by executing each program in the population. The value of fitness assigned is according to how well the program solves the problem. The best computer program that appears in any generation is designated as the result of GP [Koz92]. In brief, GP can be considered as the beginning of computer programs that program themselves.

In this book we deliberately omitted other powerful combinatorial optimization techniques such as Lagrangean relaxation, and exact enumerative techniques such as branch-and-bound and dynamic programming. These techniques, as well as others, have been included in several manuscripts [Fou84, HS84, Hu82, PS82, Ree95]. We concentrated on approximation heuristics that share several properties. Further, two of the heuristics discussed (SimE and StocE) have not previously appeared in other books. It is our belief that these algorithms, similar to others addressed in this book, are well designed and include sufficient ingenuity to make them both effective and general approximation heuristics.

References

[Brg93]   F. Brglez. A D&T Special Report on ACD/SIGDA Design Automa-
            tion Benchmarks: Catalyst or Anathema?· *IEEE Design & Test*,
            pages 87–91, Sep. 1993.

[Dav91]   L. Davis, editor. *Handbook of Genetic Algorithms*. Van Nostrand
            Reinhold, New York, 1991.

[DP80]   D. Dubois and H. Prade. New results about properties and semantics
            of fuzzy set-theoretic operators. *Fuzzy Sets-theory and Application
            to Policy Analysis and Information Systems*, 1980.

[EK97]   H. Esbensen and E. S. Kuh. A performance driven IC/MCM place-
            ment algorithm featuring explicit design space exploration. *ACM
            Transactions on Design Automation of Electronic Systems*, 2(1):62–
            80, Jan. 1997.

[Fog95]   D. B. Fogel. *Evolutionary Computation: Toward a New Philosophy
            of Machine Intelligence*. IEEE Press, 1995.

[FOW66]   L. J. Fogel, A. J. Owens, and M. J. Walsh. *Artificial Intelligence
            through Simulated Evolution*. John Wiley & Sons, New York, 1966.

[Fou84]   L. R. Foulds. *Combinatorial Optimization for Undergraduates*.
            Springer-Verlag, 1984.

[GKL95]   F. Glover, J. P. Kelly, and M. Laguna. Genetic algorithms and tabu
            search: Hybrids for optimization. *Computers and Operations Re-
            search*, 22(1):111–134, 1995.

[Glo77]   F. Glover. Heuristics for integer programming using surrogate con-
            straints. *Decision Sciences*, 8:156–166, 1977.

[Glo94]   F. Glover. Tabu search for nonlinear and parametric optimization
            (with links to genetic algorithms). *Discrete Applied Mathematics*,
            49:231–255, 1994.

[HNG94]   J. Horn, N. Nafpliotis, and D. E. Goldberg. Niched Pareto genetic
            algorithm for multiobjective optimization. *Proceedings of First In-
            ternational Conference on Evolutionary Computation*, pages 82–87,
            1994.

[HT85]   J. J. Hopfield and D. W. Tank. Neural Computation of Decisions in
            Optimization Problems. *Biological Cybernetics*, 52:141–152, 1985.

[HS84]   E. Horowitz and S. Sahni. *Fundamentals of Computer Algorithms*. Computer Science Press, Rockville, MD, 1984.

[Hu82]   T. C. Hu. *Combinatorial Algorithms*. Addison-Wesley, 1982.

[IM96]   H. Ishibuchi and T. Murata. Multi-objective genetic local search algorithm. *Proceedings of International Conference on Evolutionary Computation*, pages 119–124, 1996.

[J+92]   R. S. Judson et al. Do intelligent configuration search techniques outperform random search of large molecules? *International Journal of Quantum Chemistry*, 44:277–290, 1992.

[Kar96]   S. V. Kartalopoulos. *Understanding Neural Networks and Fuzzy Logic – Basic Concepts and Applications*. IEEE Press, New York, 1996.

[Kas92]   I. Kassou. *Amelioration d'ordonnancements par des methodes de voisinage*. Doctoral dissertation, INSA, Rouen, France, 1992.

[KCGV83]   S. Kirkpatrick, Jr., C. Gelatt, and M. Vecchi. Optimization by simulated annealing. *Science*, 220(4598):498–516, May 1983.

[KHN95]   H. Kim, Y. Hayashi, and K. Nara. The performance of hybridized algorithm of GA, SA and TS for thermal unit maintenance scheduling. *Proceedings of the IEEE International Conference on Evolutionary Computation*, pages 114–119, Nov. 1995.

[Koz92]   J. R. Koza. *Genetic Programming: On the Programming of Computers by Means of Natural Selection*. Cambridge, MA: The MIT Press, 1992.

[M+96]   L. D. Merkle et al. Hybrid Genetic Algorithms for minimization of a polypeptide specific energy model . *Proceedings of the IEEE International Conference on Evolutionary Computation*, pages 396–400, May 1996.

[MI95]   T. Murata and H. Ishibuchi. MOGA multi-objective genetic algorithms. *Proceedings of International Conference on Evolutionary Computation*, pages 289–294, 1995.

[MM92]   R. Männer and B. Manderick, editors. *Lamarckian Evolution, the Baldwin Effect and Function Optimization*. North Holland, 1992.

[MWSK94]   K. E. Mathias, L. D. Whitley, C. Stork, and T. Kusuma. Staged hybrid genetic search for seismic data imaging. *Proceedings of the IEEE International Conference on Evolutionary Computation*, pages 356–361, June 1994.

[Osm93]   I. H. Osman. Metastrategy simulated annealing and tabu search algorithms for the vehicle routing problem. *Annals of Operations Research*, 41:421–451, 1993.

[PS82]   C. Papadimitriou and K. Steiglitz. *Combinatorial Optimization: Algorithms and Complexity*. Prentice-Hall, 1982.

[RB94]   J.-M. Renders and H. Bersini. Hybridizing genetic algorithms with hill-climbing methods for global optimization: Two possible ways. *Proceedings of the IEEE International Conference on Evolutionary Computation*, pages 312–317, June 1994.

[Ree95]   C. Reeves, editor. *Modern Heuristic Techniques for Combinatorial Problems*. McGraw-Hill Book Co., Europe, 1995.

[S+95]   S. M. Sait et al. Timing influenced general-cell genetic floorplanner. In *ASP-DAC'95: Asia and South-Pacific Design Automation Conference*, pages 135–140, 1995.

[Sch85]   J. D. Schaffer. Multiple objective optimization with vector evaluated genetic algorithms. *Proceedings of International Conference on Genetic Algorithms*, pages 93–100, 1985.

[SH87]   H. Szu and R. Hartley. Fast simulated annealing. *Physics Letters A*, 122:157–162, 1987.

[SW87]   D. J. Sirag and P. T. Weisser. Towards a unified thermodynamic genetic operator. In John Grefenstette, editor, *Genetic Algorithms and their Applications: Proceedings of the 2nd International Conference on Genetic Algorithms*, pages 116–122. Lawrence Erlbaum Associates, Hillsdale, NJ, 1987.

[SY95]   S. M. Sait and H. Youssef. *VLSI Physical Design Automation: Theory and Practice*. McGraw-Hill Book Co., Europe, 1995.

[SyA99]   S. M. Sait, H. Youssef, and H. Ali. Fuzzy simulated evolution for multi-objective optimization. *Proceedings of the Congress on Evolutionary Computation*, Washington, DC, July 1999.

[SYSA97] E. Shragowitz, H. Youssef, S. M. Sait, and H. Adiche. Fuzzy genetic algorithm for floorplan design. In B. Bocacchi, J. C. Bezdek, and D. B. Fogel, editors, *Applications of Soft Computing, SPIE'97*, Vol. 3165, pages 36–47. The International Society for Optical Engineering, July 1997.

[TWF95]   E. Tsoi, K. P. Wong, and C. C. Fung. Hybrid GA/SA algorithms for evaluating trade-off between economic cost and environmental impact in generation dispatch. *Proceedings of the IEEE International Conference on Evolutionary Computation*, pages 132–137, Nov. 1995.

[UM93]   R. Unger and J. Moult. Genetic algorithms for protein folding simulations. *Journal of Molecular Biology*, 231:75–81, 1993.

[Was89]   P. D. Wasserman. *Neural Computing—Theory and Practice*. Van Nostrand Reinhold, New York, 1989.

[WM97]   D. H. Wolpert and W. G. Macready. No free lunch theorems for optimization. *IEEE Transactions on Evolutionary Computation*, 1(1):67–82, Apr. 1997.

[Yag77]   R. Yager. Multiple objective decision-making using fuzzy sets. *International Journal of Man-Machine Studies*, 9:375–382, 1977.

[Yag88]   R. R. Yager. On ordered weighted averaging aggregation operators in multicriteria decision making decision making. *IEEE Transactions on Systems, Man and Cybernetics*, SMC-18(1):183–190, 1988.

[Yu89]   M. L. Yu. A study of the applicability of Hopfield Decision Neural nets to VLSI CAD. *Proceedings of 26th Design Automation Conference*, pages 412–417, 1989.

[Zad65]   L. A. Zadeh. Fuzzy sets. *Information Contr.*, 8:338–353, 1965.

[Zim91]   H. J. Zimmermann. *Fuzzy Sets Theory and Its Application*. Kluwer, Boston, 1991.

Exercises

Exercise 7.1

1. Write a program to generate traveling salesman problem instances of user specified number of cities for which the optimal solution is known. Assume the cities to be located on a square grid.

2. Repeat the above assuming that the cities are located equidistantly on a circle of a given radius.

Exercise 7.2

What are the weaknesses and strengths of the individual heuristics discussed in this book?

Exercise 7.3

1. The performance of simulated annealing is hindered by its slow convergence to optimal or near optimal solutions, while genetic algorithm suffers from premature convergence. Suggest how the two techniques can be combined to design a hybrid heuristic that will introduce more diversity into the GA population, and also avoid the long computation times required by simulated annealing.

2. Can tabu search be included into your hybrid? What do you expect to be the improvement in terms of runtime and solution quality?

Exercise 7.4

1. All algorithms discussed in this book are forgetful, that is, they do not remember where they were, and therefore may revisit the same states during the search. Tabu search partially avoids this problem by relying on a memory component (tabu list). For each of GA, SA, SimE, and, StocE, suggest strategies to make them keep track of some of the previously visited states.

2. Implement and experiment with the suggested strategies on the TSP problem.

Exercise 7.5

Design a hybrid heuristic which combines features of:

1. Simulated Evolution and Stochastic Evolution.

2. Simulated Annealing and Stochastic Evolution.

3. Simulated Annealing and Simulated Evolution.

Illustrate your hybrids on the traveling salesman problem.

Exercise 7.6

What do you understand by the term Pareto Optimality? For multiobjective optimization, how does this concept differ from the goal directed search strategy discussed in this chapter?

Exercise 7.7

1. Given a graph with nodes of varying sizes, it is required to seek a two-way partition that is balanced and which has a minimum number of edges cut. Use fuzzy logic as discussed in this chapter to formulate a suitable cost function. Identify suitable linguistic variables, linguistic values, and related membership functions.

2. Repeat the above while following the fuzzy goal directed search approach suggested in this chapter. Assume that the user will specify the optimal goal vector $O = (cutsize, imbalance)$ which represents estimates of lower bounds on the size of the cut set and the magnitude of imbalance, and $G = (g_c, g_i)$ which indicates the relative acceptable limits for each objective.

3. In your opinion, how can one come up with reasonable estimates of the lower bounds needed by the optimal goal vector O?

Exercise 7.8

Repeat Exercise 7.7 for the case of $k - way$ partitioning problem.

Exercise 7.9

Do artificial neural networks constitute a reasonable optimization approach? Justify your answer.

Exercise 7.10

How does optimization using ANNs differ from optimizing using iterative heuristics discussed in this book? Address aspects such as run-time complexity, difficulty of formulation, robustness in reaching (near) optimal solutions, capability of escaping from local minima, and so forth.

Exercise 7.11

Complete Example 7.4 and obtain all the elements of the synapse matrix.

Exercise 7.12

Given n circuit modules and a connectivity matrix $C = [C_{ij}]$, where C_{ij} denotes the connectivity between module i and module j; the objective is to divide the modules equally among sets X and Y such that the following cost function is minimized.

$$EW = \sum_{i \in X} \sum_{j \in Y} C_{ij} \qquad (7.14)$$

Explain how an ANN (artificial neural network) can be set up to solve the two-way circuit partition problem. (Hint: To solve this problem, a network consisting of a $2 \times n$ matrix of neurons can be set up. Each column of this matrix corresponds to a circuit module. The two rows correspond to the two sets X and Y).

Exercise 7.13
In this chapter, fuzzification was proposed as an alternative approach to deal with multicriteria optimization problems. Some of the operators and parameters of the algorithms discussed in this book are inherently fuzzy, and therefore, fuzzy algebra can be employed. For example, the temperature parameter of SA is initially very high, and the SA search stops when temperature becomes very low. These are fuzzy linguistic values that can be described using membership functions. Suggest a fuzzy cooling scheme for the SA algorithm.

Exercise 7.14
For the QAP problem discussed in Chapter 5, fuzzify the *allocation* step of simulated evolution.

Exercise 7.15
As discussed in Chapter 4, a small tabu list size is preferred for exploring the solution near a local optimum, and a larger tabu list size is preferable for breaking free of the vicinity of a local minimum. Varying the tabu list size during the search process provides one way to take advantage of this effect. Suggest a strategy that uses fuzzy logic to dynamically choose the size of the tabu list. (Hint: Identify key words that are in fact linguistic terms required to express appropriate fuzzy rules).

About the Authors

Sadiq M. Sait (S'87, M'90) obtained a Bachelor's degree in Electronics from Bangalore University, India, in 1981, and Master's and Ph.D. degrees in Electrical Engineering from King Fahd University of Petroleum and Minerals (KFUPM), Dhahran, in 1983 and 1987, respectively. He is currently a professor in the Department of Computer Engineering of KFUPM. Sait has authored over 85 research papers in international journals and conferences. He is the coauthor of the book *VLSI Physical Design Automation: Theory and Practice*, published by McGraw-Hill, Europe (also copublished by IEEE Press), January 1995. He has also contributed two chapters to a book entitled *Progress in VLSI Design*. He served on the editorial board of *International Journal of Computer-Aided Design* between 1988 and 1990. Currently he is the editor of *Arabian Journal for Science and Engineering* for Computer Science & Engineering. His current areas of interest are in digital design automation, VLSI system design, high-level synthesis, and iterative algorithms.

E-mail: sadiq@kfupm.edu.sa

Habib Youssef (S'86, M'90) received a Diplome d'Ingenieur en Informatique from the Faculté des Sciences de Tunis, Tunisia in 1982 and a Ph.D. in Computer Science from the University of Minnesota in 1990. He is currently an Associate Professor of Computer Engineering at King Fahd University of Petroleum and Minerals, Saudi Arabia. Habib Youssef has authored more than 45 journal and conference papers. He is the coauthor of the book *VLSI Physical Design Automation: Theory and Practice*, published by McGraw-Hill, Europe, (also copublished by IEEE Press), January 1995. His main research interests are CAD of VLSI, computer networks, and performance evaluation of computer systems, and general stochastic and evolutionary algorithms.

E-mail: youssef@kfupm.edu.sa

Index